American Popular Music

American Popular Music:
Readings from the Popular Press
Volume II:
The Age of Rock

Edited by
Timothy E. Scheurer

Bowling Green State University Popular Press
Bowling Green, OH 43403

Copyright © 1989 Bowling Green State University Popular Press
Library of Congress Catalog Card No: 89-062346
ISBN: 0-87972-467-6 Clothbound
    0-87972-468-4 Paperback
Cover design by Laura Darnell-Dumm

For my son Andy, whose
enthusiasm and love of rock 'n' roll is a
constant reminder to me of what the music is all about.

Contents

GENERAL INTRODUCTION | 1

COUNTRY, FOLK AND THE ROOTS OF ROCK 'N' ROLL

Introduction | 9
The Mythology of Woody Guthrie | 13
   J.L. Rodnitzky
Country Music and American Values | 24
   John Buckley
Ten Thousand Acres of Bluegrass:
   Mimesis in Bill Monroe's Music | 34
   Robert Cantwell
Bright Lights, Big City:
   A Brief History of Rhythm and Blues, 1945-1957 | 46
   Tom McCourt
From ASCAP to Alan Freed:
   The Pre-History of Rock 'n' Roll | 63
   Reebee Garofolo and Steve Chapple

ROCK 'N' ROLL: THE 1950S AND EARLY 1960S

Introduction | 75
The Evolution of Pop Music Broadcasting: 1920-1972 | 78
   R. Serge Denisoff
"Teen Angel": Resistance, Rebellion, and Death—Revisited | 94
   R. Serge Denisoff
Elvis Presley and the Myth of America | 102
   Timothy E. Scheurer
The Evolution of the American Protest Song | 113
   Jerome Rodnitzky

FROM ROCK 'N' ROLL TO ROCK: THE 1960S

Introduction | 124
Trends in Lyrics in the Annual Top Twenty Songs
   in the United States, 1963-1972 | 129
   Gary Burns
The Lyrics of American Pop Music: A New Poetry | 144
   Harold F. Mosher, Jr.
Iconic Modes: The Beatles | 151
   Ralph Brauer
Me and the Devil Blues: A Study of Robert Johnson
   and the Music of the Rolling Stones | 160
   John D. Wells

Soul Music: Its Sociological and Political
   Significance in American Popular Culture   168
    Portia K. Maultsby
"If Ya Wanna End War and Stuff, You Gotta Sing Loud"—
   A Survey of Vietnam-Related Protest Music   179
    H. Ben Auslander
Sex Role Standards in Popular Music   185
    Kathleen L. Endres

LET IT BE: ROCK IN THE '70S AND '80S

Introduction   197
Twilight of the Age of Aquarius?
   Popular Music in the 1970s   201
    Hugh Mooney
Pop, Punk and Subcultural Solutions   220
    Julian Tanner
Reggae, Rastafarians and Revolution:
   Rock Music in the Third World   225
    James A. Winders
Disco: A Music for the 1980s?   240
    Hugh Mooney
Music Videos: From Performance to Dada-Surrealism   252
    Joan Lynch
The Price You Pay: The Life and Lyrics of Bruce Springsteen   258
    Julie Lyons and George H. Lewis

General Introduction

By all counts and standards it was a certifiable revolution. It not only changed the music to which we listened, but it changed the way we dressed, groomed, talked, and, most importantly, the way we looked at the world. It was the third musical revolution in less than a century, the others being Ragtime (1890-1917), Jazz (c. 1917), and Swing (1935), and like those revolutions there was a song that signalled the change, that portended the anarchy to be loosed upon the world as it were.

There were, of course, other songs that had profound influences on the emergence of rock 'n' roll, but "Rock Around the Clock" is the song that we associate with the beginning of it all. The song itself, moreover, is a metaphor for the entire revolution: it is like it really shouldn't have happened at all. First, it never should have been heard beyond a small club somewhere in the Northeast or maybe Chicago, you know, the places where one clandestinely (almost in twenties speakeasy style) went to hear rhythm and blues. That's where music like it had been played for years, and there was no reason to suspect it would move beyond that realm. There was, after all, the institution of Tin Pan Alley; it was large, and, although not as centralized as it had been fifty years before, it was ubiquitous and its influence could be felt throughout all the media and the business world. It was, moreover, well organized (mostly through organizations like American Society of Composers Authors and Publishers (ASCAP) and the American Federation of Musicians (AFM), and it didn't usually give a lot of credence or recognition to this type of tune. The diet it fed the consumer was relatively the same in 1955 as it was in 1935. Why change? Even though there were more "hillbilly" songs being heard in some quarters and kids seemed to like this new "race" music, the general population, the popular musical establishment perceived, still had its head screwed on right and still wanted songs like "Melody of Love" (written in 1903, but a hit in 1955) and "Love is a Many Splendored Thing."

Then there was the song itself. There was nothing spectacular about it. It had a fairly conventional backbeat rhythm, the progressions were hopelessly amateur (by Tin Pan Alley standards), the sound of the group had been around since rhythm sections splintered from big bands, and the leader of the group was not of the matinee idol variety. Its major public exposure, moreover, was on a limited number of radio stations which played rhythm and blues and rock 'n' roll and in a movie, *Blackboard Jungle*, where it was associated with a group of juvenile delinquents and not the heroes. But then there wasn't anything particularly spectacular about Irving Berlin's "Alexander's Ragtime

Band" (1911), the Original Dixieland Jazz Band's "Livery Stable Blues" (1917), and Benny Goodman's concert date at the Palomar Ballroom in Los Angeles on August 12, 1935. Like those other musical events, however, it meant something special to the kids. For them it *was* spectacular because it broke with convention, and, perhaps more importantly, because it was *theirs*. And so there the song was, perched precariously at number nine on the year-end charts in 1955. The next year, what the Tin Pan Alley establishment would call a "hillbilly" singer by the name of Presley would record with RCA and things would never be the same.

Why? That subject has been explored extensively by dozens of scholars, fans, enthusiasts, historians, sociologists, and we have brilliant analyses of the evolution and triumph of rock. There still remains, however, a sense of mystery and wonder as to how it happened. For instance, Ed Ward in *Rock of Ages: The Rolling Stone History of Rock and Roll*, notes that in 1957, one of the strongest early years in the history of rock, teens only comprised 12% of the total audience for popular music (156). So then, how could this music, largely regional and largely ethnic, come, in less than ten years time, to completely dominate a market so controlled by the forces of Tin Pan Alley, Broadway, and Hollywood? As noted, in-depth studies exist of the history of rock, and the essays contained in this volume will also help to answer that question. The essays in the first chapter will provide readers with some background on the musical forms of country, blues and rhythm and blues that contributed so much to rock's distinctive sound. Subsequent chapters are arranged by decade so we can look at rock in the context of the 50s, the 60s, and, finally the 70s and 80s. From rockabilly to 1980s retro-rock, through the seismic tremors of the Beatles, the Stones, protest music, acid rock, punk rock, disco and MTV, major developments, styles, and themes in the history of rock will be dealt with. Before looking at the individual essays, however, let us review some of the major factors in rock's popularity throughout its over thirty year history.

In looking at rock's triumph much has been made of youth and rebellion. Indeed, youth of the 50s, like their 1920s forebears, were looking to carve out a niche for themselves in a world which held out as many frightening prospects as sunny ones. Although there was not the feeling after World War II, like there was after World War I, that we were left with but a sad remnant, a, to quote Ezra Pound, "botched civilization," there was a feeling of discontent.[1] Youth, like there 20s forebears, acted out some of their discontent with stunts and gimmicks (stuffing college students into telephone booths and Volkswagens being two major ones). Movie heroes, on the other hand, gave voice to this discontent as well as their more serious incohate feelings and *angst*. Marlon Brando is asked in *The Wild One*, "What are you rebelling against?" To which he responds, "Whataya got?" And James Dean, in *Rebel Without a Cause*, given an opportunity by a detective to "let go" explodes in the police station, hammering an officer's desk with his fists. We do not know where Jim's rage comes from and how it will be channelled and/or diverted. The family seems inept, a dinosaur of another time. His father is ineffectual—bossed hopelessly by Mom and grandmother. At one point in the film as his family squabbles, he screams that they are tearing him apart. The film is largely about Dean's character and his peers (Natalie Wood and Sal Mineo as surrogate Mom and son) trying to find meaning for their lives amidst the wreckage of the adult world. In short, there is a new order emerging; youth are staking out their own territory. They have their own rituals, codes, values; it will, moreover, be a different and, as the film suggests, *better* world than Mom and Dad's.

This feeling carried over into the 60s where, as in the 50s, the rebellion began as a matter of style and attitude (Beatle haircuts, blue jeans, surfing styles, facial hair) and evolved into a political stance where Mom and Dad's world must be rejected for its tendency to breed racism, sexism, and war. Simon Frith has written of 1960s youth culture:

The class relation was reversed: middle-class teenagers were deliberately adopting lower-class values and styles that, by now, had a power and glamour of their own. And they were doing this as an aspect of an explicit opposition to both peer-group and adult middle class norms. Nineteen-sixties youth culture was still campus-based, but in rejecting the rules of fraternity and panty-raid and Big Game, student rebels had to draw on values from outside campus, from a wider context of generational struggle against the established political, economic, and sexual system (hence the radicalizing role of the civil rights movement, for example).[2]

Rock and roll was there as the music of the new order. From Pete Townshend's, "Meet the new boss/Same as the old boss," to Dylan's "Look out kid/It's something' you did," all the way back to Chuck Berry's "Hail, hail rock 'n' roll/Deliver me from the days of old," rock music has concerned itself with the preoccupations and values of teenagers. And so it was with previous musical revolutions. Tin Pan Alley, however, lying as it did at the heart of the business, was eventually able to co-opt the revolutionary forces (i.e., Paul Whiteman or even a Glenn Miller in swing) by continuing to provide the basic musical product and by adapting it to the prevailing trend. Thus, one very well might hear "Tea for Two" (1925) done by a jazz combo in the 20s, a swing band in the 30s, and, perhaps, the progression might form the basis for a bebop composition/improvisation in the 40s. Tin Pan Alley's dominance of the market provided a unifying factor in popular music until the age of rock. The sentiments expressed in swing songs of the war years ("Don't Sit Under the Apple Tree," or "Boogie Woogie Bugle Boy" etc.) are not appreciably different from those of World War I songs. However, the sentiments of "Hound Dog," "Tutti-Fruitti," "Whole Lotta Shakin'," and "Maybelline" are different from their Tin Pan Alley counterparts. In short, the revolution was clearly a musical one. The Alley would once again get back in the game, but it was clearly stunned by events in 1955 and 1956.

Over the years only one really adequate answer to the music's power has been developed, and it came to us via Dick Clark's *American Bandstand*: it's got a good beat, and you can dance to it. Ah, but what that phrase says. It was a rhythmic revolution. The first emphasis of the music, in contrast to let us say what Richard Rodgers was doing in 1955 with *Pipe Dream*, was on the beat. Niceties of harmony (major 7ths, 9ths, chromatic mediants, etc.)

are moot points in rock; melody was nice, but you didn't have to have Sinatra's, Bennett's, Ella's, or Jo Stafford's pipes to sing along with Jerry Lee, Chuck, and Buddy Holly. But you had to be able to dance to it; it had to be associated with fun and leisure time. The music had to reject the world of work, school, bedtime hours; it had to be loud and just a little dangerous. There was something exciting and slightly magical about sitting up late with a transistor or, if you were not so fortunate, a cheap crystal with ear phone, picking up a faraway station like WLS in Chicago. Through that tiny speaker the pounding triplets of Fats Domino and Little Richard, the vocal swoops and piano glissandos of Jerry Lee Lewis, the driving guitar work of Chuck Berry, those elegant harmonies and mellow I-vi-IV-V progressions of the Five Satins, and Elvis's vocal catches, cries, and passion were palpable symbols of the new order, "our" music. And if the minister didn't like it and mom told you not to watch that Mr. Presley on TV, that was even better. The Beatles, too, were ushered in on the revolution of the beat, on the Mersey Beat, loud, at times dissonant, with chords Dylan called "outrageous." In the 70s Disco kept the beat going at a steady 135 a minute, and heavy metal's continued popularity is evidence that the beat and the danger must always be there for rock 'n' roll to exist. The beat is rock's legacy and its fountain of youth. The lyrics did not have to deal directly with rebellious issues, the music itself was all the rebellion one needed.

Most importantly, however, and most ironically, the music was a return to the early roots of Tin Pan Alley. In the early days of the Alley, composers like a Harry Von Tilzer would catch snatches of dialogue on the streets ("Wait till the Sun Shines Nellie"), borrow an appropriate heading ("Just As the Ship Went Down," a song about the Titanic), see a new fashion, and then translate them immediately into musical terms. Similarly, as rock developed it drew on the values of teenagers for its inspiration. In almost a throwback to the early days of Tin Pan Alley, rock dealt with all kinds of themes from teen romance ("Puppy Love"), to rebellion ("Yakety Yak"), to death ("Teen Angel" and others), and even our fascination with UFO's ("Purple People Eater"). Chuck Berry's music alone is a virtual celebration of teen life and values ("Sweet little Sixteen" "School Days," "Rock 'n' Roll Music," etc.). The Beatles music in the 1960s chronicled our changing attitudes towards love; from the innocence of "I Want to Hold Your Hand"; to the confused and botched sexual assignation on the frontier of the nascent sexual revolution in "Norwegian Wood," to the communal utopian vision of "All You Need in Love," to the mature realization of love's narrower and but more powerful focus in "Hey Jude," they told us what we were feeling, thinking, and aspiring to. And when they told us to "Let It Be" they set the stage for the "Me decade" and we really let it be.

Youth, furthermore, had new and, in some cases, evolving forms of entertainment available to them for the perpetuation of *their* music. Record players became progressively more portable. So the partying celebrated in Haley's "Rock Around the Clock" could also be a moveable feast. World War II helped technology, not the least of which was the emergence of the 45 rpm (a line of demarcation was drawn: grownups largely bought 78s or the new 33 1/3 long playing records, kids bought 45s). This, wedded to a portable record player, meant a lot to a teenager. The other innovation was the development of the transistor radio. As *Rock of Ages* reported, by 1955, $25.00 to $50.00 could buy one of these new radios. Leisure time available, furthermore, increased as the economy improved through the 50s and into the 60s, and consequently, the transistor radio became a symbol of the convergence of money and leisure; although a fairly expensive item, *Rock of Ages* cites a study that showed that by 1956, 100% of households had one.[3] In the early days of rock's history the radio also provided youth with some minor culture heroes in the form of disk jockeys; people such as Alan Freed who, like co-conspirators in a shady operation, spun those disks late at night for "the kids" and howled and carried on quite unlike anybody else on radio. Eventually radio would initiate a mini-revolution in the late 60s with the growth of free-form progressive radio, and the form of the music itself would change. The three-minute single could give way to the record-side quasi-symphonic movement of something like Yes' *Tales From Topographic Oceans* (1973). Whatever the case, it was always "The Kids' music," and youth had their own systems on which to play their music.

Finally, there was the matter of numbers. If indeed the voices of the old guard such as Billy Rose and Columbia A & R man Mitch Miller might have been heeded at one time, by 1960 they were mere whispers on the wind. The baby boomers were coming of age. Born in the years following the war, by 1960 many were well into their teens. The economy was fine tuned, Kennedy told them they were the hope for the future, and they inherited rock 'n' roll and in the intervening years helped transform it into ROCK. They became the country's single largest block of consumers—consumers, moreover, who had the discretionary income for leisure products. By 1964, with Phil Spector at his peak, the Beach Boys celebrating the good life on the coast, Motown reinvigorating rock with "The Sound of Young America," and the Beatles arriving on February, the revolution was complete. Those heading out to the "new frontier" had their own music, the beginnings of their own myths and heroes (some of whom were musicians), and the rest of the industry as well as the culture fell in line.

Rock, today, remains a vital force, a revolutionary one. It has a tougher task these days: appealing to those who grew up with it while still speaking to the needs of the teenager. It is fragmented into folk-rock, country-rock, retro-rock, punk rock, new wave/new music, techno-pop, rockabilly, heavy metal, psychedelic, soul, funk, disco, and so forth, but it remains socially engaged (John Cougar Mellencamp, Bruce Springsteen, U-2 being three of the best known examples) while still celebrating fun and the joy of being young. It still has a good beat and you can still dance to it.

Notes

[1]David Dalton in his *James Dean: The Mutant King* (New York: Bell Books, 1974) masterfully captures the restless atmosphere of the 1950s.

6 American Popular Music

[2]Simon Frith, *Sound Effects: Youth, Leisure, and the Politics of Rock 'n' Roll* (New York: Pantheon Books, 1981), p. 192.

[3]Ed Ward, Geoffrey Stokes and Ken Tucker, *Rock of Ages: The Rolling Stone History of Rock and Roll* (New York: Summit Books, 1986), p. 123.

References

As with the first volume, I offer here some general histories of popular music as well as some general histories of rock. I will, again, emphasize books throughout this volume but I want to mention briefly some notable magazines and journals which feature useful information about rock: *Rolling Stone, Crawdaddy, Creem, New Musical Express* (British publication), *Melody Maker* (British), *Musician, Popular Music and Society, Downbeat*, and, of course, *Billboard* and *Variety*, especially for news about the music industry.

Belz, Carl. *The Story of Rock*. New York: Harper and Row, 1971.
Eisen, Jonathan, ed. *The Age of Rock*. New York: Vintage, 1969.
Ewen, David. *All the Years of American Popular Music*. Englewood Cliffs, NJ: Prentice-Hall, 1977.
Frith, Simon. *Sound Effects: Youth, Leisure and the Politics of Rock*. New York: Pantheon, 1982.
Gambaccini, Paul. *The Top 100 Rock 'n' Roll Albums of All Time*. New York: Harmony Books, 1987.
Gillett, Charlie. *The Sound of the City*. Rev. and expanded. New York: Pantheon Books, 1983.
Goldstein, Richard. *The Poetry of Rock*. New York: Bantam Books, 1969. A collection of rock lyrics.
Grossman, Lloyd. *A Social History of Rock Music*. New York: David McKay Co., 1976.
Hamm, Charles. *Yesterdays: Popular Song in America*. New York: W.W. Norton, 1979.
Macken, Bob, Peter Fornatale and Bill Ayres. *The Rock Music Source Book*. Garden City, NY: Doubleday Anchor Books, 1980.
Marcus, Greil. *Mystery Train: Images of America in Rock 'n' Roll Music*. Rev. ed. New York: E.P. Dutton, 1982.
Miller, Jim, ed. *The Rolling Stone Illustrated History of Rock and Roll*. Rev. and updated. New York: Random House, 1980.
Pareles, Jon and Patricia Romanowski, eds. *The Rolling Stone Encyclopedia of Rock and Roll*. New York: Summit Books, 1983.
Roxon, Lillian. *Rock Encyclopedia*. New York: Grossett and Dunlap, 1969.
Stambler, Irwin. *Encyclopedia of Pop, Rock and Soul*. New York: St. Martin's, 1977.
Ward, Ed, Geoffrey Stokes and Ken Tucker. *Rock of Ages: The Rolling Stone History of Rock and Roll*. New York: Summit Books, 1986.
Whitcomb, Ian. *After the Ball: Pop Music from Rag to Rock*. new York: Simon and Schuster, 1973.

Country, Folk and the Roots of Rock 'n' Roll

Introduction:
Country, Folk and the Roots of Rock 'n' Roll

At the outset it is important to say that no one chapter can do justice to these forms of American music. But the purpose here is not so much to concentrate on these forms as discrete units, but to look at them from the perspective of rock's development and triumph. They are, indeed, important forms unto themselves, but they also are part of the larger fabric of American popular music. Consequently, it is my hope that these essays will achieve two purposes: first, that they will make the uninformed aware of these wonderful forms of music and, perhaps, encourage them to listen to them and it is hoped read more on the subject; second, that they will provide the reader with some historical and cultural contexts for understanding the form and style of rock.

Proponents of country, folk, and rhythm and blues probably can all make claims for their music to be "the" distinctive American music. That is one reason they are important to study. But another reason is that they are vital to the development of rock. Rock 'n' roll, in the process of seemingly rejecting one whole strand of American culture (i.e., traditional popular song), proved itself to be as assimilative as that earlier form. It is not that rock rejected certain musical norms, it just reconfigured them and reconstituted them in a new musical framework. Returning to our symbol of Bill Haley's recording of "Rock Around the Clock" we see rock's assimilative nature at work. Charlie Gillett quotes Haley describing the music as "a combination of country and western, Dixieland, and the old style rhythm and blues"[1] Moreover, Elvis Presley's style of rock, "rockabilly," is according to Gillett, "...a Southern white version of 12-bar boogie blues, shouted with a minimum of subtlety by ex-hillbilly singers over an accompaniment featuring electric guitar, stand-up bass, and—from 1956—drums, still taboo in Nashville."[2] In short, early rock was largely formed out of the confluence of the musical forms under consideration in the following essays.

Rock has been and still is today constantly reinvigorated by these forms. Country broke out of its regional bounds long before rock, but it became a force in popular music through Elvis, the Byrds, the Eagles, and Linda Ronstadt to name just a few. It has been used for comic effect by The Beatles ("Act Naturally") and for comment by the Talking Heads; it even dominated the charts in the early 1980s with the success of *Urban Cowboy*. As popular music has been jolted by one phenomenon and one trend after another, country remains one of the most conservative forms of popular music. The basic ensembles of the Skillet Lickers, The Carter Family, or Jimmy Rodgers have undergone additions and electrification, but they are still largely string bands with pickers, pluckers, and strummers. It is perhaps the most conservative form of music today and has stayed that way during the age of rock through the efforts of performers such as Waylon Jennings and Willie Nelson in the 1970s and Ricky Scaggs, Randy Travis and The Judds in the 1980s, who have reminded Nashville of its roots. By staying on course, while the other parts of the music industry hustle and bustle around it, it is always in one place ready to attract new fans. Our essay by John Buckley explores country's deep-rooted appeal to traditional values and, consequently, how it is able to attract those fans. Robert Cantwell's essay on Bill Monroe and Bluegrass highlights a more specialized form of country music, but one which has a devoted following and which broke into national prominence in the late 60s with *Bonnie and Clyde* (music by Flatt and Scruggs) and then later with the film *Deliverance* ("Duelling Banjos" set off a flurry of interest in the banjo).

Rhythm and blues' place in rock and roll's history is secure and profound. It provided not only the basic musical ensemble for early rock, but it provided the beat, the structure and form of many of the songs, the harmonic progressions, the vocal styles (for everything from doo-wop to rockabilly), and the melodic and riff formulae used by musicians. In the context of the whole history of popular music, Rhythm and Blues is but the most recent chapter in the chronicle of black America's contribution to our country's musical life. From the time of W.C. Handy (the teens and 20s), through Armstrong, Ellington, and Bessie Smith in the 20s and 30s, up to Joe Turner in the 40s and 50s, black Americans played vital roles in the creation of popular music. Isaac Goldberg, in an early work on Tin Pan Alley, addressed the issue of black America's contribution to popular music by concentrating on the emotional content of the music of blacks. There is an ineffable almost indefinable quality in the great forms of music pioneered by blacks such as Jazz, Blues, Rhythm and Blues. In the 1960s it was called *Soul*—and that is perhaps what it has always been—soul. There was a vitality and energy and a feeling in the music of black Americans that often was not found in the works of the Tin Pan Alley tunesmiths. Black Americans taught us that the finest expression of feelings in song is the one that comes from the deepest recesses of one's being.

But there is even more than that. The music of black Americans' reminds us of the role of creativity in music making, of the lively spontaneous, and sometimes slightly dangerous quality of *making* music. These ideas are explored in the historical context of Tom McCount's essay on the history of Rhythm and Blues. This essay provides not only a good preface for the age of rock, but also good insight into rock's ability to animate its audiences.

The popular folk revival, which Woody Guthrie and the Weavers helped initiate in the 40s and early 50s, attracted the college age crowd to popular music. And so, in the 1960s, when Dylan and the Byrds pioneered the melding of the forms of rock and folk there was more than just a little enthusiasm for what emerged. Folk brought to the music scene a social and political consciousness that was largely absent from popular music except for some occasional tunes and works in the 1930s (*Pins and Needles*, "Brother Can You Spare A Dime," etc.). Its renaissance in the 50s and 60s, furthermore, coincided with a growing political and social consciousness on college campuses. Folk was at the center of civil rights marches in the 50s and 60s, and it was a Dylan lyric line that inspired a splinter radical group (The SDS Weathermen were born of "You don't have to be a weatherman/To know which way the wind is blowing"). It, moreover, introduced (re-introduced) to popular music acoustic instruments and unique styles of performance (strumming and picking styles, unusual guitar tunings, unusual instruments). Today the presence of acoustic instruments ranging from 12 string guitars to mandolins is commonplace on many rock albums (to say that the Hooters use of the mandolin can be traced back to rock's folk and country roots is hardly hyperbolic).

The figure behind much of this is Woody Guthrie. Guthrie's legacy can still be felt today in the works of John Mellencamp, U-2, Sting, and Bruce Springsteen, who often performs "This Land Is Your Land" in concert (see *Bruce Springsteen and the E Street Band Live/1975-85* [Columbia records]). There is, in fact, no better figure to highlight than Woody Guthrie in assessing the impact of "folk" music and the protest tradition on rock. If all of philosophy is a footnote to Plato, so all of protest music is a footnote to Woody Guthrie. It is not that he was the first, it is just that he was among the best and the most ambitious. Joe Klein's fine biography masterfully places Guthrie in his times and shows how Woody's own talents, drives and commitment to causes merged with current academic interest in folk and protest (i.e., Alan Lomax) and growing social unrest fostered largely by communists in the 1930s. J.L. Rodnitzky's essay deals with the single most important aspect of Guthrie—the most important, that is, for the later development of rock's social consciousness—the mythology surrounding the man.

Finally, as important as the forms of country, R & B, and folk were to the development of rock, there were events that took place in the music industry itself which dramatically shaped the face of popular music in the twentieth century. One such event was the quasi-guerilla war that was waged between the powers of American Society of Composers Authors and Publishers (ASCAP) and broadcasters and American Federation of Musicians members in the 30s, 40s and even 1950s. These events, coupled with the rise of television and revamping of radio formats where the disk jockey was king, wrought great changes in the tapestry of musical America. Reebee Garofolo and Steve Chapple's "From ASCAP to Alan Freed: The Pre-history of Rock 'n' Roll" will show how these events within the industry helped pave the way for the introduction of country, Rhythm and Blues and folk into the musical mainstream and ultimately led to the triumph of rock 'n' roll in the 1950s.

Notes

[1] *The Sound of the City: The Rise of Rock and Roll*, rev. and expanded (New York: Pantheon Books, 1983), p. 24.

[2]Gillett, p. 27.

References

Country

Green, Douglas. *Country Roots: The Origins of Country Music*. New York: Hawthorn, 1976.
Guralnick, Peter. *Lost Highways: Journeys and Arrivals of American Musicians*. New York: Vintage, 1979, 1982.
Horstman, Dorothy. *Sing Your Heart Out, Country Boy*. New York: E.P. Dutton, 1975. Collection of country lyrics.
Malone, Bill. *Country Music U.S.A.* Rev. ed. Austin: Univ. of Texas Press, 1985.
Malone, Bill and Judith McCulloh. *Stars of Country Music*. Urbana: Univ. of Illinois Press, 1975.
Rosenberg, Neil V. *Bluegrass: A History*. Urbana: Univ. of Illinois press, 1985.
Tosches, Nick. *Country: The Biggest Music in America*. New York: Stein and Day, 1977.

Blues and Rhythm and Blues

Charters, Samuel. *The Country Blues*. New York: Rinehart, 1959.
Epstein, Dena J. *Sinful Tunes and Spirituals: Black Folk Music to the Civil War*. Urbana: Univ. of Illinois Press, 1977.
Heilbut, Tony. *The Gospel Sound: Good News and Bad Times*. New York: Simon and Schuster, 1971.
Keil, Charles. *Urbana Blues*. Chicago: Univ. of Chicago Press, 1966.
Oliver, Paul. *The Story of the Blues*. New York: Chilton, 1973.
Palmer, Robert. *Deep Blues*. New York: Penguin Books, 1981.
Shaw, Arnold. *Honkers and Shouters: The Golden Years of Rhythm and Blues*. New York: MacMillan, 1978.
Southern, Eileen. *The Music of Black Americans*. New York: W.W. Norton, 1971.

Folk

Brand, Oscar. *The Ballad Mongers: Rise of the Modern Folk Song*. New York: Funk and Wagnalls, 1962.
Denisoff, R. Serge. *Great Day Coming: Folk Music and the American Left*. Urbana: Univ. of Illinois Press, 1971.
_____ *Sing A Song of Social Significance*.
Klein, Joe. *Woody Guthrie: A Life*. New York: Alfred A. Knopf, 1980.
Lomax, Alan. *Folk Songs of North America*. New York: Doubleday and Co., 1960. Collection of folk songs.

The Music Industry

Austin, Mary. "Petrillo's War." *Journal of Popular Culture*, 12 (Summer 1978), 11-18.
Chapple, Steve and Reebee Garofalo. *Rock 'n' Roll is Here to Pay: The History and Politics of the Music Industry*. Nelson-Hall, 1977.
Denisoff, R. Serge. *Solid Gold*. New Brunswick, NJ: Transaction Books, 1975.
Stokes, Geoffrey. *Starmaking Machinery: The Odyssey of an Album*. Chicago: Bobbs-Merrill, 1976.

The Mythology of Woody Guthrie

J.L. Rodnitzky

I hate a song that makes you think that you're not any good. I hate a song that makes you think that you are just born to lose. No good to nobody. No good for nothing. Because you are either too old or too young or too fate or too slim or too ugly or too this or too that....[1]

Woody Guthrie was a complicated man and his life and songs are filled with contradictions. However, the above passage catches the basic theme that makes Guthrie a folk hero to successive generations of rebels, bohemians, and defenders of the oppressed. Whatever arguments rage about Guthrie's personal ideas and motivations, few would deny that he loved people and had an instinctual feel for the dignity of every human being. Labeling Guthrie a socialist, commune radical, or folksinger misses his universal appeal. No contemporary black militant could read the above passage and fail to see that Guthrie knew the importance of cultural pride. No radical organizer could miss Guthrie's optimistic "can-do" faith in people's ability to successfully control their destiny. Black militant, woman liberationist, SDS member, labor organizer, student power advocate, Chicano, farmer, or hard hat—all would sense that Woody was one of theirs. Guthrie died in 1967, and his long losing struggle with Huntington's Chorea (a progressive disease of the nervous system) had kept him confined to a hospital room since 1955, yet his spirit could be seen everywhere in the radical 1960s.

There is good reason for going into some detail on Guthrie's life.[2] Guthrie was more than the product of his life; he was his life. His songs were his life and his life was his song. Just as Thoreau worked out and lived out his ideas in the woods, Guthrie worked up his ballads on the road. Both Thoreau and Guthrie fit securely into the American pragmatic tradition. Both sought to drive life into a corner—to taste life as its bitterest or most sublime. However, Guthrie, unlike Thoreau, was never insular. Thoreau was rooted in the settled East and foreign to the wild West. Guthrie's mind and travels embraced the continental United States. From the "redwood forests" to the "gulfstream waters," the land was indeed Guthrie's. Woody was not unlike the thousands of other rootless young Americans in the Thirties—traveling, but without a

Reprinted with permission from *Popular Music and Society*, Volume 2:3, Spring 1973), pp. 227-243.

specific destination. It was natural for these young men to feel that anywhere was better than their sad, discouraged communities. It was easy for him to believe that out beyond their State lines, there was a young vibrant America waiting to be discovered. But whereas thousands made Guthrie's journey, Woody was one of the few who wrote both constantly and passionately about his experiences. In his songs, newspaper columns, and homely prose, he was a sounding board for an inarticulate other America—used to hard times but stunned by the despair of depression. Today these people might be called disadvantaged. In those days they called them poor.

Yet as important, dramatic, and sweeping as Guthrie's life was, it is his legend and not his life that makes him the "Father of the Now Generation." Behind the post-war, protest-song phenomenon was the dramatic rise of a new type of social agitator—the protest balladeer; and most of the current folk writer-performers see Guthrie as the seminal practitioner of the art. The successful writers of the Sixties had demanded an authentic folk hero. They could hardly have worshipped the early commercial folk successes like the Kingston Trio or Burl Ives. Joe Hill was too obscured by myth (and distant in time) to be a flesh-and-blood idol. Guthrie was the logical choice. It is quite ironic that Woody never became famous until his illness forced him to retire as a writer. Only then could his more commercial imitators and worshippers elevate him to the status of historical father and make his name a household word:

Guthrie was easy to venerate since you could always interpret his life and ideas to suit any preference. Woody forcefully spoke against discrimination of any type. He declined to sing "any songs that make fun of your color, your race,...the shape of your stomach or the shape of your nose." Instead he sought to sing about people fighting "to win a world where you'll have a good job at union pay, and a right to speak up, to think, to have honest prices and honest wages and a nice clean place to live in and a good safe place to work in."[3] Hard-hat and college student, McGovernite and Wallacite, black and white, may easily say amen to those sentiments. Above all else, Guthrie had a universal outlook and he felt his songs were a universal message in a universal language—music. As he noted:

> Some people liked me, hated me, walked with me, walked over me, jeered me, cheered me, rooted me and hooted me, and before long I was invited in and booted out of every public place of entertainment.... But I decided that the songs was a music and a language of all tongues.[4]

Woody's son Arlo related that "Woody used to say that the worst thing is to cut yourself loose from people and the best thing is to sort of vaccinate your self right into their bloodstreams." Thus, Arlo observed that when he was born, "Woody told the nurse to put down 'All' on my birth certificate where it says 'Religion.' They wouldn't do that so Woody told them it was either 'All' or 'None.'"[5]

If Guthrie's world view was universal, his political view was partisan. For Woody there was only one struggle—"the fight of the work to win his fair share from his owner (boss, etc.)." To engage in this battle, any folksinger had "to turn his back on the bids of Broadway and Hollywood to buy him and his talents out." Woody was certain beyond doubt that he was on the side "that every child knows is the right side."[6] Thus, Guthrie like Walt Whitman saw himself as the voice of the inarticulate and powerless poor, or from the Marxist historical viewpoint, an edge of the historical wave. He once explained his art in these explicit Whitmanesque terms:

You may have been taught to call me by the name of a poet, but I am no more of a poet than you are. I am no more of a writer of songs than you are, no better singer. The only story that I have tried to write has been you.... You are the poet and your everyday talk is our best poem by our best poet.... I am nothing more nor less than a photographer without a camera. So let me call you the poet and you the singer, because you will read this with more song in your voice than I will.[7]

Ironically, Pete Seeger came across a comment in Guthrie's notebooks that warned: "I got a steer clear of Walt Whitman's swimmy waters."[8] The comment suggests that Guthrie drew quite heavily on Whitman's style and indeed Woody was more of a painter of uniquely personal visions than a taker of still photographs. Yet many performers see him as everyman. Thus, Country Joe McDonald, the sometime rock star, sometime interpreter of Guthrie, prefaced his version of Guthrie's "This Land Is Your Land" by explaining that Woody "was just an ordinary man" who "made all the mistakes, had all the vices...that every ordinary person has. He never gave you the feeling that he was better than you" or "worse than you"; but that "he loved you because you were just like him and he was just like you." McDonald concluded that Guthrie "tapped the reality" of "what it meant to be an American."[9]

If Woody was ordinary, he had more than ordinary partisan political fervor. In 1948, at least, he was rather down on the Republican Party in general and Thomas Dewey in particular. Guthrie observed: "I have spent ten years thinking up reasons why I didn't like Herbert Hoover, and now I multiply by nine and I've got Dewey." Now the picture was clearer for Woody. The enemy was "out there in plain sight." The Union men and voters had driven fascists and bosses "out of their ten thousand little hiding holes, and forced them, herded them, corralled them, all over into one big Republican Camp." Guthrie felt that "all of the Fascist-lovers and Nazi-lovers" had "sent Dewey valentines on his day of nomination."[10]

Guthrie's various exaggerated political statements put him squarely in the radical camp, but his political image has been twisted beyond belief by those trying to depict him as a hip, modern radical. For example, in 1967 Irwin Silber, an early organizer of People's Songs, wrote that you could not really understand Guthrie unless you understood "he was, in the most fundamental sense, a totally-committed, 24-hour revolutionary, determined to turn this whole world upside down." For Silver, Woody had a general outlook that "ultimately required the complete destruction of the world he knew." Silber noted that like Woody, Che Guevara "was some kind of nut." Silber asked if there were a Woody Guthrie somewhere "in this nightmare land we call the U.S.A." who could "write and sing the real Ballad of Che Guevara." Similarly, Silber asked if there was a Che Guevara somewhere "in this midnight" who could "raise his machine gun high above his head and inspire a people to take this land and make it their land."[11] Thus, Silber creates Guthrie...the Guerilla fighter. After all Woody did say this land was your land; he did inscribe on his guitar: "This Machine Kills Fascists." Yet, somehow the picture of Woody and Che walking down the road-machinegun and guitar in their respective hands—strains the imagination. However, it is not surprising that Silber felt that in 1966 during the heyday of the Vietnam War it was obscene for the Secretary of the Interior to name "a dam or power station for Guthrie."[12]

The Right also had an easy time seeing Guthrie's radical, pernicious side. In 1966 the Reverend David Noebel, a fierce anti-Communist, complained that the image projected of Guthrie was that he had written some "Dust Bowl songs, kid songs, union songs....a book called *Bound For Glory* and presumably went to Sunday School the rest of the time." Noebel asked: "What about the Woody Guthrie that wrote columns for the *People's World* and *The Daily Worker?*" Noebel's answer was that Guthrie was significantly involved "in the Communist subversion of American folk music." Noebel charged that Guthrie had been "identified under oath as having been a member of the Communist Party" and that his efforts in support of international Communism were "well-known."[13]

Between these two extremes of love and hate for Guthrie the revolutionary, there is a whole range of tolerant admiration for Woody the displaced American and creative songwriter. For Pete Seeger, Guthrie was a symbol of honesty born out of "just plain orneriness." Like Popeye, Seeger felt that Woody's self image was: "I am what I am, and I ain't gonna change." Thus, Guthrie "was going to cuss," and was not "going to let New York make him slick and sleek and contented." This involved resisting the pressure to make him stop writing for *The Daily Worker* and losing a number of lucrative jobs. For Seeger, this was all part of Woody's remaining "a rebel until the end." Pete also learned style from Guthrie. He admired Woody's "ability to identify with the ordinary man and woman, speak their language without using the fancy words and never be afraid—no matter where you were; just diving into some situation, trying it out."[14] Tom Paxton, a younger singer, learned a similar lesson. "Woody, above all, gave us courage," Paxton said. "He taught us that we can't run fast enough or far enough to stay out of trouble if we are going to be honest in our writing."[15] The conclusion was clear: To be an honest folksinger, Guthrie-style, was to be poor, and Woody surely met the test of poverty. It was his self-confessed followers—Dylan, Ochs, Paxton—who had self-indicted themselves by their commercial success. The times really had changed when Bob Dylan could get rich singing "The Times They Are A-Changing'." If Guthrie had helped change the times, there was little evidence of his effect during his singing and writing career. Only after his forced retirement, did his songs become widely known, or his personage revered. His honored position was obviously a symptom of the folk revival and not one of its causes.

Guthrie's music is hard to classify since it covers so much ground. However, there are four main categories of song which were largely chronological in development—dust bowl songs, union, songs, federal government propaganda songs, and children's songs. The dust bowl ballads are represented by such songs as "Blowing Down That Old Dusty Road" and "So Long-It's Been Good To Know You" (which tell of men driven from the land) and "Tom Joad," Woody's song about John Steinbeck's fictional Okie hero. These songs are simple and stark and their style lends them authenticity. "Pastures of Plenty," Guthrie's melodic hymn to the migrant farmworkers, bridges the gap between the dust bowl ballads and his union songs, while its allusions to America's physical beauty are a foretaste of his most famous song—"This Land Is Your Land." The union songs run from quite specific songs like "The Union Maid," a tribute to union women to much more abstract ballads that depict the plight of the poor in earthy parables. A good example of the latter is "Pretty Boy Floyd," which makes a Southwestern depression-era bandit into a Robin Hood and in which Guthrie testifies that he "never saw an outlaw drive a family from their home." Another song is "Jesus Christ," which adapts the views of the more extreme social gospelists and turns Jesus into a radical organizer of the poor and a thorn in the side of the wealthy. His federal propaganda songs included ballads supporting New Deal projects, like the Bonneville Dam songs the government commissioned him to write (the best known of these is "Roll On Columbia"). They also included songs urging on America's World War II effort—ballads like "The Sinking of the Reuben James," "Dirty Overhalls," and "Round and Round Hitler's Grave." A large group of children's songs like "Grassey Grass Grass," "Riding In My Car," and "Why Oh Why" testify to Woody's love of children.

Guthrie's songs do not lend themselves to simple verbal analysis, since his style was always more important than his message. His grainy voice, simple musical arrangements, crude musical accompaniments, understated lyrics, steady prolific output, and lack of commercial success, all lent credibility to his work. He wrote about what he saw, but more importantly, he composed songs for a purpose. He was one of the first Americans since the Wobbly writers to really believe in songs as a weapon in the class struggle. In the words of the title of a book of songs that includes many of Guthrie's compositions, Woody wrote *Hard Hitting Songs for Hard-Hit People*.[17] This was the truly heroic and historic aspect of his life. To play down Guthrie as a propagandist of the lower class and to center on his numerous, individual strengths, weaknesses, and quirks is to lose his real significance.

However, for many, Guthrie became a lifestyle model, divorced from his songs and his thoughts. Guthrie, the man of the people, became Guthrie the mod singer. Woody, the blood-and-guts union man, became Woody the existential hero. The hearts of the new folkniks were with Woody guthrie, but their eyes and ears were open to Bob Dylan and Jack Elliott. Perhaps Paul Nelson, editor of the *Little Sandy Review*, caught the ridiculousness of the Guthrie-oriented folk scene best of all. In reporting on the 1962 Newport Folk Festival, he observed:

Gone were the sailors...in their places were the fraternity folklorists, the Bronx Baezes and Ramblin' Jack Somebodies...the stars-in-their-eyes worshippers....
Neophyte non-conformists, the young men were courteous, polite, affected in a sort of pseudo-Western manner, all dressed in blue or tan jeans, all trying hard to look, walk, talk, act in a way both highly humane and casually road-weary. The hair was erratic, the clothes as rumpled as parents would allow; the accent was drugstore cowboy, that non-regional dialect of the Shangri-La West that Bob Dylan and Jack Elliott hail from, that mythical nowhere where all men talk like Woody Guthrie and are recorded by Moses Asch.[18]

Bob Dylan's approach to Guthrie was typical of the adulation and emulation Woody received from aspiring folksingers in the 1960s. If Guthrie, like Dylan Thomas, had already died, perhaps Bob Dylan would have named himself Woody Zimmerman. Instead, singers like Dylan borrowed other names and contented themselves with adopting Guthrie's style. That style included faded denim clothes, nomadic wandering, a colloquial rural-American dialect, and an identification with oppressed minority groups. More importantly, it included writing songs about things you either experienced or read about. Thus to imitate Guthrie was to eventually become a topical singer.

From 1959 to 1961 Dylan became a self-created facsimile of Guthrie. He had liked Guthrie's songs earlier, but now he read Woody's autobiography, *Bound for Glory*, and discovered Guthrie the hard traveler. Dylan began to invent a hobo's heritage. He vaguely alluded to being from Oklahoma; he constantly stressed he had been drifting around the country almost all his life. More importantly he began to make Guthrie songs his specialty. According to one early acquaintance, Dylan "knew more Guthrie songs than Guthrie knew."[19] Finally, Dylan got to New York and visited Guthrie. Ironically, Dylan's Guthrie phase had been run through a decade earlier by folksinger Jack Elliott. Elliott, whose real name was Elliott Adnopoz, was the son of a wealthy Brooklyn doctor. In 1951 he had traveled around the country with Woody and picked up the whole spectrum of Guthrie mannerisms and the spirit of Woody's music. During the 1950s Adnopoz emerged as Ramblin' Jack Elliott and even as "the son of Woody Guthrie." Dylan had met Elliott in New York and had picked up some of Guthrie's style second hand. It was not entirely unfair to refer to Dylan at this time (as some observers did) as "the son of Jack Elliott and the grandson of Woody Guthrie."[20] It is equally true that whereas Arlo Guthrie was once known as Woody's son, now Woody is more likely to be described as Arlo's father.

For every Elliott or Dylan there have been and continue to be hundreds of pseudo-Guthries who have not made the bigtime. Rejecting their urban, middle-class backgrounds, they drift from campus to campus (or around a single campus) guitar in hand, passing themselves off as earthy, world-weary, men of the soil. Early in the Sixties they were a subtle protest against the pseudo-intellectual sophistication of the academic community. They exuded a homey, nonconformist individuality, and presumably were at peace with both nature and their own nature. Without a guitar, these "natural men" might easily be labeled beatniks. Armed with a guitar they were instantly transformed into "folkniks" or "folkies." By the 1970s the new stress on naturalism in dress, outlook, and bodily function would give the earlier hard-traveling lifestyle a new base of support—but now the guitar was incidental.

Guthrie is prized as painfully honest and frank, but there was always a part of him that was pure put on. He passed himself off as a country bumpkin, in much the same way Will Rogers and Abraham Lincoln had. His prose was self-consciously filled with simple dialect. His songs, straightforward and simple to understand (at least on the immediate level), were performed with spartan simplicity. Yet Pete Seeger and others testified that although Guthrie ridiculed literary jargon and allusions, he was extremely well-read—ranging from medieval to modern literature.[21] Why then the consistent, tenacious "just folks" quality of his work? The answer is that Guthrie was a self-made myth. To identify with the masses, he had to remain one of the people. His power to influence, he believed, depended on his credibility. In part, his credibility depended on his continued folky ways. Yet, Guthrie was far from a Madison Avenue con man. He did not create one image as a mask while actually pursuing a contrary lifestyle. He self-consciously forced himself to adhere to his chosen image. Just as Abraham Lincoln retained his frontier mannerisms to maintain his political hold on the people, Guthrie retained his rural Oklahoma mannerisms to maintain his artistic hold on the people.[32]

There was yet another similarity between Guthrie and Lincoln. They both shared a militant faith in the average man's ability to shape society for the better. More precisely Guthrie had the 19th-Century American brand of optimism and affirmation. Woody was far closer to the mystic, confident individuality of Emerson than to the pragmatic social planners of his own era. It was after all Emerson who proclaimed: "I am defeated all the time; yet to victory I am born." It is no accident that Guthrie titled his autobiography, *Bound For Glory*, and his collection of writings was titled, *Born to Win*. Both Guthrie and Emerson attacked the political and economical establishment of their times. Both were sickened by American materialism and dismayed by America's moral blight. More importantly both felt that man was born free with limitless powers. However, the difference between Guthrie and Emerson was also the crucial difference between Emerson and his contemporary, Andrew Jackson. Both Emerson and Jackson were for the people, but Jackson was of the people. Guthrie too, perhaps more than any artist of his time, had earned his common-man image. With all his faults and contradictions, he was clearly the quintessential proletarian man.

There are few who would deny that Woody Guthrie has been mythologized, but there is little agreement on what part of him is myth. Almost everybody agrees that Guthrie is relevant, but there is no consensus on how he is relevant. Some observers, like musical arranger Milton Okun, simply see Guthrie as a classic American song writer. Thus, for Okun, "This Land Is Your Land" becomes "our national folk anthem" and "So Long, It's Been Good to Know

You" becomes "a parting song on a par with "Auld Lang Syne."[23] Some, like Irwin Silber, constantly stress that Guthrie was a true revolutionary whose current, indirect popularity "thru the voices of contemporary radiclib culture heroes represents not triumph but travesty," since his really radical writing has been blocked from view by concentrating on a few of his most popular songs.[24]

Several more balanced, less involved interpretations of Guthrie have appeared over the years, but even these tend to center on narrow aspects of Guthrie's life that are of particular interest to his interpreters. Thus, John Greenway in his pathbreaking *American Folksongs of Protest* (1953) saw Guthrie largely as a logical development of the rural hard-times school of folk protest. Although Greenway is a general Guthrie admirer, he goes out of his way to note Guthrie's all too human faults, especially his infidelity to his wives and children. Guthrie supporters are often quite sensitive about any criticism of Woody by those they consider his moral inferiors. Thus, Gordon Friesen, editor of *Broadside* scored Millard Lampell, a former member of the Almanac Singers, for describing Woody as a "bastard," "irresponsible," a drunkard "deserting those he cared for most," a man "looking for something he couldn't name." Friesen insisted that Guthrie "knew exactly what he was looking for" and "named it in almost everything he wrote."[25]

Later, in 1966, Greenway wrote an impassioned article on Guthrie that centered on what Woody's artistic genius represented and reflected. Here, Greenway set forth the theory that Guthrie's radicalism and poetic creativity both could have stemmed from the genetic disease which had made him an invalid. Greenway believed that Guthrie's most creative period was between 1939 and 1948, and that while Woody had written some 1400 songs during his life, the important thing was that from "fifty to a hundred" of the songs were as good as one could "find in all American folksong." Greenway could not imagine a "more harmless, more innocent captive of the cynical Left" than Guthrie. Thus, Greenway's final judgement of Guthrie was that "he had genius as a poet-composer, mediocrity as a singer, and gullibility as a proletarian."[26] Similarly, in 1971, R. Serge Denisoff, a sociologist, presented a detached, balanced interpretation of Guthrie's place in the political folksong movement. In his book, *Great Day Coming: Folk Music and the American Left*, Denisoff depicts Guthrie as a somewhat quixotic individual—torn between his own career ambitions and a feel for the proletarian struggle. Thus, as a communist, Guthrie was an outsider looking in, just as he was outside the mainstream of the entertainment world as a singer.[27]

Most popular accounts of Guthrie see him as a quaint rural drifter who loved America and loved people—especially poor people. Oddly enough that superficial assessment is not far off. However, the important thing is not only what Guthrie was really like, but what people thought he was like. It is Guthrie the legend rather than Guthrie the man that excites this generation of Americans. No amount of cool detailed scholarship can destroy a legend which is born anew everytime a teenager listens to a Guthrie song or reads *Bound For Glory*. As Lillian Roxon noted, Woody was "the man you sang like in the early

Sixties."[28] For a smaller but important number of singers, the legendary Guthrie will remain if not the man to sing like, at least the man to look and act like. His lifestyle has been passed on now for two generations, but it is far from shopworn. Indeed, its relevance seemed to grow throughout the past decade.

From our vantage point, Guthrie appears as a prophet. His lifestyle songs, and writings, clearly outlined the social battleground of the 1960s and 1970s. Who can doubt that the writer of "This Land Is Your Land," would be in the thick of the fight against pollution? Likewise, it is inconceivable that the Guthrie who condemned American intervention in Korea from its beginning would not have fought against American involvement in Vietnam even more vehemently. And would it not be fitting for the man who wrote "Pastures of Plenty," "Deportee," and other moving songs about the plight of migrant workers to be standing on the line with Cesar Chavez's strikers? Could the original devotee of hard traveling have resisted the freedom rides into the heart of Dixie? Could Woody, the enthusiastic exponent of the sit-down strike, have stood aloof from the sit-ins against segregation? While Guthrie's body was chained to a bed, his style pervaded the slogans and strategies of recent American radicals. Power to the People, Right-On, Shut It Down, Make Love—Not War; did not, of course, come from Guthrie's pen, but these chants seem to spring naturally from his lips.

Moreover, Guthrie's physical presence peers at us from all corners of the youth culture. The wild long hair, the faded denims, the careless and outlandish combinations of clothes, and the profanity were all natural to Woody long before they became mod symbols for studied counter culturists. In short, Guthrie was an original alienated man and a natural enemy of bourgeoisie society. He was a living counter culture and perhaps the one American of the 1940s who could step into the Broadway cast of *Hair* and be perfectly at home. Simple, poetic, bawdy, militant, and erratic—Guthrie was Bob Dylan, Jerry Rubin, and Alan Ginsberg rolled into one.

Nevertheless, Guthrie is a prophet without honor among the young. Contemporary youth know only a few of his most famous songs. The hip sub-culture is now overwhelmingly urban, while Guthrie was essentially a piece of rural Americana reacting to the Depression. Thus, the affluent now generation largely find Guthrie's songs corny, artless, and irrelevant. Yet, the Guthrie legend continues to be passed on by a small, esoteric, but influential group of folksingers, and folklorists. To them, Woody is an idol, not because he was a classic model, but because he was so obviously authentic. Guthrie has in one way or another influenced all of America's leading folksingers—Bob Dylan, Joan Baez, Phil Ochs, Pete Seeger, Judy Collins, and Tom Paxton, to name a few. With the exception of Seeger, they do not carry on Guthrie's music or ideas, but they do carry on the Guthrie legend of the folk writer-performer as a social and cultural hero. They speak Woody's name with reverence and accept him unthinkingly, as children accept the Puritans and George Washington. At the same time folk purists have embraced Guthrie as the one artist who did not prostitute his art for commercial gain. Testimonials to his genius and virtue continue to roll in—from the pages of folk periodicals and scholarly journals and from the lips of folksingers. Only a few academicians have seriously considered Guthrie's weaknesses, and even they have been captivated by his influence and my mystique.

Yet, it is less important what Guthrie was really like, and more important that singers like Dylan, Baez, and Ochs think Guthrie was like. For these contemporary artists are the models for youth, and Guthrie now influences largely through his musical heirs. There are a few current performers who traveled with Woody and knew him well, namely Pete Seeger and Jack Elliot. However, these sidekicks never became commercial successes and like Guthrie, they influence largely by their influence on the commercial stars of the folk field.

In sum, Guthrie was on the road before Kerouac, howling before Ginsberg, and on the left when it was really dangerous to be there. He had been militantly anti-establishment before there was a popularly-defined establishment. He undramatically pursued his unique lifestyle long before "doing your own thing" became *de rigeur* for commercial singers. Could he view contemporary America, Guthrie would inevitably recognize that he had, indeed, "been there and gone." Those who knew him personally and those who knew him only through his songs and imitators could indeed say at his death in 1967, so long Woody "It's Been Good To Know You."

Notes

[1] Woody Guthrie (edited by Robert Shelton), *Born to Win* (New York, 1965), p. 223.

[2] Woody Guthrie's life, from his birth to 1942, is vividly traced in his autobiography, *Bound For Glory* (New York, 1943). Additional information on his earlier life, along with comments on his career during and after World War II are found in Woody Guthrie, "My Life," in *American Folksong*, edited by Moses Asch (New York, 1961).

[3] Guthrie, *Born to Win*, pp. 222-223.

[4] Quoted in Donald Myrus, *Ballads, Blues, and the Big Beat* (New York, 1966), p. 45.

[5] Quoted in "Woody's Boy," *Newsweek* LXVII (May 23, 1966), p. 113.

[6] Quoted in *Sing Out!* XVI (December-January, 1967-1968), p. 5.

[7] *Ibid.*, p. 4.

[8] Pete Seeger, "Woody Guthrie and the Gift to Be Simple," *Little Sandy Review*, no. 5 (August, 1960), p. 20.

[9] Remarks quoted in an advertisement for McDonald's record, *Country Joe McDonald Thinking of Woody Guthrie* in *Rolling Stone*, November 29, 1969, p. 9.

[10] Woody Guthrie, *Born to Win*, pp. 162-163.

[11] Irwin Silber's column in *Sing Out!* XVI (December-January, 1967-19678), p. 55.

[12] *Ibid.*

[13] David A. Noebel, *Rhythm, Riots, and Revolution* (Tulsa, 1966), pp. 134-136. Richard Reuss, a Guthrie scholar, argues there is no evidence that Guthrie was actually a Communist Party member. However, he was obviously very sympathetic to the American Communist Party. On this point see R. Serge Denisoff, *Great Day Coming: Folk Music and the American Left* (Urbana, Illinois, 1971), p. 137.

[14] Pete Seeger, "Woody Guthrie—Some Reminiscences," *Sing Out!* XIV (July, 1964), pp. 26-28.

[15] Paxton quoted in Gordon Friesen, "Something New Has Been Added," *Sing Out!*, XIII (October-November, 1963), p. 16.

[16] Woody's early albums, especially for Folkway Records, never sold well. However, since 1960 several companies have released collections of his previously recorded songs. One of the best and most representative collections is the two-record album, *The Greatest Songs of Woody Guthrie*, Vanguard Record no. VSD-35/36 (1970). The album includes Guthrie songs sung by Woody and interpreted by such singers as Jack Elliott, Cisco Houston, The Weavers, and Joan Baez.

[17] *Hard Hitting Songs For hard-Hit People* (New York, 1967). A Collection of 150 songs from the 1920s and 1930s.

[18] Paul Nelson, "Newport: Down There On a Visit," *Little Sandy Review*, no. 30 (September, 1962), p. 51.

[19] For a comprehensive, if uneven, treatment of Guthrie's influence on Dylan, see Anthony Scaduto, *Bob Dylan: An Intimate Biography* (New York, 1971), especially pp. 39-54, 56-57, 62-67, 78-86. Scaduto's book is based almost entirely on the comments of people who knew Dylan personally.

[20] *Ibid.*, p. 57.

[21] Pete Seeger, "Woody Guthrie and the Gift to Be Simple," p. 20.

[22] For this interpretation of Lincoln, see Richard Hofstadter, *The American Political Tradition* (New York, 1948), pp. 93-95.

[23] Milton Okun, *Something to Sing About* (New York, 1967), p. 17.

[24] Silber quoted in *Broadside*, no. 118 (March-April, 1972), p. 4.

[25] Friesen quoted in *Ibid.*

[26] John Greenway, "Woody Guthrie: The Man, The Land, The Understanding in *The American Folk Scene*, edited by David A. De Turk and A. Poulin, Jr. (New York, 1967), pp. 184-202.

[27] Denisoff, *Great Day Coming*, pp. 97-99, 135-137.

[28] Lillian Roxon, *Rock Encyclopedia* (New York, 1969), p. 214.

Country Music and American Values

John Buckley

In recent years, country music has become an increasingly popular form of entertainment. Its audience has been steadily expanding for the last decade and a half. In 1961, only 81 out of 4,400 radio stations in the United States broadcast country music full-time. In 1974, the number had grown to 1,020 out of 6,900 with another 1,450 programming three or four hours of country music a day. Altogether it is estimated that about half of the radio stations in the nation play some country music.[1] There is a country music station in every major market in the United States.[2] Record sales are also increasing. In 1973, slightly more than half of the single records purchased in this nation were country music.[3]

Despite this popularity, much of the public thinks of country music as an artistic and intellectual wasteland. The music has been criticized for being both too vacuous and too reactionary. It is, moreover, often seen as a persuasive medium for the transmission of rural conservatism. Both *The Nation*[4] and *The Saturday Review*[5] have, in recent years, described country music as reinforcing the values of its listeners, while a *Harper's* article concluded that "It is not too farfetched to say the violence of the 1973-74 truckers' strike was fired, in part, by the Nashville sound."[6]

It is the purpose of this paper to examine the relationship between country music, as expressed in its lyrics, and the values of its audience. It is suggested that country music does not reinforce or alter attitudes. Instead, it offers a symbolic world with which audience members may identify.

Since there is no exact agreement as to what is "country music,"[7] only songs are studied which appeared on the *Billboard* "country" charts after January 1, 1973. Some songs recorded prior to 1973 and some songs recorded after 1973, but which did not appear on the *Billboard* survey, are included when particularly illustrative. *Billboard* surveys are drawn from record sales and radio play and, as such, provide a general index of the public's conception of "country."[8] Consequently, some songs of performers such as Kris Kristofferson and Linda Rondstadt are treated as country music while others are not.

Reprinted with permission from *Popular Music and Society* Volume 6:4 (1978), pp. 293-301.

It is worth noting that, although banjos and fiddles are still an important part of the "Nashville sound," not all of country music is the stereotyped steel guitars and whining vocal. A number of country recordings have "crossed-over" to the pop charts, becoming hits in two different markets simultaneously.[9] Both country and pop audiences are usually unaware of this process and selectively perceive such songs to fit their preconceived notion as to what is "country." Different groups may listen to the same song for different reasons; country fans enjoy the qualities they identify with "country," and pop fans hear the elements they believe characteristic of "pop." John Denver and Olivia Newton-John, for example have received major awards in both country and pop music in recent years.

Attention is confined to the lyrics for three reasons. First, country music lyrics are meant to be heard. In general, the melody is the more important factor in the selection of material in rock music,[10] while lyrics are the more important consideration in country music.[11] The instrumental is subordinate to the vocal.

Second, the lyrics are unambiguous. Unlike some other musical forms, there are no allegories and no double-meanings. Both performer and audience clearly understand the meaning of a song.

Third, the lyrics are often an attempt at identification. The landscape, people, and situations encountered in country music, unlike much of popular music,[12] are intended to be realistic reproductions of life. That relatively few listeners have experienced some of the situations described in the music (i.e. going to prison, committing murder) is less important than that the music attempts to elicit universally shared emotions. Loneliness, trust, suffering, insecurity, human weakness, and personal dignity are all constant, integral parts of the country idiom.[13]

In order to examine the relationship between country music and audience values, this paper will (1) sketch the characteristic themes of country music, (2) outline the perspectives toward personal and social relations displayed in the music, and (3) describe the country music audience and its relationship to the music.

Country Music Themes

Eight basic themes characterize country music. Sometimes songs contain only a single theme, but, more often, they are crowded with several. The pattern, however, is for one to dominate, while the others assume a subordinate role. Consequently, the central theme of a song determines its classification.

(1) Satisfying and fulfilling love relations. Like popular music,[14] the majority of country songs deal with love. In a content analysis of country songs from selected years, 1960-70, DiMaggio, Peterson, and Escoe found that seventy-five percent of the songs deal with love in its various forms.[15] A minority of these songs treats satisfying and fulfilling male-female relationships.

Such relations are almost always depicted as within the frame-work of marriage. While both sexes are forever "slip'n around" and "hav'n one night stands," there are no hymns celebrating the joys of cohabitation. Songs treat relationships between men and women, not boys and girls. Except for an occasional song reminiscing about an old high-school sweetheart, adolescent courtship is wholly ignored. Songs tell of the relations, good and bad, of adults. Consequently, marriage is a pivotal consideration.

Sex is an integral, but not a dominant, part of satisfactory relationships. The chorus of Charlie Rich's "Behind Closed Doors" suggests the sexual dimension of the relationship while the stanzas describe the public dimension. The same attitude is expressed more concisely by Ronnie Milsap when he sings, "I'm not just her lover; I'm her friend."

(2) Unsatisfactory love relationships. Easily the single most prominent theme in country music is unsatisfactory love relations.[16] An earlier study of popular music found expressions of romantic discord to be common.[17] In country music, however, the audience not only knows that the singer is unhappy but is candidly told why. If satisfactory male-female relations are equated with good marriage, then unsatisfactory relations are most often associated with a marriage that is going, or has gone, wrong. One or both partners are unfaithful, weak, or inattentive which leads to divorce, regrets, and, in some cases, repentance.

Sex is a more volatile factor in unsatisfactory relations. It is frequently emblematic of other interpersonal difficulties. Titles such as "Barrooms to Bedrooms," "I'd Rather Be Picked Up Here Than Be Put Down at Home," and "Out of My Head and Back Into My Bed" are representative of the emphasis. Male-female relations, in sum, do not go awry because of lack of money or meddling in-laws but because of loneliness, jealousy, and human weakness.

(3) Home and Family. Family relations, while not given anything like the attention devoted to male-female relations, are seen as equally complex. When set in an identifiable locale, these songs are most likely to tell of a farm family and rural life. Typical is David Allen Coe's "Family Reunion," the narrative of a mountain family gathering to play fiddle tunes. Like many other songs in which the family is sympathetically portrayed, Coe is recalling an earlier time.

Home, however, is also the setting for unhappiness. Life is hard for both parents and children, and the problems encountered are not easily solved. "Rocky Mountain Music," for example, tells of a a father's death, the mother's subsequent illness and bad temper, and a little brother whose mental illness causes him to be "taken away." Like the male-female relationship, the family and home present the individual with a range of experience, some rewarding and some debilitating.

(4) Country. It is no accident that family life is more likely to be better in the country; there is a positive agrarian image in country music. "Country" may be a recognizable physical location, but it is more than this; it is a state of mind, a way of life. "Country is," as Tom T. Hall sings, "workin' for a livin,' thinkin' your own thoughts, lovin' your town," but, above all, "country is all in your mind."

(5) Work. Country music does not feature traditional work songs so much as it does songs about work. "The Workin' Man Blues" and "One Piece At A Time" describe dull, repetitive physical labor "with the crew" or "at the factory." There are no songs about school for, as Charlie Daniels notes, "A rich man goes to college/and a poor man goes to work." Work in country music is almost exclusively a male purview. Women are mothers, wives, lovers, barmaids, and truck-stop waitresses. Housework, to be sure, is drudgery, but, with rare exceptions, is discussed only when justifying a love affair.

(6) Individual worth. Country music is rooted in a belief in the worth of an individual. People live lives of quiet dignity, their strength and character not always appreciated by others. They meet and come to terms with, but do not always conquer, blindness, death, poverty, alcoholism, and being orphaned. MacArthur's Hand, for example, tells the story of an old man being sentenced for vagrancy. Once decorated for heroism by the General himself, the proud veteran is now destitute. The old man summarizes his case for the judge, "I was fit to fight your wars,/Am I not fit to walk your streets?" The quality of the man's life is not measured by his conventional accomplishments but by the content of his character.

(7) Rugged individualism. Not only is the individual important, but he, for it usually is a man, controls his own destiny. As Charlie Daniels boasts, "I ain't ask'n nobody for noth'n if I can't get it on my own." Travel, violence, prison, and drink constitute the world of the rugged individualist. The jobs of these men are more expressions of their personality than sources of income. The cowboy has given way to the trucker as mythic hero, symbolizing self-reliance and personal independence. The danger, the uniqueness of the life, and the sense of camaraderie are evident in songs such as "White Knight" and "Big Mama." The trucker is answerable only to himself.

Barroom fights, time in jail, wild parties, and getting drunk are seldom glorified as ends in themselves but, instead, as rites of the rugged individualist. They are actions emblematic of a life style.

There are, however, occasional doubts as to whether the life style really brings happiness. Titles such as "Here I am Drunk Again" and lyrics such as "Today I'll face the big fight/ But I really had a ball last night" express an ambiguous love-hate relationship for the wild life, albeit a minority one.

(8) Patriotism. Perhaps no aspect of country music has received more attention than its patriotic theme. The aggressive militancy of the Vietnam era, when approximately ten percent of country music dealt with social or political issues,[18] will be discussed later, but, suffice to say here, that contemporary songs are overwhelmingly non-polemical. Indeed, social and political issues have almost entirely disappeared as song topics. Of the eight themes, the patriotic currently receives the least emphasis.

Of course, country performers are not alone in singing about true love, the wild side of life, or love of country. Not all the themes in country music, to be sure, are unique to the idiom. What is unique is the symbolic world that is sketched by these themes. It is peopled almost exclusively by adults in the prime of life. Affairs of significance center around the male. The rural life, which has been recently embraced by other genres, has been a favorite image of country writers for over fifty years. Adolescence is infrequently recalled. College, like business and the professions, is all but non-existent, and work is dull, physical, and unrewarding. Marriage, whether good or bad, is at the center of romantic relations. In this world, people, above all, retain their individuality, whether struggling for control over their own destiny or preserving through inner dignity.

First, although it uses some of the same themes as other genres, only country music features all eight themes described here. These themes form a symbolic world that is endemic to country music. Some aspects of the landscape are found in other musical idioms, but nowhere else are social relationships exactly so constituted.

Second, these themes do not change over time. Writers may fashion new and different ways to present the themes, but the themes themselves remain essentially unchanged year after year. Whether the setting is the railroads, mines, or Harlan County in the '30s, or highways, factories, and urban bars in the '70s, the message is the same.

Third, the presence or absence of certain instruments, generally, does not make music country. To be sure, many country songs may be identified by the stylized steel guitars and fiddles. Traditional instruments and instrumentation, however, are not the reliable trademark that they once were. Guitars, fiddles, and banjos have been appropriated by other genres. Some country performers, in turn, added electricity to their instruments and engineering to their voices. At the same time, an increasing amount of recording is done with orchestral accompaniment.

Fourth, the appeal of country music, like other musical idioms, is not always confined to its own listeners. Successful songs may "cross-over," achieving popularity in more than one genre, by attracting a country as well as a non-country audience. Glenn Campbell and Ann Murray are as much country entertainers as pop celebrities. Some "progressive country" and "country rock" performers, such as Charlie Daniels and Jimmy Buffet, have both a rock and a traditional country following, with each group drawing something different from the music.

Country Music Perspectives

These eight themes unambiguously express daily problems and primal emotions. In addition, song lyrics provide perspectives on the social and personal relations represented in the themes. Perspective is provided when the audience is informed of the singer's attitude toward the primary theme in a song. For example, what is the performer's attitude toward being a trucker? Basically five perspectives appear to characterize country music. Although most perspectives can be, and are, taken toward all eight themes, certain perspectives are more closely associated with particular themes.

(1) Expressive. The performer's purpose in a number of songs is merely to express or describe his/her feelings. An exuberance for life and a need to communicate one's satisfaction undergird the expressive impulse which occurs

most frequently in the extremes of rugged individualism and the satisfactory love relationship. Songs like "Dear Woman," and "I've Got a Winner in You" so obviously disparate from "The Red-neck National Anthem," spring, nonetheless from a shared desire to glorify life choices.

The need to communicate feelings is also manifest in narrative songs. These three-minute morality plays are most often employed in describing unsatisfactory love relationships or instructing the audience on the importance of individual worth. George Jones and Tammy Wynette's "Golden Rings" follows the prescribed formula, the first verse describing a couple's purchase of a wedding ring in a pawnshop, the second their marriage "later on that afternoon," and culminating in the break-up of the marriage in the third verse. The expressive perspective is common, but not preeminent, in country music.

(2) Utopia. Many of the people who are not happy with their current situation imagine affairs as being, or having been, better at some other time and/or place. If life is somehow insufficient, it was better in some other place or at some other time. "Paradise," for example, looks back on an agrarian utopia. "A backwoods old town" in western Kentucky is nostalgically recalled as the setting of childhood memories. Its idyllic landscape, however, is a thing of the past since "Mr. Peabody's coal train has hauled it away." While most songs are not so explicit, performers, nonetheless, express an acute awareness that there are conditions which are more desirable than the one in which they currently find themselves. Past and present utopias can be found in most characteristic themes.

Other themes are sometimes also approached from a utopian perspective as, for example, lost love in "The Most Beautiful Girl in the World" and trucking on "Convoy." The latter song is a saga of a cross-country truck convoy that evades the law and violates the speed limit. Utopias are real or fictive, occurring in the present and the past, but it is singular that there are almost no future utopias in country music. Emmy Lou Harris's "One of These Days," a general reaffirmation that things will be better in the future, is a rare exception.

(3) Escape and fantasy. Perhaps the most prevalent attitude expressed in country music is escape and fantasy. Sometimes the flight is physical, but, more often, it is psychological. It characterizes unsatisfactory male-female relations, rugged individualism, and work. Assignation is often portrayed as flight from an unsympathetic spouse. Titles such as "Help Me Make It Through the Night," "She's Helping Me Get Over You," and "From Woman to Woman" are suggestive of the attitude. Work is confronted with psychological fantasy as well as physical escape. In "Daydreams About Night Things," Ronnie Milsap, for example, sings, "While my hands make a livin'/My mind's home lovin' you." Fifteen years in the factory have cost Johnny Paycheck his "woman" and given him nothing in return. He fantasizes that he will hit his foreman and walk out, after telling the boss to "take this job and shove it." Much of rugged individualism is also escape and fantasy. The destination is less important than the trip in songs like "Ridin' My Thumb to Mexico," while the bar, with its attendant drinking and fighting, appears as a refuge from daily problems.[19]

(4) Forbearance. Forbearance, the determination to persevere, is often an indication of individual worth as well as being a perspective that is frequently adopted in family relations. People in these songs do not conjure visions or try to escape into fantasy but confront their problems directly. Like the veteran in "MacArthur's Hand," they continue to strive, although the tide of events may run against them. When laid-off "down at the factory" before Christmas, Merle Haggard recalls how he had "wanted Christmas to be right for daddy's girl" but now hopes only to "make it through December." He does not recall better days or get drunk, but instead, makes plans for the family's future.*

(5) Polarization. Although the polarized perspective is almost entirely absent from contemporary country music, the attitude deserves attention since it played such a prominent role in the songs of the 60s. Polarization is, of course, a rhetorical strategy as well as a perspective, but the concern here is with its function as perspective, with what it suggests about people's attitudes and world view.

Country music has long defended the values of its audience, and its defense has been most aggressive when those values were most seriously challenged. Comparing the advantages of farm and city life is an old theme in country music, but the social upheaval of the 1960s, with songs like "I Wouldn't Live in New York City if You Gave Me the Whole Darn Town," introduced a shrillness seldom heard before. New issues, like the changing role of women, were cast in extremist alternatives. Tammy Wynette, for example, sang the polemical "Love Me, Don't Liberate Me" as well as the more traditional "Stand By Your Man."

But it was the Vietnam War and domestic dissent that elicited the strongest reaction from country artists. From December 1965 through August 1966, "there were always at least four Vietnam songs on the *Billboard* country charts."[20] Most defending the justness of the War and the wisdom of American involvement. The lyrics of these songs, frequently set to martial music, often conveyed a "love it or leave it" tone. By December 1969 and the release of "Oakie from Muskogee," comment was channeled into attacking dissenters, defending traditional American values, and generally ignoring the propriety of American involvement.[21] If some country music frequently presented a polarized perspective during the 1969s, it was reflecting political and social attitudes of the day.[22]

The Country Audience

To say, as some critics have, that country music is "Southern white, working-class music"[23] is only partially true. Its following has grown in recent years until, today, it is more national than regional. This is only one characteristic that emerges from a rough profile that it is now possible to draw of the country

---

*The release of "If We Make It Till December" coincided with the Arab Oil embargo and a Detroit auto strike in the fall of 1973. Although coincidence, the timing may have influenced audience perception of the lyrics.

music audience. It is clear that the average country music fan is increasingly likely to live in the North. Moreover, research indicates that he/she will not be a transplanted Southerner but a native Northerner.[24] This trend enabled radio station WHN in New York City to increase its audience 50 percent within eight months to 1.2 million after adopting an all-country format.[25] The shift is also reflected in record sales. Approximately 10 percent of Loretta Lynn's records are sold in the New York metropolis area.[26] Furthermore, "there is no regional difference between the South and the rest of the nation in the distribution of country music listeners by age, occupation, years of schooling, and family income."[27]

Evidence suggests that the country music audience clusters between the ages of 25 and 49.[28] Country music also has the greatest appeal for the less well educated. As years of education increase, the probability that one will be a country music fan decreases so that high school, and especially grade school graduates are significantly over represented in the country audience.[29]

If country music is no longer a primarily Southern idiom, it remains predominantly working class. It is the rare executive or professional who is a country music fan. More common, but still disproportionately small, are the numbers of fans among the ranks of managers, clerical and sales workers.[30] Peterson and Davis in their 1974 study of "The Contemporary American Radio Audience" point out that "fully 45.5 percent of country music listeners are craftsmen, skilled or semi-skilled workers." They also report that unskilled workers (farm and manual laborers, cooks, porters, bartenders, service workers, etc.) are overrepresented in the ranks of country fans. The country audience, therefore, is concentrated in the "middle income category," earning a family income of between $5,000 and $15,000 in 1975.[31] Few of the very poor or the very wealthy are attracted to country music.

Part of the attraction of country music for this audience would appear to be in the lyrics. Its themes and perspectives reflect common experiences. It is music of identification, written for and about working class adults. Like the people portrayed in the songs, country fans also get married, raise a family, hold a job, take pride in their country as well as confront marital and family problems, illness, and death.

Marriage and family are probably fulcrums of everyday experience. Their real work holds out as much opportunity for personal enrichment as do the fictional jobs of Ronnie Milsap and Johnny Cash.[32] It is not surprising, therefore, that negative perspectives outnumber positive in country music and that any type of future utopia is almost non-existent.

The growth of country music in recent years, however, has attracted increasing numbers of Northerners, urbanites, and even some college students,[33] groups less likely to identify with some traditional country themes. Nonetheless, the music is able to express the values of both its old and new constituencies. That it is able to do this is attributable to the audiences' perception.

Popular culture materials, such as music, may serve different purposes for the same, or different, audiences.[34] It would appear that country music, by communication values of newly acquired significance, is mirroring an important portion of Northern urban opinion. As the Program Director for New York City's WHN explains, "There is a back-to-the soil feeling among urbanites now-a-days. People are ecology conscious. They long for simple days when music reflected love and loneliness and death and going to jail, the stuff country music is all about.[35]

Recent converts in Northern cities, then, are attracted by the ability of the music to articulate their problems. They can identify not only with the common themes of marriage, home and family, and individual worth, but they can also appreciate the importance of self-reliance, forbearance, the agrarian lifestyle, and the general emphasis on the quality of life. In this, they are not appreciably different from their counterparts in the South where "apparently, a larger number of working and lower-class urban whites dream of some day resigning from their jobs and moving to the country to earn a living on a small farm."

In sum, the lyrics of country songs reflect the values of its audience. The fictive world created by country music is not the same as the real world of audience members, but it is one they can easily understand and with which they can identify.

Notes

[1]"Why Country Music is Suddenly Big Business," *U.S. News*, 29 July 1974, p. 59. Benjamin Stein, "Forget the Beatles, Here's to Tom T. Hall," *Wall St. Journal*, 24 Dec. 1973, p. 4.

[2]Steve Toy, "C & W Road Widening $300-Mil Nationwide: Biz As Appeal Soars," *Variety*, 275, 12 June 1974, p. 41; Paul Hemphill, *The Nashville Sound* (New York: Simon and Schuster, 1958), pp. 180-184.

[3]George H. Lewis, "County Music Lyrics," *Jour. of Comm.*, 26 (1976), 37.

[4]Paul Dickson, "Singing to Silent America," *The Nation*, 23 Feb. 1970 pp. 211-213; Florence King, "Rednecks, White Socks, and Blue-Ribbon Fear," *Harper's*, July 1974, pp. 30-34.

[5]John Rockwell, "Blues and other Noises, in the Night," *Sat. Rev.* 3 (4 Sept. 1976), 32.

[6]Florence King, "Rednecks, White Socks, and Blue-Ribbon Fear," *Harper's*, July 1974, p. 34.

[7]"Cross-overs to Country Music Rouse Nashville," *New York Times*, 4 Dec. 1974, p. 75.

[8]James T. Carey, "The Changing Courtship Patterns of Popular Songs," *Amer. Jour. Socio.*, 64 (157). 723.

[9]Bruce Cook, "Nashville's Counter-culture," 3, *Sat Rev.* (4 Oct. 1975), 48-49; "Country Goes Pop," 20 *Horizon* (Nov. 1977), 52-57.

[10]Richard A. Peterson and David G. Berger, "Entrepreneurship in Organization: Evidence from the Popular Music Industry," *Admin. Sci. Q.*, 16 (1971), 99.

[11]Lewis, p. 38.

[12]S.I. Hayakawa, "Popular Songs vs. the Facts of Life," *Mass Culture: The Popular Arts in America*, eds. Bernard Rosenberg and David Manning White (Glen Coe, Ill.: Free Press, 1957), p. 399.

[13] Legal regulations and community standards of good taste prevent the overt expression of certain audience values. Most notable is the underground market for racist records. Jens Lund, "Country Music Goes to War: Song for the Red-Blooded American," *Pop. Music and Soc.*, 1 (1972), 221-223; John D. McCarthy, Richard A. Peterson, and William L. Yancey, "Singing Along with the Silent Majority," *Side Saddle on the Golden Calf*, ed. George H. Lewis (Salt Lake City: Goodyear Pub., 1972), p. 59.

[14] Richard A. Peterson and David G. Berger, "Three Eras in the Manufacture of Popular Music Lyrics," *The Sounds of Social Change: Studies in Popular Culture*, eds. R. Serge Denisoff and Richard A. Peterson (Chicago: Rand-McNally, 1972), pp. 288-289; Carey, "Courtship," p. 721.

[15] Paul DiMaggio, Richard A. Peterson, and Jack R. Escoe, Jr., "Country Music: Ballad of the Silent Majority," *Social Change*, p. 41.

[16] *Ibid.*

[17] Donald J. Horton, "The Dialogue of Courtship in Popular Song," *Amer. Jour. Socio.*, 62 (1957), 576.

[18] DiMaggio, Peterson, and Escoe, p. 44.

[19] Ivan M. Tribe, "The Hillbilly vs. the City: Urban Images in Country Music," John Edwards Memorial Fund Quarterly, 10; Pt. 2 (1974), 44.

[20] Lund, pp. 211-223.

[21] Lund, p. 224.

[22] *Ibid.*

[23] Charles Portis quoted in Mike Reagan, "The Pious Rhetoric of Country Music," *Music Jour.*, 27 (1969), 67.

[24] Richard A. Peterson and Paul DiMaggio, "From Region to Class, The Changing Locus of Country Music: A Test of the Massification of Hypothesis," *Social Forces*, 53 (1975), 497-506.

[25] Stein, p. 4; *U.S. News*, p. 48.

[26] Stein, p. 4.

[27] Peterson and DiMaggio, p. 502.

[28] Richard A. Peterson and Russell B. Davis, Jr., "The Contemporary American Radio Audience," *Pop, Music and Soc.*, 3, 4 (1974), 307.

[29] Peterson and Davis, p. 308.

[30] DiMaggio, Peterson, and Escoe, pp. 49-50.

[31] Peterson and Davis, p. 310.

[32] John D. McCarthy, Richard A. Peterson, and William L. Yancey, "Singing Along with the Silent Majority," *Side-Saddle on the Golden Calf*, ed. George H. Lewis (Salt Lake City: Goodyear Pub., 1972), p. 59.

[33] Phillips McCandlish, "Leaders in Country Music See Chance to Win City," *New York Times*, 16 April 1973, p. 1.

[34] David Reisman, "Listening to Popular Music," *Mass Culture*, p. 409.

[35] Allen Hotlen quoted in Allen Krebs, "WHN Joins Camp of Country Music," New York Times, 26 Feb., 1973, p. 62.

Ten Thousand Acres of Bluegrass: Mimesis in Bill Monroe's Music

Robert Cantwell

The morality of art consists in the perfect use of an imperfect medium.
                                                                Oscar Wilde

What is now widely called bluegrass music, which reached its maturity in Bill Monroe's band on the Grand Ole Opry in the mid nineteen-forties, offered a successful solution to the practical problem of marketing an essentially rural, old-fashioned and traditional music to public audiences increasingly unresponsive to the old-fashioned music except as parody, or burlesque, modes of self-consciousness which for twenty years had been generally encouraged in rural performers by radio and recording entrepreneurs. But it was a practical problem with moral implications: to preserve in the marketplace without self-parody a form not originally or inherently commercial was symbolically to affirm the essential dignity of the way of life from which that music had come, and of which it was the expression—a way of life whose erosion by social and economic change had a vivid illustration in the evolution of the Grand Old Opry, which by the forties had acquired network status and a national reputation, and had relegated the genuinely rural and traditional musician to the background.[1]

By interposing himself between a public audience and a string-band whose music has a traditional character, and by cultivating intensively the essential features of that music so that a more remote audience might more readily discern them, Bill Monroe negotiates the meeting of one phase of culture and another, and makes of that negotiative or mediating process an aesthetic third dimension which is in effect mimetic: just as we make moral inferences about a dramatic character on the basis of his actions, so do we make moral inferences about the musician according to his management of his materials. "I think you can watch people," Monroe says, "any kind of work they do in the way of music, and tell pretty well through their life what they've gone through, if you watch it close enough."[2] A musical performance is potentially, then, a kind of dramatic action, "mimetic" in the sense that the musician "represents" or "figures forth" a character in action who is, whatever his relation to actuality, essentially a fiction.

But the power of a musical instrument, style or kind to "figure forth" is colored by a complex burden of historical, social and cultural associations from which our response to music can never be entirely separated. It is plausible, I think, that a self-conscious traditional musician, for whom the range of those associations is not controlled by formal convention, as it is in classical performance, might expand his field of artistic choice to include them, establishing, in effect, his own conventions, and creating an expanded art which includes both musical and dramatic elements. That Bill Monroe has in fact done so is powerfully suggested by the widely imitated and rigorously consistent pattern of his stage performance, over which he appears to exercise almost complete control. It is also suggested, I think, by a certain disproportion in his reputation among those who have seen him perform as contrasted to those audiences, primarily urban, who have only heard him on record. I suspect that the intense allegiance Monroe inspires as a performer, though obviously a tribute to the power of his music, testifies also to those features of his art which cannot be conveyed on a phonograph record.

The complex effects of Bill Monroe's performance are difficult to describe; but its more obvious features have frequently been noted. Monroe himself is a striking figure—dashing and patrician, presenting that peculiar clarity of image one associates with public, particularly political figures. While offstage he might easily be mistaken for some popular rural evangelist or Southern senator, onstage he is, perhaps, the prosperous and genteel Kentucky planter of the recent past. By whatever subtle means one represents himself to the world—Bill refers to it as "the way a man carries himself"—he conveys the impression of a profound natural dignity which seems to have arisen from the habit of reflection upon matters of principle. However one interprets the message of his person, it is clear that the sheer amplitude of that message places him in a sensory foreground to which the Bluegrass Boys provide a background; the consequence of this arrangement is a three-dimensional acoustic and pictorial space which resonates socially and morally to the intellectual and physical activity of the musicians.

Aristotle likes the pleasure we take in mimesis to the pleasure of learning: "This," the artist has affirmed, "is that."[3] In the later stages of a mimetic art, as its audience grasps the laws of the evolving mode, the artist may struggle to conceal himself, conferring an apparently independent life upon his subject; but at the outset he must persistently intercede, offering his own imagination as a medium through which an otherwise indefinite idea might be resolved. He is, in other words, a teacher and his art has scholarly overtones:

> If you study music deep enough, old time music, why you get to learn what's good for it and what's not good for it. You just can't play it now and not pay any attention to it and do that. You've got to be thinking about it, maybe when you're working doing other things; you've got to keep your mind on that music and really get deep in it. I think I've studied old time music deeper than anybody in the country....[4]

The relationship an audience perceives between Monroe and his band, in whom his music is both represented and embodied, might be compared, albeit imperfectly, to the relationship between, say, a Lomax or Seeger who has brought a folk musician out of the field to the attention of an urban or intellectual audience. The important difference is that for Monroe, the relationship is the subject matter of a dramatic art which symbolically emphasizes the voluntary reintegration of the mediating figure, in what might be called an act of condescension, with the life he has economically, socially and artistically transcended but in which his imagination is rooted, and to which, therefore, he must periodically return in art.

That a moral inference might be made about Monroe on the strength of this act of condescension—I use the term in its primary sense—I think its obvious, and however we might describe that inference, it is certainly the moral foundation of bluegrass music. Monroe's art—his sensitive interpretation of old-time music, his intellectual grasp of the social implications of representing that music to a contemporary audience—demands that the mastery of it, within certain limits of course, include mastery over the style, range and originality of his musicians; and because his four musicians, the Bluegrass Boys, are also a tiny community of men, Monroe's governance of them has the appearance of, and often is in fact, the exercise of moral authority. To the force of such authority in him much of his audience is highly responsive, and it provokes metaphors such as the "father" of bluegrass music, or more extravagantly, the "master" of it: a term whose religious thrust is, I think, lost on no one.

Urban audiences unfamiliar with bluegrass music will sometimes naively suppose that the Bluegrass Boys are not professional musicians, and would no doubt feel betrayed to discover that in spite of testimony to the contrary, Kenny Baker, Monroe's superb fiddler, is not a coal-miner, though he has mined coal. This is a sure sign of the success of the fiction, which, like many fictions, modifies reality only slightly, but with a precision that accomplishes a thorough separation from it. Bill Monroe's sidemen are in fact never anything less than experienced and expert—almost without exception the best in bluegrass; in order to play in Monroe's band a musician must have complete command not only of Monroe's material and of the heavily syncopated, driving rhythms typical of his music, but of the delicate economy of expression which, it seems, a bluegrass musician can learn from Bill Monroe alone and whose purpose, I think, is to promote an overall unanimity or singularity of effect. "Nobody can say they play bluegrass," reports former Bluegrass Boy Bob Black, "until they play it with Monroe."5

What is important for us, though, is that Monroe's paternal role becomes in performance a subject of dramatic representation. In harmony singing Monroe will carefully modulate his powerful voice to the voices of the others; often he will move among individual members of the band during instrumental breaks, or drop behind them to observe the whole, taking care that his own variations on the melody—he calls it "getting the most out of a tune"—do not duplicate any of theirs. Occasionally he will address his mandolin directly to a banjo or guitar picker who has fallen off the pace. "Monroe knows what everybody's doing at all times," Black continues. "He has a thousand ears under that hat."[6] At times one cannot help but feel that were Monroe to relax his grip upon the operations of the band for an instant the entire phenomenon would dissolve before our eyes.

Among many young musicians Bill Monroe is notorious for his insistence upon wholesale good-looks and good grooming in the members of his band; the figurative sons or disciples of the father of bluegrass, of course can be no less. Monroe's sovereignty over them—and from this one must partially exclude fiddler Kenny Baker, who as a kind of right-hand man in the management of Monroe's ten thousand acres of music is intermediate between Monroe and the rest—is implied by the poker-faced expressions of the members, whose immediate audience is, of course, Monroe himself, whose approval for various reasons they wish to solicit; the actual audience, whatever its ethnic character, often seems to arouse terror in them. That a band member should address the audience directly, except by Bill's implicit invitation in an instrumental break, or in any other way call special attention to himself, is unusual and unseemly. The membership of the Bluegrass Boys is, moreover, constantly in flux, and in recent years many of the Bluegrass Boys have been boys in the literal sense: young enough to be Monroe's sons or even grandsons. This flux has been explained in various ways: Bill wishes to populate the field with musicians trained in his style; or he does not pay them enough; or he becomes quickly dissatisfied with them; or they wish to thrown off his yoke. Perhaps all are true. But the formal explanation is that young and newly professional musicians remain in that psychological and aesthetic background which mimetically the music requires; their individual excellence seems somehow to attach to Monroe, as a son's to a father's.

The acoustic instruments upon which Bill insists—banjo and fiddle especially—quite obviously belong, moreover, to the parochial or even domestic background of the music. They are historically connected to a species of Southern music which predates the Civil War and in the popular imagination are emblematic of both the region and the period—Bill calls them "antiques" even if one happens to have been manufactured yesterday in Tokyo. The systematic structure of bluegrass admits each of them in turn into the public or secular foreground, where, as Bill's own remarks suggest, they are played in a fashion that somehow captures the essence of the old-time styles and of the special character of the instruments themselves. We must have, for example, the characteristic tolling of the five-string banjo, the bass runs of the guitar, and the rhetorical wail of the fiddle constantly before us.[7] To thus sharpen or amplify the auditory texture of traditional styles by devices peculiar to bluegrass, and not strictly speaking, traditional, transforms the instruments—If I may offer a conjecture—into representations of themselves. In presenting the particular music of his instrument the musician is at the same time representing it as a class or kind. "This," the banjo-player seems to affirm, "is the banjo." And "This," says the fiddler, "is the fiddle." The vigorously compressed vocal phrasing of bluegrass, too, which draws sentences upon into dense parcels of words, seems designed to represent an impassioned mode of speech, particularly

Southern speech, through the emotional contour of song; its heavily accented pattern of emphasis reflects the singer's effort to preserve the phonetic integrity of the phrase within the constraints imposed by rhythm and melody. Bluegrass singers call this "singing with feeling," a style which often resembles pulpit oratory with its intense conviction and unnerving directness of address. To that intensity lyric is usually subordinate—as, indeed, it is in the churchhouse, where the preacher's message is always and ever the same.

If Bill Monroe did not actually invent this style, he certainly consolidated it for bluegrass. Lord and Parry long ago pointed out that illiterate epic singers think of language in phrases and word-groups, not as discrete words for which they lack an alphabetic image.[8] Bill Monroe, of course, is not illiterate; but his speaking voice has the lovely melodic quality typical of semi-literate or illiterate speech, and he reads with a sub-vocal moment of the lips.[9]

For his accompanying instrument, Monroe has chosen the most anomalous of all, the mandolin, which among the many stringed instruments that have passed from traditional into commercial music has most stubbornly resisted such a transformation (how many electric mandolins are there in Nashville?), and whose role even in traditional music was a modest one. It is Bill Monroe's tirelessly inventive, aggressive, blues-influenced style alone that has brought it into prominence. For the mandolin, like the banjo, cannot readily produce tones perfect enough to qualify it for the fine arts—not, at least, as we have come to know them. No formal techniques are available which will arouse in the mandolin the intensity and brilliance of the violin; nor are further technical improvements likely to give to the banjo the resonance of the guitar or the nimbleness of a mechanically more sophisticated stringed instrument such as the harpsichord. Consequently the emotional impact of the mandolin or banjo is the issue of the musician's struggle to advance ideas sufficiently complex to draw the instrument out of its background of associations—but not at the expense of that background. The predominantly urban practice of confining oneself to melodic elaboration becomes swiftly tiresome; what distinguishes the great bluegrass musician is the subtlety of rhythm and depth of tone that joins idea to association in a single transcendent effect, upon an instrument which in spite of its many charms is not inherently subtle or deep.

Generally speaking then, the bluegrass style emphasizes the tension between the imagination of the musician and the available means of expressing it, a tension which implies that in playing his old-fashioned folk instrument with the expressiveness, energy and drive necessary to move a public audience, the musician has made the best possible use of limited resources. He has made a little go a long way. In this resourcefulness an alert observer will detect the agrarian ethic of strict economy with which the national ideals of self-sufficiency and independence are often associated. This is perhaps why Bill Monroe and other bluegrass musicians insist that bluegrass is the only true "country" music; the insight is a moral one, not sociological or historical. One cannot help but note the yawning gulf between Monroe's music and the country-western music of Nashville, which, with its electric instruments and ostentatious costumes implies a repudiation of the rural ethic—or perhaps a

Saturday-night holiday from it. We might somewhat speculatively extend the principle and suggest that the vocal tension characteristic of bluegrass and other folk-singing styles, like the sexual repression with which Alan Lomax has associated it,[10] reflects underlying economic conditions, particularly conditions of scarcity. The rich, full operatic voice, and the mellow, ingratiating voice of a jazz singer, have little place in bluegrass; rather the singer must sing against the restrictions imposed by high pitches, or, ideally, through some natural flaw—a faint hoarseness such as Ralph Stanley's. Earl Taylor can sing, it appears, without opening his mouth—or if he must through one side of it only.

One final note on the mandolin: Monroe is in possession of many fine antique mandolins, including at least one exceedingly rare Gibson F-5 in mint condition conspicuously autographed by Lloyd Loar, the designer of the delicately carved, scroll-cornered flatback mandolin now chiefly identified, through Monroe's influence, with bluegrass music. There is little doubt that of the many mandolins available to Monroe many sound as good at least as the battered and mutilated instrument he chooses to play on stage, the most important attribute of which is that it is *his* mandolin. As he plays, the unmistakable relish and pride, his eyes fixed on the fingerboard, the instrument thrust forward or held up where we can see it, he actually seems to be *teaching us how to play it;* nor can we help but wonder that Bill has somehow got the broken down old thing freshly arrived from the attic to work, and in so doing has, like Aladdin rubbing the ancient lamp, evoked the spirit of a lapsed existence which imaginatively we long for.

Which brings me to the actual subject matter of Monroe's music. The process of sharpening or amplication in bluegrass has parallels in other art forms which are recapitulations, reconstitutions or summaries of obsolescent styles or kinds. In literature we find analogies in renaissance recreations of ancient epic and romance; in music we find them, perhaps, in the development of chamber music and fugue out of 16th century antecedents. Often such recreations, deliberately or not, are parodies of the original: because parody ridicules by exaggerating what attaches to the object by association, and caricature through disproportion, a distorted or superficial conception of one's model will appear to ridicule it. In country music we have parody in blackened teeth and bib overalls, and caricature in excessively high pitches, accelerated tempos, or fake southern drawls. Monroe's music, however, is a kind of caricature without ridicule; it seems to strike at what is fundamental or seminal, has theoretical force and amounts to a generalization or type: which is simply to say, perhaps, that bluegrass is what Monroe calls "the old southern sound"— a distillation or purification of southern string-band music. As such it is highly abstract, with an enormous capacity to absorb subject matter, and may as easily provide an occasion for technical innovation as become a repository of traditional songs or commercial and sentimental songs composed along traditional lines. The *impulse* to purify, however, to invite the imaginative leap of which we have been speaking, as well as the impulse to accept it, is not abstract; it is antiquarian and even reactionary: the characteristic modes of the romantic imagination. I use the term "romance" loosely to refer to all those kinds of art which employ rigorous formal conventions as a device for containing the free and spontaneous play of the imagination, spontaneity being, as psychoanalysis recognizes, the mode of expression most congenial to the unconscious mind. Thus defined, the term refers not only to those kinds of poetry, music and painting normally called romantic, but to many popular and folk arts, including the folktale and the ballad. Usually associated with the remote, the exotic, or the antique, romance contemplates a human action in an idealized natural setting at a distance sufficient to discover its typical or perennial patterns, or what are often called archetypes or myths. To place its subject matter at a suitable distance, romance will typically interpose some mediating agent through whom the audience must apprehend the matter second-hand.

Nelly Dean, the dramatized narrator of Bronte's *Wuthering Heights*, is such an agent, as is the mysterious cabbalist whom Coleridge invents to annotate his *Rime of the Ancient Mariner*. Northrop Frye describes the romantic world[11] as one "idealized by reverie" in which good and evil are sharply discriminated; characters in romance consequently may "expand into psychological archetypes" so that we find in hero, heroine and villain figures upon whom, in Jung's terms, *libido, anima* and *shadow* might readily be projected: thus the romanticism of most popular literature, with the "suggestion of allegory...constantly creeping in around its fringes." With its reliance upon the understructure of the individual psyche, Frye goes on, romance "radiates a glow of subjective intensity" which inclines toward the "tragic emotions of passion and fury" from which "something nihilistic and untamable" is likely to escape. The social affinities of romance, he adds, with its "grave idealizing of heroism and purity," are with—think of Byron—the aristocracy.

In these sense, I think, bluegrass is romantic. The grave idealism and subjective intensity are everywhere apparent in bluegrass and in the personalities of bluegrass musicians, as is the untamable thing that howls like a banshee in some of the more acute and concentrated efforts of bluegrass tenor singers. In the singer himself we have a hero, in the *persona* of the solitary pilgrim reminiscent of Bunyan's folk allegory, or, closer to home, of the disconsolate rambler touring a nightscape of honky-tonk and tavern; in a more carefree spirit he may become the yodeling cowpoke of the Western plains. Our heroine is a maiden descended nearly without modification from the ballad tradition and bound up with an indefinite longing for lost places and times:

> Oh in dreams I see my darling
> In a gingham dress she looked so sweet;
> Oh I long for old Kentucky
> And my darling once more to meet.[12]

But the grown woman in bluegrass lovesongs is far more likely to betray than to love you; she partakes of an evil expressed mutually in songs of romance shattered by infidelity as of households broken up by death—the severing of human ties, particularly family ties with their foundation in sexual love. Rarely do we meet the Prince of Death face-to-face—but we do meet him. His profoundest expression echoes the Christian imagination at its most primitive, as in "The Little Girl and the Dreadful Snakes": I ran as fast as I could through the dark and dreary wood/But I reached our darling girl too late.[13] Evil has a more effete expression, too, in a landscape inherited from the 19th century bourgeois preoccupation with the grave—dreary and funereal, sometimes in bluegrass vaguely associated with city streets, in which the disoriented soul, whose symbol is often an orphaned child, confronts an earthly existence from which all light has withdrawn to the ineffable glory beyond, itself accessible only through death.

Altogether, of course, these themes represent the immediate background of bluegrass, which includes Anglo-Irish folk tradition, evangelical religion, turn-of-the century popular song, rural blues, and the beginnings of the country-western motif, which through Jimmie Rodgers exercised strong influence on Monroe. But what is more to the point, perhaps, is the material which bluegrass does *not* absorb from its background or from other kinds of music: it largely rejects the trivializing or antiseptic treatments of love common in popular music, for example, while at the same time rejecting the sexual innuendo of the blues; from country-western music it rejects the tendency to treat contemporary social, political or domestic problems. There are telling exceptions, of course: John Prine's "Paradise," which is about strip-mining in eastern Kentucky, joined the bluegrass repertoire almost at once. Though its themes may occasionally range into the northern urban present, the thematic center of bluegrass remains the southern rural past, especially the mountain past, which since the days of Cecil Sharp has been a subject for romantic contemplation. And if the affinities of romance, finally, are aristocratic, then Bill Monroe, costumed as a prosperous southern landowner, offers to his audience an image cleansed of vulgarity in which it can identify a social and economic ideal: "someone they can look up to," Monroe says, "a gentleman."

Like the peasant balladeers who saw the outlines of human passion in the lives of their betters, and those aristocrats who for the same reason idealized the rustic or pastoral life, Bill Monroe has translated social distance into aesthetic distance, particularly the vast social distances which are the stuff of romance. In doing so, of course, he objectifies himself—the image we behold in Bill Monroe is beyond us whatever our social status; it is beyond us the way sculpture is beyond us. But, like a Byzantine icon, it is an image that stares back at its beholder. By placing himself imaginatively on an aristocratic plane, Monroe climbs to a prospect from which he can contemplate his own life, and by extension the entire way of life his own represents, at a distance. "Way down in the Blue Ridge Mountains..." "Back in the hills of old Kentucky..."[14] The narrator of these lines has been figuratively expelled from the world of which he sings, so that in Monroe's music, subject matter and the manner of its representation meet in the fact of exile. The three-dimensional configuration of the bluegrass band, the tension between musician and instrument, and the distance between singer and subject—in this interplay resides, I think, a single unitary purpose.

If bluegrass is somehow romantic, with the romantic emphasis upon the simplicity as well as the extremity of human experience, perhaps we can describe with some precision, at the risk of seeming a bit fanciful, what species of the many possible romantic effects bluegrass attempts to produce. I've tried to suggest that if in a mimetic art moral inferences can be made on the basis of a human action, then the bluegrass style, with its antique instruments, its vigorously syncopated phrasing and tonsil-busting pitches, is an ordeal designed to challenge, and in challenging expose, the artist's intellectual, imaginative and moral resources. All serious music, of course, presents such a challenge; but bluegrass exploits it for mimetic ends. No doubt we admire Itzhak Perlman, and may make certain moral inferences about him on the basis of his playing—indeed, since we suppose that such qualities as imagination and intelligence manifest themselves in any violinist's performance, we *must* make such inferences. But *that* we do is peripheral to his art. Perlman's aim is to join our souls to the soul of the composer, Monroe's to set forth a moral ideal. Perlman's relationship to the composer's text, which can be said to be held in common by its typical audience, somewhat resembles the relationship between, say, an epic singer and his materials, which are traditional and communal. Thus, surprisingly, the art of classical music, with respect at least to the relationship among composer, performer and audience is much more like a traditional art than is Monroe's music, which, though it calls upon traditional materials, is essentially original and individual.[15]

We should conclude then by considering Monroe's astonishing voice, which has been compared to everything from a railroad whistle to a bowl of fresh cream. Its power, like unto a jet-engine, is obvious to anyone; not so obvious, perhaps, is its delicacy and lustre: "Bill's got a pearl in his voice," Ralph Stanley says. According to Bill Keith, the well-known chromatic banjo-player who traveled with the Bluegrass Boys in the sixties, Monroe in riding from show to show would attempt to sing the songs of one performance a half-tone higher for the next. This is not high singing for its own sake; rather it is an effort to preserve the morally-grounded tension between the vocal powers and the demands the singer makes upon them. Where that tension is lost, in singers for whom high notes pose no difficulty, though the broader mimetic effect of the style may remain in force, its *moral* dimension is lost. Were this not the case bluegrass music would be dominated by eunuchs or sopranos or both. Moreover to sing *above* one's range—to sing, that is, where the only feature of the voice still under control is pitch, which cannot properly be called singing at all, is to invite an uncomplimentary inference. "If you sing *too* high," Bill says, "people'll say, 'Now that man's used bad judgment'." *Judgment*. Bill Monroe's judgment consists in knowing, among other things, at what point in his vocal range on a given day or evening a song can be attacked to produce a certain emotional effect popularly called "the high lonesome sound"—and if that should happen to be in B-flat, well then, let the fiddler, who would no doubt prefer to play in A, play in B-flat. For the "high, lonesome sound" occurs only at the apex of an arc which describes the line of equilibrium between vocal force and what might be called vocal flavor or value.

What is the "high, lonesome sound"? I wonder if it is not a musical equivalent of that characteristically romantic effect produced by the conjunction of beauty and terror called the Sublime. Certain of our romantic art comes to mind, such as the painting of the Hudson River School, which by miniaturizing the human figure isolates it in a landscape of immense proportion and ineffable detail, an image whose poignancy consists in our recognition that the painter has placed us at a distance from our subject so vast that our powers of observation have been in effect supernaturally expanded. This recognition is accompanied, I think, by a sensation of exile and solitude, which by virtue of the union of the emotions of isolation and expansion arouses a powerful conviction of intellectual or spiritual growth measured by the headlong fall of the eye into an impossibly remote vanishing point. The scale of the earth has been expanded, and there is no foreground; we have the giddy sensation of being held aloft by an invisible support—nor will the painter allow us to look down at our feet. By taxing the powers of perception to the limits of what pleasure which can be taken in beauty, the sublime intensifies the painful disproportion between what we can imagine—and thus desire—and what we can actually possess.

What the romantic painter achieved pictorially, Monroe achieves musically: though I hesitate here to make too sharp a distinction between auditory and visual experience. Auditory impressions are seldom unaccompanied by some phantom and fugitive visual interpolation, and since in human perception kinesthesia is the norm we are justified, I think, in attempting to understand one sense in terms of another.

In the psychic universe through which the romantic imagination moves—again I follow Frye[16]—heights, and, if the metaphorical extension will be permitted, high-pitched sounds, are perennially associated with intellect and spirit, with moral purity and ultimately with the divine. All organic processes, including thought and feeling, establish sensations in and are traditionally identified with various points in the body; the highest operations of the mind seem to take place (of course I know this only by report) *above* the top of the head: "I know I have read a poem," says Emily Dickinson, "when I feel as if the top of my head has been blown off." Moreover the figures we apply to high-pitched sounds—sharp, keen, pure, piercing and the like—are generally the same ones we apply to wit, intelligence and moral sensitivity. In the kinesthetic sensorium, the high-pitched note for which the jazz trumpeter of bluegrass singer has exchanged his soul moves us toward a point at the center of experience, a point without dimensions and therefore out of time that organizes attention and sharply resolves the will. Visually that point is literally a vanishing point—it flings the singer back into the distant hills from which he came, miniaturizes him, as it were, freeing him from imperfections and placing him in a field of immensities which for a fleeting moment of psychic unity—what might be called a momentary arrest of thought—we grasp; but *from which we must depart.*

It is the way Bill Monroe conducts himself on this rarified plane of high notes that his mimetic genius shines forth most brilliantly. Other singers, perhaps, can reach their vocal *primum mobile*, and do it with ease, precision and grace. But Bill Monroe, one might say, does it bravely—leaping, not climbing, not clinging by the fingernails but standing solidly upon two feet—only for a moment, but long enough to breathe the air and plant a flag. Nor, having arrived, will he depart carelessly or in haste; rather he soars away like an eagle, imitating, in certain absolute performances such as "Goodbye Old Pal" or "Muleskinner Blues," the natural decline of receding sounds—the Doppler effect—and thus provoking an inestimable sensation of loss of that to which, according to the momentum of musical expectation, we have become deeply committed. The emotion is bereavement, and we find an expression of it in the pearl in Bill's voice to which Ralph Stanley referred: a vocal image which I myself have heard only in the voices of certain elderly people and in voices, especially children's, struggling to hold back tears.

And *that's* what makes us feel lonesome.

One wonders if bluegrass music is not the complex response of an inspired hill-country musician who early in a professional career found himself behind a proscenium arch in the vast, dark spaces of a public auditorium, with a sea of impersonal faces spread out before him—wonders, especially, when one recalls that Bill Monroe has been visually impaired all his life. In giving birth to bluegrass, Monroe must somehow have redefined his relationship to his inheritance of traditional music, must have expanded his awareness, perhaps, as I have suggested, under the influence of a crisis at once practical, social and psychological, sufficiently to make of those cultural boundaries which formerly enclosed him a formal design which is the content of a newly-formulated and more abstract medium. The simple presence of formal design suggests visualization: hence the usefulness of a visual analogy. In some respects bluegrass seems an auditory exploration of terrestrial space; the very name implies it. In his singing and playing Monroe generates a hypothetical perspective which does away with the actual setting—auditorium, nightclub, park—and establishes an imaginative landscape, sunlit, boundless and green, of which the band—itself a neat and compelling picture—is the center and source.

Bluegrass is not more than thirty-five years old. But it essentially captures a richly variegated and more ancient world of traditional and popular music—"ancient tones," in Monroe's phrase—which would otherwise have been forgotten, whose sources are commingled with the sources of our national life. As a coherent ensemble style, bluegrass provides the basis for what could conceivably become, with further refinement, a native classical music; indeed in Bill Monroe's band at least it is already a classical art. Though its implied tense is the past, it discovers our humanity in retrieving from the past facts of imagination that are immune to time and change.

Notes

[1] Bill Malone, *Country Music U.S.A.: A Fifty-year History* (Austin, 1968), pp. 72 ff.

[2] Quoted in Ralph Rinzler's notes to "The High Lonesome Sound of Bill Monroe and His Bluegrass Boys," MCA-110 [formerly Decca DL7-47801]. I should like to acknowledge at once a sweeping and profound debt to Ralph Rinzler, who has made a more intimate acquaintance with Bill Monroe possible for me, and whose deep understanding of and enthusiasm for Monroe has helped me better to appreciate his genius. All of Monroe's remarks quoted here are taken from conversations between 15 and 18 April 1977, a four-day period during which Rinzler and I traveled with Monroe's band.

[3] See *Poetics*, Chap. IV.

[4] Rinzler, op. cit.

[5] Quoted by Dix Hollobaugh in "Iowan Bob Black Grazes on Nashville's Bluegrass," *Des Moines Sunday Register Picture*, September 19, 1976, p. 31.

[6] Ibid., p. 31.

[7] Suggested to me by Bill in an interview on 17 April, 1977.

[8] Albert B. Lord, *The Singer of Tales* (New York, 1960), p. 25.

[9] I observed this while traveling with Monroe in April.

[10] Alan Lomax, *Folk Song Style and Culture* (New York, 1968).

[11] My discussion here follows Frye's essay "Specific Continuous Forms," in the *Anatomy of Criticism* (Princeton, 1957), pp. 303 ff.

[12] Bill Monroe, "Rose of Old Kentucky," BMI.

[13] Albert Price, "The Little Girl and the Dreadful Snake," BMI.

[14] The opening lines of the refrains of Monroe's "Little Georgia Rose" and "On My Way Back to the Old Home," respectively.

[15] See Robert Kellogg, "Oral Literature," *New Lit. History*, 5 (1973-74), 55-56.

[16] See especially *The Secular Scripture: A Study of the Structure of Romance* (Cambridge, 1976).

Bright Lights, Big City: A Brief History of Rhythm and Blues 1945-1957

Tom McCourt

The decade following the end of World War II appeared to be a placid time for America. Henry Luce's "American Century" reached its apex as business recognized and then rushed to fill postwar marketing gaps both here and abroad. Per-capita income soared from 596 dollars in 1940 to 1506 dollars in 1950,[1] and abundance flowed like the fresh ribbons of concrete carrying families to the promise of the suburbs, where the din of the city would be replaced by the drone of softly whirring appliances. But underneath its surface sheen of tranquility and tedium, the mosaic of American society was shifting into patterns that would result in a fundamental redefinition in the next quarter-century.

World War II drastically altered the shape of the work force and abetted the assimilation (at least economically) of minority groups into the mainstream of American society. Displaced by the growing mechanization of Southern agriculture and attracted to the prospect of unskilled wartime labor, over 1,600,000 blacks migrated to the urban North in the 1940s.[2] Three migratory routes predominated—from Mississippi and the Delta states to Chicago, from Texas and the Midwest to California and from Georgia and the Carolinas towards Boston and New York.[3] The prosperity fostered by World War II engendered the rise of an urban black middle class, and business discovered this new class possessed a great deal of economic power. While the media income of blacks continued to lag far behind that of whites, studies indicate that the economic position of blacks grew at a faster rate between 1940 and 1954 than at any future time.[4]

The recording industry recognized the market potential of minorities long before the civil rights era of the early sixties. The first record by a black artist, Mamie Smith's "Crazy Blues," was released by the Okeh Recording Company in 1920 and briefly sold a phenomenal 7500 copies a week.[5] An almost exclusively black audience purchased jazz and blues releases at the rate of five million records annually in the twenties and companies like Okeh, Paramount and

Reprinted with permission from *Popular Music and Society*, Volume 9:2 (1983), pp. 1-18.

Columbia engaged in heated competition for the "race record" market. They were joined by several small black-owned labels, including Black Swan, Oriole and Black Patti. The Depression decimated the recording industry, however and by 1934 only Columbia, ARC-Brunswick and RCA's Bluebird subsidiary were issuing "race records."[6] Columbia reportedly survived largely on revenue generated by blues singer Bessie Smith,[7] and by the late thirties the surviving companies and newcomer Decca Records were thriving in the "race" market.

For a number of reasons, the years during and immediately after World War II saw a dearth of black recordings. Fearing the jukeboxes would curtail the demand for live musicians, in July, 1942 the American Federation of Musicians instigated a two year moratorium on recording.[8] Coupled with government restrictions on record production due to a scarcity of shellac, the major record companies dumped the "race" market to concentrate on more profitable mainstream pop. In spite of these constraints, the war years saw rapid changes in black music. Although traditional blues retained some following among recently transplanted Southerners, many were anxious to reject the stoic resignation and despair that ran rich through country blues. According to Mike Rowe, "as the postwar migrants settled down to urban life there was an undoubted reaction to the 'cottonfield' nostalgia that the blues was supposed to represent."[9] The urbanization of black America was reflected in the popularity of swing bands led by Jimmie Lunceford, Count Basie and others, but postwar economic pressures reduced the size of many touring bands. Bandleader Johnny Otis explained the origins of small-group rhythm and blues:

Around '47, jobs became increasingly scarce for big bands.... When I put together a new group, I was still thinking of a brass section, reed section. So I used two saxes, trumpet and trombone and piano/bass/drums/guitar. This became like the standard rhythm and blues ensemble.[10]

But rhythm and blues ensembles, emerging simultaneously on the East and West Coasts and upper Midwest, were much more than attenuated big-bands. Their music may be described as a fusion of gospel music, "jump" or shuffle rhythms derived from boogie-woogie pianists and the shout-styled blues of big-band singers Joe Turner and Jimmy Rushing. Vocalists like Clyde McPhatter and Jackie Wilson later emerged with deep roots in gospel and rhythm and blues appropriated such gospel elements as melisma vocal techniques, ritualized call-and-response and the vocal quartet format adopted by the Five Royales, the Dominoes and many others.[11] Ray Charles, for one, achieved an artistic and commercial breakthrough (as well as the enmity of traditional gospel singers) by adapting secular lyrics and strident arrangements to gospel standards (i.e., "I Got a Woman" from "My Jesus is All the World to Me.")[12]

The saxophone became a primary solo instrument in the wake of reduced brass sections and newly-electrified guitars and basses contributed a jagged intensity. The sheer physical exuberance of rhythm and blues was considerably removed from the staid rhythmic conventions of Tin Pan Alley and virtually all components of the music were subjugated to the quest for "danceability." Arnold Shaw noted that "words were frequently employed and manipulated for their rhythmic properties, giving rise to the cry that [rhythm and blues] lyrics were incomprehensible."[13] At times, lyrics could seem inconsonant and repetitious, but Ian Hoare found that "[rhythm and blues] often uses words in a spontaneous manner—part of a wider pattern in black music whereby the act of expression took precedence over the artifact as the final goal."[14] Cecil Grant's ballad "I Wonder" is widely credited with breaking open the rhythm and blues recording book in 1945. But Grant was soon outshown in popularity by Louis Jordan and his Tympany Five, whose "Caldonia" and "Open the Door, Richard" each had over one million dollars in sales. Jordan was the first consistently successful rhythm and blues artist—his sunny demeanor and upbeat (if often self-depreciating) recordings and performances dovetailed perfectly with the needs and attitudes of many blacks in the mid-to-late-forties.

Rhythm and blues was performed by and for residents of the postwar black ghettoes and its artists initially made few concessions to a mass audience. Consequently, the music's nascent raucousness was not universally welcomed by the public. Peacock Records' head Don Robey remembered, when "rhythm and blues was felt to be degrading and not heard by respectable people."[15] The years before World War II had seen isolated instances of black performers achieving popularity with white audiences, but early crossover success either sang in a manner similar to white performers of the era or accommodated stereotypes of "funny" and "childlike" black behavior. Dismissed by whites and radio programmers, rhythm and blues gained exposure among blacks through jukeboxes. By 1940, 350,000 jukeboxes were in service around the country and in 1945 a leading record manufacturer claimed that 75 percent of his output was slated for jukeboxes, with only 25 percent apportioned for retail sales.[16] Cosimo Matassa, head of New Orleans' most successful recording studio, attested to the enormous effect of jukeboxes on sales:

A hit record would get worn out each week on the jukebox, because shellac supplies were scarce and record formulations were poor...it got played 100/110 times and it was worn out. So a hit record kept on selling and selling.[17]

Juke joints, cramped and frequently delapidated bars featuring jukeboxes for dance music, were primary sources of entertainment for many blacks due to the zealous segregation of white bars and theaters. Black musicians had played to strictly segregated audiences at a few white establishments in the thirties and early forties, but after the war most performers ground out endless strings of one-nighters on the "chitlin circuit" of black theaters across the country. Harlem's famed Apollo Theatre, the "flagship" of the circuit, presented such fledgling performers as Ella Fitzgerald, Billie Holiday and the Drifters at its Wednesday night amateur contests. Other noteworthy theaters on the tour included the Royal in Baltimore, the Regal in Chicago, the Paradise in Detroit and Washington D.C.'s Howard Theater. The majority of American halls, however, were off-limits to blacks. The musicians' union was segregated and in 1944 the NAACP found that only 32 of 673 locals were "colored." A few had segregated subsidiary branches, but the majority excluded blacks altogether.[18] Black musicians were often subjected to humiliating treatment at the hands of white clubowners and those who objected to such treatment faced harsh consequences. For example, Cab Calloway was pistol-whipped by a security guard and booked by police on charges of intoxication and resisting arrest when he tried to enter a white Kansas City ballroom where Lionel Hampton was performing.[19]

Blacks only made inroads into the entertainment industry after World War II, when their economic clout could no longer be ignored. Many clubs sought black patronage when clubowners discovered that black acts often cost less to book than comparable white groups. Record sales figures revealed that blacks spent a higher percentage of their income on records than did whites. Ahmet Ertegun of Atlantic Records told Arnold Shaw:

> Black people were clamoring for blues records, blues with a sock dance beat. Around 1949, that was their main means of entertainment. Harlem folks couldn't go down town to the Broadway theaters and movie houses. Black people had to find entertainment in their houses—and the record was it.[20]

Black music gained radio airplay after the war as ghetto communities gained sufficient economic strength to support black-oriented programming. In addition, the advent of television forced many radio stations to devise alternative formats as the formerly homogenous radio market became segmented and specialized. In 1948, Memphis station WDIA became the first 50,000 watt station to devote itself exclusively to black music. Encouraged by the success of WDIA's format, by 1951 most large Southern cities had a radio station devoted to black programming with Northern cities following suit shortly thereafter.[21] Independent white-owned stations began hiring black deejays in an effort to garner black audiences and in 1953 *Variety* found over 500 deejays across the country devoting their shows to rhythm and blues.[22] Their names reflected the funk and flash of rhythm and blues—Fatman Smith, Poppa Stoppa, the Jet Pilot of Jive and others were instrumental in exposing the music to a broader audience.

By the end of World War II, the major record companies had largely abandoned "race records" as well as "hillbilly" music due to wartime restrictions on materials and the limited sales potential of specialized markets. Independent labels, such as Exclusive, Beacon, Varsity and Keynote, had featured jazz, pop and gospel in the late thirties, but these companies also suffered from the wartime supply crunch. As a result, postwar conditions were ripe for the emergence of a profusion of virtual one—or two-man operations to fill the void. The advent of portable tape recording eliminated the necessity of elaborate recording facilities and independently-run pressing plants opened their facilities to anyone with cash in hand. An estimated four hundred record companies started operations in the forties and 100 lasted until 1952.[23] Their hold on the rhythm and blues market was so strong that a *Billboard* survey found that only two of the top 50 rhythm and blues records released between 1949 and 1953 were issued by major companies.[24] Many of these new labels were started by shrewd white businessmen solely because the music promised quick and substantial financial rewards.

The founders of Atlantic Records, however, were notable exceptions. Ahmet Ertegun, the record-collecting son of a Turkish diplomat and Herb Adamson started their label in New York in 1947. Atlantic initially issued jazz instrumentals but steered its course towards rhythm and blues after scoring its first sizeable hit, Stick McGhee's "Drinking Wine Spo-Dee-O-Dee," in 1949, Singer Ruth Brown's success for the label illustrates Atlantic's early grasp of the crossover potential of rhythm and blues. Ahmet Ertegun admitted:

The blues we made with Ruth Brown came out like urbanized, watered-down versions of real blues. But we discovered white kids were buying them because the real blues were too hard for them to swallow. Distributors started telling us that they were selling these records as pop.[25]

Atlantic's frequent use of New York-based jazz musicians and sophisticated instrumental arrangements resulted in what were probably the most polished rhythm and blues recordings of the era and the label racked up hit after hit with artists like La Vern Baker, the Drifters, Joe Turner and the Clovers. The company enjoyed a positive reputation among its artists because Atlantic's management avoided the unscrupulous methods employed by many other labels. According to Charlie Gillet, major record companies often stole songwriter credits and cheated artists out of any royalties from sales.[26] Many artists, fearing record company machinations, rejected royalties in favor of outright payments and lost potentially sizeable earnings if their records became hits. It is no surprise, therefore, that performers were drawn to Atlantic, which guaranteed them royalties of five percent on sales. Ahmet Ertegun recalled a visit by a Columbia representative that illustrates the major label's contempt for rhythm and blues artists:

He wanted to make a deal whereby Columbia would distribute for Atlantic Records because we seemed to be very good at what he called 'race records.' So I said, 'Well what would you offer us?' He said, 'Three percent.' 'Three percent!' I said. 'We're paying our artists more than that!' And he said, 'You're paying those people royalties? You must be out of your mind!' Of course he didn't call them 'people.' He called them something else.[27]

Atlantic revitalized the moribund careers of performers like Ray Charles and Joe Turner and the company also relied heavily on Southern field trips to discover artists. Atlantic became preeminent among rhythm and blues labels, with grosses ranging from one million dollars in sales in 1953 to 20 million dollars in 1963. The company scored over 100 top-ten rhythm and blues hits between 1950 to 1966,[28] and its mid-to-late fifties roster of artists such as the Drifters, the Coasters, Chuck Willis, Clyde McPhatter and Ray Charles illustrates the depth of Atlantic's contribution to American music. Atlantic remained one of the leading independent labels until its sale to Warner Brothers in 1966.

Chess Records was another giant among the early rhythm and blues labels. Polish immigrants Phil and Leonard Chess ran the Macamba Lounge in Chicago, and the bar's success led them to establish Aristocrat Records in 1947. Their first release, after changing the label's name to Chess, was Muddy Waters' "Rolling Stone" in early 1950. The record sold approximately 70,000 copies, phenomenal for a straightforward country blues. The Chess brothers were convinced that they had a solid business proposition and Leonard Chess undertook a series of field trips through the South to establish relations with small Southern labels.[29] Record leasing and reciprocal promotion agreements were common among independent companies lacking extensive distribution networks.[30] Chess leased a number of blues sides from Sam Phillips of Sun records, including "Rocket 88" by Jackie Brenston and the Delta Cats in 1951. The song, fused "jump" rhythm, distorted electric guitar and a squealing saxophone in a manner that has led man to hail "Rocket 88" as the first rock and roll record.[31] While arch-rival Atlantic smoothed and buffed its rhythm and blues to a high gloss, Chess stood at the cutting edge of recording technology with its pioneering use of tape delay and echo effects. But the Chess legacy is built largely on the recordings of Muddy Waters, Howlin' Wolf, Little Walter and Sonny Boy Williamson, the monumental figures who defined electric blues.

Chess also had a couple of early successes with pop ballads by the Moonglows and the Flamingos, but the company had its greatest success in the burgeoning crossover market with the swaggering "hoodoo" of Bo Diddley and Chuck Berry's sly portrayals of "motivatin" and other teenage pastimes. Berry delineated the popular culture of the late fifties perhaps more successfully than any other performer of the era, but his color caused him to remain an outsider. Chuck Berry almost singlehandedly defined rock and roll with his consummate craftsmanship, and his records retain their striking originality and exuberance today. Despite the crossover success of Berry and Bo Diddley, however, Chess preferred to strengthen its domination of the electric blues scene and spurned Elvis Presley on the grounds that he was "too hillbilly."[32] Chess usually dealt fairly with its artists, but the company's business practices were somewhat suspect. According to Pete Guralnick, Chess was the only record company to deduct "payola" as a legitimate business expense.[33] Chess successfully weathered several extensive investigations into its business dealings, but the company's distinguished career was effectively ended when the GRT Corporation bought it out after the death of Leonard Chess in 1969.

An abandoned Cincinnati icehouse served as headquarters to King Records, founded in 1954 by ex-furniture salesman Sid Nathan. King's first success came with "hillbilly" artists Moon Mullican, the Delmore Brothers and Cowboy Copas, but the company swung increasingly to rhythm and blues in 1947 after the success of Bull Moose Jackson's "I Love You, Yes I do." Nathan quickly signed the Dominoes, who hit in 1951 with "Sixty Minute Man." The group generated such stars as Clyde McPhatter and Jackie Wilson and for all purposes originated the vocal ballad style known as "doo-wop."[34] Another early King success was Hank Ballard, whose 1954 hits with the Midnights "Work With Me, Annie" and followup "Annie Had a Baby" were widely blasted for allegedly debauching the minds of unsuspecting youths. Although he started his career with Aladdin Records, Wynonie Harris cut a number of wonderfully salacious records at King, beginning with Roy Brown's "Good Rockin' Tonight" and continuing with "All She Wants to Do is Rock," "Sittin' On It All the Time" and "I Like My Baby's Pudding." Illinois Jacquet, founder of the "Honk and Screech" school of sax playing, was an occasional sideman to Harris. Arnold Shaw recalled Jacquet's days with Lionel Hampton in the early forties:

The story is told of a gig that the Hampton band played on a barge on the Potomac River. At the peak of a rousing rendition of 'Flying Home,' a Hampton hit noted for Jacquet's frenzied tenor solo, Hampton shouted to his bass player, 'Hit the water!' The cat was so stirred up that he took the exhortation literally and leaped overboard.[35]

Not all of King's artists were purveyors of raunch, however. The label released many graceful ballads by Ivory Joe Hunter and Little Willie John and "Soul Brother Number One," James Brown, had his first hit on King—"Please, Please, Please" in 1956. The Five Royales (previously the Royal Songs) made the transition from gospel to rhythm and blues and signed with King in 1954, scoring with 1957s "Think" and "Dedicated to the One I Love" a year later. King also enjoyed great success with dance instrumentals by Earl Bostic and Bill Doggett, whose "Honky Tonk" sold over four million copies in 1956 and 1957. Sid Nathan co-wrote many of King's bestselling titles and the company declined rapidly after his death in the mid-sixties.

Atlantic, Chess and King were based in the East and upper Midwest, but the West Coast and South also saw a flurry of activity by independent record companies after World War II. Leo, Edward and Ida Menser founded Philo Recording in July 1945 and began issuing jazz records by Lester Young and Helen Humes. After a name change to Aladdin Records, the company concentrated on the budding rhythm and blues market with the Five Keys, Charles Brown and country bluesman Lightnin' Hopkins. But Aladdin's greatest early success came with former Texan Amos Milburn, who released a series of sodden titles in 1950 including "Bad, Bad Whiskey," "Thinkin' and Drinkin'," "Let Me Go, Whiskey" and "One Bourbon, One Scotch and One Beer." Milburn also recorded a number of "jump" blues, including "Let's Rock Awhile," "Rock, Rock, Rock" and "Let's Have a Party," whose ultimate influence far exceeded their sales. Aladdin began selling to white teenagers in the mid-fifties with Shirley and Lee, the "Sweethearts of the Blues," whose records detailed their reported, though non-existent, romance. The company was absorbed by Imperial Records in 1959.

Modern Records was another family-owned label, started in March, 1945 by Jules, Joe, Saul and Lester Bihari in Los Angeles. Modern's blues-oriented catalogue featured John Lee Hooker, Etta James, Jimmy Witherspoon and Elmore James, but its biggest seller was former disc jockey Riley "B.B." King, whose first hit, 1951 "Three O'Clock Blues," was recorded on a portable tape recorder at the Memphis YMCA.[36] Don Robey formed Peacock Records in 1949 in order to record Clarence "Gatesmouth" Brown while the guitarist was appearing at Robey's Houston nightclub the Golden Peacock. Robey also recorded many gospel artists, but his star was balladeer Johnny Ace, whose popularity sky-rocketed after Ace shot himself in a game of Russian roulette on Christmas Eve, 1954 before a scheduled appearance in Houston. Ace's posthumous release, "Pledging My Love," promptly soared to number one on the rhythm and blues, country and pop charts. Robey proceeded to buy out Duke Records and obtained the services of Bobby Blue Bland, whose enormous success carried the label well into the 1960s. Don Robey was black and undoubtedly encountered more difficulties with the recording industry than did his white colleagues. His engineer, Walter Andrus, described Robey:

He was just like a character out of 'Guys and Dolls.' He'd have a bunch of heavy guards around him all the time, carrying pistols and that kind of stuff, like a czar of the Negro underworld.[37]

Robey died of a heart attack at age 71, June 16, 1975.

Savoy Records covered almost all the bases in postwar black music. Founded in 1939 by Herman Lubinsky, the Newark, New Jersey-based label was preeminent in the North with gospel artists like James Cleveland, pioneered "bebop" jazz with Charlie Parker and was vital in establishing much of the tenor of early rhythm and blues with singers Little Esther, Big Maybelle and Nappy Brown and "honking" saxists Big Jay McNeely and Illinois Jacquet. Savoy has been hailed by Arnold Shaw as "the first rhythm and blues label of consequence, in terms of both the artists it developed and its longevity."[38] Few performers recorded exclusively for Savoy or other labels, however. Rhythm and blues artists lacking long-term contracts frequently switched companies out of fear (often justified) that management was depriving them of royalties or recording opportunities. Also, according to Mike Rowe:

Working with new or rejected talent, a small record company would persist in the hopes of the elusive big hit. If it came, the company would establish itself or more likely, the big-selling artist would be snapped up by one of the bigger companies.[39]

Art Rupe started Jukebox Records in 1944 after undertaking an exhaustive study of marketing practices in the Los Angeles area. His research apparently paid off when the company's first release, the Sepia Tones' "Boogie Number One," sold 70,000 copies.[40] In 1946 he changed the label's name to Specialty Records and continued his success with Roy Milton and his Solid Senders, as well as gospel groups the Swan Silvertones and the soul Stirrers (featuring lead vocalist Sam Cooke, who went on to near-mythic status as a solo artist in the early sixties). Rupe journeyed to New Orleans in 1952 and came away with Lloyd price, whose "Lawdy Miss Clawdy" hit number one and stayed in the rhythm and blues charts for six months. Price later switched to ABC, but Rupe compensated for his loss with Little Richard (nee Richard Penniman of Macon, Georgia), the rocker nonpariel responsible for such fervid whoops as "Tutti Frutti," "Lucille" and "Rip It Up." From all reports, Richard was quite a flamboyant entertainer—Jerry Lee Lewis claimed that he would have to wipe pools of fingernail polish off the keyboard before following Richard onstage. Although Richard was a leading exponent of the "devil's music," he was also a deeply religious man who renounced rock and roll in the late fifties after glimpsing Armageddon on a trans-oceanic airplane flight. He staged a relatively successful comeback in the mid-sixties, but has since regained his religious calling.

Imperial Records was another Los Angeles-based label that struck it rich in the South. Lew Chudd, who started Imperial in 1945, was informed by disc jockey Poppa Stoppa of "a fat kid whom he heard in Good Town, an unpaved black section of New Orleans."[41] Chudd checked out the kid, was suitably impressed, and promptly signed young Antoine "Fats" Domino to his label. The first release by Fats, 1950s, "The Fat Man," hit the rhythm and blues top-ten and Fats began cranking out hit after hit, all cut in a style as benign as his enormous bulk. Fats crossed over to the pop charts in 1956 with "I'm In Love Again," "My Blue Heaven" and "Blueberry Hill," and proceeded to sell over 30 million records by 1962.[42] It was a rich and happy "fat man" who blithely told a reporter "when things go right I can make records all day. After all, I like to make them."[43] New Orleans was a hotbed of rhythm and blues activity in the fifties, producing Smiley Lewis for Imperial, Professor Longhair for Atlantic, Huey "Piano" Smith for Ace and a host of others. The ebullience of Crescent City rhythm and blues is typified by the loping refrain of "gooba, gooba, gooba, gooba: in Huey Smith's hit "Don't You Just Know It" and the chorus of "oh, she baldhead" in Professor Longhair's classic "She Ain't Got No Hair."

The major record companies began casting covetous glances at rhythm and blues in the early fifties when the success of independent labels became too strong to ignore. After an initial period of postwar prosperity the major companies found themselves in the doldrums as the big bands waned in popularity and nothing came along to fill the gap. The crooners of the early fifties and their vapid ballads offered little to teenagers who suddenly possessed a great deal of of disposable income as a result of the booming postwar economy. As they fiddled with their radio dials, many suburban kids inadvertently stumbled upon a marvelous and alien thing—rhythm and blues broadcasts from the inner cities. Big Joe Turner booming "Shake, Rattle and Roll" may well have been a transcendental experience for many listeners after years of Tin Pan Alley treacle. Teenagers were drawn to the immediacy and vitality of this new music and began seeking out rhythm and blues records. Ahmet Ertegun and Jerry Wexler reported the phenomenon in a 1954 issue of *Cashbox:*

As far as we can determine, the first area where the blues stepped out in the current renaissance was in the South. Distributors there about two years ago began to report that white high school and college kids were picking up on the rhythm and blues records, primarily to dance to. From all accounts, the movement was initiated by youthful hillbilly fans rather than the pop bobbysoxers and the latter group followed right along. A few alert pop disc jockeys observed the current, switched to rhythm and blues formats and soon were deluged with greater audiences, both White and Negro, and more and more sponsors.[44]

It may seem surprising that whites first began listening to rhythm and blues in the South, given the vehement segregation of the area, but contact between poor rural Southern blacks and whites was frequent—many white sharecroppers worked alongside blacks in the fields.

Listeners in the upper Midwest and West Coast quickly followed suit and the Dolphin Record Store in Los Angeles reported in May, 1952 that its patronage, until that time almost exclusively black, was now 40 percent white.[45] These young white buyers mainly sought rhythm and blues instrumentals because of their "danceability." A survey by Key Records in mid-fifties Los Angeles revealed that 61.7 percent of those polled said "rhythm" was the most important influence i choosing records.[46] It was virtually impossible for black performers to have a million-selling record without a significant amount of sales to whites, but artists often found their music compromised by efforts to appeal to white teenagers who treated their work largely as a novelty. Johnny Otis explained to Pete Welding.

When the white audience appeared and we saw it and knew it was there, it didn't take us long before we realized what they preferred. We found that if we played a blues or a very bluesy thing, we lost them. But when we played very spirited rhythm and blues things, we captured them. And when we did a caricature of rhythm and blues, we really got to them. Like if the cats laid down on the ground, kicked their feet up in the air and went 'rawf, rawf' on the saxophones—something we wouldn't do unless we were just kidding—Well, *that* is what they liked, that is what they wanted.[47]

One can easily commiserate with Otis (a white man) on the vissitudes of the music industry, but one must also wonder if such pandering on the part of musicians did little but reinforce the preconceptions of their audience.

Perhaps the best testimonial to the growing popularity of rhythm and blues occurred June 25, 1949 when *Billboard* changed the heading of its "race" record chart to rhythm and blues. Two years later, a classical music deejay on Cleveland's WJW began broadcasting rhythm and blues at the urging of a local record store owner.[48] Alan Freed's "Moon Dog House Rock and Roll Party" caught on quickly with area teenagers and Freed promoted a "Moondog Coronation Ball" in Cleveland on March 21, 1952. The show, publicized exclusively on Freed's nightly broadcasts, featured the Dominoes, the Orioles, the Moonglows and others. Eighteen thousand tickets were sold in advance and an estimated 25,000 people showed up for the concert, which was held in a hall that could seat only 10,000.[49] The inter-racial success of such an event would have been inconceivable five years earlier and its promoter made news across the country. Although other white deejays had programmed rhythm and blues, Freed is credited as one of the first to play black music for a largely white audience. Freed later moved to New York City and annihilated his competition in the ratings until the payola investigations destroyed him.

The rapid changes of the early fifties resulted in a scramble for scapegoats by forces hostile to integration. A backlash soon developed against rhythm and blues—"race music" had been tolerated as long as it was confined to ghettoes and the rural South, but rhythm and blues was perceived as a direct threat to social mores when white teenagers began listening to it. Russ Sanjek of Broadcast Music, Incorporated recalled:

It was a time when many a mother ripped pictures of Fats Domino off her daughter's bedroom wall. She remembered what she felt towards her Bing Crosby pinup and she didn't want her daughter creaming over Fats.[50]

Racist organizations distributed handbills throughout the South that proclaimed:

The screaming, idiotic words and savage music of these records are undermining the morals of our white youth in America.[51]

Many authorities recoiled in horror at the rampant miscegenation and anomie they supposed would surely accompany the airplay of rhythm and blues records. The North Alabama Citizen's Council attempted a ban of rhythm and blues broadcasts on grounds the music "brings out the base in man, brings out the animalism and vulgarity."[52] Alan Freed's nationally televised "Rock and Roll Dance Party" was yanked off the air when a black boy and white girl were shown dancing together. Self-proclaimed "highbrows" also cocked their snoots at rhythm and blues, exemplified by Stan Freberg's 1956 denunciation of the music as being "dirty and as bad for kids as dope."[53]

Much of the furor surrounding rhythm and blues concerned the frequently double-entendre nature of its lyrics. As Michael Haralambos has indicated, few rhythm and blues songs openly hinted at racial oppression. Male-female relationships frequently served as metaphors for the black social perspective and lyrics were often quite explicit.[54] In 1953, *Variety* editor Abel Green launched an acrimonious attack on what he dubbed "leerics." Citing such titles as "Sixty Minute Man" and "Work With Me, Annie" Green piously asserted:

Even the most casual look at the current crop of 'leerics' must tell even the most naive that dirty postcards have been translated into songs.[55]

Another *Variety* writer proclaimed:

Their lyrical concoctions belong in the more difficult honky tonks and should never be heard on the air.[56]

A Mobile, Alabama deejay told *Variety*:

Between forty and fifty percent of rhythm and blues discs make the trash basket. Filth in both title and words make their destruction a must.[57]

Bright Lights, Big City   57

Attacks on rhythm and blues lyrics by *Variety* and other publications were somewhat blunted when it was pointed out that even the most innocuous Tin Pan Alley pap wasn't always pure in intent. Songwriter Al Stillman wrote:

> Practically all lyrics, except 'Barney Google,' have been dirty—with the carriage trade practitioners Cole Porter, Lorenz Hart, etc. contributing their share...the object of all 'leericists' outside of W.S. Gilbert has always been to get as close to the Main Subject as possible without stating it and/or 'cleaning it up' by marrying them in the last line.[58]

The rhythm and blues fray carried over to music publishing. Until the early forties, ASCAP (American Society of Composers, Authors and Publisher) dominated music publishing. When ASCAP attempted to raise its rates with a boycott of broadcasters in 1940, independent writers and radio networks retaliated by forming Broadcast Music Incorporated and banning ASCAP—licensed songs from the air for 22 months.[59] BMIs catalogue was comprised of uncopyrighted standards and public domain material as well as "hillbilly" and "race" titles—all of which ASCAP had spurned as noncommercial. Tensions between the two companies were heightened in the early fifties and it is reasonable to suspect that much of the backlash to rhythm and blues was engineered by ASCAP. In 1956, Alan Freed told an interviewer:

> The oldtimers who formerly controlled the music publishing business wouldn't even license rhythm and blues material until about a year ago. By that time, a new group of writers and publishers had gotten the inside track on rock and roll and now the newcomers are making the money.[60]

ASCAP consistently tried to quash rhythm and blues until economics forced them to reconsider their policies. In 1954, ASCAP succeeded in banning Johnny Ray's "Such a Night" from airplay because of its "suggestive" lyrics and according to *Variety*:

> ASCAP songwriters...take credit for switching the spotlight [of Congressional investigations] from TV quiz rigging to disc jockey payola.[61]

Rhythm and blues songs accounted for eight of the top 25 records on *Billboards* 1954 pop charts and record companies competed fiercely for airplay. Low-salaried disc jockeys occasionally accepted stipends and gifts" from struggling independent labels lacking regional offices and large promotional staffs. "Payola," as it was called, was nothing new. Payoffs were frequent as early as World War I and the practice was widespread throughout the record industry by the mid-fifties.[62] But a House of Representatives committee investigating the situation in 1959-1960 singled out independent broadcasters, ignoring such network practices as license trading and "fixing" advertising rates. Arnold Shaw claimed:

Not the least significant factor was the struggle of older-generation publishers, songwriters and recording artists to halt the onrushing tide of rhythm and blues and rock and roll that was sweeping them out of the market. It was a question of economics and power, not morality.[63]

In spite of public and industry efforts at suppressing rhythm and blues, the music accounted for an estimated 15 million dollars worth of sales in 1952.[65] While publicly shunning "race music," the major companies desperately tried to seize the increasingly lucrative rhythm and blues market away from independent labels. Many major record companies re-activated their "race" labels in the early fifties—Columbia with Okeh, Decca with Brunswick and RCA with its Bluebird and Groove subsidiaries. Records were tested in rhythm and blues markets and if successful, put into general release. The major labels reduced their output of singles in hopes of raising the odds that a release would "hit." Subsidiary labels were distributed independently on a regional basis, all to no avail. In 1954, 23 of the year's top-30 rhythm and blues discs were released on independent labels.[66] *Billboard* proclaimed 1955 as "the year rhythm and blues took over the pop field," and records by black artists garnered ten percent of all pop music sales.[67] Although the independent companies had maintained their grip on rhythm and blues, they were hurt by technological developments. Shellac-based 78 rpm records, the mainstay of the record industry, were rendered obsolete by RCAs introduction of unbreakable 45s in the mid-fifties.[68] Seventy-eights persisted in rhythm and blues until 1957, but 45s were cheaper for the major companies to produce and ship. Independent labels were forced to reduced their prices to remain competitive, leading many labels to bankruptcy in the late fifties. In addition, independent labels were often at the mercy of unscrupulous distributors. Nick Tosches explained:

When an independent had a hit, that meant many more copies of the record had to be manufactured than usual. If the hit sold two million units, the company owed whatever pressing plant it used a whole lot of money...but often when the company went to its distributor to collect the money its million-seller had made, the response was, 'What hit? It sold twenty thousand units.' Most independents had neither the money nor the courage (for some distributors long, long ago were tied with The Boys) to initiate legal action.[69]

In the meantime, having largely given up on developing their own rhythm and blues talent, the major companies developed another tactic—white performers "covering" successful rhythm and blues songs.

Cover versions were not isolated to rhythm and blues. "Hillbilly" music, long ignored by the major labels, was inundated with a spate of laundered country and western standards by mainstream performers like Tony Bennett when the music began showing sales promise in the early fifties. Adapting this formula to rhythm and blues, the major companies began releasing "acceptable" treatments of rhythm and blues material by suitable no-threatening performers like Pat Boone. These cover versions purged the music of any content deemed objectionable and also robbed it of any vitality. Perversely enough, many independent record companies encouraged cover versions. The independent labels frequently owned the publication rights to titles and made up in song licensing royalties what they stood to lose in sales.[70] The victims in all this were the original performers, who helplessly watched their royalties wither as major labels, with the benefit of a larger distribution network and increased airplay, beat their originals to markets and sales: "Fattening frogs for snakes," Sonny Boy Williamson called it.

The fate of Arthur "Big Boy" Crudup is one of the most distressing examples of an artist's abuse at the hands of a record company. Crudup, a bluesman from Mississippi who set up housekeeping in a crate underneath a railroad overpass after his arrival in Chicago, recorded extensively for RCAs Bluebird subsidiary in the forties. Bluebird was run by Lester Melrose, who also served as Crudup's manager, Mike Rowe notes:

In a field noted for honesty Melrose was probably more scrupulous than most; he paid the artists for the sessions and their expenses and was ready with a hand-out when they were in need of it. But as Melrose published all the songs one wonders whether they received their copyright dues.[71]

Arthur Crudup certainly did not. For all practical purposes, Melrose stole the rights to Crudup's songs and excluded Crudup from thousands of dollars in royalties after Elvis Presley, who acknowledged Crudup's profound influence on his style, successfully covered his songs in the rock and roll market.[72] Crudup died virtually penniless before litigation could transfer the royalties that rightfully belonged to him. He did, however, receive an appreciative plaque (but no money) from Presley.

The practice of covers peaked between 1954 and 1956 and waned with the rise of rock and roll and the increasing sophistication of white record buyers. The emergence of rock and roll, in conjunction with the payola investigations, marked the end of the rhythm and blues era. Black artists like Chuck Berry, Fats Domino and Little Richard triumphed over covers and found themselves topping the pop charts. The same thing was occurring in black music—in 1957, white artists had nine of the sixteen number-one songs on *Billboard's* rhythm and blues charts.[73] Early rockers like Elvis Presley, Carl Perkins and Jerry Lee Lewis had much in common with their black counterparts. Both groups were, for the most part, products of poor Southern backgrounds and these white artists had absorbed a great deal of black culture through economic and other ties. As rock and roll achieved preeminence, many of the older rhythm and blues performers slipped into obscurity, replaced by artists who held more relevance to the young white audience whose tastes were beginning to dominate the music industry. If the schism between cultures was so great that rhythm and blues was never really embraced by the whites who found promise of liberation that lay beneath the surface of rhythm and blues—the proud cry of a neglected people affirming their existence as if for the first time. That is why, perhaps, so many hated it and though it profane. It was what Ahmet Ertegun called "big foot, mud, red clay—real black music in a black environment under the worst possible conditions. Because of its obvious innocence and sincerity, it captivated the world.[74]

Summary and Conclusions

It is possible to claim that rhythm and blues did promote and reinforce a substantial and far-reaching change in post-World War II American society, by virtue of the minority culture that produced rhythm and blues and society's reaction to the music as a manifestation of that subculture. New forms of popular music are the products of interplay between economic and social elements, as exemplified by the chain of events that led to the creation of rhythm and blues.

Increasingly mechanized Southern agriculture and the industrial demands of World War II resulted in the urbanization and corresponding economic growth of black America. Wartime supply shortages caused the leading record companies to cease issuing records oriented towards blacks, resulting in a marketing gap after the war that small, specialized record companies were easily able to fill, and the lack of interest in black music on the part of established record companies created an insular environment for the development of rhythm and blues. The new independent record companies, in search of quick returns, issued records in a variety of styles, including gospel, jazz and blues. This resulted in a great deal of musical experimentation in hopes of tapping the potential market of newly-urbanized blacks. In conjunction with a recession-induced reduction of "big bands," this musical hybridization resulted in rhythm and blues.

Primary exposure of rhythm and blues took place through jukeboxes in the absence of black-oriented venues. But clubowners began to realize that the demand for rhythm and blues was growing and coupled with the relatively low salary demands of rhythm and blues artists, began booking black performers into previously all-white clubs. The popularity of television after the war, as well as the growing number of small radio stations unaffiliated with networks, segmented the radio industry and postwar black prosperity created a lucrative advertising base for black-oriented programming.

It is clear, then, that social change precipitated rhythm and blues, rather than vice-versa. But rhythm and blues did reinforce the culture from which it came by crystallizing and articulating the concerns of that culture. According to Michael Haralambos:

Particular forms of music respond to particular needs, which are the product of particular social contexts...music is a dependent variable. It reflects rather than directs, it is changed rather than changing anything.[75]

Notes

[1]*Statistical Abstract of the United States* (Washington, D.C.: GPO, 1951).

²*Report of the National Advisory Commission on Civil Disorders* (New York: E.P. Dutton, 1968), p. 240.

³Michael Haralambos, *Right On: From Blues to Soul in Black America* (New York: Drake, 1975), p. 100.

⁴Charles Killingsworth, "Jobs and income for Negroes," in *Race and the Social Sciences*, ed. Irwin Katz and Patricia Gurin (New York: Basic Books, 1969), p. 204.

⁵Steve Chapple and Robert Garofalo, *Rock and Roll is Here to Pay* (Chicago: Nelson Hall, 1977), p. 2.

⁶Mike Rowe, *Chicago Breakdown* (London: Eddison Press, 1973), p. 14.

⁷Ralph Gleason, "Rhythm and Blues(Rock and Roll) Makes the Grade," in *The Negro in Music and Art*, ed. Lindsay Patterson (New York: Publishers Company, 1967), p. 116.

⁸Rowe, *Chicago Breakdown*, p. 25.

⁹Rowe, *Chicago Breakdown*, p. 191.

¹⁰Arnold Shaw, *Honkers and Shouters* (New York: Macmillan, 1978), p. 156.

¹¹Ian Hoare, "Mighty, Mighty Spade and Whitey: Black Lyrics and Soul's Interaction with White Culture," in *The Soul Book*, ed. Simon Frith (London: Eyre Methuen, 1975), p. 157.

¹²Haralambos, *Right On*, p. 100.

¹³Arnold Shaw, *The World of Soul; Black America's Contribution to the Pop Music Scene* (New York: Cowles, 1970), p. 96.

¹⁴Hoare, *The Soul Book*, p. 154.

¹⁵Shaw, *The World of Soul*, p. 95.

¹⁶Shaw, *Honkers and Shouters*, p. 128.

¹⁷John Broven, *Rhythm and Blues in New Orleans* (New York: Pelican, 1978), p. 106.

¹⁸Shaw, *Honkers and Shouters*, p. 124.

¹⁹Shaw, *Honkers and Shouters*, p. 397.

²⁰Shaw, *Honkers and Shouters*, p. 397.

²¹Lawrence Redd, *Rock is Rhythm and Blues: The Impact of Mass Media* (East Lansing: Michigan State University Press, 1974), p. 26.

²²Redd, *Rock Is Rhythm and Blues*, p. 27.

²³Chapple and Garofalo, *Rock and Roll is Here to Pay*, p. 29.

²⁴Shaw, *The World of Soul*, p. 104.

²⁵Shaw, *The World of Soul*, p. 129.

²⁶Charles Gillet, *Making Tracks: Atlantic Records and the Growth of A Multi-Billion Dollar Industry* (London: W.H. Allen, 1975), p. 65.

²⁷Chapple and Garofalo, *Rock and Roll is Here to Pay*, p. 236.

²⁸Shaw, *Honkers and Shouters*, p. 373.

²⁹Peter Guralnick, *Feel Like Going Home: Portraits in Blues and Rock 'n' Roll* (New York: Outerbridge and Dienstfrey, 1971), p. 220.

³⁰Gillet *Making Tracks*, p. 88.

³¹Robert Palmer, "Rock Begins," in *The Rolling Stone Illustrated History of Rock and Roll*, ed. Jim Miller (New York: Random House, 1976), p. 11.

³²Guralnick, *Feel Like Going Home*, p. 235.

³³Guralnick, *Feel Like Going Home*, p. 223.

³⁴Greil Marcus, *Stranded: Rock and Roll for a Desert Island* (New York: Alfred A. Knopf, 1979), p. 267.

³⁵Shaw, *Honkers and Shouters*, p. 58.

³⁶Shaw, *Honkers and Shouters*, p. 204.

[37] Shaw, *Honkers and Shouters*, p. 488.
[38] Shaw, *Honkers and Shouters*, p. 344.
[39] Rowe, *Chicago Breakdown*, p. 103.
[40] Shaw, *Honkers and Shouters*, p. 180.
[41] Shaw, *Honkers and Shouters*, p. 261.
[42] Shaw, *Honkers and Shouters*, p. 264.
[43] Shaw, *Rhythm and Blues in New Orleans*, p. 70.
[44] Broven, *Rhythm and Blues in New Orleans*, p. 36.
[45] Chapple and Garofalo, *Rock and Roll is here to Pay*, p. 31.
[46] Gleason, "Rhythm and Blues (Rock and Roll) Makes the Grade," p. 117.
[47] Pete Welding, "Johnny Otis: The History of Rhythm and Blues," in *The Rolling Stone Interviews Volume Two*, ed. Ben Fong-Torres (New York: Warner Paperback Library, 1973), pp. 314-315.
[48] Redd, *Rock Is Rhythm and Blues*, p. 28.
[49] Shaw, *Honkers and Shouters*, p. 507.
[50] Chapple and Garofalo, *Rock and Roll Is Here to Pay*, p. 47.
[51] Paul Oliver, *The Story of the Blues* (New York: Chilton, 1973), p. 167.
[52] Redd, *Rock Is Rhythm and Blues*, p. 49.
[53] Shaw, Honkers and Shouters, p. xxv.
[54] Haralambos, *Right On*, pp. 71-72.
[55] Abel Green, "Leer-ics," *Variety*, 189, 9 March 1955, p. 44.
[56] Jimmy Kennedy, "Fears U.S. Will Make Negative Global Impression Via R&B Tunes," *Variety*, 189. 9 March 1955, p. 49.
[57] "Mobile Station Quotes 'Variety' on Leerics—Will Not Broadcast 'Em," *Variety*, 189, 23 March 1955, p. 1.
[58] Shaw, *Honkers and Shouters*, p. xxv.
[59] Broven, *Rhythm and Blues in New Orleans*, p. 3.
[60] George Leonard, "The Great Rock 'n' Roll Controversy," *Look*, 20. 26 June 1956, p. 48.
[61] Chapple and Garofalo, *Rock and Roll is Here to Pay*, p. 24.
[62] Shaw, *Honkers and Shouters*, p. 511.
[63] Shaw, *Honkers and Shouters*, p. 511.
[64] Shaw, *Honkers and Shouters*, p. 517.
[65] Chapple and Garofalo, *Rock and Roll Is Here to Pay*, p. 24.
[66] Chapple and Garofalo, *Rock and Roll Is Here to Pay*, p. 24.
[67] Chapple and Garofalo, *Rock and Roll Is Here to Pay*, p. 35.
[68] Chapple and Garofalo, *Rock and Roll Is Here to Pay*, p. 23.
[69] Nick Tosches, *Country: The Biggest Music In America* (New York: Dell, 1977), pp. 242-245.
[70] Shaw, *The World of Soul*, p. 164.
[71] Rowe, *Chicago Breakdown*, p. 19.
[72] Shaw, *Honkers and Shouters*, p. 32.
[73] Shaw, *The World of Soul*, p. 164.
[74] Shaw, *Honkers and Shouters*, p. 396.
[75] Haralambos, *Right On*, p. 9.

From ASCAP to Alan Freed: The Pre-History of Rock 'N' Roll

Reebee Garofalo and Steve Chapple

Rock 'n' roll, as everyone must know by now, did not simply spring full blown from the spit curl of Bill Haley. The evolution which yielded this new music was first and foremost a process whereby grassroots writers and performers, a great many of whom were black, were brought to the attention of a mass audience. Or, as described by long-time editor of Billboard magazine Paul Ackerman, "a process by which the root music of America entered the mainstream."(1)

It is a very complex process, dating back to the late thirties, which involved initially a challenge to the music publishing establishment of the time as well as changes within the performance hierarchy. It is a David and Goliath story which pitted the fledgling independent record companies like Atlantic, Modern, and Chess against corporate giants like RCA and CBS. It is a tale of changing priorities in broadcasting which strengthened the role of local radio and turned the independent deejay into the central figure in the recording industry. Finally, it is a process involving such diverse variables as populating migrations, material shortages, and technological advances. The emergence of rock 'n' roll can only be fully understood in terms of the convergence of the results of this myriad of forces in the early fifties. The purpose of this paper is, thus, to provide a brief historical overview of the preconditions of rock music.

Most historians are quick to point out that rock 'n' roll cannot be understood simply as a music; that it must be understood as a social phenomenon. The better known rock histories—Belz (2), Gillett (3), Guralnick (4), Lydon (5), and Cohn (6)—trace the music not only artistically, but socio-culturally as well. Belz introduces a discussion of the difference between folk art and fine art. Gillett's groundbreaking analysis of major vs. independent record companies adds a structural dimension to the discussion. And, any number of works on black culture notably *Blues People* by Leroi Jones (Imamu Baraka) (7)—offer an understanding of the dynamics of racism. In all of these pioneering works there is the hint that there is more to music than meets the ear. Yet, the actual

Reprinted with permission from *Popular Music and Society*, Volume 6:1 (1978), pp. 72-80.

functioning of the businesses which mediate the artist and the audience remains something of a mystery.

More recently such books as *Apple to the Core*, by McCabe and Shonfeld (8) Denisoff's *Solid Gold* (9), Gillett's *Making Tracks* (10), *Star Making Machinery* by Stokes (11), and our own *Rock 'n' Roll is Here to Pay* (12), have attempted to locate the music firmly within the context of the huge culture industry which produces it. These more recent works provide a sophisticated understanding of the music industry as it currently operates, but in relatively few cases deal with the broader context of rock's pre-history. *Making Tracks* is a history of Atlantic Records which, of course, predates rock 'n' roll. And *Here to Pay* brings together a number of sources in an introductory chapter dealing with the corporate history surrounding the beginnings of the modern music industry.

Another book which touches on the subject of rock's pre-history is the somewhat exaggerated, witty and currently (it seems) out of print *After the Ball* by Ian ("You Turn Me On," 1965) Whitcomb. (13) In one paragraph, he encapsulates the history of the forties as follows:

Here are the changes: the BMI-ASCAP war, the renaissance of the record, the appearance of independent record companies, the fall of the big band, the rise of the solo singer, the start of the teen frenzy, the spread of hillbilly music. The end of the old Tin Pan Alley. (14)

Whitcomb's list is not exhaustive, but he mentions a number of issues which clearly paved the way for rock 'n' roll. We will begin our analysis with the war between ASCAP and BMI.

BMI Takes on the Music Publishing Establishment

ASCAP (The American Society of Authors, Composers, and Publishers) and BMI (Broadcast Music Incorporated) are known as performing rights organizations. They are the organizations which recover royalty payments from the performance of copyrighted music. This is usually accomplished through the issuance of blanket licenses allowing the user unlimited access to any selection in the catalogue for a set fee. Royalty revenues are then distributed to the membership according to a complex system of credits. The war between ASCAP and BMI, an extended controversy which ultimately precipitated the payola hearings of 1959 and went on well into the sixties, had its beginning in 1939, the year BMI was founded.

Earlier in the century, after a hard-fought battle, ASCAP had established in practice the legal principle articulated in the 1909 Copyright Law—that writers are entitled to compensation when their work is performed in public for profit. At first, revenues came from the sale of sheet music, recordings, and live performances in hotels, nightclubs, and ballrooms. It wasn't until the legal principle was extended to include radio broadcasts, another hard-fought battle, that ASCAP began to realize its full economic potential. Whereas in 1931, ASCAP received a total of one million dollars in royalty payments

The Pre-History of Rock 'N' Roll

from all sources, the society recovered more than four times that amount from radio alone in 1939.

To understand fully the importance of this situation, one must first understand something about the character of music publishing at the time. Until 1939 ASCAP was a closed society with a virtual monopoly on all copyrighted music. Membership in the organization was limited to the most "literate" writers of the Broadway-Hollywood axis of popular music—Rodgers and Hart, Cole Porter, George Gershwin, Irving Berlin, George M. Cohan, etc. Since there did not yet exist any regulatory guidelines, the organization was free to set any fee for a license. As proprietor of the compositions of its members, ASCAP could prohibit any medium from using its catalogue. Aside from being able to exercise considerable power in the shaping of public taste, the financial possibilities of the organization seemed limitless.

By the 1940s, ASCAPs 1250 or so composers, authors, and publishers had become very greedy, so greedy in fact that after more than a year of rock negotiations with radio, they announced their intention of doubling the fee for a license when the existing agreement expired on December 31, 1940. For the broadcasters, who had always considered ASCAP's demands excessive, this was the last straw. The National Association of Broadcasters, representing some 600 radio stations, decided to boycott the entire ASCAP catalogue, which as we have noted, was virtually all copyrights music. For almost the whole of 1941, no ASCAP music was heard on the radio. The publishers finally came to terms, but only after a federally-initiated criminal anti-trust action forced ASCAP into a "consent decree" regulating its dealings with its clients.

Negotiations had actually broken down back in the fall of 1939. Expecting ASCAP to exploit its recent victory over radio to the fullest, and dissatisfied with their own weak position at the bargaining table, the broadcasters had decided then to form their own performing rights organization. Broadcast Music Incorporated was born on October 14, 1939.

Taking advantage of ASCAP's stringent membership requirements, as well as its relative indifference to the popular and folk music being produced outside of New York and Hollywood, BMI sought out and acquired its support from the 'have not' publishers and writers in the grassroots areas. (15)

By the time the 1941 boycott rolled around, BMI was ready with a catalogue of its own. For the next ten months the United States was treated to its first earful of its own root music. Authentic regional styles were broadcast to a mass public intact—not yet flattened in the national pop melting pot. Though, in its initial stage, BMI came up with few songs of lasting significance, the Broadway-Hollywood monopoly on public taste was publicly challenged for the first time. Without this challenge, we might never have heard from writers like Huddie Ledbetter, Hank Snow, Roy Brown, Ivory Joe Hunter, Johnny Otis, Fats Domino, Hank Williams, Ernest Tubb, and Wynonie Harris, whose songs began to reach the top of the charts at the end of the decade.

Population Migrations Open New Markets

The creation of a national audience for these regional musics was aided significantly by the population migrations associated with World War II. Large numbers of southern blacks and poor whites moved north and west to find work in defense plants, and they brought their music with them. At the same time many midwesterners and easterners were stationed in southern military bases where they were bombarded by some 600 country music radio stations. These new audiences must have liked what they heard. Detroit juke box operators reported that "hillbilly" records were the most popular, and in Europe, The American Armed Forces Radio Network voted Roy Acuff more popular than Frank Sinatra.

Black music was limited by a separate and unequal marketing structure, but, in the forties, it too showed potential for national expansion. The "race" market was first discovered when Mamie Smith's 1920 recording of "Crazy Blues" shocked the Okeh Recording Company executives by selling 7500 copies per week. The advent of radio in 1922, however, temporarily decimated the record business; sales dropped off steadily from a high of $106 million in 1921 to a low of just $6 million in 1933, at the height of the Depression. With the exception of "classic blues" records by women artists like Victoria Spivey, Ida Cox, and Bessie Smith which continued to sell, black music developed primarily in live performances. And although radio broadcasts utilized only live performances, the medium was specifically limited to white musicians. Even as developing black music ushered in the "big band" era, it was still only white orchestras that could be heard playing it on the radio.

The black exodus from the south during World War II contributed to the loosening of radio's restrictive programming. In the forties, more-than one million blacks left the South, three times as many as the decade before. Newly immigrated blacks had enough money from wartime prosperity to establish themselves as an identifiable consumer group. Particularly in areas which received a high concentration of black immigrants, it was in the interest of radio to introduce some programming that would cater to this new audience. Gradually, some black-oriented programs (usually slotted late at night) began to appear on a few stations. It was this kind of "specialty" programming during the early fifties which would finally tear down the walls of the "race" market.

The Big Bands Become a Casualty of the War

Having already alienated the music publishing establishment of the day, the broadcasters—which is to say, radio—managed to arouse the anger of established musicians as well. It was around the early forties that radio began to program recorded music—records. This was also the era of big bands, fancy ballrooms, and most important for the musicians, live music only on the radio. Radio was their own electronic ballroom; it provided very steady work. They would not give it up to records without a fight. In 1942 the American Federation of Musicians went out on strike. Nobody recorded. Nobody but the singers, that is.

Vocalists are covered by a different union—currently called the American Federation of Television and Radio Artists—and AFTRA didn't join the strike. The AFM itself thus aided the rise of solo vocalists—who were becoming the main attraction of the big bands anyway—by giving them free reign of the recording studios. After months of striking the musicians returned to the studio only to find the vocalists in charge. Somebody like Frank Sinatra no longer simply "fronted" the Tommy Dorsey Band. The vocalists were now the headliners. According to Gillett, "Records by the bands dominated the best selling lists in 1937 to 1941. During this period band recordings accounted for twenty-nine of the forty-three records that sold over a million copies each." (16) With the rise of the vocalists, the pop charts were gradually taken over by the likes of Bing Crosby, Perry Como, Dinah Shore, Vaughn Monroe, Frankie Laine, Doris Day, and Jo Stafford.

If the rise of the solo vocalist was a psychological blow to the big bands, it was the post-war economy which dealt the death blow. In the return to normalcy it was no longer feasible to support the elaborate production of 20 piece orchestras as a regular diet. Ballrooms disappeared. Unable to find steady work, the big bands gradually disbanded. As told by Whitcomb:

Miller died in a wartime plane crash, but Herman, James, and Dorsey had folded their original bands in late 1946, together with Benny Goodman and many others. The straighter, less jazzy bands like Lawrence Welk's and Guy Lombardo's survived (for a specialist and aging public) but the Big Band Era, just over a decade, was finished. (17)

The black big bands, who had provided much of the impetus for the big band sound and who are conspicuous in Whitcomb's account by their absence, limped along for a while on one-nighters in the decaying dance hall circuit. The better known black bands like Basie and Ellington could also count on an occasional hit record to fall back on such as Basie's recording of "Open the Door, Richard" for Victor which made the year-end pop charts in 1947. Although some of the bands were able to make something of a comeback later via television, it was clear by 1947 that a musical era in the United States had come to an end and it was reflected in record sales. Between 1947 and 1949 sales dropped off more than $50 million, which at the time represented more than 20 percent of the dollar volume of the industry.

Rhythm and Blues Rushes into the Breach

Gearing up for Korea, the economy was fueled once again and, like other industries, the music business was destined to expand. With the big bands no longer recording, however, there was something of a void in popular music. As always, the industry was looking for a new trend. A less cumbersome music was needed, and much to the dismay of the major record companies, "rhythm and blues" filled the bill.[1] The major companies—Columbia, Victor, and Decca—had gained a firm control of the "race" market during the Depression with the failure of independent labels like Paramount and Black Swan. The independents either had their catalogues bought out by the majors or disappeared completely. As the "race" market came to be dominated by big bands in the late thirties, the most famous like Basie and Ellington were simply signed by the majors. For all practical purposes, independent record companies had ceased to exist.

The population migrations mentioned above had opened up the possibility of a nationwide market for black music, which prior to World War II did not exist. The "race" records of the twenties and thirties sold well, but primarily in regional markets. The majors never exploited this new market during the war because a shellac shortage caused significant cutbacks in the number of records which could be manufactured. Shellac is the principle ingredient that was used in making the old 78 rpm records. During the war it became almost impossible to obtain the market from India where it is secreted by a tree-crawling scale insect. At the height of the shortage, in order to buy a new record it was often necessary to turn in an old one so that it could be recycled.[2] Since the pop market alone was capable of absorbing virtually all the records that could be produced, the major labels concentrated their efforts there. The specialty fields, especially blues, jazz and gospel, bore the brunt of the cutbacks and were essentially abandoned by the major labels.

Whereas the shellac shortage had seriously limited the supply of specialty music, the war had, if anything, increased the demand. Thus, after the war ended, the majors tried to regain control of the specialty markets. In the country and western field this proved to be relatively simple. According to Gillett,

> ...the companies responded by heavily promoting various songs performed in versions of country and western styles. One tactic was to promote the strong southern accent of most country and western singers as a 'novelty' as Capitol did successfully with Tex Williams' "Smoke That Cigarette" in 1947, and as Columbia did for several years with various Gene Autrey songs, including "Rudolph, the Red-Nosed Reindeer" (1950).
>
> Alternatively, the country and western songs that were closest to the melodramatic or sentimental modes of conventional popular songs were promoted as popular songs— or, more frequently, recorded by popular singers in a style that was halfway between country and pop. (18)

Performers such as Frankie Laine, Guy Mitchell, and the more authentic Hank Williams often fit this latter category. Through these various manipulations, the country field was soon firmly back in the hands of the majors, where it remains today.

The black market proved much more difficult. Having ignored black music for a number of years, the majors had lost touch with recent developments in the rich and constantly evolving black culture. While the majors contented themselves with connections to the most prominent black innovators of the big band sound, other black musicians based in the Southwest were developing styles that were much closer to the blues. As the era of big bands declined one music that was brought to the fore is described by Baraka as "huge rhythm units smashing away behind screaming blues singers." (19) This was rhythm and blues. Since it did not lend itself readily to the production styles of the major labels, they decided to ignore the relatively smaller black market.

The Pre-History of Rock 'N' Roll   69

This situation made it possible for a large number of independent labels to enter the business. It is estimated that by 1949 over 400 new labels came into existence. Most important among these were: Atlantic in New York, Savoy in Newark, King in Cincinnati, Chess in Chicago, Peacock in Houston, and Modern, Imperial, and Specialty in Los Angeles. These R&B independents were generally hampered by a shortage of materials, lack of funds, and inadequate distribution, yet with a hit, profits could be substantial. Modern was able to sell its blues singles for $1.05 in the late forties while the majors were only getting 78 cents for pop singles. Particularly with the increased affluence provided by the war, black people were willing to spend more for their music. The relatively small number of independents that survived the forties gained a foothold in the industry that would not be dislodged.

Technology Makes it All Possible

A number of technological advancements set the stage for the growth and further expansion of rhythm and blues music and its eventual takeover of the pop market as rock 'n' roll evolved. The first of these was the introduction of magnetic tape, stolen from the Nazis during WWII. Prior to this innovation, quality recording was tied to elaborate studios and cumbersome equipment not to mention a substantial capital investment. Recording facilities were located in relatively few city centers and were firmly under the control of established corporate powers. Magnetic tape and its more versatile hardware changed all that. Aside from bringing the obvious technical advantages of editing and better sound reproduction, magnetic tape made it possible for anyone to record anywhere. It was now possible for a Buddy Holly to be recorded in Clovis, New Mexico. Operating out of a small studio in Memphis, an enterprising young engineer named Sam Phillips could record B.B. King, Howlin' Wolf, Junior Parker, and Rufus Thomas, on the way to discovering Elvis Presley. The new technology clearly encouraged independent production and the formation of independent labels.

In 1948, Columbia's Dr. Peter Goldmark invented high fidelity. In what was to become known as the "battle of the speeds"— a contest which pitted Columbia's 33 against RCA's 45—competition between the two giant firms yielded discs of excellent quality, and more important for our purposes here, maximum durability. The introduction of the unbreakable record was particularly important to the development of rock 'n' roll because, as Carl Belz has pointed out,

> ...rock has existed primarily on records. In this, the music is rather different from jazz and from the traditional folk music to which it is related. Although jazz and other types of folk music exist on records, they did not originate in that medium. For the most part, they originated and developed through live performances. Rock, it seems to me, has generally done the opposite. Records were the music's initial medium. (20)

Most audio and visual media—television, film, and to a lesser extent, radio— are capital intensive industries. They require huge sums of money for production. Records, on the other hand, do not depend on an elaborate transmission system as does television, and they are not affected by government decisions concerning, say the assignment of frequencies on the electromagnetic spectrum. Particularly in the late forties, records emerged as a relatively inexpensive medium.[3] In part for this reason, it was not as easy for a few giant electronics firms to monopolize the business. Records soon became the staple of the music industry, surpassing sheet music as the major source of revenue in 1952 at around the same time that radio overtook juke boxes as the number one hit maker.

A final technological development strengthened local radio as the main vehicle for the popularization of rock 'n' roll. It involved a major media policy decision which had been made earlier in the century but which came to fruition in the early fifties. As early as 1935, RCA had announced plans to commit its research capabilities to the development of a then unheard of broadcast medium—television. In the late forties TV became accessible as a consumer item, and by 1951 RCA had already recovered from its years of research and development and the initial period of programming television stations at a loss. By 1957 there were 39 million TV sets in use in the United States, filling 80 percent of the homes. Television very quickly attracted most of the national advertising and network radio fell off, but local radio grew as an effective medium for local advertisers.

In this way the emphasis that RCA and CBS placed on television provided the context in which independent record companies and rock 'n' roll could develop. RCA's preoccupation with TV, for instance, made it pay less attention to its relatively less important record division. The lack of top executive emphasis given to network radio in comparison to network TV allowed independent radio stations to experiment successfully with new music, new programming, and new personalities. These independent stations eventually pushed aside the more staid network stations and in the process helped to revitalize the then smaller record industry.

Local Radio Brings it Home

Local Radio in the early fifties was a very loosely structured scene. The independent deejays—"personality jocks," as they were called—were in control. There were no music directors and nothing approaching the tightly structured programming and restrictive playlists that we see today. In the search for cheaper forms of programming, records provided the obvious answer. Record programming soon became the rule for radio and the disc jockey replaced the live entertainment personalities who had dominated radio in the thirties and forties. Until the 1959 payola hearings curtailed their power and Top 40 programming rationalized the AM format, the independent deejays were the central figures in the record industry. They could and did make hits. Relying on their own inventiveness for popularity, the independent deejays often experimented with "specialty" musics as an antidote for the trivial pop fare of network radio. Rhythm and blues music proved to be quite popular with white as well as black audiences. As early as 1952, Dolphin's Hollywood Record

Shop, a black retail outlet, reported that its business was all of sudden 40 percent white. They attributed it to independent deejays playing R&B records.

As the market for black music expanded, so did the number of stations playing it. At first, the deep south was the center for R&B radio. On white owned "negro stations" black deejays like "Professor Bop" in Shreveport, "Jocky" Jack Gibson in Atlanta, and "Sugar Daddy" in Birmingham were important in popularizing R&B music. Blues performers like Howlin' Wolf, B.B. King, and Rufus Thomas, all had shows in Memphis.

Gradually, white music stations began programming some R&B shows to accommodate the potential audience for black music in northern cities. As record sales indicated the growing popularity of rhythm and blues among white teenagers, white stations made a growing commitment to the music and black deejays were soon followed by white R&B jocks. Among many others there was "Poppa Stoppa" Clarence in New Orleans, Phil McKerman of Berkeley (who sired the late Pigpen of Greatful Dead fame), George "Hound Dog" Lorenz in Buffalo, and, of course, the now famous Bob "Wolfman Jack" Smith of Shreveport.

The most famous of the white R&B deejays at the time was a classical trombonist from Salem, Ohio, named Alan Freed. He is often remembered as the father of rock 'n' roll and even claimed to have invented the term. Based in Cleveland, his show, "Moon Dog's Rock 'n' Roll Party", became so popular that he was soon hired by SINS in New York which he made the number one popular music station in the city. Typical of those who saw the R&B surge and its evolution into rock 'n' roll firsthand, Freed once said: "Anyone who says rock 'n' roll is a passing fad or a flash-in-the-pan trend along the music road had rocks in his head, Dad!" He knew whereof he spoke. A *Billboard* headline reported: "1955—THE YEAR R&B TOOK OVER POP FIELD", and the rest is history.

Notes

[1] The term "rhythm and blues" represents both an authentic development within black music and a marketing category adopted by the music industry in 1949 as a catch all phrase for all black music. As such, it replaced the former designation, "race music."

[2] It is interesting to note that it is also possible to recycle vinyl, the main ingredient used in the manufacture of 33 rpm records. Yet no such program was initiated in the early seventies when the industry claimed a severe vinyl shortage. As the quality of 33's declined and suggested list prices rose to $6.98, whole warehouses of cutouts were simply being destroyed, a practice which continues to this day.

[3] Since the sixties, when the music industry became much more centralized, the production of records has become more and more tied to sophisticated electronic equipment, lavish multi-track studios, and enormous promotional budgets.

References

1. Steve Chapple, Interview with Paul Ackerman, 1973.

2. Carl Belz. *The Story of Rock*, New York: Oxford University Press, 1969: 2nd ed., Harper Colophon Books, 1973.
3. Charlie Gillett. *The Sound of the City: The Rise of Rock and Roll*. New York: Outerbridge and Dienstfrey, 1970; Dell, 1972.
4. Peter Guralnick. *Feel Like Going Home: Portraits in Blues and Rock 'n' Roll*. New York: Outerbridge and Dienstfrey, 1971.
5. Michael Lydon. *Rock Folk: Portraits From the Rock 'n' Roll Pantheon*. New York: Dell, 1968.
6. Nik Cohn. *Rock From the Beginning*. New York: Stein and Day, 1969; Pocket Books, 1970.
7. Leroi Jones (Imamu Baraka). *Blues People*. New York: William Morrow, 1963.
8. Peter McCabe and Robert D. Shonfeld. *Apple to the Core: The Unmaking of the Beatles*. New York: Pocket Books, 1972.
9. R. Serge Denisoff. *Solid Gold*. New Brunswick: Transaction Books, 1975.
10. Charlie Gillett. *Making Tracks*. New York: Sunrise Books, 1974.
11. Geoffrey Stokes. *Star Making Machinery: Inside the Business of Rock and Roll*. New York: Vintage Books, 1977.
12. Steve Chapple and Reebee Garofalo. *Rock 'n' Roll is Here to Pay: The History and Politics of the Music Industry*. Chicago: Nelson-Hall Publishers, 1977.
13. Ian Whitcomb. *After the Ball: Pop Music from Rag to Rock*. New York: Simon and Schuster, 1972.
14. Ibid., p. 197.
15. Nat Shapiro. Volume 2, 1940-1949 Popular Music: *An Annotated Index of American Popular Songs*, New York: Adrian Press, 1965.
16. Gillett, *The Sound of the City*, op. cit., p. 3.
17. Whitcomb, op. cit., p. 200.
18. Gillett, *The Sound of the City*, op. cit., p. 9.
19. Jones (Baraka). op. cit., p. 168.
20. Belz, op. cit., p. VIII.

Additional Sources

Lee Berk. *Legal Protection for the Creative Musician*. Boston: Berklee Press, 1970.
Arnold Passman. *The Deejays*. New York: MacMillan, 1971.
Russ Sanjek. "The War on Rock" (mimeo) 1971.
Ortiz M. Walton. *Music: Black, White, and Blue*. New York: William Morrow, 1972.

Rock 'n' Roll: The 1950s and Early 1960s

Introduction

When one thinks of the history rock in the 1950 s it is sometimes difficult to remember that we are roughly talking about a five year period. And when you consider the fact that some of the major figures were out of the picture by 1958 it is even more incredible. The first half of the decade was still firmly in the grasp of the Tin Pan Alley oriented musical establishment. But there were signs that its influence was fading. A comparison of the top songs of 1945 and 1955 shows that many of Tin Pan Alley's major songwriters like Harold Arlen, Johnny Mercer, James Monaco, Rodgers and Hammerstein, Hoagy Carmichael, Jimmy McHugh, Frank Loesser, Harry Warren, and John Green were represented in the rollcall of hits for 1945; in 1955 none of these names would be present in the hit song list.[1] The following year would see the debut of *My Fair Lady*, Frank Loesser's daring *Most Happy Fella*, Jule Styne's *Bells Are Ringing*, and *Li'l Abner*, but it would also see the national debut of Elvis Presley, a presence who, because of his simultaneous mastery of recordings, movies, and TV, was destined to have more influence than any Broadway show could ever imagine. So it was that those early hits, especially those of Haley and Presley were like an explosion that rocked and reverberated throughout the musical and cultural world. It was but a moment, in retrospect, an original dramatic blast and then, shockwaves, and the fallout which came afterward.

That dramatic blast gave birth to the dominant and influential styles of rock 'n' roll, as outlined by Charlie Gillett: New Orleans dance blues (Fats Domino); Northern rhythm and blues (Bill Haley), Chicago rhythm and blues (Chuck Berry), rockabilly (Elvis, Carl Perkins).[2] These styles, of course, echo throughout the next three decades of the sound. The blast also gave birth to a new style—not just a musical style, but a cultural one as well, a style that would enable a new generation to give expression to their own unique values and beliefs. The music became associated with important rituals (dancing, cruising in automobiles, eating—i.e., the jukebox in the diner), dress (blue jeans, leather, DA's), myths (romance, sexuality, cars, leisure, youth in general); and it gave us heroes, heroes, who furthermore, embodied and articulated our myths. Elvis was the first rock 'n' roll hero, but he was also our first rock icon: he was a *presence*, the first to articulate and then symbolize the potential (good and bad) of the music.

Chuck Berry was another hero, and he was the first griot of youth culture, the first youth advocate of the music. He almost singlehandedly, as he said, delivered popular music from the days of old. His music tenuously held on to the rhythmic, harmonic, and melodic forms of the old rhythm and blues while pushing it into new lyric terrain, a terrain inhabited only by the teenager. As the decade worn on, the music, following the lead of Berry, shook off the vestiges of its rhythm and blues progenitors and established itself as music for a younger generation. It is important to remember that the 1950's was the only age that actually featured what we know as rock 'n' roll, a type of music where the primary value was that it had a good beat and you could dance to it.

Rock 'n' roll also attracted tragedy—as will happen with any explosion. The event that is probably foremost in people's minds is Buddy Holly's untimely death in 1959. This, however, had been preceded by Jerry Lee Lewis's marriage scandal (it seems folks didn't think much of Jerry Lee marrying his 14-year-old third cousin), and by Little Richard's desertion of the music as he had a vision and saw his future lie with God and not with Mammon singing ditties like "Tutti Frutti" and "Long Tall Sally." Disk jockey Alan Freed, a pioneer of rock 'n' roll programming, was making $75,000 by 1957, which is hardly tragic, but it did make him a target for muckrakers and rock's enemies.[3] Finally, in 1959, he became a tragic footnote to the first golden age as he was indicted on payola charges and income tax evasion. For all intents and purposes, after 1960, Freed's career was over, and the voice one of rock's greatest champions was neutralized. For many teens there was also tragedy in Elvis' induction into the army in 1958—"The Presence" lost some of his presence. Finally, Chuck Berry was caught in a Mann act violation. Hard times for rock 'n' roll.

Ironically, with rock at its weakest point, in stepped Tin Pan Alley primarily in the form of Brill Building (one of the last actual buildings of the old Tin Pan Alley) songwriters like Neil Sedaka, Paul Anka, Carole King, and Phil Spector. They did not turn the music back over to the "days of old" but recast the teen fantasies and preoccupations pioneered by Chuck Berry into smartly styled—if sometimes overly slick—tunes. Meanwhile on television, Dick Clark provided a wholesome antidote to Alan Freed, and rock, altered but still largely in tact, slid smoothly into the turbulent sixties. The thunder of the explosion however reverberated in foreign places like Liverpool and London and those aftershocks were about to set off another series of blasts that would renew rock music in the States in the 1960's.

The essays in this section begin with R. Serge Denisoff's essay on the evolution of popular music broadcasting; the thrust of his discussion is directed toward the dramatic changes that have taken place in the industry since the 1950's and the role radio played in the evolution of rock music. Denisoff's other piece, on "Teen Angel," deals with some key themes in 1950's popular music and how they are related to youthful rebellion. Interestingly enough, the theme of death, although popular in 19th century music, fell out of the canon of themes during the heyday of Tin Pan Alley. The theme, however, was quite popular in the early days of rock, and Denisoff deals with the implications of the return of this theme to popular music. The essay on Elvis Presley attempts to place his achievement in the context of the larger mythology of our popular culture. It is an attempt to account for Elvis' appeal as well as to offer another perspective on his status as the supreme hero-icon of rock 'n' roll. Finally, Jerome Rodnitzky's essay picks up where the essay on Woody Guthrie left off as he chronicles the merger of folk and rock, the emergence of Bob Dylan, and the rise of protest music during the folk revival of the late fifties and early sixties.

Notes

[1] See Julius Mattfeld, *Variety Music Cavalcade: Musical-Historical Review, 1620-1969*, 3rd ed. (Englewood Cliffs, NJ: Prentice-Hall, 1971).
[2] Gillett, *Sound of the City*, chapter two.
[3] See Mike Jahn's chronology of news items dealing with rock in 1958, in his *Rock: From Elvis Presley to the Rolling Stones* (New York: Quadrangle Books, 1973), pp. 71-72.

References

Berry, Chuck. *Chuck Berry: The Autobiography*. New York: Harmony Books, 1987.
Goldrosen, John. *Buddy Holly*. New York: Putnam, 1979.
Hopkins, Jerry. *Elvis: A Biography*. New York: Warner Books, 1971.
Tosches, Nick. *Hellfire: The Jerry Lee Lewis Story*. New York: Delacorte Press, 1982.

The Evolution of Pop Music Broadcasting: 1920-1972

R. Serge Denisoff

The American Federation of Television and Radio Artists (AFTRA) asserts that the number of disk jockeys can be found by "multiplying the number of AM and FM Stations by an average of four." According to this formula, at least 25,000 persons are employed as disk jockeys. This evidences a 500 percent increase from 1957 when *Time* reported a figure of 5,000 deejays pontificating over the airwaves. Not only has the number of record spinners changed over this time span, but also the role of the disk jockey.

The term disk jockey is believed to have been coined in a *Variety* cover story of Jack Kapp, where the Decca executive used the term "record jockey." As Arnold Passman was later to observe, the label came to connote "jockeying or riding a record toward success."[1] A more typical definition is "the art of announcing records on a program of nothing but records."[2]

A series of conflicting claims not withstanding, the evolution of the disk jockey can be traced to the inception of radio where announcers played gramophone records and chatted informally with their unseen audience. The practice of broadcasting records was attractive, especially to smaller stations, considering the minimal investment necessary to fill air time.

The opposition of sheet music publishers and a number of performers such as Fred Waring and Bing Crosby at the outset hampered the broadcasting of gramophone records, but did not end it, since, as Judge Learned Hand was to rule, copyright control ended with the sale of the record. Therefore, radio stations "could not be restrained from using records in broadcasts." This interpretation of the 1909 Copyright Law coupled with the publishers realization that radio could provide a forum for their songs, began to uplift the power of disk jockeys as the central avenue for public recognition of the songwriters' product, a sentiment the bandleaders of the swing era were quick to recognize.

Radio announcers, prior to the arrival of Al Jarvis to KFWB, Los Angeles, were aptly described as "The same staff spieler who read poetry announced each disc solemnly, impersonally, and formally enough to qualify as an adept funeral director." Jarvis personalized the announcer's role with the addition

Reprinted with permission from *Popular Music and Society*, Volume 2:3 (Spring 1973), pp. 202-26.

of a conversational and friendly microphone style. The approach, perfected by Arthur Godfrey on the East Coast, elevated the announcer from a mere stylized reciter of poetry, ads, and record introductions into a "personality" who commanded the attention of his listeners, thus adapting an equal, if not superior, status to the music he played. Jarvis also pioneered a format within which his "liberated" radio personality could function with success The Make Believe Ballroom. The program structure was simply to play dance tunes and simulate an atmosphere of a marathon ballroom with real or contrived conversations with the performers and dancers. Martin Block, a library assistant at KFWB, seeing the success of the Jarvis vehicle, moved it to WNEW in New York. Block, a former pitchman, parlayed this framework into a medium-wide phenomenon which in time would spawn *Your Hit Parade* and *Lucky Lager Dance Time.*

Arthur Godfrey's approach to his audience was similar to Block's but confined to the early morning hours where he used "earthiness, independence, enthusiasm," and irreverence to announce disks and a growing list of profit hungry, but masochistic, sponsors awaiting his barbs. By the late 1930s, it was clear that the record-playing radio personality was a force to be reckoned with in the dissemination music. Benny Goodman, in 1937, reportedly paid Al Jarvis the sum of $500 to play his latest recordings. In turn, Ballroom listeners increasingly insisted that the bandleader's public appearances be exactly as on record. For the road band, this meant "gritting one's teeth and playing the trademark arrangements note for note."[3] Swing historian, George Simon, has noted the role of the disk jockey in the big band era:

Some (bandleaders) romanced disk jockeys with intense and sometimes nauseating ardor. Some jocks reacted in kind...not stymied, as many of their successors in the sixties were to be, by strict adherence to a 'top forty' type of programming, many disk jockeys actually sought our records by new, upcoming bands and promoting such discoveries remained a labor of love for many a big band disk jockey.[4]

The success of the Jarvis-Block format induced the American Tobacco Company to nationally sponsor *The Lucky Strike Hit Parade,* adding the dimension of ranking records as to their popularity. In the early 1940s Martin Block was to write "If the platter is a good one, the most effective type of direct marketing has taken place. And sales are sure to reflect the airing of the disk."[5] After nearly twenty years of sporadic attempts to contravene radio, few singers, musicians, record companies, or sheet music publishers would dispute the merit of this claim.

In the early "ballroom" days, Jarvis and Block were forced to purchase the records they aired. However, the war-time rationing of shellac, as well as the growing recognition of radio impact upon music taste, found programmers receiving *gratis,* personalized sample records. Glenn E. Wallichs, a co-founder of Capitol Records, recalled:

We typed special labels with their (top 50 deejays) names on both sides, pressed them on expensive lightweight, unbreakable vinylite compound and then had our limited employee force drive around and distribute each sample personally.

It was a service that created a sensation. *We made the jock a Big Man*, an Important Guy, VIP in the industry.[6]

Capitol not only formally recognized the importance of the deejays but also introduced the freebee "exclusive record" which was a precursor of the payola of the 1950s. The "exclusive" was a form of reward to important deejays in the industry. As Norman Prescott noted in his Congressional testimony:

...it was more important for a jockey at that time to get an exclusive record and be able to shout, "I have got it," where nobody else had it on the one or two other stations, than money...as the disk jockey grew into a businessman, he realized his power. At that time, he did not know what his image was, because he was just starting in a relatively new business. So he went into the areas of personnel management, publishing, putting his name on songs, and whatever it is.[7]

The advent of the "exclusive" and the "freebee" underlined the recognition that in the path of a handful of major record companies a new obstacle, with power, had been inserted. To reach the public, a cultural gatekeeper must be coped with. The Blocks, Jarvis' and Godfreys were not mere announcers who would fill up air-time with the handiest record around. The sponsoring of records by bandleaders, and "exclusives" were the opening scenes of what was to become the "cost of doing business."

The importance of the disk jockey was even further enhanced by the diversification of the record and sheet music industries. The rise of Broadcast Music Inc. (BMI) to successfully challenge the all-powerful American Society of Composers, Authors, and Publishers (ASCPA), and the ensuant emergence of independent or "indie" record companies made air-time, or "exposure," all the more precious and difficult to obtain. The disk jockey was the gatekeeper of air-time and the arbiter of economic success and failure for recording companies and songwriters. A *Newsweek* correspondent in 1947 cynically chided deejays reporting: "With all the power in their programs, and no directors to ride herd on them, some are unrestrained in swiping ideas from anyone. They mercilessly play the records that will do *them the most good*..."[8] Dexter attributed even greater influence to the triumphant jock, "his ever-rising power turned the jukes from hit makers to meek little machines that...offer only the music the local jockey ordains. Not even television...can affect the nation's music tastes."[9] Despite disclaimers by prominent deejays, then and now, that they are merely reflections of public taste, there is little question that broadcast exposure is the key to a record's success.[10] One observer noted "If they don't know about a record, they sure as hell are not going to buy it." A program director adds "people don't know what they like, they like what they know." This was especially true for "name" disk jockeys in key market areas of the country since these regions greatly determined which songs placed upon the *Billboard* Hot 100. A Cleveland, Boston, or New York jock who "got on a record" could easily help place it on the August list. The Hot 100, especially for proponents of the Top Forty format, was the barometer of public opinion. Consequently, only a handful of jocks in key market cities could determine the fate of a record. This made payola even more attractive to the donor, since it could assure airplay, especially for the smaller or independent companies. Payola was a trade euphemism for an honorarium for special consideration or what *Billboard* termed "play for pay."

The significance of the "Payola scandals" of the late 1950s lay not in the morality of the practice nor in the "feet of clay" posture of Dick Clark or Alan Freed. Rather, the import of payola was the industry's abortive attempt to control its market in a manner similar to its non-entertainment counterparts listed on the New York Stock Exchange.

Payola: Gatekeepers For Sale

Norman Prescott, the opening witness before the Harris Sub-Committee investigating "deceptive practices in the broadcasting field," aptly described the reason and function of payola. He explained:

...the tremendous output of records, and the fierce competition that exists within the industry, it is a matter of who can play, what, when there is limited amount of play on the air...payola, has become the prime function of this business to get the record on the air at any cost and dispose of it, because if you do not...you cannot get individual income (profits).[11]

Prescott, a former deejay in a top market area, went on to emphasize this statement observing that his four-hour popular music show aired 50 to 52 records per day. Many of these records remained on play lists for four to six weeks. The difficulty lay in the fact that the industry over-produced some 200 new singles per week all in the hope of breaking into the magic circle of *Billboard's* Top Twenty-Five. To further compound the situation, a single that received airplay in a major market area such as Boston, Cleveland, Detroit, or Lost Angeles was nearly guaranteed a spot on the *Billboard* Hot One Hundred, thus nearly assuring its exposure throughout the rest of the nation. The pressure, as the witness noted, was "tremendous." Payola was one device by which the manufacturer could have some semblance of control over his product. Payola promised he would reach as many taste publics as possible out there in mythical "air land."

Payola, as it existed prior to the "scandal," evidenced two dominant forms: "play for pay" and the "consultantship." "Play for pay" was simply "how many dead presidents (twenty dollar bills) are there for me?" This mode of payola was direct payment from the industry to the gatekeeper for air time. The most spectacular practitioner was *American Bandstand* host Dick Clark. The "breaking" or introducing of "Get A Job" and "All American Boy" aptly illustrate "play for pay" on the Clark program. The Silhouettes "Get a Job" was originally produced by Philadelphia disk jockey, Kay Williams, on his Junior label. The disk was purchased by Ember Records. During the transition, the song copy-right was transferred to the Wildcat Music Co.[12] Wildcat Music was controlled by *Bandstand* producer Tony Mammerella. Then the national television show "broke the record." "All American Boy", written by Orville Lunsford, was a talking blues about the rise to fame by Elvis Presley. Lunsford took his song to Fraternity Records. He was urged to have the song processed by Mallard Pressing Company owned by Dick Clark. As soon as 50,000 disks were ordered, the song received extensive airplay on *American Bandstand*. Although the song was actually recorded by Bobby Bare, the non-singing Billy Parsons was provided with appearances on the Dick Clark show to promote the record. The money he was paid for the appearances was charged against his royalties at Fraternity as "promotional expenses."[13] Overall, Clark played 50.4 percent of the records available through the companies in which he had an interest. Of these, 65.4 percent were played prior to the time they appeared on a *Billboard* chart listing. Clark "broke" records on his network dance show for personal gain indicating the exposure power of *American Bandstand*. In the concluding moments of Clark's testimony, chairman Orin Harris told the beleaguered television personality, "You are a product of that system, not responsible for it. You took advantage of a unique opportunity to control too many elements...in the popular music field, through exposure of records to a vast teenage audience."[14] This overt type of payola was unique in that few disk jockey's commanded the power of Dick Clark or indeed Alan Freed. "Play for pay" was generally found in large market areas and was not widespread. More common was the subtle and covert practice of consultantships.

William B. Williams told *Life*, "If a disk jockey had to listen to all these records, he'd go to the kookie house." A fellow jock added, "No broadcasting company expects its men to listen to each and every record. It is just a physical impossibility."[15] The problem, as Paul Ackerman, the music editor of *Billboard*, correctly indicated, was "the abundance of product." Over 130 singles and 100 long-playing albums were being released each week. Consequently, as the *Billboard* editor told the probers, "Competition for exposure is extreme, for without wide public exposure, the potential buyer would never hear most of these records. This is true not only at the broadcast level, where payola enters into play, but also at the retail level."[16] To circumvent the sheer numbers, the music industry, through its local distributors, in fact hired "name" deejays to listen to their product. The jock was listed on ledger sheets as a "consultant." A 1959 sample of 23 major cities found a total of $263, 244 being paid to deejays for consulting and other services. Some distributors and indeed recipients of these fees interpreted them as bribes and acted accordingly; however, the large number of records, from ten to fifteen companies, physically precluded the jocks ability to play all of them. One consultant, Charles Young, observed, "One of their problems was on labeled records by unknown artists...he (distributor) would send these records to my house, and he would call me and ask me what I thought of these records...it did not influence me in one way or another.[17] The distributors perceptions of this exchange was not dissimilar. Donald Dumont explained consultants fee as being partially for "equal consideration in listening to my new releases." Another distributor said, "We made payments...for these people who gave us their time and attention in listening and helping us evaluate our new releases."[18] "Play for pay" predicted an outcome, while consulting provided preferential treatment. Obviously, a record familiar to a jock had a better chance than one he had not heard of, especially where new artists were concerned. After nearly a year of exposures, the Congress passed a bill making payola a crime punishable by a fine up to $10, 000. Both the industry and the disk jockey were somewhat dismayed by the entire episode. A "indie" record manufacturer told *Billboard*, "Today, it's more difficult to tell if you're actually getting anything for your money. There's absolutely no guarantee your record will be played." Disk jockeys added, "There are still too many records. And payola still flourishes," and "payola is practiced in practically every business I know of. The biggest example and most glaring example I can think of is 'lobbying' in Washington."[19] Payola, after the Harris investigation, continued in an altered form since the structure of the music business remained the same. Nonetheless, the perceived autonomy of the individual deejay was altered. The scandals indirectly hastened the awareness of job standardization, particularly in the major market areas. The freedom of the jock was already severely limited in the mid-western and southern states due to the injection of Top Forty radio into the region in the middle 1950s. In 1955, Todd Storz introduced the concept of Top Forty radio at WTIX, New Orleans, and applied it throughout an entire chain operated by a southern pharmaceutical company. Top Forty radio consisted of the repeated play of those songs found on the *Billboard* chart. Interspersed with these continuous hits were jingles and patter in what can best be described as a carnival or medicine show atmosphere. The philosophy underlying this concept was that the airing of material from the *Billboard* chart, then containing C & W and R 'n' B material, would attract the largest audience, then the index of success in radio. For Storz and his imitators, the formula worked. In the beginning deejays in the Storz chain were controlled not by policy but the mechanics of the format. As one former Storz employee noted, "an announcer was required to que six turntables with ET's (transcribed commercials and newscasts) records, give time and temperature." He had time to do little else. In time, what he did say was monitored by the home office. One executive order was to avoid "excessive talking" thus the rapidity of delivery. As comedian George Carlin, then a jock, recalled, the policy was "Shut up and play the music." The home office of the Storz chain automatically built the playlist behind the established charts. For this reason, Storz personnel missed out on the payola given their big city counterparts. Bribing a Storz jock would be a waste of money since he had no control over the songs he played. The payola scandals consciously inserted similar controls into the major market cities such as Cleveland, Boston, New York, and Detroit where the practice of payola had been rampant. It was in these areas that the charts were most effected. Bill Drake's streamlining of many of Storz gimmicks into a rigid format was the ultimate in playlist control. The introduction of demographics in polling further tightened up what the jock should play or say as he was now concerned not with large numbers of listeners but rather a specific limited and affluent segment of the audience. Other stations merely shifted the responsibility of compiling a play list to support personnel such as the program director or the music director.

In most cases, the result was the same, the era of freewilled deejays was rapidly drawing to a close. The idiosyncratic mike styles of the Niagras, Millers, Carneys, Hancocks, Biodis, and Russ Knights would be synthesized into one: the Boss Jock. The "wild and screaming" jock now "does nothing but announce the records, he does this in a hysterical style with fast talk and pitched sell."[20]

With the dimunition of direct payola, the industry representative or promo man was restored to a position of importance. His task was to gain exposure for his acts. In part, this restored the "majors" to a place of competitive advantage over the indies since the smaller companies, having relied heavily upon payola, did not have a promotional apparatus of any magnitude. Nor could they afford to develop one.[21]

The payola scandals provide one important glimpse into the mechanics of music marketing and the function of gatekeepers. The manufacturer, in order to reach the public, has to go through the radio station, the central vehicle for product exposure. In the case of "play for pay," this was a simple procedure removing nearly all risk by purchasing exposure time. "Play for pay" aborted the gate-keeper role. Consulting—being paid to listen to records—provided less risk in the quest for precious air time, but it did not insure it. The disk jockey in this instance maintained his discretionary powers as gatekeeper. The payola hearings greatly curtailed the "play for pay" system and shifted the gatekeeper role from the individual to the collective of station management, with staff, or the dictates of formula radio.

Collectivized Gatekeeping: Boss Radio vs. The Underground

Al Jarvis and Martin Block originated formula radio with their Make-Believe Ballroom Shows. *Your Hit Parade* sponsored by a cigarette company added the next ingredient of ranking songs as to popularity. Top Forty and Boss Sound radio are the end products of a synthesis of record ranking, microphone technique developed by Block, and structured time usage perfected into an art by Bill Drake and Ron Jacobs at KHJ in Los Angeles. Formula radio was a structure into which all of these pieces fit. Deejays, songs, even commercials, and news were designed to fit the mold; if they did not, they were not aired.

AND THE HITS KEEP COMIN'... Boss radio first appeared in the Los Angeles area on May 5, 1965, two weeks prior to the opening scheduled by Bill Drake and Ron Jacobs. The catalyst for this unanticipated event was a dejected KHJ newsman. Dick Splanger, in search of another position, approached KFWB, a competitor, and told them "I know what they're going to be doing at KHJ." On the morning of May 5, Robert W. Morgan ran up to the KHJ program director, Ron Jacobs, and announced "Turn on KFWB, they're calling themselves Boss Radio and they have 20-20 News and the disk jockeys are called the Boss Jocks." In order to save the emerging KHJ identity, Don Steele began to broadcast the same afternoon. KFWB retreated from the new format leaving the Boss Sound to the Drake station. The unexpected introduction of the Boss Sound in the late spring of 1965 was symbolic of what came before to the "nth degree." One of its founders, Ron Jacobs, indicates "most of that stuff was ad lib or created out of necessity."[22] It was not as some would have it a cool calculated and restricted format, at least in the beginning. The generic title itself was adopted as a convenience. KHJ's original slogan in the 1920s was "Kindness, Happiness, and Joy." This slogan gave way to an unsuccessful attempt at programming rock during the 1950s which was overshadowed by "Color Radio" at KFWB. In order to differentiate the KHJ of the 60s from its predecessor, the management searched vainly for a new supporting slogan. One of many suggestions was "Boss Radio KHJ." "Boss" at that time was considered an old fashioned term. Not able to find another catch-word the adjective was a-fixed on billboards and in newspaper and trade ads, but not on the air. Three and a half hours after KHJ was forced on the air by its competition, the station aired an identification jingle followed by the deejays name and the time. Ron Jacobs recalls "So we had the jingle 'KHJ, Los Angeles and the guy comes in and says' it's 6:30 in Los Angeles' I was standing there in the booth and said 'That's redundant. We just said Los Angeles,' so I said try saying 'Boss Angeles' so he did it the next time, and thereafter, we did it every half hour, 169 hours a week, forever."

Other refinements were brought in by this haphazard manner. The first year's play list was borrowed from a rival station. The famous formula was drawn up on a cocktail napkin in a Los Angeles bar by Bill Drake, Ron Jacobs, Gary Mack and Les Turpin. The format consisted of airing 33 records. As these 30 songs were taken from established charts. The KRLA chart was the model for the first year, then the *Billboard* "Hot One Hundred" became the guideline. Three singles were picked by the program director as "hit bounds." Intermixed with these records were approximately 1,000 oldies which were termed "goldens." On weekends, especially during rating sampling periods, "goldens" predominated. Each hour operated on what has come to be called the Drake Clock. The first single was aired at the top of the hour. Three minutes later a commercial or station plug would follow, then seven minutes after the hour something else would happen and then another slot until the 20-20 news. The numerical sequence for spots was "3-7-11-16-20...30-33-37..." The deejay patter was highly stylized and in time predictable: "Boss Radio...handling you the heavy hits, around the clock...where the hits always happen first...the hits just keep on coming!" With the exception of the rapid-fire and structured deejay delivery, Boss Record was an extension of the Top Forty format developed in the 1950s as Jacobs is quick to observe:

> KHJ was just a refinement. If it had the appearance of going faster...it was because we were just starting out like crazy with less of the extraneous stuff.... There had been a tendency with people like McClendon and Storz, when they got successful, not to protect the amount of music they could play. They would get successful and if somebody could sell another spot to a used car dealer, they would put on another spot.

The station kept its rigid commercial limit which would only allow about twelve minutes per hour of commercial fare. The station also strictly enforced its policy of minimizing the chatter by its disk jockeys. Jocks were told "Brian Wilson has just spent nine months of his life wrestling with this thing that takes two minutes and forty seconds. So unless you got something really terrific to say, for your eight seconds, shut up." The better deejays at KHJ such as "Humble Harv" Miller "The Real" Don Steele and Robert W. Morgan complimented the format. Steele, for example, possessed the ability to provide a continuity within the contrasts in the Drake format. According to Jacobs "He was very loud, and he can rise above all the production things that are engineered, the elements that surround him. That's quality...(he) really understands this parade of sounds, and that it is a contextual series of contrasts." However, Miller, Steele, and Morgan are exceptional radio personalities within that format. Others are merely imitators captive in a formula which dominated the AM music idiom. While KHJ never resorted to buzzers that went off after eight seconds other stations may have thus generating the belief that in Boss Radio a jock is little more than an appendage to a Top Forty chart. The programming power at KHJ was in the hands of the program director and the music librarian, Betty Brenemann who assisted him.

A majority of songs aired at KHJ were charted, that is, were currently on the *Billboard* list or had been as with the goldens. The opportunity to "break" a new record at the station was statistically very small. Open programming slots in a given week ranged from one to five. At least fifty or more singles competed for these slots. Songs were picked on the basis of "pacing the tempo of the record, the category of the record as to musical configuration, emotional mood at the time, what people are going for, who's happening in television...the criteria is what the hell sounds good."[23] In other words, a song was chosen if it possessed a number of qualities and met several conditions, come of which transcended the intrinsic quality of the or the "in the grooves" doctrine so widely quoted in the record industry. Drake and Jacobs considered "momentum" the key. Momentum referred to an act or record which was visibly on the ascent or was, in industry argot, "hot." Sonny and Cher, the Supremes, and the Beatles in the mid-1960s all possessed momentum. A song by an established performer following a previous success more often than not was made a "hit bound" on KHJ. The value of exposure for a proven group was really quite minimal. Ron Jacobs, the recipient of numerous golden records thanking him for making X record a hit, considers many of these awards superfluous since "some of them would have been a hit regardless because the group is so big."

Even momentum, however, was not a guarantee of KHJ airplay. Timing was equally important. KHJ had three musical categories which facilitated the pacing of records. Pacing involved the structuring of an hour, that is, two records of similar style, volume, sex of singer, etc. would not be played one after another. As a result the injection of a new record in the field of 33 charged the entire complexion of the playlist. To illustrate, Jacobs would not put three R & B songs on his playlist in a given week regardless of the quality of the record or the momentum of the performer. He recalls "there would never be a week that we would put on Wilson Pickett and the Temptations and Otis Redding no matter if all three had made their greatest record." In this sense a group with a sound similar to another with a chart item was doomed to failure. Why play Zagar and Evans when Simon and Garfunkle "have something going?" Only in rare instances does imitation or similarity help a new performer. America's "Horse Without A Name" in 1972 was an instantaneous hit because the trio's music was identical to that of the super-group Crosby, Stills, Nash, and Young which had not made a record in over a year thus ignoring an established audience for their countrified songs. America was able to capitalize on this situation. It is widely believed that had "Horse" been released at the same time as a CSNY record the group no doubt would have remained an obscure trio. Timing, therefore, is an important variable in a records ability to break into a Boss Sound playlist. While timing can help a group, the clock itself frequently works against it as well. The time of a program director is valuable. Consequently, the screening of records at KHJ worked against most performers. Ron Jacobs was able to review up to a hundred singles in a half-hour simply by listening to the first bar or opening four seconds of a song. If the opening was not infectious and fitting the immediate needs of the format it was rejected. "I can afford to disqualify anything that's going on my station if it doesn't make it in context, and if it makes it in context, it has to come on strong in the beginning." Many record producers, being aware of this review policy, would stress strong bass runs as in "Green Onions" or "You Really Got Me" for an opening thus providing the attention getting sound. This rather cavalier technique is a product of the excessive volume of product that the PD was faced with. Citing the statistic that a new album appears every 90 minutes in America Jacobs explains that he "doesn't have the real time capability to listen to all the songs."

The importance of KHJ lay considerably beyond its immediate market area, since the *Billboard* chart, as well as the Bob Hamilton and Bill Gavin tip sheets, are based upon the air play offered records in the major market area. Los Angeles is perhaps the most important of these areas. Songs not introduced in these areas rarely are played in the so-called secondary markets as their playlists are based upon what is popular in the major markets. The Catch 22 aspect of this is most distressing to promotional people who have devised numerous channels to get around program directors such as Ron Jacobs.

While acknowledging the power of a gatekeeper at KHJ, Jacobs does mildly dissent from the importance of getting a record played on Boss Radio: "I'm sure I could give you an example of ten incredible records that were played routinely as hit bounds for 2-3-4 weeks—nothing happened to them, absolutely nothing...." He could not cite any and added "there are *very few* that we stuck our neck out just because we liked it, that were totally unknown. I think *those probably comprise the ones that we got burned on.*" Consequently KHJ basically programmed records with momentum, that is, those by name artists. In recent years, KHJ has utilized it's smaller sister stations in the Drake Chain to air-test singles that are believed to have potential thus eliminating the risk factor in the major market area. Still, getting a record on the KHJ playlist is a major achievement for any promotion man. Jay Lasker, the flamboyant president of ABC-Dunhill, has erected a large Oriental gong in the executive hallway to be rung by promotional personnel when one of their acts breaks on a major market AM station. A dull buzz is used to announce secondary breakouts.

Free Form Radio...underground, progressive or free form radio was born in the still of the San Francisco night. Originally, Russ "The Moose" Syracuse, who held forth on the Number One Top Forty station, KYA, during the midnight to dawn shift played material never aired during the day time "ratings" hours. *All Night Flight* was a staged space voyage with music, exotic characters, and satire. In conducting this simulated "air trip" the deejay tapped a reservoir of musical material ignored by the formula stations: the long playing album. Devotees of the *Billboard* "Hot One Hundred" and other charts in 1965 would be oblivious to Bob Dylan, Joan Baez, and all of the other artists never having a hit single. In San Francisco, especially, many of the local favorites had not yet signed a recording contract. During the daylight hours there was little incentive to change the KYA format as Tom "Big Daddy" Donohue and other "boss jocks" were leading the Drake managed KFRC in the ratings race. Syracuse in the wee hours of the morning violated nearly all of the cannons of Boss Radio. He did not "shut up and play the music." Much of the music he did air was generally not found on any chart. He played tapes of the Grateful Dead, the Great Society, Big Brother, and the Jefferson Airplane. During the day, as Airplane bassist Jack Casady observed "KYA refused to play our first RCA single." Due to his unique time slot, "The Moose" was free of most station management interferences, he was able to demonstrate a fact aptly illustrated by the Beatles and Stones that albums were no longer just a one hit single with eleven fillers. Each of the Beatles' album was a total package which frequently outsold hot "hit" singles. Big Daddy Donohue explained his disaffection with the AM format as partially attributable to "the fact that the Byrds LP, or the new Bob Dylan album, was out selling the single records on their playlists, in most cases Top Forty programmers choose to ignore them rather than attempting to determine cuts." Few Top Forty program directors deluged in 1966 with 7,086 singles had the time or inclination to plow through some 3,752 albums containing twelve cuts each. Syracuse could and did review material during his six hour air stunt literally "bombing" those he did not like. The new format worked with college students and "street" people indicating that a youth audience existed which preferred musical fare besides the normal AM material. This fact was not lost upon advertisers increasingly concerned with demographics.

Demographics became important in radio industry early in the 1960s when some radio stations either unable or unwilling to compete with Top Forty acceded "numbers" to stations as KHJ and KYA. The Top Forty philosophy was "if we had the kids listening, we figure we could be Number One because the stations in L.A. before then had gotten to be Number One by making the kids listen...demographics are absolutely silly for programmers to consider."[24] But, as the demographic profiles indicate the major consumers of singles and Top Forty radio in the mid-1960s were in the lower age brackets ranging from 9 to 24 with an emphasis on the teeny-bopper or 9 to 15 bracket. While avid consumers of pimple cream and American International films this

The Evolution of Pop Music Broadcasting   89

age group did not purchase many products their older brothers and sisters, the major consumers of albums, did. Top Forty radio centered upon the 9 to 18 audience, while so-called "Middle of the Road" (MOR) stations concentrated upon those 35 to 49, thus leaving the highest consumption demographic of 18 to 34 unattended. This economic fact alone lent indirect legitimacy to the Syracuse format. A large specialty audience in a major city is not to be ignored especially when the taste group buys most of the autos, appliances, and stereos, in the United States. The identification of this alternative audience especially when *Time's* "man of the year" was the "under-25 youth" lent considerable support to formats other than Top Forty. As if to underline the existence of an alternative taste public, the Federal Communication Commission in 1966 ruled that AM and FM Stations under common ownership separate their programming formats as of January 1, 1967. The rise of the LP, more sophisticated sampling techniques, as well as industry awareness of a youth culture were all conditions which provided the soil in which underground radio was flourish.

KMPX-FM in San Francisco was a foreign language specialty station on the verge of bankruptcy. The station listed "vanity" programs ethnic shows where the announcer was also the sponsor. For a time, the station held an "announcing school" where part of the training was conducted on the air. Only Roy Trumbull's Sunday evening folk music show featuring Dylan, Paxton, Ochs, Baez, and others had any youth appeal. Trumbull, who also broadcast on the Pacifica station KPFA, chatted informally and played requests usually from university students. This was KMPX first exposure to the emerging "new community" in the city. A Detroit deejay Larry Miller was imported to do an all night rock program. It was the only one on the station. The show was to become the "style-setter" of the underground radio format. The management originally knew nothing about rock music instead their forte was the Portuguese or Italian Hour. Consequently, Miller was afforded considerable leeway. He chose records, asked for requests, introduced songs with the precision of a jazz-announcer detailing group personnel. The "patter" was "street rap" with a quiet restrain, in part due to the lateness of the hour. Students crammed for exams with KPMX in the background and others smoked dope. The playlist was huge in comparison to the Boss Radio's 33 selections. Miller used 200 to 300 records by Frisco bands, bluesmen, folksingers, poets, and whatever else seemed appropriate. The show was a success. A year after the initiation of the Miller show, Tom Donohue joined KMPX as the program director of the first FM "free form" station. The programming format embraced "rock 'n' roll, folk traditional and city blues, raga, electronic music, and some jazz and classical selections, "I believe music should not be treated as a group of objects to be sorted out like eggs with each category kept apart from the others, and it is exciting to discover that there is a large audience that shares that premise."[25] Donohue hired a number of ex-KYA people who complied their own playlists. An all girl engineering staff was employed. Advertising revenues rose from $3,000 a month to $25,000. Donohue's evening show became the top rated program in the Bay Area appealing to the magic demographic of 18 to 34.

An FM show had done the impossible, it got bigger "numbers" than it's AM counterparts. The success of KMPX spawned a vast number of so-called "free form" stations of which there are an estimated 400 nationally.

For the record industry the success of underground radio was like a breath of fresh air. An entire new avenue for the exposure and marketing of product had opened up. A hit single, while remaining the most effective catalyst for fame, was no longer the *only* way to break an act. The success of Warner/Reprise in the late 1960s is attributed by many of its executives as being directly connected to the rise of "free form" radio. As noted, Warner/Reprise originally was an MOR album lavel with nearly 80 percent of it's catalogue representing Dean Martin, Frank Sinatra, Petula Clark, Trini Lopez and Peter, Paul, and Mary. Rarely did these artists break into the exalted Billboard top twenty. When Warners/Reprise moved into the youth music sphere its reliance on albums did not change. Singles were taken from albums rather than the other way around. Consequently, as an album label the company greatly benefited from "free form" which stressed the specialty album as opposed to the Top Forty single. Indeed, all of alternate media established the Warners Communications Corporation as the company with the "hot hand" in the early 1970s. Other companies were equally delighted with the shift away from the dominant singles emphasis of AM radio. A Columbia Records executive added, "Thank God for underground FM stations because that's given an outlet for the artist who wouldn't be played on Top Forty or might not get broken on Top Forty. One saving light on the horizon. But again, the Top Forty stations are in the position the buyer is in. If they've got, in the case of KHJ, 300 singles to choose from in one week, obviously if they're only gonna be able to add 3-4 singles to their playlist that week, and there's a new Santana or a new Bob Dylan or new Chicago, those are the ones that are going to be the first shot." While underground radio has in fact liberalized and opened up playlists and allowed deejays to get away from the Drake Clock, the "freedom" of this idiom has been an issue since the advent of KMPX.

On March 18, 1968 Tom Donohue and Milan Melvin resigned from KMPX thus beginning a long strike and facilitating the emergence of KSAN as a major "free form" station. A major issue, besides money, was artistic freedom. The strikers accused Crosby-Pacific Broadcasting Corporation, which took over ownership of the station, of interference. Melvin claimed he had been asked to cut his shoulder length hair if he wished to be station manager. He choose to strike. A deejay was told not to play classical cuts longer than five minutes as to maintain program balance. Other complaints centered upon the banning of some songs from airplay as "The Pusher" by Steppenwolfe and "Parchment Farm" by Blue Cheer.

Meanwhile, in New York, Murray "The K" was being fired from his "free form" show on WOR-FM. The reason was the takeover of the Drake syndicate. In leaving Murray claimed, "The music's back in the hands of the people who don't care. There's no personality on the air and the station is developing a routine and a format."[26] Drake's interjection did, indeed, raise WOR's ratings, a fact many AM Top Forty program directors quote anytime a hint of

The Evolution of Pop Music Broadcasting 91

liberalization of play lists is mentioned. The assertion that the progressive format has taken on the same rigidity of Boss Radio has some merit. Some FM stations have replicated to the last decibel the original KMPX and KSAN sound. The purchase of KSAN by Metromedia, a large communications network, found its philosophy being used in Philadelphia, New York, and other major cities.

A 1972 *New York Times* survey indicated a considerable standardization of the progressive format had taken place. In some cases the stations had reverted to Boss Radio. The major catalyst for the decline of "free form" was the so-called "Love" network on the ABD-FM chain. Stations on the Love chain were supplied with tapes and radio spots produced in New York. *Rolling Stone* described these affiliates as featuring "a 24-hour anchorman called 'Brother John' who reads poetry, ala Rosko, and presides over the format's bland blend of 'progressive rock' seemingly guided by the trade magazines."[27] All seven FM affiliates instituted this policy and program directors dictated the playlists and the time that certain records were to be played. A network vice-president commented, "We feel that in the last year [1971] there has been a major shift among young people away from radicalism and esotericism."[28] A record company executive sadly noted "the free form stations are non-existent with the exception of 2 to 3. KMET here (Los Angeles) WBCN in Boston. There are not very many others that I can think of that are either profitable or visible. So it isn't going to change." The so-called "open air" policies of the latter half of the 1960s, outside of campus stations, were rapidly disappearing.

Allen Shaw, president of ABC-FM, after a brief fling at free form, introduced his version of the Drake Clock. The Shaw formula was to create a playlist of pre-selected songs taken from charts, oldies, and cuts from successful albums. These are then inserted into a time-table as the Clock. The deejays are tightly controlled and monitored. They are told to say "Hi, this is...." Shaw explained, "It's good radio principles: little DJ talk, careful spot placement, call-letter frequency, weather.... The jingles are not a limitation." The selection of the playlist on ABC-FM is quite similar to the Boss Radio formula:

We operate on two premises: certain recording artists are more popular than others. Two, a station can choose to present the new, less popular music to a segment of an audience or present only the more popular—without reproducing Top Forty. We've been accused of turning into an FM Top Forty. What's wrong with it? If that's what people want, then there should be one station in town to do that.[29]

This formula has been described as the "Chinese Menu"; that is, a song is chosen from an album, another from the Top Forty chart, another from the oldies list and so on. For the record company attempting to break an artist the move away from free form greatly inhibits their ability to break an act.

In 1973 there are still some independent FM stations which adhere to free form. The Metromedia chain still allows its deejays some editorial control. WPLJ in New York is one example, although it is consistently beaten in the ratings by the Drake-controlled WOR-FM. Don Morehouse at KMET in Los Angeles runs a "free form" station where deejays still pick what they will play. WARX-FM in Detroit also leaves much of the programming discretion in the hands of its announcers. Dennis Fawley, a WABX jock, comments "You have to be aware of everything that's coming out and decide whether or not to put it on the air. Each person here on this staff is aiming at a different audience depending on his *own tastes and personality.*"[30] Such discretion is becoming increasingly restricted even on FM radio.

AM radio has been affected by the rise of the progressive stations. This has been especially true with the move away from free form. A rather typical reaction by AM programmers has been to dismiss the progressive format. George Wilson, of the Bartell Broadcasting Chain with number one rated stations in Milwaukee and Denver, is a typical example. Wilson refused to play album cuts on his Top Forty stations as LP cuts "lose ratings for you." "People," he insists, "who're into album cuts...aren't into Top Forty radio."[31] Furthermore, Wilson cites the demographic that only the 18-24 year old age group listen to progressive. Consequently, he feels Top Forty commands a greater market. It would be safe to say that a vast majority of AM popular music program directors would concur with Wilson's sentiments. Don Armstrong of WOHO in Toledo totally supports this notion. Having worked in the Southern, mid-West, and Canadian markets, Armstrong feels the audience is "unhip" and desirious of familiar material. He says "You can't keep an audience with new material unless they're locked in a building." "People don't know what they like, they like what they know. They know those songs that you can hum, sing, whistle, tap your foot too, preferably all four."

Notes

[1] Arnold Passman, *The Deejays* (New York: The Macmillan Company, 1971), p. 64.

[2] "A Jockey's Life," *Newsweek*, December 16, 1946, p. 71.

[3] Passman, *op. cit.*, p. 76.

[4] George Simon, *The Big Bands* (New York: The Macmillan Company), 1967, p. 56.

[5] Block, *op. cit.*, p. 45.

[6] Wallichs, quoted in D. Dexter, "1930-1945, Disk Jockey: Origin of the Species," *Billboard*, December 27, 1969, p. 58.

[7] Testimony of Norman Prescott, *Responsibilities of Broadcasting Licenses and Station Personnel*. House of Representatives 86th Congress (Part I) 1960, p. 39.

[8] *Newsweek*, *op. cit.*, p. 72.

[9] Dexter's position while generally valid, does ignore a spate of songs popularized through the medium of television. The most noteworthy is Joan Weber's "Let Me Go Lover" featured on a *Studio One* play. Themes from several shows also have reached the Number One spot on the Hot One Hundred such as "Davy Crockett."

[10] Nearly all of the press reports before and after the payola hearings stress the "mirror" thesis. Howard Miller told *Time*, "I play the things they want to hear. Unless I do, I don't have an audience, and, therefore, I have denied my station, my second integrity, an audience. And the station loses the account of my advertiser, my third integrity." "What Makes Howard Spin," *Time*, April 29, 1957, p. 50.

[11] Testimony of Norman Prescott, *op. cit.*, p. 7.

¹²Ben Grevatt, "More Ready to Make Like Canaries as Scandal Grows," *Billboard*, November 23, 1959, pp. 2, 51.

¹³Testimony of Billy Parsons, Part II, *op. cit.*, pp. 1083-1095.

¹⁴Mildred Hall, "Clark Winds Up Testimony with Stout Payola Denials," *Billboard*, May 9, 1960. p. 3.

¹⁵"Gimme, Gimme, Gimme on the Old PAYOLA," *Life*, November 23, 1959, p. 45; and Testimony of Joseph Finan, Part I, *op. cit.*, p. 145.

¹⁶Testimony of Paul Ackerman, Part II, *op. cit.*, p. 904.

¹⁷Testimony of Charles Young, Part I, *op. cit.*, pp. 203, 205.

¹⁸Testimony of Donald Dumont, Part I, *op. cit.*, p. 532; and Testimony of Harold Dinesten, *op. cit.*, pp. 355-356.

¹⁹June Bundy, "Payold NOT Dead Now Underground," *Billboard*, August 29, 1960, p. 1; and "Deejays Tab Payola Probe as Bootless Political Football," *Billboard*, December 19, 1960, pp. 1, 4.

²⁰A Bester, "New Age of Radio," *Holiday*, June, 1963, p. 56.

²¹Bob Rolontz, "Promotion Man Back in Saddle as Payola Tide Ebbs," *Billboard*, August 8, 1960, pp. 1, 33.

²²Interview

²³Interview

²⁴Interview

²⁵Donohue, quoted in Jerry Hopkin's *Rock Story* (New York: Pocket Books, 1970), p. 141.

²⁶Bob McClay "Murray the K on WOR-FM (They screwed it up)" *Rolling Stone* 1 November 9, 1967, p. 10.

²⁷"FM Underground," *op. cit.*, p. 6.

²⁸"New Trends Alter Underground Radio," *New York Times*, January 10, 1972, p. 46.

²⁹Shaw quoted in Ben Fong-Torres "Radio: Ups and Downs in the FM Ozone," *Rolling Stone*, July 6, 1972, pp. 22, 24.

³⁰Patti Johnson "WABX-FM," *Phonograph Record Magazine*, June, 1971, n.p.

³¹"George Wilson Propounds His Potent Programming Technique," *Billboard*, August 12, 1972, p. 20.

"Teen Angel":
Resistence, Rebellion and Death—Revisited

R. Serge Denisoff

Popular songs, particularly since the late 1960s, have increasingly attracted the attention of serious writers as opposed to fan magazine biographers. Books and articles in scholarly journals have appeared bearing the methodological imprimatur of American studies, history, sociology and English. Most of these new works concentrate upon the ideational and intellectual aspects of popular music and its metaphysical leaders such as Lennon, Dylan, Morrison, Springsteen and Townsend. They do, however, ignore what is considered intellectually declasse as *kitsch* or low-cult. Articles appearing in *Popular Music and Society*, for example, strongly reflect this bias.[1] Nonetheless, it is precisely this segment of rock music that dominates the charts and the Boss Radio airwaves.[2] Consequently it appears useful that students of rock music look at the intellectually commonplace in order to understand the entire spectrum of popular songs and their possible social significance. While the rise of overt sociopolitical statements on the top 40 charts during the 1960s appeared unmistakable it should not be assumed, as many have, that popular songs prior to the Beatles and Dylan were void of social criticism and dissent.[3] The classic illustration of sociological impact being present in music *kitsch* is, perhaps, found in the so-called teenage coffin songs of the early 1960s

The teenager coffin songs—narrative ballads performed in a pseudo-operatic style of crooning—have customarily been portrayed as representing the Dark Age of popular music. Influential New York rock critic Richard Goldstein frequently characterizes the emergence of the Liverpool Four as saving the world from "death songs, pretty boys, and payola."[4] Richard Meltzer takes a similar track, in part, arguing that the rock and roll of the early 1960s was an attempt to return to the golden roots of rock observable in the 1950s. He writes:

To rock 'n' roll, renaissance is merely necrophilia, and this notion has frequently burst forth into the very content of rock song. Mark Dinning's "Teen Angel" is such a song, as is nearly everything recorded by Dicky [sic] Lee.[5]

Reprinted with permission from the *Journal of Popular Culture* Volume 16:4 (Spring 1983) pp. 116-22.

Meltzer's major thesis, supported by the subsequent popularity of the disco sound and country music, misses the point that coffin songs had a significance—sui generis—of their own. They were not *ipso facto* just an uncomfortable way station from Elvis Presley to Lennon and McCartney.[6] The teenage coffin song instead may be interpreted within the framework of Camus' thesis on the nature of rebellion. In the prototype coffin song the protagonists—Tommy and Laura, Jimmy and Mary—are placed in conflict with the expectations of adolescent social status. Consequently the antagonists customarily are symbols of adult society—the parents, economic institutions and the like. In confronting these obstacles, tragedy, in the form of death, strikes. The conflict, as perceived in coffin songs, is a product of the unique status of youth. Lewis Feuer suggests that generational conflict is entirely different from that of class struggle in that one's gerontocratic status is both temporary and diffuse.[7] Moreover, the conflict between generations is more a competition since either wishes to destroy existent dominant—submissive relations. Therefore, the adolescent does not overtly proclaim his superiority over adult society. As Friedenberg indicates, the teenagers of the early 1960s did exist in a colonial status with one significant qualification:

The maintenance of a colonial system requires that the native accept enough of the dominant culture to meet its schedules, work for payment in its smaller currency, desire and consume its goods, and fight in its armies.... But the native is not expected—indeed, not usually permitted—to actually 'pass'; he is never granted full membership in the dominant culture, and the dominant culture does not depend for its survival on his ultimate willingness to accept it.[8]

Unlike the proletarian, slave or peasant, the teenager through the passage of time becomes part of the gerontocratically dominant group. The teenager does not have a permanent stake in generational revolution. The teenage role is tied to working within established channels. For example, the singer in "Summertime Blues" chronicles the tribulations of youth, but concludes "there ain't no cure for the summertime blues."[9] Tommy in "Tell Laura I Love Her" loses his life in his adherence to the "get rich quick" theme. Beyond absolute revolution and conformity to the "colonial" adolescent role lies a middle-range of dissent outlined in Albert Camus' conceptualization of rebellion, and evolution or existence and death. Existence involves rebellion, "I rebel therefore we exist."[10] Death is the absolute act of resistance in that it involves a total withdrawal. Death both negates existent relationship of power—parent and child—but also finalizes the positive relationship. Death at the physical level negates. At the metaphysical level it stabilizes. For example, life is perceived by theologians and philosophers as transitory. Life after death, on the other hand, is permanent. The truncation of life, opting for death is rebellion since it negates existence. Camus writes:

Metaphysical rebellion is the movement by which man protests against his condition and against the whole of creation. It is metaphysical because it contests the ends of man and of creation.[11]

So it is with the teenage coffin songs. The actor cuts short his subservient "colonial" role and rejects the potential of adulthood by asserting a higher power or option available to him. In choosing life the subject, while in a subservient position, affirms the status quo. In death the physical withdrawal of services become rebellion since the outcome is final.

The early coffin songs found on the pop charts were transfers from the country music genre. The first of these was Jody Reynolds' "Endless Sleep" which was a precursor of things to come. The story line was partially summarized by the chorus: "I heard a voice crying in the deep; Come join me baby in my endless sleep" (c. Johnstone-Monter-Inc./Elizabeth Music). Reynolds, in exhorting Presleyian tones, documents how an external force—the sea—has taken away his girlfriend, who in turn implores him to "come join her" in death. This basic Romeo-Juliet theme is a staple motif in coffin songs. Immediate adversity can be overcome with the absolute of death. Even the last second revelation that the heroine is saved from drowning does not lessen the impact of the song since nearly all those following, with the exception of "Bobby" and Roy Orbison's "Leah," do not end happily.

"Endless Sleep," perhaps because of the rock-a-billy singing style, did not start a trend although several songs did capture elements of the original. Thomas Wayne's recording of "Tragedy" lamented the departure of a loved one: "All that's left is the dark;/You've gone from me oh, oh tragedy" (c. Bluff City Music BMI). Wayne's youthful semi-operatic style laced with highly pained and throbbing "oh's" left little doubt in the listener's mind that this was unmistakably a teenage tragedy. Mark Dinning's "Teen Angel" combined the dominant features of both the Reynolds and Wayne recordings. "Teen Angel" had a clear story line: A car is stalled on a railroad track and the girl inside is killed while searching for her boyfriend's high school ring—which he had given her. The singer's response to the accident paralleled Wayne's haunting "oh, oh tragedy." However, as in "Endless Sleep" the grief-stricken suitor attempts to re-establish the relationship. The singer mournfully asks if the "loved one" can see or hear him and is he still her "own true love" concluding "teen angel answer me please" (c. Acuff-Rose).

"Teen Angel" reached the top position on the *Billboard Hot 100 chart*. As with any song that accomplishes this feat and remains on *Billboard*'s list for 18 weeks, "Teen Angel" generated several imitations. On June 13, 1960 "Tell Laura I Love Her" by Ray Peterson began to climb the same *Billboard* ladder of success. In the Independence Day issue, the trade paper alerted its readers with " 'Tell Laura' Leaping Charts."[12] "Tell Laura" was cast in the classic mode of an English ballad with all of the audio embellishments of its predecessors, and the addition of screeching brakes and an automobile crash. As with all teenage coffin songs the conclusion was preordained, however the ideology of the song was clear.

Tommy, the protagonist, was killed pursuing the Horatio Alger ideal. More importantly, love did not conquer all, especially economics. Tommy wishes to buy Laura a wedding ring, but does not have enough money. He enters a stock car race which offers a thousand dollar prize. He is, as the lyric notes, "the youngest driver there." During the race Tommy is killed. He tried and failed, at least within the ideological context of the colonial power. In the last verse we find Laura kneeling in a chapel praying for her departed lover, she can hear him repeat his dying words: "Tell Laura I love her/Tell Laura I need her" (c. E.B. Marks Music Corporation, BMI). While "Tell Laura" did not reach the exalted Number One ranking on the *Billboard* chart, it did stay on for 14 weeks. The song also introduced the thesis that death was an outcome caused by a social problem in the here and now. Indeed, the final solution in "Tell Laura" may be portrayed as a worthy endeavor to transcend the Governor—Colonial aspects of adolescence. As Camus suggests, this is the highest and noblest form of resistance since death curtails the master's power and also, the willingness of the resistor to rebel with his life affirms the validity of these rights for him and for all human beings.[13]

The Everly Brothers' rendition of "Ebony Eyes" was both in style and structure a country and western death ballad as opposed to teenage coffin song. It did, however, reiterate the "external intervention—death—reunited in afterlife" framework. A young soldier on leave arranges to have his fiancee join him so they can be married. The plane crashes. Ebony Eyes is taken away. But in heaven, when death comes to the soldier, they will be rejoined "and I'll know she will be my beautiful ebony eyes" (c. Acuff-Rose Publications, Inc.). "Ebony Eyes" was a commercial success also, and was emulated by Jim Reeves' "The Blizzard," Neil Scott's "Bobby," Pat Boone's "Moody River" and the Fleetwoods' remake of the Thomas Wayne song "Tragedy." In the country field songs such as Tex Ritter's "Hillbilly Heaven" and Wilma Lee and Stony Cooper's "Wreck on the Highway" received some air play. By the fall of 1961, the original wave of coffin songs was exhausted.

In the waning days of summer, 1962, three songs dealing with the subject of death appeared on the Hot 100 chart. Roy Orbison's song "Leah" was structurally and lyrically similar to "Endless Sleep" and "Laura." In the melodramatic place, Hawaii, a skin diver dreams he is drowned while fetching pearls for "his lost love." The other two "hits" added another dimension to death and resistance. Rex Allen, the veteran of numerous "singing cowboy" films, recorded "Don't Go Near the Indians" in the so-called "Tex-Mex" style of Marty Robbins' "El Paso." In true narrative ballad form the song chronicles the experience of an Indian boy who is raised as a white. He is unaware of his ancestry and despite the warnings of his adopted father does associate with the local Indians. He falls in love with an Indian maiden and asks his father's permission to marry. In reply, the authority figure relates how the hero is an Indian and that his object of affection is "...your sister/and that's why I've always said: 'Son don't go near the Indians please stay away/Son don't go near the Indians please do what I say' " (c. Acuff-Rose Publishing). Implicitly "Indians" revived the Romeo-Juliet theme of dissent to societal impositions upon romantic relationships between adolescents. The motif was based upon social endogamy and propinquity. The polarization along the lines of Camus' "them and us" had entered the consciousness of popular songs. Songs such as Crystals' "He's a Rebel," produced by Phil Spector and Ann Cole's "Don't Stop the Wedding" decried parental interference in love rites. "Indians" inversely introduced the social class barrier in absolutist terms. For Rex Allen's unfortunate Indian only reincarnation or a spiritual after-life could possibly transcend the barriers of incest. Dickey Lee and the Shangri-Las saw death as an outcome to equally unsolvable problems. Dickey Lee in appearance could in no way be classified as a rebel. Posing as a college letterman with a crewcut he was reminiscent of the Pat Boone image during the Presley rock-a-billy period. With songs such as "I Saw Linda Yesterday" and other rating-dating musical statements Lee's image was that of America's big brother. Nonetheless his two most popular records were classics in the coffin song genre. "Patches" was a documentary of social injustice. Patches was a Shanty-town girl who is in love with a middle class youth. The youth's parents disapprove of the relationship. The parental interference into the relationship causes Patches to throw herself into the river and drown. Upon overhearing the news of the drowning, the singer announces he will join her: "It may not be right/But I'll join you tonight" (Aldon Music, Inc.). In an act reflecting both guilt and protest the youth commits suicide. In a future recording Lee relates the tale of a teenage boy who "falls in love with Lauri." Laurie, at the time of this encounter had been dead a year.[14] Dickey Lee's longevity on the pop charts was fleeting at best; however, his downfall was not directly caused by the emergence of the Beatles as some observers have claimed.[15]

The unit which epitomized the "death as rebellion" genre was the Shangri-Las, a female trio named after James Hilton's *Lost Horizon*. The name of the group was designed to connote "...a place where everything was quite perfect, a restful place of contemplation, a true Utopia."[16] Mary Weiss was the lead singer with the Ganser twins, Margie and Mary Ann, providing the harmonic background. The Shangri-Las were an existential contradiction. They dressed and appeared middle class WASP, yet their singing style was distinctively Black and modeled on the Shirelles and later the Crystals. As one observer noted they were "the tough mama goes soft." Yet their songs transcended the Mailer "White Negro" posture since they came on as white middle-Americans who painfully were attempting to cope with a world not of their making.[17] The first Shangri-Las production, "Remember" (Walkin' In the Sand) was a standard torch song, as all their records were. However, the influences here were the Donald Wood rhythm and blues hit "Death of an Angel" (c. 1955) with a touch of "Endless Sleep." The lyric of a discarded woman contained all the elements of a "weeper" not to mention the sound of a crashing ebb tide. "Remember" did moderately well on the charts.

"Leader of the Pack" totally surpassed "Remember" and actually pushed a Beatles record out of the high spot on the "Hot 100" in 1964. "Leader of the Pack," a 45 record, was a mammoth production akin to the American International films of the time. The production opened with several of the singers describing the honored status of the heroine, Betty, who was dating the leader of a motorcycle gang.[18] Betty in short order notes the disapproval of her parents and her humanitarianism in relating to Jimmy—the leader of the pack. Betty's father then orders her to dissolve the relationship, and she does. Upon telling Jimmy of her father's command: amidst the sounds of shattering glass and bending steel, Jimmy is killed. Betty's friends commiserate but "now he's gone." As in Janis Ian's song "Society's Child," the lyric ends not on a note of resignation but implicit accusation and internal self-righteousness. Had not the colonial rulers interfered, Jimmy would still be alive! In death, victory, however shallow, was present.

Ray Peterson in June of 1964 attempted to recreate "Tell Laura" with another coffin song "Give Us Your Blessing" written by Barry and Greenwich, later the lyrical brains behind the Shangri-Las Red Bird Productions. The song reached No. 70 on the Hot 100 and remained on the chart for six weeks. In music industry circles this ranking is, for established performers, a mediocre effort. Two years later the Shangri-Las covered this song with a much greater degree of success. "Give Us Your Blessing" incorporated all of the variables and indices noted and added the DeMille touch of record-making. The song opened with the sound of thunder clapping, and three shrill voices changing "Run, Run, Run, Mary/Run, Run, Run Jimmy...." A sad but very youthful voice began to recite the ensuing tale of tragedy. Jimmy and Mary are young lovers. The teenagers approach the girls' parents requesting permission to be married and rebuffed. During the song it is made readily apparent that resistance and defiance are the young couple's only choices, and they elope during a rainstorm. The next day they are found in critical condition after a highway crash. The elopers in the song, nonetheless, appear to triumph. The parents are blamed for the dual fatalities: "Give us your blessings; Please don't make us run away" (Trio Music, Inc. BMI).

The group's next song "Out In the Streets," was a restatement of the "Leader of the Pack" theme. This time, however, the boyfriend is not potentially rejected, but rather accepts the conventions of middle class America. "He don't comb his hair like he did before/He don't wear those ole black boots no more... [but]...his heart is out in the street." It is a Promethean plot with a protagonist attempting to accommodate the normative societal prescriptions. His past in Pavlovian or behaviorist terminology prohibits this endeavor. "Out in the Streets," while in the "Dawn," "Society's Child" genre of exogamous relationships between rich and poor, city and suburb, and black and white, brought together the social dissent found in both Dickey Lee's "Patches" and the Shangri-Las' previous successes. "Streets" transcended the customary rating-dating themes of endogamy, but unlike the other compositions finds the relationship failing on the basis of sociocultural differentiation rather than adult intervention. As in the George Stevens film *Shane* the "marginal man" can attempt to acculturate, but in time he must return to the role of being a gunfighter who will "die by the sword." This fits neatly with the storyline in "Leader of the Pack" where Jimmy, the Hell's Angel-like suitor is killed in a motorcycle accident.

Several death songs in the latter half of the 1960s—"Ode to Billy Joe" and "Honey"—sold quite well. Still, the teenage coffin song did not return after 1965. The demise of coffin songs correlates with the introduction of overt statements of social dissent as found in Barry McQuire's "Eve of Destruction," and Glen Campbell's version of "Universal Soldier." Conversely the "He's a Rebel," "Tell Laura I Love Her," "Patches" oriented songs were *passe* with the advent of the counterculture and its disavowal of the social ethic of the 1950s, and indeed parental authority.

The coffin songs of the early 1960s were quantitative novelties, no doubt, but to discount them as a meaningless nodal point in rock music history is to miss a significant aspects of its evolution. For in the early 1960s seemingly the only viable form of rebellion for many adolescents was withdrawal in running away or in death. Drugs, politics and changing economic standards, perhaps, have temporarily mediated Camus' ultimate question of existence or death. But as Marshall Fishwick suggests there is "lots of blood in popular culture."[19]

Notes

[1]John Bridges and R. Serge Denisoff, "PMS in Retrospect: A Look at the First Six Volumes," *Popular Music and Society*, Vol. 7, No. 1 (1979), 2-7.

[2]See John Bridges, "Changing Courtship Patterns in the Popular Song: A Replication of Horton and Carey," M.A. Thesis: Bowling Green State University, 1980.

[3]See D.K. King, "Protest Song in the United States." *Folklore Forum*, X (1978), 9-25.

[4]Richard Goldstein quoted on "How the Beatles Changed the World," *CBS Tuesday night*, May 28, 1968.

[5]Richard Meltzer, *The Aesthetics of Rock* (New York: Something Else Press, 1970), 61. Also c.f. H.F. Mooney, "Just Before Rock: Pop Music 1950-1953, Reconsidered," *Popular Music and Society*, Vol. 3, No. 2 (1974), 65-108.

[6]See John C. Thrush and George S. Paulus, "The Concept of Death in Popular Music: A Social Psychological Perspective," *Popular Music and Society*, Vol. 6, No. 3 (1979), 219-228.

[7]Lewis S. Feuer, *The Conflict of Generations: The Character and Significance of Student Movements* (New York: Basic Books), pp. 7-35.

[8]Edgar Z. Friedenberg, *Coming of Age in America* (New York: Random House), pp. 3-8.

[9]R. Serge Denisoff and Mark H. Levine, "Generations and Counter-Culture: A Study in the Ideology of Music," *Youth and Society* 2 (Sept. 1970), 35-38; and Richard Staehling, "The Truth About Teen Movies," *The Rolling Stone* (Dec. 27, 1969), 34-48.

[10]Albert Camus, *The Rebel: An Essay On Man in Revolt* (Translated by Anthony Bower; New York: Knopf, 1956).

[11]*Ibid.*, p. 23.

[12]"Ray Peterson's 'Tell Laura' Leaping Charts," *Billboard* (July 4, 1960), p. 20.

[13]Camus, 13-22.

[14]"Laurie" was on the *Billboard* "Hot 100" for a period of 13 weeks in late spring 1965.

[15]The popularity of "Laurie," "Leader of the Pack," "Last Kiss," "Give Us Your Blessing" and other coffin songs during 1963 to 1965 empirically refutes the notion that these songs were a respite between Presley and the Beatles. This fact also questions Belz' thesis that the Beatles' popularity was due to a search for some collective happiness after the Kennedy assassination.

[16] Liner notes, *Golden Hits of the Shangri-Las* Mercury Records (SR 61099).

[17] There is little doubt that the intellectual significance of the group was primarily a product of the wisdom of Phil Spector and the writing talents of Jeff Berry and the Crystals.

[18] Cf. John Johnstone and Elihu Katz, "Youth and Popular Music: A Study in the Sociology of Taste," *American Journal of Sociology* 62 (May 1957), 563-568.

[19] Marshall Fishwick, "Popular Culture as Art," Presentation at Bowling Green State University, Dec. 3, 1970.

Elvis Presley and The Myth of America

Timothy E. Scheurer

I'm going to Graceland Poorboys and Pilgrims with families
And we are going to Graceland

Paul Simon, "Graceland" (1986)

The new habits to be engendered on the new American scene were suggested by the image of a radically new personality, the hero of the new adventure: an individual emancipated from history, happily bereft of ancestry, untouched and undefiled by the usual inheritances of family and race; an individual standing alone, self-reliant and self-propelling, ready to confront whatever awaited him with the aid of his own unique and inherent resources.

R.W.B. Lewis, *The American Adam* (1955)

Lord please save his soul
He was the king of Rock and Roll

Robbie Robertson, "American Roulette" (1987)

Revolutionaries are reconcilers. As they push into new frontiers, as they challenge our preconceived notions and force us to look at the new, they also, Janus-like, reaffirm the traditional and cast their gaze deliberately on the past. Beethoven forever altered the symphony, but he did so within the confines of the sonata-allegro conventions of his predecessors. The French Revolution overturned the monarchy, but saw the new order modeled on the virtues of Republican Rome. Ragtime forced a rhythmic revolution in American popular music at the turn-of-the-century, but the ragged rhythms were almost invariably grounded in the classical structure of the rondo form. Elvis Presley, similarly, stood at the center of the rock 'n' roll revolution, but he achieved his rebel-hero status by also reaffirming traditional American values.

When he burst upon the scene in 1956 Elvis finally and incontrovertibly altered the shape of American popular music. Elvis was a revolutionary for the fifties generation, but, like other revolutionaries, he was also a reconciler. In this essay I hope to show how Elvis' tremendous popularity and his impact on music was due to his ability to push popular music into new frontiers while at the same time offering young Americans a new version of the Myth of America and the American Dream. His vision of the myth was grounded in the ideals of our forefathers, but it was also unique to the youth of the 1950's. Consequently, in his career he passed from being a hero figure to icon, a presence who transcended "the moment" and came to represent a more profound reality than his mere presence would suggest.

The hero figures of any civilization or generation contain the myths of that culture. Heroes, through significant action, articulate those myths. Myths, moreover, are central to the consciousness of all cultures. Myths, according to James Oliver Robertson:

> ...are the patterns—of behavior, of belief, and of perception—which people have in common.... They provide good, "workable" ways by which the contradictions in a society, the contrasts and conflicts which normally arise among people, among ideals, among the confusing realities, are somehow reconciled, smoothed over, or at least made manageable and tolerable (xv).

Myths are part of our daily rituals, our worship, our habits, and, within the realm of popular culture, myths are crucial because they provide a deeper level of meaning than history would normally accord certain activities. The Myth of Success, for instance, transforms the pursuit of wealth and material goods into a capitalist version of the Grail quest. The Myth of the West, similarly, transforms an historical moment into a cosmic battle between the forces of nascent civilization and the retreating forces of the savage wilderness.[1] In the process, the values that emerge triumphant from this struggle form what could be termed "sacred history," to borrow a term from Mircea Eliade. Eliade has written of myth:

> Its function is to reveal models and, in so doing, to give a meaning to the World and to human life. This is why its role in the constitution of man is immense. It is through myth...that the ideas of *reality, value, transcendence* slowly dawn. Through myth, the World, can be apprehended as a perfectly articulated, intelligible, and significant Cosmos (145).

Heroes are a vehicle whereby this world is made intelligible and significant because their lives, adventures, skills, and talents remind us of our most cherished values and our highest ideals. They live out the deepest, fullest and greatest notions of what it is to be human. As we look at Elvis' career we will see how he gave meaning to the lives of a new generation of Americans, and how that generation, through rock 'n' roll, embraced a new reality, adopted "new" values, and achieved a sense of transcendence.

Elvis was able to take the basic stuff of the myth of the America, the heightened sense of promise, to quote F. Scott Fitzgerald, and make it viable for a new generation. Elvis, as a rock 'n' roll hero, suggested a new vision for kids while anchoring his ethos in the past. He had a new look and dress style; his music was new and it expressed new values. But there is illusion here—perhaps the Easterner is right: all is *maya*—for as radical as he appeared, he actually articulated some deeply rooted values in regards to success, community, the country, utopian and egalitarian ideals (in short, the component parts of our American myth). Where Elvis differed from his mythic forebears, however, was that he reified the promises of opportunity, equality, property, and self-reliance in the context of the values of youth culture such as spontaneity, emotionalism, sexuality, freedom, and possibility. For the first time in the country's history, the myth was truly a youthful vision.

In the past, when young people worked out the myth of America they did it almost as a rite of passage; for instance, the Alger hero's drive to succeed is actually an exercise in achieving the values of adult society: thriftiness, responsibility, position, power. Even Ruby Keeler's articulation of the myth of the American Dream in *42nd Street* (1933) represents a movement from the world of childhood to adulthood as she is told by director Julian Marsh, "Sawyer, you're going out there a youngster, but you've got to come back a star." In short, to be a star is to be an adult, is to have achieved the socially accepted norms of success established by adults. With Elvis it is not so. The values he embodied as an early rock 'n' roll hero remain the eternally youthful. Let us then look at the factors that enabled him to reconcile the values of youth culture and the myth of America: his image and his music. First, his image.

Elvis fulfills the classic American definition of the success myth. He was indeed the poor boy who, through luck, pluck, and a bit of talent, rose to the top. The son of a truck driver who had difficulty making ends meet for his family, Elvis planned to become a truck driver himself. He was a bit of an outsider, wearing his hair pompadour style and playing music generally associated with blacks; he, in short, seemed to run counter to not only the traditional values of the old South, but to the traditional values of mainstream white culture in the 1950's. And so, perhaps, when he finally made it big, he struck a chord in many who also saw themselves as disenfranchised from the mainstream culture; they saw in Elvis the promise and the potential that they knew lay within them all.

An important element of Elvis' image was his look. He made the hairstyle of the "greaser" acceptable. When he performed he wore a suit like other performers and crooners before him, but somehow he made it look dangerous. And after he was a success, he made the suit gold, wearing his success in a bold, hopelessly adolescent fashion. There is also the mythic Elvis garbed in black leather. When did he actually wear that outfit? It doesn't matter if it was when he was eighteen or thirty, the image is the only thing we have and the only thing that mattered. In short, many of the styles that seemed to lurk on the fringe of our culture and which symbolized rebellion and danger (even for teenagers) finally became acceptable when worn by Elvis. Somehow the dangerous element was slightly mitigated and was replaced by feelings of spontaneity and freedom—freedom from social conventions, especially the conventions of the world of parents.[2]

Youth are ripe for change but they need moorings. Elvis could challenge the dress code of the fifties because he brought some other seemingly positive values into play. He was, as suggested above, the poor boy made good. His roots lay in the agrarian South, and so he seemed a modest, loving son who took some of his first earnings to buy mom a car. And he seemed to handle all the hoopla with a goodly dose of humor and self-deprecation. In fact, one of the images of Elvis that resonates most in our memory is the incomparable

Elvis Presley and The Myth of America   105

sneer. Is it disdain for what he is doing? For his audience? For the whole system that made him a star? Or is it just the poor boy trying to reconcile his humility and the lure of the fame? Whatever it is, it reminds us of how very young he was and how innocent he seemed of the dangers that attend success.

What of his success? He did, after all, represent the myth of success in his meteoric ascent to superstardom. But here too he was revolutionary, or so it seemed. It was more than Alger-like rags-to-riches and "pluck and luck." The very rapidity of his rise in the music and entertainment world seemed to belie our most cherished notions about hard work, frugality, perseverance. Elvis redefined work in a sense; it didn't really seem like work, and it had about it that evanescent aura of spontaneity. Robert Pielke writes: "...his very success pointed out the outrageous disparity between the quantity and/or quality of effort on the one hand and social rewards on the other; there was no correlation whatsoever, no justice at all" (142). The notion of effort, however, is largely illusory; it's just that his effort wasn't understood by the average person on the street (the artist's effort never is). That hedonistic abandon and rough vocal style couldn't possibly be work, could it? The kids accepted it as work however, and, in this regard, Elvis was clearly in the mainstream of twentieth century rebel figures. James Oliver Robertson has described the contemporary hero in the context of corporate America:

The focus in modern stories is on individual success despite the bureaucracies. Success is measured by ingenuity, courage, expertise, physical prowess, and the employee's ability to snatch personal pleasure, reward, and a hedonistic life style out of the pressures of employment and employers. Large quantities of money, private pleasure, and consumption, and public acknowledgement of the individual's abilities, personality, and luck are the rewards at least of the fictionalized heroes and heroes of modern life (211).

And so it was with Elvis. He represented a new breed of hero, grabbing the rewards of the system without—seemingly—playing the game. His sense of abandon and shy, self-effacing personality told us that he wasn't taking all of this too seriously. Consequently, he stood as proof positive that Dad's way— of holding down two jobs and running himself into the ground on his daily trek from suburbia—was not the only way, that one could, indeed, grab success without hard work, frugality, and perseverance, without capitulating one's youth. Success and the attendant work ethic, finally, was not defined by adult values but by youthful values.

Another aspect of Elvis' image crucial to his heroic status and his reification of the myth of America is his performance style. Of course, it is here where all the early rock 'n' rollers were on the New Frontier. Theirs was a style completely antithetical to that of their mainstream music forebears. One cannot imagine Sinatra grinding his pelvis to the strains of "All Or Nothing At All" or "Come Fly With Me." His style, and that of Crosby, was of the cool crooner, conversationally addressing his audience via the microphone.[3] Yes, in another time Al Jolson and Eddie Cantor were known for their energy and dynamism on stage, but nothing prepared America for Elvis—except, perhaps, images of lindy-hopping teens of the 40s. Some thought Johnnie Ray was too much as he lay his emotions bare for all to see; for some it was too much and actually made them squirm. Elvis made them blush.

It was, after all, sexuality. His hips moved almost as if controlled by a force beyond him—or, perhaps better, within him—that knew no bounds. Some may recall a favorite Elvis move: he would stand still and the leg would seem to twitch automatically. Or he would be doing an animated dance across the stage, stop dead, grab his leg, pick it up and move it over a few inches and then it would take off as though all it needed was a little push to get it going. It was kinetic sex. He had a relationship with the microphone as well, but it wasn't like Bing and Frank's. Those men established an intimacy, as Henry Pleasants has noted, with their audience via the way they sang into the microphone.[4] Elvis obliterated that relationship; he, to use Robert Pielke's notion, negated it. So did all of rock as it turned music into public utterances; it was electric music that negated the necessity of the electrical connection to its audience. The impact was immediate, sensual, palpable. The performer seemed wide open, raw, part shaman and part griot. Only when he sang a ballad, was the relationship to the microphone different, it was more Sinatra-like. He cradled it, gently caressing it as he would the face of one he loved. And through it all it hardly seemed like work, any of it, it was so natural, so spontaneous. He took youthful emotions and sexuality and made them dangerous and wonderful at the same time. The performances were transcendent moments where one experienced the untrammeled expression of freedom from restraints and of possibilities—it was fun.

It was through his music, however, that Elvis most completely embodied the myth of America. Elvis's music is an almost perfect synthesis of American culture and mythic ideals and a celebration of the myth of the melting pot. His music reaffirms the egalitarian ideals of the myth, it crosses and blends the music of black and white subcultures with that of the musical mainstream. Henry Pleasants has written of two of the most famous sides coming out of the legendary Sun sessions, "That's All Right" and "Blue Moon of Kentucky": "They represented the convergence in one small-town boy, born at the right time, in the right place, in the right environment and under the right circumstances, of all the musical currents of America's subcultures: black and white gospel, country-and-western, and rhythm-and-blues" (269). The Sun sessions indeed did define Elvis. Sam Phillips said if he could find a white man who could sing like a black man he could make millions. Elvis proved to be that man for Phillips.

The Sun sessions, a celebration of that which we call "rockabilly," range over the entire field of popular music with an urgency, a freshness, and a sense of promise. It is as though it has never been done before—but, of course, it had all been done before. For in the Sun sessions you not only hear the voice of popular music's future, but you also hear echoes of its past. Among the influences who echo through the sessions are, according to Peter Guralnick, country performers such as Roy Acuff, Eddy Arnold, Jimmie Rodgers, Bob

Wills and the white gospel group, The Blackwood Brothers; but you also hear Big Bill Broonzy, Big Boy Crudup, the Ink Spots, and, perhaps most interestingly, Billy Eckstine (23). These are the voices and sounds that shaped Elvis. And what he did was bring them all together in the nervous, uptempo sounds of rockabilly, a melting pot style of music, a hybrid: country/bluegrass in sound, rhythm-and-blues in feel and energy. It was hoedown and low-down. It was country and urban all rolled into one. Elvis said that he didn't sing like no one else and his music affirms that. It is virtually impossible to nail down the genre for "That's All Right"; it is, to be sure, a blues based song, but the feel of it in Elvis' hands is that it has gone beyond being "merely" rhythm and blues. It seems at once to be a country tune as that opening guitar jangles in a straight strumming pattern. Scotty Moore's lead work traces out established blues hooks and some country ones as well and Bill Black's slapped bass seems rooted in the sound of the hills. And over it all is Elvis' vocal. It growls with that R & B sexuality one came to expect from the form, but the voice is pitched higher. This is most definitely not Billy Ward or B.B. King. The vocal is reminiscent of Hank Williams' "Hey, Good Lookin' " and some of his other hits, but it is not pure country. The voice swoops (ala the styles of people such as Al Jolson and the crooners of the 30's and 40's), it wails and whines, and bristles tensely in a virtual celebration of Tin Pan Alley, the rural south, and the city. Greil Marcus has written of the Sun sessions:

What I hear, most of the time, is the affection and respect Elvis felt for the limits and conventions of his family life, of his community and ultimately of American life, captured in his country sides; and his refusal of those limits, of any limits, played out in his blues. This is a rhythm of acceptance and rebellion, lust and quietude, triviality and distinction. It can dramatize the rhythm of our own lives well enough (169).

These characteristics carried over to his work on RCA Victor as well. It is the work with Victor, in fact, which is most important to analyze in understanding Elvis' role in popular music. It was, after all, the material that he recorded for RCA that pushed him into the national limelight. According to *The Rolling Stone Encyclopedia of Rock 'n' Roll*, Elvis garnered ninety-four gold singles, three gold EP's, and forty gold LP's for RCA; his films, moreover, grossed $180 million.[5] The Sun sessions were largely a regional product. The Elvis Presley that listeners took to their heart was the Presley of RCA.

Looking over those song titles one can see why he triumphed. They are a veritable celebration of adolescence: there are the songs of anger and rebellion in "Hound Dog," "All Shook Up," and "Jailhouse Rock"; there are the songs of adolescent romance: "Wear My Ring Around Your Neck," "Love Me Tender," "Are You Lonesome Tonight?", "I Want You, I Need You, I Love You," and "Can't Help Falling in Love"; and there are songs, such as "Teddy Bear," and "Little Sister," which capture the innocence of being young. For many young people it was, moreover, their first genuine exposure to rock 'n' roll.

Consequently, the sound that Elvis laid down, for good or ill, established the standard for the rock 'n' roll sound.

One notable difference over the Sun sessions was the quality of the recordings. Generally they were better produced—not necessarily from an artistic standpoint, but from a technical one. The sound is cleaner, fuller, more present in many cases ("Don't Be Cruel" is one of the best for this); in short, the raw elements one generally associates with the small label are gone and the industry standard is in place. So in "Don't Be Cruel" that opening guitar, hammering out a conventional R & B riff, has an immediacy; then comes Elvis' vocal, full, rich, throaty, still pitched up as it was in those Sun sessions, but there is also a crooner's richness to the sound; then the backup vocalists make their entrance, part doo-wop chorus and part Pied Pipers (to Elvis' Frank Sinatra). Listening over the RCA recordings one has to marvel in a way that the vitality was not sapped from the performances. But this is exactly where Elvis' greatness lies: he transcended the technological and commercial refinements. Listen to "Hard Headed Woman": it starts out like a Little Richard rave-up with Elvis punching out the opening measure *a cappella*; then the orchestra enters and it is almost comical, sounding like some record producer's idea of what an R & B backup band should like. The horns slide into notes reminiscent of the way the band plays "Take Me Out to the Ball Game" in the Marx Brothers' *A Night At the Opera*. But it works. Elvis' raw energy and basic commitment to the material carry the day.

Underlying every Elvis song are the "new" rhythms and sounds that a majority of American listeners had never heard before. The R & B riffs which outline the Tonic-Subdominant-Dominant progression, the emphasis on the back beat, the aggressive use of blues harmonies are all part of the revolution. All are a part of a sound that teenagers could say was "theirs." But there is the other side as well. There is the Tin Pan Alley side. It can be seen in the material itself and in Elvis' vocal style. Some of the songs are pages ripped out of the past. "I Want You, I Need You, I Love You" could have been written anytime between 1920 and 1950, "Are You Lonesome Tonight?" was indeed written in 1926, and "It's Now or Never" is based on an old Neapolitan song, "O Solo Mio."

In terms of performance Elvis once again reconciled the worlds of the musical subcultures and the world of the mainstream musical culture. Elvis' vocal stylings are part R & B growler and wailer, part country, and part crooner. Henry Pleasants notes that at times when Elvis "eases off" as in a ballad he achieves a sound "reminiscent of Bing Crosby," and he compares Elvis' vibrato to that of Billy Eckstine (275). One does hear echoes of the great crooning tradition in Elvis' work. There is a lovely little moment early in "Love Me Tender," for instance, when he performs an appoggiatura over the word "never" in "Never let me go." One can't but help think of Bing, Frank, or even Judy Garland who did something similar in "Over the Rainbow." Later in the song he slides down the scale to hit a note, a musical gesture reminiscent of Al Jolson and many of the blues singers early in the century. Jim Curtis sees an ambivalence in this aspect of Elvis' art. Citing Linda Ray Pratt's notion of Elvis being simultaneously "King and Outsider" he sees an ambivalence between the southern tradition and the Tin Pan Alley tradition in his work, the most notable connection being between himself and Sinatra. He writes, "His affinities with both of these traditions enabled him to pull unprecedented audiences, and to evoke unprecedented adulations. Because he has so many affinities with Frank, Elvis is as much the last great crooner as he is the first great rocker" (26). It may also be for this reason that his presence on the music scene incontrovertibly altered Tin Pan Alley's role as the dominant force in American musical life. Elvis broke the boundaries, his art obliterated distinctions between Tin Pan Alley and R & B because it reconciled them in a new sound; consequently, to this day the influence of Tin Pan Alley can still be felt. He did not negate the style of the crooner and the melody years; he merely redefined it for a new generation.

Elvis, in life, quickly passed from hero to legend. His return from the Army had all the trappings of a second coming. People hoped that rock 'n' roll, which had suffered some shocks in the intervening years, and which was largely in the hands of smooth producers and Elvis-cloned teen idols such as Bobby Vee and Rick Nelson, would emerge again, to paraphrase Ferlinghetti's lines about America, in a rebirth of wonder as the rough and tumble child of the mid-50's. Such was not to be the case. Elvis settled into Hollywood, a medium which would never allow him to realize the potential and brilliance he had displayed after he signed with RCA. But the fans were undeterred. They wouldn't let go, and Elvis passed from being a bona-fide hero to becoming an icon.

An icon, as Kurt Weitzmann notes, is an object that provides the believer with a glimpse into a greater reality beyond the physical.[6] Consequently, they fit perfectly into the world of cultural mythopoesis. Icons are symbols and the concrete manifestation of our beliefs. They freeze in time, moreover, that belief and the reality behind the belief. And so it was with Elvis. Regardless of the changes and transformations that took place in his physical appearance, his performances, and the persona he projected in the different media, he was for many always the young rebel, the perfect embodiment of rock 'n' roll. John Lennon once asked a friend who attended an Elvis concert in Las Vegas how it was; his friend said, " 'Well, if you sort of half shut your eyes and pretended, it was heaven' " (Pielke 152). It had to be so. As Robert Pielke notes, "Perhaps it was unavoidable, but his countless worshippers have never been able to distinguish between the transitory and finite Elvis and the Elvis who is eternal and infinite. In all probability they never tried. If so, the only thing remaining to them is the sediment of nostalgia, a dead past" (147). His fans, and even those who formed no deep bond with his persona, needed the Elvis of 1956, the young country boy, testing the waters of the American Dream, poised on the edge of recklessness and promise; his audience saw in him something of what Nick Carraway saw in Gatsby: "...there was something gorgeous about him, some heightened sensitivity to the promises of life...."

Elvis' life, then, the fabled Sun sessions, and the subsequent recordings for RCA Victor celebrated the values of youth and their vision of the country. Robert Pielke sees in Elvis a symbol of the "negation of the prevailing attitudes [of the times] towards sex, race, and work..." (153), and Elvis, indeed, did negate the prevailing attitudes. But one must remember that in the act of negation there is usually a corresponding affirmation of alternate values. Elvis' image and music reconciled some troubling currents in the culture of the 1950's and in the process negated the prejudices and conventions of the past while reaffirming the positive regenerative forces of the myth of America. His life and performance style synthesized and reconciled the great traditions of American music: blues, country and Tin Pan Alley—all alive in a new melting pot of musical expression. He spoke a language of egalitarianism, opportunity, promise, freedom, and passion. Greil Marcus has written of Elvis:

> At his best Elvis not only embodies but personalizes so much of what is good about this place: a delight in sex that is sometimes simple, sometimes complex, but always open; a love of roots and respect for the past; a rejection of the past and demand for novelty; the kind of racial harmony that for Elvis, a white man, means a profound affinity with the most subtle nuances of black culture combined with an equally profound understanding of his own whiteness; a burning desire to get rich, and to have fun; a natural affection for cars, flashy clothes, for the symbols of status that give pleasure both as symbols, and on their own terms. Elvis has long since become one of those symbols himself. (204)

To this I would only add that Elvis did more than just personalize the contradictions of our culture. He embodied them and, consequently, reconciled them in the reification of the myth of America for a new generation. His tragic death, too, is significant beyond the mere loss to music it represented. For some, such as Paul Simon ("Graceland"), Robbie Robertson ("American Roulette"), and John Hiatt ("Riding With the King"), who have all celebrated Elvis in song, his end and, by extension, his life is a metaphor for the dangers inherent in success. He thus simultaneously becomes the embodiment of the American Dream—a real-life manifestation of Chuck Berry's "Johnny B. Goode" myth—and the American nightmare: there is everything to be gained and everything to be lost and all in an instant. In a sense, Elvis did not really die in 1974—an idea ironically affirmed in the work of the three above mentioned songwriters and made poignantly manifest in the occasional reports of those people who say they have seen Elvis since his death in 1974.[7] For, like other great movements and heroes in our culture, Elvis' "presence" meant a renewal and regeneration, and his iconic status reaffirms that spirit of renewal through successive generations. He was the embodiment of D.H. Lawrence's myth of the American sloughing off the old skin and making itself new. And even as he grew older and slowly came closer to parodying himself (that one has the capacity for self-parody is in actuality one of the definitive tests for a cultural icon) his "presence" could not be diminished; for as we watched him we knew that out there, beyond the sweating, bloated, sequined figure, and beyond death itself, lie the real America. In our dim mythic collective imagination a black-clad, baggy-trousered Southern greaser reminded us that to let go, to, as Thoreau said, place your castle in the air and reach for it, to go out to the edge just before you lost control was to grasp the essence of America, was to experience real success, was to have it all.

Notes

[1] See John Cawelti, *The Six Gun Mystique* (Bowling Green, OH: The Bowling Green State Univ. Popular Press, 1971) for an excellent discussion of the myth of the west.

[2] See Deena Weinstein's essay "Rock: Youth and Its Music" in Volume I of *American Popular Music* or in *Popular Music and Society* 9 (1983) 2—16 for an excellent discussion of rock's role in reconciling youth and adult values.

[3] See Henry Pleasants, *The Great American Popular Singers* (New York: Simon and Schuster, 1974), pp. 15-30, for a fine discussion of the crooner's style and the role of the microphone in shaping that style. See also John Rockwell, *Sinatra: An American Classic* (New York: Random House/Rolling Stone Press, 1984), pp. 51-52.

[4] See *The Great American Popular Singers*, pp. 15-30; and see also Gene Lees' discussion of Sinatra, "The Sinatra Effect," in his *Singers and the Song* (New York: Oxford University Press, 1987) where he discusses Sinatra's "naturalistic" singing technique and use of the microphone in achieving that style.

[5] These figures are from *The Rolling Stone Encyclopedia of Rock and Roll*, ed. Jon Pareles and Patricia Romanowski (New York: Rolling Stone Press/Summit Books, 1983), p. 440.

[6] *The Icon: Holy Images—Sixth to Fourteenth Century* (New York: George Braziller, 1978), pp. 7-8.

[7] During 1988 there have been numerous "sightings" and rumors about Elvis. He has supposedly been seen in shopping malls, and it is rumored that occasionally Colonel Tom Parker gets a call from "The King."

In response to the many rumors and sightings a local Columbus radio station offered a $2,000,000 reward for anyone who could bring Elvis into its station—this contest did not just run for a couple of days but for weeks. There were, however, no takers. This, however, did not probably dissuade people from their beliefs in Elvis' immortality.

References

Curtis, Jim. *Rock Eras: Interpretations of Music and Society, 1954-1984*. Bowling Green, OH: Bowling Green Univ. Popular Press, 1987.

Eliade, Mircea. *Myth and Reality*. Trans. Willard R. Trask. New York: Harper Torchbooks, 1963.

Guralnick, Peter. "Elvis Presley." *The Rolling Stone Illustrated History of Rock and Roll*, rev. ed. Ed. Jim Miller. New York: Random House/Rolling Stone Press, 1980.

Lees, Gene. *Singers and the Song*. New York: Oxford Univ. Press, 1987.

Marcus, Greil. *Mystery Train" Images of America in Rock 'n' Roll Music*. New York: E.P. Dutton, 1976.

Pareles, Jon and Patricia Romanowski, eds. *The Rolling Stone Encyclopedia of Rock and Roll*. New York: Rolling Stone/Summit Books, 1983.

Pielke, Robert G. *You Say You Want a Revolution: Rock Music in American Culture.* Chicago: Nelson-Hall, 1986.

Pleasants, Henry. *The Great American Popular Singers.* New York: Simon And Schuster, 1974.

Robertson, James Oliver. *American Myth, American Reality.* New York: Hill and Wang, 1980.

Tharpe, Jac L., ed. *Elvis: Images and Fancies.* Jackson: University Press of Mississippi, 1979.

The Evolution of the American Protest Song

Jerome L. Rodnitzky

American music has seldom been viewed as a focus for social or political struggle. Yet recently we have witnessed a veritable revolution in American popular music as protest songs and "message songs" of infinite variety compete for public attention. Like most revolutions, this phenomenon is less revolutionary than it appears. Protest songs have always been with us, although there is a natural tendency to overlook their presence. Life is always rosier in retrospect, and yesterday's protest song becomes increasingly ludicrous and irrelevant. To survive, songs of discontent must communicate universal frustrations. Since topical songs are by definition custom-made for a particular time and place, they remain rigid period pieces. Thus, there have been no classics of American folk protest—nothing remotely comparable to Hawthorne's novels or Whitman's poetry. Diverse, local, and elusive, the protest songs of the past are nowhere because they were everywhere and sprang from a multitude of now irrelevant social settings.

Topical songs had an obvious appeal to pragmatic pioneers. Unlike sophisticated European symphonies and operas, they told a simple story and vented simple emotions. From the beginning, Americans sang about politics, wars, heroes, badmen, and misery, but their style was overwhelmingly personal. In contrast to most twentieth-century protest songs, the earlier ballads lacked positive social goals. Perhaps the most subtle songs were the laments of Negro slaves which we loosely categorize as spirituals. Cut off from their natural culture, religion, and community, slaves developed the spiritual as a substitute for all three.[1] Singing in the fields constituted an invisible church service. Spirituals lamented the present, affirmed faith in the future, and often poked fun at whites through subtle lyrics.

Protest songs took a distinctly modern turn with the rise of the International Workers of the World. Better known as the Wobblies, the IWW was a militant labor group which first organized in Chicago in 1904 and included socialists, anarchists, and syndicalists. Their most cherished plan was to ultimately sign up every worker in a single union and call a general strike to decide who was going to run the world—workers or bosses. In pursuit of this goal, the

Reprinted with permission from the *Journal of Popular Culture*, Volume 3:1 (Summer 1969) pp. 35-45.

Wobblies used every possible means to foster worker solidarity, including a wide variety of songs.

At first, the IWW used classic songs of revolt such as "The Marseillaise" and "The Red Flag," which were printed on a four-page song-card. However, the old revolutionary songs contained too much ideology and not enough humor and idiom. For example, one song started out:

> Arise then, arise then,
> Ye men of the plow and the hammer,
> Ye men of the helm and the lever,
> And send forth to the four winds of the earth
> Your new proclamation of freedom.[2]

Thus, increasingly, new songs, written by Wobbly members like Joe Hill and Ralph Chaplin were added to the song-card. Hill, whose real name was Joel Emanuel Hagglund, was by far the most creative of the IWW writers. Emigrating to the United States from Sweden in 1902, Hill worked as a general laborer and joined the IWW in 1908. Over the years he had imbued both the spirit of class struggle and the evils of wage slavery, and he began to write new-style labor songs—direct, bawdy, and topical. Hill borrowed tunes, lyrics, and ideas and twisted all three into the Wobbly idiom. For example, he changed the popular "Casey Jones" ballad into a timely protest song by substituting the Southern Pacific for the Illinois Central line and turning Casey from a heroic engineer to a strike-breaking scab. Every part of the established order was fair game for his satirical songs—from industry to churches. One song noted:

> Some time ago when Uncle Sam he had a war with Spain
> And many of the boys in blue were in the battle slain
> Not all were killed by bullets, though, no not by any means,
> The biggest part that died were killed by Armour's Pork and Beans

And another titled "The Preacher and the Slave" remarked:

> Long-haired preachers come out every night,
> Try to tell you what's wrong and what's right;
> But when asked about something to eat,
> They all answer with voices so sweet.
> You will eat, by and by,
> In that glorious land above the sky.
> Work and pray, live on hay,
> You'll get pie in the sky when you die.
> (That's a lie)[3]

Hill was executed by the State of Utah in 1915 for supposedly murdering a grocer, but he quickly became a legend to many laborers and his songs found a welcome place in the IWW's *Little Red Songbook,* which was first published in Spokane, Washington in 1909. Richard Brazier, a member of the committee which published the first songbook, recalled that they wanted songs which would run the "gamet of emotions," songs "of anger and protest" that would call their oppressors to judgment along with the entire industrial profit system. These songs were to deal with every aspect of the workers' lives and "sow the seeds of discontent and rebellion." They were sure that "the power of song" would "exalt the spirit of rebellion."[4] In a few years the songbook grew to a volume of fifty songs. The books were handed out to new members along with their union cards, and on each red cover was inscribed the motto: "To Fan the Flames of Discontent."

When the IWW was discredited by its opposition to World War One, both protest songs and militant unionism hibernated during the prosperous, raucous 1920's. However, when the Depression hit, both traditions revived under the stimulus of hard times. It is an axiom of labor organization that workers sing only under great stress, and during the Thirties new unions like the CIO and United Mine Workers sang on the picket lines. With the wave of union organizing drives during the mid-1930's came a flood of protest parodies of popular tunes. Thus, when the sit-down strikers took over the General Motors plant in Flint, Michigan, they sang:

> When we walked out on you,
>   we set you back on your heels,
> Goody, goody!
> So you lost some money and now
>   you know how it feels
> Goody, goody![5]

For many newly-organized workers, especially in rural coal-mining areas, unionism was a great deliverance to be celebrated and contemplated in song, as the gospel was affirmed in religious hymns. Indeed, several famous labor songs used the melodies of popular hymns.

However, militant unionism was irrelevant during the production crises of World War Two. Furthermore, the post-war confrontation with Russia drove radicals of every persuasion out of labor organizations, and these were generally the individuals who encouraged songs of dissent. Long-term prosperity and suburban living have long since made union protest songs passe. A few unions still have songbooks, but since only a small percentage of workers attend union meetings, except during strikes, songs are seldom sung. In any case, the union protest-song tradition remained for any organized movement to draw on.

A deeper and more powerful tradition was fostered by the life and work of Woody Guthrie during the 1930's and 1940's. Guthrie, an itinerant folksinger and periodic hobo from the Oklahoma dust-bowl, roamed from coast to coast during the Thirties—writing as he traveled. His songs were traditional in style, but included a new dimension. Transcending personal plight, they subtly captured the underprivileged other America he knew first hand. His songs reflected both the failures and possibilities of the nation. Guthrie was partisan, bawdy, erratic, and perhaps a naive ideological captive of the American Left, but his simple, powerful ballads somehow rang true and captured aspects of the nation's glory and shame. Whether singing about dustbowl misery, the union struggle, America's natural beauty, or the plight of migrant workers, Guthrie's voice was one of affirmation. As Guthrie noted, he "made up songs telling what" he "thought was wrong and how to make it right, songs that said what everybody in that country was thinking."[6] Like Whitman, he celebrated the strength of the common man and proclaimed:

I am out to sing songs that will prove to you that this is your world and that if it has hit you pretty hard and knocked you for a dozen loops, no matter how hard it's run you down or rolled over you, no matter what color, what size you are, how you are built, I am out to sing the songs that make you take pride in yourself and in your work. And the songs that I sing are made up for the most part by all sorts of folks just about like you.[7]

Guthrie's optimism characteristically appears in the title of his autobiography, *Bound for Glory*, and after the war the same optimistic outlook would fire the imagination of a new generation of topical songwriters who sought a new world. Oddly enough, at one point Guthrie was subsidized by the Federal Government. In the spirit of the New Deal's Federal Arts Projects, the Bonneville Power Administration commissioned him to write some songs to celebrate, and whip up enthusiasm for, the Columbia River Project. The twenty-six songs he completed for Bonneville were among his best and included "Roll on Columbia Roll On" and a subtle song of the migrant worker, titled "Pastures of Plenty."

Just before the war, Guthrie settled in New York City and together with a small group of rural-oriented traditional folksingers planted folk music in a liberal, urban setting. This cross fertilization would produce the legion of urban folksingers whose repertory was a mixture of traditional folksongs and topical protest ditties. It would also connect the urban folksong movement to the political left. One early indication of the new mood was the Almanac Singers, a group which included Guthrie and his young protege, Pete Seeger. The Almanacs mixed traditional folksongs with liberal politics and were especially interested in singing at union rallies. Characteristically, they recorded an album of anti-war songs, but withdrew it when Germany attacked Russia in 1941. They then brought out a record urging America to enter the war, and soon Guthrie joined the merchant marine and Seeger, the army.

After the war, many enthusiasts felt that the country was ready for a folksong revival, and furthermore that it would mushroom through the union movement. Thus, in 1946 Seeger and others founded an organization in New York named People's Songs which published a magazine of the same name. The periodical stressed political action through music, and the organization produced a film-strip guide called "Sing and Win." Unfortunately, People's Songs was ignored by the unions, who now sought a more conservative image, and given comfort by the radical left, who welcomed any support. Thus, in 1948 the organization threw its weight behind Henry Wallace, even to the extent of publishing a *Wallace for President Songbook*. In its brief two year history, it became involved in enough dubious, left-wing ventures to ruin the reputation of a hundred organizations. People's Songs did not directly ally itself with radical groups, but its willingness to sing for and sympathize with groups like the American Labor Party, The Socialist Party, and the American Communist Party made radicalism and folk songs almost synonymous. One anti-communist joke of that era depicted two party members planning a meeting: "You bring the Negro," said one, "I'll bring the folk singer."[9] Above all, these writer-singers were writing protest songs which topically attacked alleged injustices from "civil rights" to "free speech." Not surprisingly, when People's Songs was investigated by Congress, the periodical called for songs to abolish the House Committee on Un-American Activities and to "militate action against an impending fascism which would mean death for all freedom in music." The editor concluded: "Let's get some brand new songs; let's rewrite some bold new ones; let's hit it from every angle with slams at the un-Americans and their activities, new exposes of red-baiting and anything else we can think of. But let's start turning them out and sing them so loud that they'll hear us in Washington."[10]

Embraced by the far left, and deserted by the unions, People's Songs folded early in 1949 with patriotic groups snapping at its heels. The song-writing survivors went underground during the 1950's, although a new magazine, *Sing Out*, gave them a means of national identity and communication. It appeared that the short-lived urban, topical-song movement had collapsed and been buried in its own radical debris. During this period, a small esoteric group of folk enthusiasts saw their folk-singer heroes investigated by Congress and blacklisted by the media. On college campuses, there was very little interest in folk music—topical or otherwise—and guitars were definitely symbols of leftist agitation. Not until McCarthyism faded and the civil-rights crusade accelerated, would folk music begin to replace jazz as the musical staple of the campus.

The cultural isolation of the early 1950's gave folksingers the opportunity to reflect, redefine their philosophy and goals, and polish their arts. Imperceptively, the focus changed from visions of a brave new world to a stress on the folk traditions of the past. Obviously, protest songs were an integral part of this tradition, but linking them with the American heritage bestowed a wholesome image. As traditional American art, folksinging quietly invaded the musical vacuum on college campuses. Jazz had floated away in the haze of its increasingly complex and abstract construction. The folk ballad, however, was extremely communicative and intelligible. At the same time, the high-school kids who were swept off their feet by rock and roll in the 1950's were ready for something more sophisticated and meaningful when they entered college at the end of the decade.

Indicative of folk music's new success were the Weavers—a quartet of People's Songs performers—led by Pete Seeger. Though they were black listed by radio and television, the Weavers sang to packed audiences at college concerts and their records were campus hits. As the Weavers opened the breech, new folk recording artists and small record companies began reaching for the college market and a new wave of folk composition resulted. The Weavers and especially Seeger had popularized the rough-hewn iconoclastic ballads of Woody Guthrie (now incurably ill and in the first stages of a hereditary disease that would eventually take his life in the Spring of 1968). Guthrie had been a poet of the unions, depression, and the common man, but above all he had been a restless man of the open road. Rejecting the security of their middle-and-upper-class backgrounds, students identified with the Guthrie tradition and began singing songs and adopting life styles that suggested "hard traveling" of all kinds.

Then suddenly in the late 1950's and early 1960's came the cataclysmic events that called folk guitarists to arms. Along with the student-led Southern civil rights movement, came a variety of songs. Northern songwriters picked up the spirit and spun out a mass of polemics against racism, the arms race, and middle-class conformity. Commercial record companies quickly sensed the drift, and pleasant melodic groups like the Kingston Trio cashed in on the new college rage and popularized the movement even further. As the torrent of popularity continued, the protest characteristics of the movement were diluted, but topical protest ballads continued to appear and continued to supply the most vivid picture of the folk craze. Thus, by 1961 *Newsweek* could report:

Basically the schools and students that support causes support folk music. Find a campus that breeds Freedom Rides, Anti-Birch demonstrators, and anti-bomb societies, and you'll find a folk group. The connection is not fortuitous.[11]

The so-called folk protestors or folkniks were generally not ideological, but they were willing to associate with non-conformist movements, despite adult warnings that such activities would endanger their professional future. In a literal sense the "silent generation" of the 1950's broke out into song. Always present was the example of Negro students in the South. Media coverage of the sit-in movement gave vivid proof that Martin Luther King's passive resistance program was a singing movement as well. As King became the leader and "We Shall Overcome," the anthem of the civil-rights struggle, northern folksingers developed leaders and anthems of their own. Dynamic new performer-composers like Bob Dylan and Phil Ochs directly assaulted the "military-industrial establishment," while gifted singers like Joan Baez and Judy Collins reached out for an ever-wider audience. The syrupy, apolitical Kingston Trio was replaced by the irreverent Chad Mitchell Trio and eventually by the aggressively-liberal Peter, Paul and Mary. Song titles like "Masters of War," "Talking World War III Blues," "I Ain't Marching Anymore," "Draft Dodger Rag," and "The Times They Are A Changing" immediately indicate what was on the minds of the new folk generation.

If topical protest conquered the campus, it failed to dent the television media. As usual, network and sponsors were intent on avoiding controversy, and several folksingers, notably Pete Seeger, were barred from commercial programs in the 1960's. Seeger had been called before the House Un-American Activities Committee in 1955 and had invoked the First Amendment in refusing to testify about his past radical associations. Had he pleaded the Fifth Amendment, he could have escaped prosecution, but Seeger chose to argue that the guarantees of free speech and association granted by the First Amendment also guaranteed the right to remain silent about one's beliefs and associations. Seeger was prosecuted and in 1961 finally convicted for contempt by a Federal District Court in New York City and sentenced to one year in prison. At his trial, Seeger pointed out that for twenty years he had sung songs for groups of Americans of every "possible political and religious opinion and persuasion" and had never refused a group because he disagreed with some of their ideas. He noted that some of his ancestors were religious dissenters who came to America over 300 years ago, and others were abolitionists in the 1840's. Seeger indicated his songs were in that tradition and asked the court for permission to sing a sing in his defense, which the judge refused. Seeger appealed his conviction, and it was set aside in 1962 by the U.S. District Court of Appeals.[12] His exoneration, however, did not make Seeger more palatable to the media. Thus, in 1963 when ABC launched a show called "Hootenanny," featuring top folksingers, Seeger was blacklisted. The more militant, and by this time the most popular, folk artist of the day rushed to Seeger's defense. Joan Baez, for example, dedicated a song to him at each of her concerts. Both Bob Dylan and Joan Baez, the King and Queen of folk protest told "Hootenanny": no Seeger, no Dylan or Baez. Peter, Paul, and Mary and other performers provided the same message.

By 1965 the tide had turned. The merger of rock and roll with folk-oriented songs, which the entertainment industry christened "folk-rock," brought message songs to the high school crowd and the best-selling-record charts. One quickly recalls the media vogue for thoughtful songs like "Universal Soldier" and idiotic songs like "Eve of Destruction" which dominated popular disc-jockey shows. The so-called teeny boppers were now dancing the newest frantic steps to pacifist and integrationist topical songs, electronically amplified by equally new and frantic rock groups. Message songs had arrived, and they seemed to be everywhere triumphant. But what kind of a triumph was it?

Back in 1961, during his darkest days, Seeger had depicted himself as a "cultural guerilla" who operated as part of the underground. He was taboo to the media, yet he could roam from campus to campus, sing a concert and move on. Above all, he prized college students the "one sector... which refused most courageously to knuckle under to the witch hunters." Thus, Seeger looked forward in confidence. He felt that the students who had learned his songs and style were "taking them to thousands of places where" he "could never expect to go." Though he could not get a job at a university, those whom he had helped motivate were now university faculty. Like fireflies, these young men were to "light up the night," or perhaps even be more potent insects. For example, Seeger recalled that once a white politician had told Sojourner Truth, the 19th-Century Negro abolitionist leader: "Woman, I care no more for you than a mosquito." "Mabbe so," said she, "But, praise God, I'll keep you scratching."[13]

Increasingly, however, it appears that the topical song has been poisoned by its own success. As civil-rights, anti-war, and student-power movements spontaneously created their own songs, the guitar-strumming singing demonstrator became a national stereotype. Once the stereotype was established, a host of commercial entertainers turned out scores of protest songs that were technically pleasing, general enough to attract various tastes, and, above all, profitable. Originally growing out of a concrete situation that called for redress, protest songs are now more likely an expression of an individual life-style. Instead of calling attention to specific evils, they radiate general alienation and a hazy non-conformist aura and content. Listen to the most popular songs of Bob Dylan, Paul Simon, or even the Beatles. They have become lost in an existentialist haze. In attempting to be all things to all people, the compositions become do-it-your-self protest songs. One can read whatever one wants into the lines. Stance has become more important than goals. The message song has been replaced by the mood song. Whether or not the medium is always the message, the medium has obviously overtaken most protest songs. However, although the content of songs are increasingly hazy and thus less powerful, their influence is far more pervasive through the simple weight of numbers and their matter-of-fact presentation. Some argue that their effects on the young may even be subliminal. Others contend that the protest song acts as a sublimation of the act of protest, and thus retards social action. In any case, one must view with alarm the tendency to treat protest as a life-style, divorced from actual goals. To freely mix pacifism with civil rights or to equate dissent against Vietnam policy with protest against marijuana restrictions, makes a mockery of responsible protest. It is quite ironic that whereas our earliest protest songs have been forgotten because they were too diverse in origin, and are nowhere because they were everywhere, our present songs probably will be quickly forgotten because by saying everything they in effect say nothing. Yet, perhaps there is something all too American in the contradiction and wild diversity of the newest protest songs. No doubt, Bob Dylan like Walt Whitman might reply to critics: "Do I contradict myself? Very well then, I contradict myself. I am large; I contain multitudes."

Notes

[1]On this point see Daniel J. Boorstin, *The Americans: The National Experience* (New York, 1965), pp. 190-199.

[2]Irwin Silber, monthly column in *Sing Out*, April-May, 1965, p. 40.

[3]*Ibid.*, p. 41.

[4]Richard Brazier, "The Story of I.W.W.'s *Little Red Songbook*," *Labor History*, 9 (Winter, 1965), p. 97.

[5]Pete Seeger, "What Ever Happened to Singing in the Unions," *Sing Out*, 15 (May, 1965), p. 29.

[6]Quoted in Donald Myrus, *Ballads, Blues, and the Big Beat* (New York, 1966), p. 45.

The Evolution of the American Protest Song

[7] Woody Guthrie (edited by Robert Shelton), *Born to Win* (New York, 1965), p. 223.

[8] *People's Songs*, 3 (February-March, 1948), pp. 2-3.

[9] Quoted in Oscar Brand, *The Ballad Mongers* (New York, 1962), p. 128.

[10] *People's Songs*, II (December, 1947), p. 2.

[11] *Newsweek*, November 27, 1961, p. 84.

[12] Quoted in *Little Sandy Review*, 13 (April, 1961), pp. 3-5.

[13] Pete Seeger, "The Theory of Cultural Guerilla Tactics," *Sing Out*, 11 (October-November, 1961), p. 60.

From Rock 'N' Roll To Rock:
The 1960S

Introduction

About midway through *American Graffiti* John Milner (Paul LeMat) and his cruising "companion" Carol (Mackenzie Phillips) get into another spat. This one is over a song on the radio. As the Beach Boys "Surfin' Safari" comes on the radio Carol turns the sound up; Milner turns it down; she attempts to turn it up and he stops her with the line "I don't like that surfin' shit. Rock 'n' roll's been going downhill ever since Buddy Holly died." She, of course, being at least six years his minor speaks glowingly of the Beach Boys, "Don't you think the Beach Boys are boss!" By 1963, when the film is set, Carol probably wouldn't care much for Buddy Holly or even Chuck Berry— in fact she might not know who they were. The two characters speak a different language and they like different music, and, although separated by less than ten years in age, they are already two distinct musical generations. The differences, moreover, are profound because they represent the first stage in the evolution of popular music from rock 'n' roll to rock.

The 1960's brought the greatest changes in popular music since the 1920's when jazz, movies, radio, and swing, in its earliest form, made themselves felt. The changes complemented the tenor of the times as well. The seeming tranquility of the 1950's[1] gave way to a decade Jim Hougan describes as "so full that most remember it as an Age."[2] The decade began with great promise as Kennedy was sworn into office. The youth of the country were told they had a role to play somewhere on the "New frontier," and they believed it. They were, after all, probably the best educated generation ever, they were living in the midst of economic security, and there were more of them—or so it seemed—than all the other generations put together. It was perhaps this illusion that led to their engagement in so many issues. Morris Dickstein has written:

> I spoke earlier of the "existential" spontaneous character of the young protesters, and of the New Left in general. It was as if the movement had been designed unconsciously to respond to the criticisms leveled at Stalinism. If the Old Left was Benthamite and materialist, the New Left was almost obsessed with "the quality of life." If the Old Left distrusted emotion and individuality and demanded organizational (even conspiratorial) discipline, the New Left was almost anarchic in its relish for individual display, in its scrupulousness about ends and means, in its moral fervor and utopianism.[3]

First they marched off as part of Kennedy's armies—to the third world as members of the Peace Corps, to the south for civil rights demonstrations, or to Vietnam to live out John Wayne war fantasies and Barry Sadler green beret heroics. Phil Och's declaration in the mid-sixties that he wasn't marching anymore, seemed odd at first, then, as the decade wore on, prophetic. By the end of the 60's, the sense of privilege the youth felt gave way to a feeling that they had been, like "Jumping Jack Flash," born in a cross-fire hurricane and that a spike was being driven through their heads. And so they took to the streets in defiance of some of the self-same forces that sent them marching off down the "yellow brick road" in the early 60's. In 1968, when it seemed like the world might explode with the deaths of Martin Luther King, Jr. and Robert Kennedy, the Chicago Convention, the riots on college campuses and in the inner cities, there at the center of the maelstrom stood young people "mobilizing" on college campuses and on the streets with the Rolling Stones' words echoing in their heads, "But it's all right now,/In fact it's a gas."

The music of the 1960's mirrors this evolution from the days of innocence to the days of awareness. The decade began with a host of teen idols singing and swinging Brill Building melodies that brought, as *Rock of Ages* has noted, a new sophistication to pop—and in fact served to redefine rock 'n' roll.[4] Paul Anka, Bobby Vee, Neil Sedaka, Rick Nelson, and others crooned melodies with well-crafted melodies and harmonic changes that their rock 'n' roll forebears would not have conceived. Another Brill Building entrepreneur, Phil Spector, broke out of the songwriting cubicle and transformed doo-wop into symphony and art song. While, in Detroit Barry Gordy parlayed great business acumen, stylish songwriting and some basic R & B licks into the "Sound of Young America" on the Motown label. On the West coast, Hollywood had Elvis and his presence seemed forever lost to us. But then we really didn't care much because we had the Beach Boys who were redefining the American Dream: it was no longer a home in the suburbs with a car and two TV's, no, the dream was "If everyone had an ocean." As though to say that if everyone had access to the sea, surfin' and a woody, life would be complete, some ineffable and wonderful goal would have been achieved.

Even the British Invasion in 1964 perpetuated the days of innocence. The Beatles, as revolutionary as they were, were also an important antidote to the too awful reality of the assassination of John F. Kennedy. Ralph Brauer's essay on the Beatles deals with their crucial role in the cultural changes that would transpire over the next six years from the time they landed in New York. The Rolling Stones's ugly and defiant image portended, perhaps, the eventual shift in consciousness in the 1960's. As John Well's essay notes, they grabbed the demonic and somewhat mystical spirit of the past in Robert Johnson's music and recast it for a new generation. It was Yin and Yang: the Beatles aspired to hold your hand, the Stones wanted you under their thumb.

The shift was gradual, but it had to come. Even the Beatles capitulated: they quickly went from saying, "If you're talking about destruction/You know you can count me out," to, on *The White Album*, adding an "in" after the "out." Confusing? Not really. It was either a classic case of equivocation or a searing moment of recognition, recognition of one's ultimate responsibility and commitment to issues beyond mere self-interest. Youth tended to read it as recognition. By 1969, in fact, one could hardly buy an album by anybody from Jimi Hendrix to John Denver which did not deal with some social issue. Ben Auslander's essay on Vietnam-related protests songs, takes a selective look at an issue that animated passions and which inspired a number of songs. Vietnam, in fact, and the music it inspired may serve as a metaphor for the entire shift from rock 'n' roll to rock. Finally, Kathleen Endres' essay on "Sex Role Standards in Popular Music" will cast some light on how popular music has, for the last twenty years, dealt with another issue that animated American youth in the 60's: feminism.

Race also was an issue in the 1960's. Some of the hardest battles had been fought in the 1950's, but the 1960's provided heroes such as Martin Luther King, Jr. and Eldridge Cleaver who inspired both blacks and whites. One felt one must embrace Dr. King's Utopia and Cleaver's often apocalyptic vision simultaneously, because both were so compelling. Regardless of what camp one fell into, however, one could not escape the sense of purpose and a growing pride in the awareness one's own racial and cultural identity. At the heart of this sense of identity was a quality Black Americans called Soul. It was a quality, moreover, most apparent in the music. White Americans bought the albums—largely because they had a good beat and you could dance to them—but the message in the music was not lost on them. When Aretha Franklin sang of "Respect" the sentiments transcended male and female relationships and went to the heart of black culture as a whole. She seemed to bring together the sacred and the profane in perfect harmony, gospel married to bawdy rhythm and blues: echoes of 200 years of oppression mixed with hopes for liberation, all in the three minute pop song. James Brown, emblematic of the times, went from master showman ("I Feel Good") to spokesman ("Say It Loud—I'm Black and Proud") by decade's end. Portia Maultsby's essay on Soul music explores the emergence of black music in the 1960's and its crucial role in shaping the culture's attitudes towards Black Americans.

The emergence of black culture in the 1960's parallels the emergence of "youth culture" in general during the decade. In both cases the use of the term *culture* is important because it suggests the creation of entities separate from the mainstream or standard culture. What was significant about the youth culture of the 60's is that it transcended sub-cultural status and, at times, seemed to be the emergent and dominant culture. The generational conflicts were more than just adolescent rejections of Mom's and Dad's rules, but a clear philosophical rejection of their values. Young men in the past may have scrapped with Dad over use of the car, but there was never any doubt that they wouldn't, like Dad, follow their leader into war. Scrapping over the car seemed childish in the late sixties and downright pathetic in 1970 when more than one parent said to offspring after the Kent State killings, "If you would have been there, you should have been shot too." It made James Dean's rebellion in the fifties seem a quaint chestnut of yesteryear. For, you see, not only could Mom and Dad be fuddy-duddyish about matters sexual, but they had made major mistakes: their world was racist and sexist, their capitulation to "establishment" values was a failure of will and morality. The gulf was wide, and drugs, sex, and protest were the symbols that made the gulf real and final.

And the music. It was no longer rock 'n' roll, a rhythm and blues based music with simple lyrics played by small ensembles of electric instruments. Lyrically, as Gary Burns' and Harold Mosher's essays will show, the distinctive teen element of rock lyrics gives way to a wider range of subjects, a heightened political consciousness, and a sense that rock lyrics, indeed, are a form of poetry—they do, after all, deal with profound issues, so why should they not be accorded the same status as poetry, or so the arguments ran. In a sense, these two essays pick up where the essay "Thou Witty" in Volume I left off. We shall see that the music itself had clearly moved onto another plane. By 1969 there were art rock collaboration between rock bands and symphony orchestras (*Days of Future Passed* by the Moody Blues), there was a rock opera (*Tommy* by The Who), there were albums featuring lieder-like song cycles (*A Tramp Shining* written by Jim Webb), there was Jim Morrison, our guide on psycho-sexual nightmares that demanded one either have firm groundings in Freudian psychology or be so high as to obliterate all meaning.

In short, the music was getting serious, it was making demands, and in those shortening days before the deaths of Joplin, Hendrix, and Morrison and the breakup of the Beatles and other groups, it was creating a second golden age of rock (on a parallel with the golden age of songwriting in the 1930's). Rock 'n' roll had grown up, had become more sophisticated, and in the process it laid the groundwork for the fragmentation of the music in the 1970's.

Notes

[1] See Todd Postol's "Reinterpreting The Fifties: Changing Views of a 'Dull' Decade," *Journal of American Culture*, 8 (Summer 1985), 39-45.

[2] "Decadence," in *The Sense of the Seventies: A Rhetorical Reader* (New York: Oxford Univ. Press, 1978), p. 13.

[3] *Gates of Eden: American Culture in the Sixties* (New York: Basic Books, 1977), pp. 267-68.

[4] Ed Ward, *Rock of Ages: The Rolling Stone History of Rock and Roll* (New York: Summit Books, 1986), pp. 216 and 225.

References

Christgau, Robert. *Any Old Way You Choose It: Rock and Other Pop Music, 1967-73*. Baltimore: Penguin Books, 1973.

Davies, Hunter. *The Beatles*. New York: McGraw-Hill, 1968.

George, Nelson. *Where Did Our Love Go?: The Rise and Fall of the Motown Sound*. New York: St. Martin's Press, 1985.

Gleason, Ralph. *The Jefferson Airplane and the San Francisco Sound*. New York: Ballantine Books, 1969.

Guralnick, Peter. *Sweet Soul Music: Rhythm and Blues and the Southern Dream of Freedom*. New York: Harper and Row, 1986.

Hirshey, Gerri. *Nowhere to Run: The Story of Soul Music*. New York: New York Times Books, 1984.

Norman, Phillip. *Shout: The Beatles in Their Generation.* New York: Fireside Books, 1981.

Rodnitzky, Jerome. *Minstrels of the Dawn.* Chicago: Nelson-Hall, 1976.

Scaduto, Anthony. *Bob Dylan.* New York: New American Library, 1979.

Shelton, Robert. *No Direction Home: The Life and Music of Bob Dylan.* New York: Oxford Univ. Press, 1985.

Whitcomb, Ian. *Rock Odyssey: A Musician's Chronicle of the Sixties.* Garden City, N.Y.: Doubleday Dolphin Books, 1983.

Trends in Lyrics in the Annual Top Twenty Songs in the United States, 1963-1972

Gary Burns

Popular songs are programmed fantasies which tell stories, directly address the audience, present opportunities to eavesdrop on make-believe thinking and conversation, and assault or soothe the nervous system through the highly abstract symbol system of music. The songs are programmed both in the sense that they are written, arranged and recorded (i.e. the music and lyrics in each song are "programmed"), and in the sense that they are played over radio airwaves in accordance with predetermined "formats." Corporate marketing and consumer choice (whichever, if either, one chooses to emphasize) of particular types of programmed song-fantasies seem in many cases to follow identifiable patterns consistent with other cultural trends. Systematic analysis of song lyrics is an area that has been neglected by researchers but which can provide significant insights into our culture. As George Gerbner has noted in relation to television, stories in the form of fiction and drama tell us "how the invisible forces of life and society really work.... The stories of a nation are the basic process by which human behavior is formed, by which how things work in life are [sic] learned, and if you can control the storytelling, you don't have to worry about who makes the laws."[1] Stories and drama create a fantasy world which the mind can select in preference to or through neglect of directly experienced reality. By studying this fantasy world and the process through which it is created and passed on, it is possible to learn much about the collective values and beliefs of a society. Although it is seldom pointed out, song lyrics, like television programs, create a fantasy world in which characters act, plots unfold, and lessons become clear. Such stylistic devices as first person narration and direct address to the audience or to an implied character involve the singer directly in the story—he or she poses as a character in a fantasy world. Although the listener has great freedom in interpreting the fantasy world as it is presented, and in selecting or rejecting it as he or she sees fit, the fact remains that the listener's choices are limited or guided by the original, rhetorical programming

Reprinted with permission from the *Journal of Popular Music & Society* Volume 9:1 (1983) pp. 25-39.

of the fantasy. This essay sets forth, in overview form, some particular interpretations of the programmed fantasies in the most popular song lyrics in the United States from 1963 to 1972.[2]

"Most popular" is defined here as the *Billboard* annual top twenty songs (for every year from 1963 to 1972).[3] Because eight of these songs were instrumentals and one ("Sukiyaki") was sung in Japanese, the total number of lyrics analyzed was 191. My view of song lyrics as stories/dramas/fantasies owes much to Ernest Bormann, whose method of "fantasy theme analysis" has shed light on how public pretending of many varieties can affect, and can be used to affect, beliefs, attitudes, and behavior.[4] My analysis of song lyrics focused on depicted characters, actions, and payoffs—that is, dramas. While previous research on song lyrics has, for the most part, concentrated on character types such as the "outsider," specific moods such as "love negative," or specific artists (e.g., Bob Dylan) or genres (e.g., protest songs),[5] my aim was to describe what Bormann calls "rhetorical visions"—configurations of mood, subject matter, assumptions, value judgments, wishes, and advocacy— traceable to recurring types of fantasy dramas.

One factor useful in describing rhetorical visions is the emotional tone of the song lyrics. Of the songs I studied, most (59%) had a positive tone. In other words, songs with happy, hopeful themes and messages were more common than songs with sad, angry, or despairing lyrics. The 59 percent figure is an average for the ten-year period. Notable departures from this average occurred in 1964 (79% positive), 1967 (75% positive), and 1971 (35% positive).[6] Thus, lyrics of the most popular songs were, on the average, unusually happy in 1964 and 1967, unusually unhappy in 1971. Examination of the specific lyrics involved leads to the conclusion that 1964, 1967 and 1971 were peak years of three coherent rhetorical visions in popular music lyrics.

The 1964 vision was primarily one of dyadic love, relieved of many of the inhibitions and requirements routinely placed on it in previous popular lyrics. The 1964 vision was swept in by the British invasion, which, as a rhetorical movement, eventually spread through such media forms as James Bond books and movies; Beatle haircuts, accents, and movies; Carnaby Street fashions and the Twiggy haircut; American importation of British TV series (*Secret Agent, The Avengers, That Was The Week That Was*); and products such as English Leather and British Sterling toiletries, Thom McAn Sohos shoes, Yardley's London Look cosmetics and Piccadilly slacks. This vision was innocently utopian in tone. The dark revelations of the Rolling Stones and the Animals were usually drowned out by the exuberance of the Beatles, the Kinks, Manfred Mann, Gerry and the Pacemakers, Freddie and the Dreamers, Herman's Hermits, the Dave Clark Five, Petula Clark, and countless lesser known talents.

In 1967, the coalescing rhetorical vision was primarily an American utopia of unfettered love, much like the utopia of the British invasion, but admitting generously of the rhetoric of evil, irrationality, and violation. This vision is closely linked symbolically with the summer of 1967, which was simultaneously the "longest summer"[7] (of several consecutive "long, hot summers") and the "Summer of Love." The "longest summer" contributed to a cultural climate that easily accommodated "dark" lyrics such as "Light My Fire" and "Ode to Billie Joe." The cultural climate was increasingly hospitable for such songs until approximately 1971. Meanwhile, the "Summer of Love" encouraged more general usage of the word "love." This more general usage is best exemplified in such songs as "People Got to Be Free" (1968), "Aquarius" (1969), and "Get Together" (1969). In these songs, "love" is something one gives to other people in general, not only to one person chosen as a mate. Simultaneously with the expressed desire for universal love came frequent statements that mainstream American culture provided a hostile environment for the kind of love depicted in the new music. The 1964 vision had been built upon the potential for having fun within the established system. The 1967 vision was based on the assumption that fun pursued through the "proper channels" of the established system was not a worthy enough goal, and that some kind of escape from or transcendence of the Establishment was necessary. The 1967 vision of universal love through escape spread through such phenomena as Haight-Ashbury, the Monterey Pop Festival of 1967, the Beatles' album *Magical Mystery Tour*, the songs of Donovan in his "Eastern" period, draft resisters' emigration from the United States, and the burgeoning drug culture. Popular music, and American culture in general, continued to resonate in response to these phenomena for many years.

In 1971, negative lyrics in my sample outnumbered positive lyrics by thirteen to seven (65% to 35%). This was the only year studied in which negative lyrics predominated. The music industry produced, and its public consumed, a musical rhetoric of defeat in love and social activism. Of course, this negative view was not the only way of looking at the world in the early 1970s. Optimism was still present in popular music, and actually regained its "majority" in the annual top twenty in 1972. However, not only was optimism less evident quantitatively in 1971 than in any other year studied, but, as subsequent discussion will indicate, the optimism of 1970 through 1972 (and possibly beyond) had significant qualitative differences from that which preceded it. Lowered expectation became a common theme in American culture throughout the 1970s, and was often exhibited in the music of the "singer-songwriter" movement. Participants in this movement included Melanie, Randy Newman, Bob Dylan, Nilsson, Neil Young, Gilbert O'Sullivan, Kris Kristofferson, Lee Michaels, Don McLean, Rod Stewart, and Carole King (all of whom were represented in my sample with negative songs); and James Taylor, Joni Mitchell, Laura Nyro, Elton John, Cat Stevens, Danny O'Keefe, Paul Simon, Barry Manilow, Jackson Browne, Neil Diamond, and Harry Chapin. As the 1960s had been a period of apparently happy and/or artistically powerful musical groups, the 1970s were a period of pessimistic individuals, whose hits were in many cases slow (Taylor, Mitchell, John, Stevens, Manilow, Diamond), spare in instrumentation (Young, Michaels, Stewart, King, Taylor, Mitchell, Stevens), or concerned with depression or despair (almost all the artists named above had hits of this sort).

In the late 1960s and early 1970s it became tempting to believe that small collectivities do not work. A major reason for this was the demise of admired rock bands. In an age of heated dispute over civil rights, student rights, drugs, clothing and hairstyle, and American foreign policy (among other things), it became difficult in many cases to remain a cooperating member of one's true family or community, especially for adolescents and young adults involved in the stressful process of passage and initiation into adulthood in America (and much of the remainder of the Western World). For many of these young people, rock bands, especially the Beatles, served as a vicarious family.[8] The Beatles spearheaded the British invasion ca. 1964 and were leaders in the psychedelic retreat ca. 1967, especially through such albums as *Revolver, Sgt. Pepper, Magical Mystery Tour,* and *Yellow Submarine.* While they were together, they and other rock bands demonstrated the viability of collective creation and quasi-familial relationships. Rock festivals and demonstrations simultaneously encouraged belief in the viability of large scale collective celebration and community. Around the time the Beatles broke up, the rhetorical vision developing from the 1964 and 1967 frameworks shattered, as will be demonstrated in subsequent discussion. Particularly unsettling were the failure of the utopian Apple Corps and the feud between John Lennon and Paul McCartney. Lennon and McCartney originally wrote their songs as a team, then began writing individually, but still listed all their songs as jointly written. The image of Lennon and McCartney as a symbiotic songwriting team was replaced in the early 1970s by a vision of the two men as mutually parasitic and competitive.[9] Country Joe and the Fish and the Doors were two other bands who experimented with shared songwriting credit and/or royalties. Both bands eventually abandoned the practice.[10] The utopian myth of collective creation succumbed to the "real world" of competition for money and fame. There is general critical agreement that none of the Beatles have been able individually to make records as artistically or intellectually significant as the best Beatles records.[11] This may be taken as evidence of the artistic validity of the 1960s utopian vision of collection creation, but also as evidence that money triumphs over art, at least in some cases.

Reunion of the Beatles became a common fantasy propagated through mass media and other channels throughout the 1970s, and even after the death of John Lennon (the remaining three Beatles were rumored to be planning a reunion album in Lennon's honor; George Harrison's "All Those Years Ago" is sometimes said to be a tribute to Lennon, with all three surviving Beatles participating in the recording—but these reports have also been contradicted). The Beatles as individuals were seen as incomplete—able to make money, but not great art capable of redirecting cultural history.

The overwhelming majority (73%) of songs in my sample pertained to familial love—usually to sex and/or romantic love. Sixteen percent pertain to society. These overall percentages are approximately equal to percentages for most of the individual years. The most significant departure from the norm occurred from 1968 to 1971. The percentage of songs pertaining to love dropped from 85 to 1967 (the highest percentage in the ten-year period) to 53 in 1968 and 1969 (the lowest percentage for songs pertaining to love). In 1970, the percentage rose again to 75, approximately normal for the ten-year period. The number of songs pertaining to society rose simultaneously with the decline of the number of songs pertaining to love. The percentage of songs pertaining to society rose from 10 (approximately normal) to 35 (highest for the ten-year period) between 1967 and 1968. The percentage then declined year by year (32 in 1969, 25 in 1970, 20 in 1971), but did not return to ten percent until 1972. These figures demonstrate a sudden rise in 1968, and gradual decline until 1972, of interest in society as a topic in song lyrics, on the part of songwriters, musicians, and the record consuming public (at least in the Top 40, 45 rpm market). Temporarily, society became of greater concern, while dyadic love became of lesser concern. All but one of the songs from my sample which pertain to society have a counterculture flavor (the exception is "Ballad of the Green Berets"). The frequent occurrence and visionary content of counterculture songs about society demonstrate that it is in these songs that the counterculture made its greatest contribution to popular music.

Chronologically, the first major rhetorical vision in popular lyrics from 1963 to 1972 can be labelled "Perfect, Permanent, and Dependent." These adjectives indicate the major attributes of love according to this rhetorical vision, which is largely a positive one. In this vision, lovers are constant companions, destined to be together forever, dependent on each other, destined to be married (although rarely already married). This kind of love is exemplified in "I Will Follow Him," "Hey Paula," "So Much in Love," and "You're the Reason I'm Living" (all 1963). In some cases, the lovers must bow to social pressure in order to cause envy among friends, save the female's reputation, prove the male's manhood, or satisfy parents or friends (examples include "He's So Fine," "My Boyfriend's Back," and "Walk Like a Man" [all 1963]). In some cases, the lovers have recently separated, causing misery (examples include "End of the World," "Rhythm of the Rain," and "Blue Velvet" [all 1963]). The Perfect, Permanent, and Dependent vision declined after 1963, which was probably the last year in a long period of dominance for it in popular music. For the most part, Perfect, Permanent, and Dependent love in popular music paralleled the dominant rhetorical visions of love found in Doris Day movies, TV situation comedies of the 1950s and marriage advice articles in mass circulation magazines in the 1950s and early 1960s.[12] Popular music applied this vision to adolescents by using "boys" and "girls" as characters (often portrayed by falsetto-voiced singers), sometimes in school settings, often with a goal of marriage.

In 1964, a new rhetorical vision of love emerged. This vision will be referred to as "British Invasion," because British records propagated it intensely beginning in late 1963. American records soon became more like these British records in style, content, or both, making what was originally a British innovation a joint British-American enterprise by 1967.[13] The British Invasion fostered in popular love songs a rhetorical vision involving being flirted with or seduced, benefitting from chance or fate, receiving gratifications, and promising nurturance. These themes are present, in various ratios to each other (with nurturance usually emphasized least), in many songs from my sample, especially between 1964 and 1967 (examples include "I Want to Hold Your Hand," "She Loves You," "Oh, Pretty Woman," and "Do Wah Diddy Diddy" [1964]; "I Got You Babe" and "Can't You Hear My Heartbeat" [1965]; "Lightnin'

Strikes" [1966]; and "I'm a Believer" and "Happy Together" [1967]). The development of the British Invasion rhetorical vision in popular music paralleled developments in content of numerous other media, including movies (the early James Bond films, *The Liquidator, Modesty Blaise, Our Man Flint, A Hard Day's Night, Help! Georgy Girl, To Sir With Love, In Search of Gregory*), TV series (*I Spy, The Man from U.N.C.L.E., The Avengers, The Monkees, The Addams Family*), and fiction (e.g., Robert Sheckley's *The Game of X* and *The Tenth Victim*). In most of the examples cited, society is a major concern, with dyadic love important only as a secondary theme.[14] Consonant with this restricted role, love is often depicted in fast-paced images of fortuitous encounter, mysterious attraction, flirtation, and gratification (with nurturance included in some cases.) Both in popular music and in the other media mentioned, the rhetorical vision of the British Invasion is almost exclusively positive. Characters usually began and ended as unusual, but accepted and nonthreatening, members of Establishment society.

This view changed around 1967 (1966 was, in many ways, a transitional year) with the advent of a rhetorical vision which will be called Counterculture. This counterculture vision is essentially a continuation of the rhetoric of the British Invasion, but with some major changes. Protagonists now could not find utopia within the context of Establishment society. Society became of greater concern, and exerted greater influence on love and other family relationships. Mainstream society became something to escape from or resist (examples from 1967 include "I Think We're Alone Now," "Groovin'," and "I Was Made to Love Her"; examples from earlier years include "Under the Boardwalk" [1964] and "Poor Side of Town" [1966]; post-1967 examples include "Make It With You," "Cracklin' Rosie," and "Candida" [all 1970]). In general, escape became less prominent as a theme, and resistance more prominent, from 1967 to 1971. Similarly, pessimism gradually replaced optimism as the dominant mood.

The year 1967 marked the culmination and final resurgence of 1960s rhetorical optimism spawned by the British invasion. The rhetoric of the British Invasion was, in fact, at the core of the Counterculture rhetorical vision of love. However, the need for lovers to escape from social pressure was also a prominent theme in the love songs of 1967. This outsider's stance rhetorically cast society as a villainous "they" and a threat to the new (since 1964) doctrine of gratuitous love. At about this same time, nurturance, became moval of certain features of the Perfect, Permanent, and Dependent vision, especially permanence. The rise of responsibility and decline of gratification as themes indicate a more ostensibly altruistic view of love in the Counterculture vision than in the British Invasion vision. (Good examples of lyrics with a theme of nurturance include, "I Was Made to Love Her" [1967]; "Bridge Over Troubled Water," "Ain't No Mountain High Enough," and "I'll Be There" [1970]; "You've Got a Friend" [1971]; and "Lean on Me' [1972]. In 1970, responsibility/nurturance and escape/resistance had become even more common themes, and gratification had once again become very common. Much of the emphasis on playfulness and good luck carried over from the British Invasion vision of love had disappeared, but in 1970 the counterculture reflected in popular lyrics still believed in love.

In this view, fulfillment was possible through a love based on devotion to another person, reliance on that person for gratifications, and alliance with that person against a hostile society.

The Counterculture vision of love in popular music diverges slightly from thematic developments in other media. In well-known "counterculture" films involving love, such as *The Graduate, King of Hearts,* and *Zabriskie Point,* and in novels such as Elia Kazan's *The Arrangement,* the endings are only tentatively or ironically optimistic, and conclude works that are, to a large extent, pessimistic. This is in contrast with Counterculture love songs, which concentrate more precisely on love, and which are almost always more optimistic and less ambiguous. More emphatically pessimistic are such films as *Medium Cool, Little Murders, Easy Rider,* and *Shampoo,* and novels such as Richard Farina's *Been Down So Long It Looks Like Up to Me.* In each of these works, a potentially utopian love or friendship is ruined by society, fate, or a tragic flaw in character (or by some combination of these). In each case, the love is posed as a drastic and positive change in lifestyle for the protagonists—a sort of dream come true. At the end of each work, the dream is over.

In popular lyrics the Counterculture rhetorical vision's view of society was most clearly stated 1968-1970. The overall mood of the "Counterculture" songs in my sample was negative in most of the isolated cases prior to 1968, predominantly positive in 1968 and 1969, and about evenly divided between positive and negative from 1970 to 1972. The approximate parity of positive and negative in the last three years is misleading because of the importance of "American Pie" and various "dream is over" songs that were extremely influential but did not reach the annual top twenty (e.g., "Won't Get Fooled Again," "God"). Even "Smiling Faces Sometimes" attacked the utopia still being proposed in other songs. In addition, 1970-1972 is a negative period compared to the euphoric one which preceded it (1968-1969).

Tables 1 and 2 below summarize essential features of the Counterculture vision of society as presented in song lyrics in my sample. Table 1 lists items viewed favorably in the rhetoric of this vision; Table 2 lists items viewed unfavorably.

"Dream is Over" is the name I use for popular music's rhetorical vision of love following the Counterculture vision. The Dream is Over vision was prominent in 1971 and 1972 (most acutely in 1971), and probably remained so for at least a year following 1972. Many love songs in this period were unhappy, for numerous reasons. The most common reasons included being abandoned ("Me and Bobby McGee," "How Can You Mend a Broken Heart" [1971]; and "Without You" [1972]); inability to attract or understand the desired person ("Just My Imagination" and "Knock Three Times" [1971]; and "Brand New Key" [1972]); one lover being "untrue" ("Mr. Big Stuff" and "Do You Know What I Mean" [1971]); inconvenient presence of third parties ("Daddy Don't You Walk So Fast" and "I Don't Want To Be Right" [1972]); inability to put up with dependence ("Baby Don't Get Hooked on Me" and "Brandy" [1972]); failure of one lover to satisfy the other ("Want Ads" and "It's Too Late" [1971]); and inability to terminate an unhappy relationship ("Maggie

Table 1
Things Viewed Favorably in Counterculture
Vision of Society

Thing Viewed Favorably	Substantiating song(s) and year(s)
openness to intimacy	Hey Jude, 1968
freedom, liberation, cutting ties	People Got to Be Free, 1968
	Aquarius, 1969
	Proud Mary, 1969
	Everything Is Beautiful, 1970
	California Dreamin', 1966
helping	People Got to Be Free, 1968
	I'll Take You There, 1972
soul	Stoned Soul Picnic, 1968
celebration	Stoned Soul Picnic, 1968
	Joy to the World, 1971
music	Stoned Soul Picnic, 1968
	Let It Be, 1970
trust	Stoned Soul Picnic, 1968
	Aquarius, 1969
drugs, being stoned	Hey Jude (?), 1968
	Stoned Soul Picnic, 1968
	Aquarius (?—"crystal revelation"), 1969
	Crystal Blue Persuasion (?—title), 1969
	Grazing in the Grass (?), 1969
alcohol	Stoned Soul Picnic, 1968
	Joy to the World, 1971
peace	Aquarius, 1969
	People Got to Be Free, 1968
	Joy to the World, 1971
love	Aquarius, 1969
	Crystal Blue Persuasion, 1969
	People Got to Be Free, 1968
	Get Together, 1969
newness	Aquarius, 1969
	Crystal Blue Persuasion, 1969
open mind	Crystal Blue Persuasion, 1969
	Everything Is Beautiful, 1970
brotherhood	Crystal Blue Persuasion, 1969
togetherness	Get Together, 1969
nature	Grazing in the Grass, 1969
	People Got to Be Free, 1968
	Proud Mary, 1969
traveling, motion	Proud Mary, 1969
	California Dreamin', 1966
living on the land	Proud Mary, 1969
spirituality, faith	Aquarius, 1969
	Let It Be, 1970
	Crystal Blue Persuasion, 1969
	Everything is Beautiful, 1970
optimism, trust in the future	Let It Be, 1970
	Everything Is Beautiful, 1970
	Crystal Blue Persuasion, 1969
	People Got to Be Free, 1968
	I'll Take You There, 1972
tolerance	Everyday People, 1969
	Everything Is Beautiful, 1970
California	California Dreamin', 1966

Table 2
Things Viewed Unfavorably in Counterculture Vision of Society

Thing Viewed Unfavorably	Song and Date	Exemplary Passage
intolerance	Blowin' in the Wind, 1963	"How many roads must a man walk down before you call him a man"
war	Blowin' in the Wind, 1963	"how many seas must a white dove sail before she sleeps in the sand... how many times must the cannon balls fly before they're forever banned... how many deaths will it take till he knows that too many people have died"
	American Woman, 1970	"I don't need your war machines"
	War, 1970	"War...what is it good for, absolutely nothing/War, it ain't nothing but a heartbreaker/Friend only to the undertaker"
	The Night They Drove Old Dixie Down, 1971	"I like my brother before me, I took a rebel's stand/ He was just eighteen, proud and brave, but a Yankee laid him in his grave"
pollution	Blowin' in the Wind, 1963	"How many times must a man look up before he can see the sky"
callousness, isolation	Blowin' in the Wind, 1963	"How many ears must one man have before he can hear people cry... how many times can a man turn his head, pretending he just doesn't see"
oppression	Blowin' in the Wind, 1963	"how many years can some people exist before they're allowed to be free"
advertising	Satisfaction, 1965	"When I'm watchin' my TV/ And that man comes on to tell me/How white my shirts can be/Well he can't be a man 'cause he doesn't smoke/The same cigarettes as me...I can't get no satisfaction"
standoffish females	Satisfaction, 1965	"I'm tryng' to make some girl/Who tells me, 'Baby, better come back, maybe next week/'Cause, you see, I'm on a losing streak'... I can't get no satisfaction"
job	Working in the Coal Mind, 1966	"Five o'clock in the morning/I'm already up

138   American Popular Music

		and gone/Lord, I'm so tired/ How long can this go on... 'Cause I make a little money/Hauling coal by the ton/But when Saturday rolls around/I'm too tired for fun"
	Thank You, 1970	"Many men are missin' much/Hatin' what they do"
prayer, religion	Mrs. Robinson, 1968	"Jesus loves you more than you will know, wo wo wo... Heaven holds a place for those who pray, hey hey hey"
institutions	Mrs. Robinson, 1968	"We'd like to know a little bit about you for our files/We'd like to help you learn to help yourself/Look around you, all you see are sympathetic eyes/Stroll around the grounds until you feel at home"
generation gap	Mrs. Robinson, 1968	"It's a little secret, just the Robinson's [sic] affair/Most of all you've got to hide it from the kids"
electoral politics	Mrs. Robinson, 1968	"Going to the candidates' debate...Ev'ry way you look at it, you lose"
commercial sports	Mrs. Robinson, 1968	"Where have you gone, Joe Dimaggio/A nation turns its lonely eyes to you"
America	American Woman, 1970	"American woman, get away from me/American woman, mama, let me be... Colored lights can hypnotize/Sparkle someone else's eyes"
ghettoes ghettoes	American Woman, 1970	"I don't need your ghetto scenes"
naive optimism	Thank You, 1970	"Looking at the devil/ Grinnin' at his gun/ Fingers start shakin'/I begin to run"
communication breakdown	Thank You, 1970	"Stiff all in the collar... Chit, chat, chatter tryin'... Many things is on my mind/Words in the way"
fear	Thank You, 1970	"Flaming eyes of people fear/Burnin' into you"
death	Thank You, 1970	"Dyin' young is hard to take"
co-optation	Thank You, 1970	"Dying' young is hard to take/Sellin' out is harder"
hypocrisy	Smiling Faces Sometimes, 1971	"Smiling faces sometimes pretend to be your friend/

		Smiling faces show no traces of the evil that lurks within... Your enemy won't do you no harm/'Cause you'll know where he's comin' from/ Don't let the handshake and smile fool ya"
loss of heroes	American Pie, 1971	"I can't remember if I cried/When I read about his widowed bride/But something touched me deep inside/The day the music died...the three men I admire most/The Father, Son, and the Holy Ghost/ They caught the last train for the coast/The day the music died"
high school	American Pie, 1971	"Well I know that you're in love with him/'Cause I saw you dancin' in the gym/You both kicked off your shoes...I was a lonely teenage broncin' buck/With a pink carnation and a pickup truck/ But I knew I was out of luck/The day the music died"
1960s	American Pie, 1971	"And there we were all in one place/A generation lost in space/With no time left to start again... And as the flames climbed high into the night/ To light the sacrificial rite/I saw Satan laughing with delight/The day the music died"
drugs	American Pie, 1971	"Helter-skelter in the summer swelter/The birds flew off with a fallout shelter/Eight miles high and fallin' fast/It landed foul on the grass"
rock music	American Pie, 1971	See "loss of heroes," "1960s" and "drugs."

May" [1971] and "Oh Girl" [1972]). Simultaneously, however, a number of other love songs included positive references to permanence ("Nice to Be With You" and "Betcha by Golly, Wow" [1972]); physical gratifications ("Treat Her Like a Lady" [1971] and "I Gotcha" [1972]); and benefits associated with "candy land" and other vague stimuli ("Candy Man" [1972]). These references indicate a partial revival of British Invasion exuberance. The return of these older utopian views of love honored relatively insignificant components of the roots of the Counterculture rhetorical vision, and contrasted with the Dream Is Over rhetoric of many negative songs. Probably more significant was the carry-over of the theme of nurturance from the Counterculture rhetorical vision. The continued occasional use of nurturance as a theme indicated a vestigial faith in the possibility of meaningful love. However, love was increasingly defined as friendship—the romantic or sexual love characterized by gratification, flirtation and insulation no longer appeared in pop music with its former frequency and positive outcomes. The positive depiction of nurturance encouraged acceptance of responsibility in interpersonal relationships, and abandonment of former utopian dreams or illusions grounded in the ideal of free movement. The new restrictions on movement signaled a period of lowered expectations. Many of the utopian songs of 1971 and 1972 actually added to the negative flavor of these years by offering as positive, musical dramas devoid of many of the delights depicted in previous years. Instead of excitement, the new positive love songs depicted a world that was "mellow," and used appropriately downbeat music as a vehicle.

Based on the foregoing discussion, it is possible to summarize the four rhetorical visions as follows:

Time Period	Prevailing Rhetorical Vision	Characteristic Fantasies (positive except where noted)
?-1963	Perfect, Permanent, Dependent	perfect love permanent love lovers dependent on each other fitting into society being left (negative)
1964-67	British Invasion	fortuitous encounter mysterious attraction flirtation sensory gratification dancing, soul
1967-71	Counterculture	sensory gratification escape from society nurturance universal love bright future war (negative)
1971-72-?	Dream Is Over	failure of counterculture (negative) being left (negative) being trapped in love (negative) friendship permanent love

Martin Pawley has argued that mass media content depicts a "secondary reality," which, he says, the audience has come to prefer over the real world "which demonstrably exists."[15] Popular music contributes to secondary reality through its form, which encourages the audience to pay attention to nonexistent people who seem to be inside a loudspeaker, and through its content, whose ostensibly trivial, slice-of-life dramas cumulatively form epic rhetorical visions. The higher meaning of pop music and the process through which form and content interact are very imperfectly understood; the proper role of institutions in the formation of culture is, or at least should be, one of the major issues of the present age. Since cultural form is to a large extent transparent to the people using it, systematic analysis of content can be a useful first step leading

Lyrics in the Annual Top Twenty Songs in 1963-1972   141

to grounded conclusions about the nature of mediated reality. This study is such a first step, which I hope will lead to further discoveries of the reasons for, and meanings and implications of, popular music form and content and their interrelationship.

Notes

[1]George Gerbner, interview in the TV program *A Death in the Family*, written and produced by James Hayden, a production of WCCO-TV, Minneapolis, n.d. (ca. 1979).

[2]For a more detailed discussion, see Gary Curtis Burns, "Utopia and Dystopia in Popular Song Lyrics: Rhetorical Visions in the United States, 1963-1972," dissertation, Northwestern University, 1981.

[3]See "Hot 100—1963," *Billboard*, 75, No. 52, 28 Dec. 1963, Section 2, p. 30; "Top Records of 1964," *Billboard*, 77, No. 1, 2 Jan. 1965, p. 6; "Top Singles of 1965," *Billboard*, 77, No. 52, 25 Dec. 1965, Section 2, p. 22; "Top Singles," *Billboard*, 78, No. 52, 24 Dec. 1966, Section 1, p. 34; "Hot 100—1967," *Billboard*, 79, No. 52, 30 Dec. 1967, Section 1, p. 42; "Hot 100 Singles—1969," *Billboard*, 81 No. 52, 27 Dec. 1969, Section 2, p. 16; "Top Pop 100 Singles," *Billboard*, 83, No. 52, 25 Dec. 1971, p. TA-36; and "Top Pop 100 Singles," *Billboard*, 84, No. 53, 30 Dec. 1972, p. TA-20.

[4]See Ernest G. Bormann, "Fantasy and Rhetorical Vision: The Rhetorical Criticism of Social Reality," *Quarterly Journal of Speech*, 58 (Dec. 1972), 396-407; Ernest G. Bormann, "The Eagleton Affair: A Fantasy Theme Analysis," *Quarterly Journal of Speech*, 59 (April 1973), 143-159; and Ernest G. Bormann, "Fetching Good Out of Evil: A Rhetorical Use of Calamity," *Quarterly Journal of Speech*, 63 (April 1977), 130-139.

[5]See, respectively, B. Lee Cooper, "The Image of the Outsider in Contemporary Lyrics," *Journal of Popular Culture*, 12 (Summer 1978), 168-178; Bruce Anderson, David G. Berger, R. Serge Denisoff, K. Peter Etzkorn and Peter Hesbacher, "Love Negative Lyrics: Some Shifts in Stature and Alterations in Song," *Communications: International Journal of Communication Research* (West Germany), 7 (1981), 3-24; Gregg M. Campbell, "Bob Dylan and the Pastoral Apocalypse," *Journal of Popular Culture*, 8 (Spring 1975), 696-707; and Robert A. Rosenstone, " 'The Times They are A-Changin': The Music of Protest," *Annals of the American Academy of Political and Social Science*, 38 March 1969), 131-144.

[6]Exactly *how* notable these statistics are is a matter of interpretation. Ten years is a short period over which to chart yearly trends. Nevertheless, if deviations from the average percentage of positive songs (59%) are plotted chronologically over the ten-year period, the result is:

1963	0
1964	plus 20
1965	minus 1
1966	minus 9
1967	plus 16
1968	0
1969	plus 4
1970	plus 6
1971	minus 24

1972   minus 9

The average absolute value of the deviations in 1964, 1967 and 1971 is almost five times (4.83) as great as the average absolute value of deviations for the other years. Even allowing for subjectivity and error in sampling and classificaiton, the deviations in 1964, 1967 and 1971 seem so sharp as to warrant classifying these as years of special interest.

[7] Paul Sann, *The Angry Decade* (New York: Crown, 1979), p. 204.

[8] On the Beatles as a vicarious family, see Wilson Bryan Key, *Subliminal Seduction* (1973; rpt. New York: New American Library, 1974), pp. 61-63.

[9] Lennon seemed to resent the fact that McCartney was assumed by the press and public to be the major or solo writer of "Eleanor Rigby." Lennon maintained that he, Lennon, had played a significant part in the writing of the song. (Jann Wenner, "The Rolling Stone Interview: John Lennon. Part Two: Life with the Lions," *Rolling Stone*, No. 75, 4 Feb. 1971, p. 38.) In addition, there was an air of competitiveness in Lennon's insistence that it was he, not McCartney, who had first seen that the Beatles had outlived their usefulness and he, not McCartney, who had first wanted to leave the Beatles. (Jann Wenner, "The Rolling Stone Interview: John Lennon. Part One: The Working Class Hero," *Rolling Stone*, No. 74, 7 Jan. 1971, pp. 37-38.)

[10] Country Joe and the Fish did not share songwriting credit; however, Country Joe McDonald recalled: "I was splitting up all my copyright royalties with the band, and...I was...pretty insane for doing it." (David Felton and Tony Glover, "The Rolling Stone Interview: Country Joe McDonald," *Rolling Stone*, No. 83, 27 May 1971, p. 35.) The Doors shared songwriting credits on their first three albums, listed individual songwriters on the next three, then returned to crediting the entire group on *L.A. Woman*, their last album recorded while Jim Morrison was alive. Jerry Hopkins and Daniel Sugerman explained the Doors' approach to songwriting, royalties and decision-making in *No One Here Gets Out Alive* (New York: Warner Books, 1980): "They had an unusual partnership agreement whereby everything was to be shared equally. Jim was writing nearly all the songs, but when they recorded, he said, the Doors would be listed as composer, and royalties and all other income would be divided equally four ways. All creative decisions would be made not by majority rule but by unanimous vote." (p. 82). Hopkins and Sugerman imply that the later practice of crediting individual songwriters was evidently intended to prove that other band members besides Morrison wrote songs (Morrison having become the "star" of the band): "By June [1969] the Doors' fourth album [*The Soft Parade*] was finally complete. A full year in preparation, this album had been the most frustrating yet, with Jim contributing only half the material. His energy obviously, was being directed more toward poetry than lyrics. For this reason, and because Jim didn't want anyone to think he wrote the song that would be their next single, 'Tell All the People,' individual writer's credits replaced the traditional, 'Songs by the Doors'." (p. 246)

[11] For an early indication of this critical trend, see Robert Christgau, "Living Without the Beatles: IPMC," *Village Voice*, 16, No. 37, 16 Sept. 1971, pp. 42-43; and Robert Christgau, "Now That We Can't Be Beatle Fans Anymore," *Village Voice*, 16, No. 39, 30 Sept. 1971, pp. 40-42, 48, 57.

[12] See Virginia Kidd, "Happily Ever After and Other Relationship Styles: Advice on Interpersonal Relations in Popular Magazines, 1951-1973," *Quarterly Journal of Speech*, 61 (Feb. 1975), 31-39.

Lyrics in the Annual Top Twenty Songs in 1963-1972   143

[13]This alliance was presented to the public through pseudo-British, American bands packaged by American promoters, e.g., the Sir Douglas Quintet, the Monkees (which included a British pop singer, Davy Jones), Sam the Sham and the Pharaohs, and Paul Revere and the Raiders; events such as the 1967 Monterey Pop Festival, which featured both British and American acts; British-American collaboration in bands such as the Jimi Hendrix Experience; and other transatlantic exchanges of people, musical styles, costumes and lyrical themes (e.g., Donovan's interest in Dylan's folk style, flower power and Jefferson Airplane; Van Morrison's move to America; Johnny Rivers' performance of the theme song on the British TV series *Secret Agent*).

[14]A parallel example from popular music, not included in the sample, but in many ways exemplary of British Invasion rhetoric, is the Yardbirds' "Over Under Sideways Down," 1966, which begins with the line "Cars and girls are easy to come by in this day and age."

[15]Martin Pawley, *The Private Future* (1973; rpt. New York: Pocket Books, 1977), p. 164.

The Lyrics of American Pop Music: A New Poetry

Harold F. Mosher, Jr.

In recent years rock music has increasingly come to be treated as the poetry of the 1960's.[1] Beginning with Richard Goldstein's *The Poetry of Rock*, the first "respectable" book on the subject, the trend has blossomed into many "relevant" texts in English literature and poetry courses.[2] Some of these works have ignored the obvious fact that music helps to illuminate the poetry. Words and music complement each other, and separating words from music will detract from the song's total effect.[3] Nonetheless, the lyrics appear indicative of the *zeitgiest* of the 1960's. The often cited example of the Jefferson Airplane's "White Rabbit" is illustrative since it mirrors the surrealism and drug induced experientialism of that decade. Pills, "a hookah smoking caterpillar," and mushrooms encourage the listener to "Feed [his] head": that is, when "logic and proportion have fallen sloppy dead," when the objective world seems to fail you, "turn on" and "drop out," in hippy slang. Like Carroll's book, Donovan's "Sunny Goodge Street," or Bob Dylan's "Fourth Time Around," "White Rabbit" is full of funny, surrealistic images with "the White Knight...talking backwards" and the dormouse announcing slogans. The song proposes no constructive way of life such as, say, One Nation Underground's "drop out" does, advocating self-reliance, or such as Steve Miller's "Children of the Future" does, promoting acceptance of love. "White Rabbit" merely suggests an escape through drugs, or it may be implying, as the surrealists and dadaists did, that to construct a new world we need first to destroy the old. So down come "logic and proportion" in a prophetic vision. Playing with words, the counters of reality, rearranges reality and makes it possible to see the world in a new way. "White Rabbit," though, instead of stating this philosophy discursively, performs it, imitates this disorder.

"White Rabbit" puts us in the "greening" stream of consciousness and reduces that distance between us and the psychological action that a nineteenth century editorial-omniscient novelist would create. Its nonsense is more faithful to the psychedelic philosophy which distrusts logic and even words as too limiting, as preventing freedom of the psyche to expand. Tom Wolfe in *The*

Reprinted with permission from *Popular Music and Society*, Volume 1:3 (Spring 1972), pp. 167-176.

Electric Kool-Aid Acid Test suggests that the rational intellect filters out too much experience and prohibits man from enjoying the full life of the senses. So anything like drugs or happenings or rock music that breaks down this barrier will permit man to experience life more directly and thus more fully. Art should imitate sensory experience as closely as possible, and, in the extreme, a novelist like Ken Kesey gives up writing entirely and turns to creating a sort of living art. Such an aesthetic brings us to the end of literature. One way of tracing the history of art in the twentieth century is to see it evolving from forms imitating outside reality to structures imitating man's inner perception of the world, and then becoming the experience itself. In literature, for instance, the movement is from realism (Thackeray's chronological depiction of events) to the variation by time-shift imitating the way a person remembers a narrative (Conrad) to surrealism, or the reality which the individual mind imposes on the outside world. Always the purpose has been to bring art closer to life. The counterpart in painting to such a mimetic form as automatic writing, recording a mind thinking, might be the surrealists' *objets trouvés* or the contemporary pop artists' soup cans.

Two generalizations can be made about the form and content of these mimetic songs. First, they express their meaning, as most good poetry does, obliquely, whether by simple implication, ambiguity, irony, symbolism, surrealistic devices, or by dramatic means. As Richard Goldstein points out, "rock poets are beginning to regard ambiguity as an enchancement of their lyrics' effectiveness. An undertone of irony is often cultivated, and sometimes lyric and melody are pitted against each other in emotional counterpoint."[4] As an example of this counterpoint Ned Rorem cites the beginning of the Beatles' "A Day in the Life" where the overwhelming poetry-"He blew his mind out in a car"-is set to calm music.[5] In "Ode to Billie Joe," Bobbie Gentry emphasizes the uneventful narrative background of eating and working with simple rhymes and monotonous melody as a counterpoint which keeps the sensational events of death and suicide from appearing too melodramatic. Often images work ironically against each other also; T.S. Eliot and calypso singers mix surprisingly in Dylan's "Desolation Row." Second, many of these songs seem to develop the philosophy of non-conformity and independence by describing the restrictions of daily living. They tell their adherents to be themselves whether they drop out into their own solipsistic, hallucinatory world, the one of "White Rabbit," or even further into mind-blowing sound, or whether they "turn on" to an imaginative new life, that of "Drop Out," or go so far as to try to form the outside world according to their convictions, as the son does in "The Great Mandella." Perhaps the most convincing way to demonstrate that the best of rock lyrics are effective poetry is to show how skillfully certain techniques are used to develop themes which these techniques are organically suited to treat. The relatively more objective poems employ drama, irony, implication, and ambiguity to treat the theme of daily restriction, whereas the more subjective songs present their worlds solipsistically and surrealistically to develop the themes of non-conformity and independent thinking. Both types often rely on setting to reveal states of mind.

To illustrate these trends in popular music, I have chosen the hybrid genre of folk-rock as performed by Paul Simon because the lyrics found in this idiom often provide the best examples of those songs that dramatize objectively their theme, that of restriction and failure.[6] Let us begin, then, with songs that view the world more from the outside than within a mind and that use the more traditional poetic devices of drama, irony, ambiguity, and implication; then let us move from these to songs that describe worlds which individual minds form solipsistically and surrealistically. An example of a dramatic song is Paul Simon's "America" which portrays by means of a monologue and through a short conversation the failure of communication between the speaker and his girl and between the speaker and his country, or what that country stands for—the American Dream.

The poem begins casually and mockingly, the speaker poking fun at his fortune which consists probably of some clothes in his bag, some cigarettes, and some pies. His girl Kathy joins in the spirit of light-hearted adventure, and the two friends, not really serious lovers, talk and laugh at the other people on their bus, probably all of them middle-class and middle-aged. But the feeling of gaiety soon fades, dramatized by their acts of first smoking the last cigarette together, then turning separately to reading and watching the scenery. Finally, Kathy sleeps and the speaker has to talk to himself, confessing his loneliness and unexplainable emptiness. Paul Simon even uses the setting, as an objective correlative, with the moon alone in a wide open sky over a flat plain in the wasteland of New Jersey to reveal that the emptiness of the land is matched by the speaker's emptiness. New Jersey, the so-called "Garden State," represents the commercialization of the American country-side, where oil refineries have replaced farms. It is the perfect symbol for the failure of the American Dream, which once represented the freedom for self-fulfillment but has come to mean the license for exploitation. One suddenly realizes that the imagery of finance—"fortunes" and "real estate"—together with the seemingly off-handed remark—"Michigan [as described, say, by Hemingway's *In Our Time*] seems like a dream to me now"—the imagery and the remark about the dream link the failure of the friends' communication with the larger failure of any American, played by the speaker, to achieve the promise of his nation. The boy jokingly refers to love in business terms, but by the end of the poem, as he sits sad and bewildered counting the cars on the turnpike, we perceive that the corruption of the American Dream has affected his communication with the girl and the land, and that he, like the lonely souls in the bus and in their cars, is also riding down the turnpike vainly searching for America, for fulfillment. The refrain—"They've all come to look for America" with its sad musical tone—takes on an increment of meaning as it is repeated: he is just as desolate in his search as the others. Thus, through actions and words the poem dramatizes very simply, but also very subtly, the loneliness of a boy and a girl and thereby the dilemma of all Americans cut off from each other and therefore from one source of self-development—that of sharing with others. The development of the self cannot be easily effected in a climate where the true self, one's real character, is ignored by others. Human relations cannot be reduced to business dealings.

The dramatic technique manages to imply a good bit about the theme of restriction.

The dramatic opposition of two voices is a familiar device in rock. Paul Simon uses it in "Seven O'Clock News/Silent Night" and in "Scarborough Fair/Canticle." Formally the two parts of this latter song seem to belong together. The meter of both poems is roughly four-stress, and the stanza length in each is the same—eleven lines—if one excepts the beginning and ending choruses of "Scarborough Fair." Thematically and dramatically the two poems are related. If the two poems do belong together, one reason is that the speaker of "Scarborough Fair" is the soldier described in "Canticle." This conclusion is based on an interpretation both of the drama of these ballads and of their themes. One of the appeals of the good ballad is that much remains unstated, and the listener has the pleasure of supplying missing information to help the bard compose his piece. An examination of what is implied by the dramatic juxtaposition of the two songs by Paul Simon, "Scarborough Fair/Canticle," uncovers their meaning.

The chorus of "Scarborough Fair" tells us that a girl had once been the speaker's "true love" and thus implies that she is no more. The body of the poem then presents her with various impossible tasks to accomplish in the medieval tradition of the ordeal. Its refrain states that the completion of these tasks will once more make the girl a true love of the speaker, but the implication is that because of the impossible nature of the ordeals—finding land between the sea and the beach, for instance—she will never become his true love. Why not? The ambiguous answer lies in "Canticle" which, in my opinion, describes the speaker of "Scarborough Fair." Repetition calls our attention to "Sleeps unaware of the clarion call" which links the "child of the mountain" to the soldier as does the hillside on which they both repose and where there is a grave. By juxtaposing the child with the soldier, by associating them both with sleep and the hillside, and by implying the traditional metaphor of sleep for death, the poems suggest that the person described in "Canticle," the speaker of "Scarborough Fair," is, if not physically dead, at least spiritually dead. Though he polishes and cleans his gun, he does not join the fighting (not that this inaction alone would make him spiritually dead). Though he thinks of his former love, he does not go to give her his message. The image of a loitering soldier on a hillside bemused by his lost love reminds one of the knight in Keats's "La Belle Dame Sans Merci." The lute music, the four-stress line, and the alliteration ("War bellows blazing in scarlet battalions") of "Canticle" further suggests the middle ages and the setting of Keats's poem. One conclusion might be that because the soldier is sick with lost love, he cannot act. Another is that because he is engaged in a senseless war whose cause has been forgotten, he cannot return to his former love. Both conclusions imply that love and war are incompatible, also the implication of another ballad "Cruel War," and the medieval music and setting imply the eternalness of this problem: what has been true in the past and is true now will probably always be true. "When will they ever learn?" asks Pete Seeger's "Where Have All the Flowers Gone?" The dramatic juxtaposition of "Scarborough Fair/

Canticle" might even suggest a third and quite different interpretation: just as girls cannot be forced to love by impossible tasks, so boys cannot be forced to fight for forgotten causes. The dramatic method allows multiple meanings, none of which really contradicts the others; they all deal with the failures of love and war, another variation on the theme of restriction.

Let us now consider another group of songs which like most good lyric poetry also communicate indirectly but less by drama and irony and more, rather, by implication and ambiguity. Most of them still deal with the theme of restriction in various forms.

A humorous song, on the surface at least, is Paul Simon's "At the Zoo," whose casualness and bouncy rhythm might throw one off the scent. The key to the poem's deeper meaning is at the center: "Something tells me it's all happening at the zoo." What is happening? Animals, the remainder of the song tells us, masquerade as humans or stand for different human characteristics like honesty, insincerity, and stupidity. The effect is that the humor and satire are not directed at the animals, who after all are not supposed to possess these human characteristics, but it is directed at the humans, who are supposed to have them. To give to animals human traits is to degrade humans. Perhaps the poem also suggests an application of the law of evolution. If "it's all happening at the zoo," the animals, as man's progenitors, have already played all men's roles, and these roles are just that—poses, masks. That monkeys "stand for" honesty rather than that they "are" honest is significant. Why, for instance, should zebras be reactionaries necessarily? Simon means us to see this role as simply arbitrary. It is significant that the list of animals begins with monkeys who most closely resemble men. We are thus put on the trail for Simon's method and meaning; men like animals long before them have been assuming false identities for centuries, fooling others and themselves. The same history of dishonesty, insincerity, etc., repeats itself in our "civilized" age when we take "fancy rambles" to look at the animals in the cages—that is, at ourselves. By putting the human mask on the animals, Simon has made humans see themselves for what they really are. The mirror is a more effective teacher than bare statement especially when the subtleties of implication at first becloud the mirror and then suddenly leave it clear to reveal the spectator laughing at himself.

Likewise, Paul Simon's "Mrs. Robinson" is a poem which obscures at first its unpleasant portrait of a restricted life only to make its point more striking as the picture comes into focus. What is wrong with Mrs. Robinson? What secret must she hide from her children? What grounds seem alien to her? What information does the speaker want from her for the "files"? Why does Mrs. Robinson need reassurance when everybody around her is "sympathetic"? For what reason must she learn to help herself? These questions suggest that Mrs. Robinson is psychologically maladjusted, perhaps paranoid. But the horrible truth that we slowly realize is that she is probably just as well a typical suburban housewife. Her life represents the wasteland of America's affluent society, which is responsible for the emptiness and hypocrisy of such organizations as the Harper Valley PTA, to cite Jeannie C. Riley's version of Peyton Place. Mrs. Robinson's meaningless life consists of such activities as receiving on Sunday afternoon and going to occasional political rallies. Because she must feel the irrelevance of it all, she needs reassurance, and the song gives it mockingly to her, parodying the child's prayer—"Jesus loves me that I know, for the Bible tells me so"—with the refrain—"Jesus loves you more than you will know/(Wo wo wo)/God bless you please, Mrs. Robinson,/Heaven holds a place for those who pray/(Hey hey hey)." But Mrs. Robinson's god is Joe DiMaggio, to whom the whole nation "turns its lonely eyes." Unfortunately even this baseball hero, whose legends have assumed the proportions of religious myth for this decadent society, has deserted it. No wonder Mrs. Robinson, and others like her, are lonely, insecure, loveless members of a latter-day wasteland, whose god has "gone away/(Hey hey hey)." By the end of the song the echo of this laugh rings menacingly in our frightened minds, for the poem implies that all our lives could become like Mrs. Robinson's.

Paul Simon's "A Hazy Shade of Winter," one of his more subjective poems, goes deep into the psyche to investigate imaginative independence as a solution to the restrictions imposed on the individual by society. Its world is seen subjectively—solipsistically and even surrealistically. It advises to "live your life behind your eye,/Your own skies, your own tomorrow," as One Nation Underground's "Drop Out" says. In other words, do not allow the world to impose its own ways on you because, in living by the world's standards, you die by its defects. If more people reject the world's killing pace, its calendar will crumble. See the world in your own way, and you will live in your own world. The failure to live by such a solipsistic vision is dramatized by "A Hazy Shade of Winter." As in "America" and "I Am a Rock," Paul Simon uses the landscape to reveal inner states of mind, but in "A Hazy Shade of Winter" we see the landscape change as his mind, following his mood, alters it. In "America" and "I Am a Rock," the landscape is objectively real and is stable; in "Hazy Shade" it is a projection of the narrator's mind and changes according to what happens there. When the despondent narrator pretends that he can re-create his hopes, his landscape changes from the brown leaves and "hazy shade of winter" to the grass and ripening crops of summer. His "scene" changes the season, weaves time into his own tapestry, not vice versa. In the tradition of Buddhism (with an assist by Maharishi Mahesh Yogi) and American Transcendentalism, the song shows how the self can control its own environment. But this narrator is not schooled enough in this philosophy, and, depending on someone else to remember him, the narrator forgets his self-reliance, he confronts his writing failures, he drinks, and he sees the springtime of hope fade into his winter of despair. He is controlled by the outside world and its insistent tolling of "Time,/Time,/Time," which dominates the opening mood of the poem.

Although most rock songs have been admired for their music, many of them have lyrics with remarkable poetic qualities. Their form is generally loose, often to accommodate the music. Nevertheless, their drama, irony, ambiguity, and symbolism put them in the tradition of "serious" poetry, and they have something interesting and important to say about the restrictions of modern life and the ways of gaining freedom from these restrictions. What is more, they use their traditional poetic devices to present their themes in imaginative, original, and sometimes quite extravagant forms. In the best of them, one never gets the impression that they are written for the sake of either technique or content alone; their techniques, no matter how unusual, seem organically suited to their themes. The judgment of the lasting value of rock poetry depends not, as Murphy and Gross seem to imply, on their skill in handling traditional techniques alone nor on the relevance of their themes only but rather in their ability to put established poetic methods in the service of songs about contemporary problems.[7] Their art and relevance are renewing poetry and an interest in it. Time and time again in these songs one finds beneath a disarmingly simple and entertaining surface a studied art and considered thought organically unified to create something worthy of the name of "new poetry."

Notes

[1] See Richard Goldstein, *The Poetry of Rock*, New York: Bantam Books, 1969; Stephanie Spinner, *Rock Is Beautiful*, New York: Dell Books, 1970; and Barbara Farris Graves and Donald J. McBain, *Lyrics Voices: Approaches to the Poetry of Contemporary Song*, New York: John Wiley and Sons, Inc., 1972. For a critique of this approach cf. Robert Christgau, "Rock Lyrics Are Poetry (Maybe)," in J. Eisen, ed., *The Age of Rock, Vol. I*, New York: Vintage Books, 1969, 230-243; and R. Serge Denisoff and Mark H. Levine, "The One Dimensional Approach to Popular Music: A Research Note," *Journal of Popular Culture IV* (Spring, 1971), 911-919.

[2] A review of these books is found in Tony Glover, "Bound to Rock," *Creem 3* (January, 1972), 51-56.

[3] See James D. Graham, "Rhythms in Rock Music," *Popular Music and Society* 1 (Fall, 1971), 44-50; and Karen Murphy and Ronald Gross, " 'All You Need Is Love, Love Is All You Need'," *New York Times Magazine*, April 13, 1959, 50.

[4] Richard Goldstein, "Wiggy Words That Feed Your Mind," *Life*, June 28, 1968, 70.

[5] Ned Rorem, "American Music and the Beatles," *Dialogue* I (1968), 52.

[6] For a background see Bill C. Malone, *Country Music U.S.A.: A Fifty-year History*, Austin: University of Texas Press, 1969; Oscar Brand, *The Ballad Mongers*, New York: Funk and Wagnells, 1963; and R. Serge Denisoff, *Great Day Coming: Folk Music and the American Left*, Urban: University of Illinois Press, 1971, 164-197.

[7] Murphy and Gross, *op. cit.*, 50. See James T. Carey, "The Ideology of Autonomy in Popular Lyrics: A Content Analysis," *Psychiatry*, 32 (May, 1969), pp. 15-164; Robert A. Rosenstone, "'The Times They Are A-Changin' ': The Music of Protest," *Annals*, 381 (March, 1969), 131; and Jerome L. Rodnitzky, "The New Revivalism: American Protest Songs, 1945-1968," *South Atlantic Quarterly, 70* (Winter, 1971), 13-21.

Iconic Modes: The Beatles

Ralph Brauer

Reprinted with permission from *Icons of America*, by Ralph Brauer, edited by Browne and Fishwick, Bowling Green University Popular Press, 1978, pp. 112-23.

"Yeah, well, if there is a God, we're all it."

John Lennon

"God," noted Pogo from his vantage point in the comics, "is unemployed." Words have been discarded, retooled, or vulgarized accordingly. "Idol" now pertains to anyone or anything to the group doing the idolizing. For example, a high school sports hero can be an idol to a grade school sand-lot jock while his older sisters "just idolize Paul Newman's eyes." Charisma is no longer a word applied only to religious figures who have received a special grace from God; instead a political hero like John Kennedy can be said to have "that special grace" and a TV newscaster like Walter Cronkite is spoken of as having charisma. Icon has come to be a word used by cultural analysis to describe images which in Marshall Fishwick's words "are admired artifacts, external expressions of internal convictions, everyday things that make everyday meaningful."[1]

It is a pointed comment on our world today that some like Fishwick believe icons can only be objects. Although the religious figures of the medieval icons were materially dead, they were still spiritually alive and their presence was felt as surely by their devotees as if they had been living. Death and life did not have the same meaning then as they do now. To see our contemporary icons as being only objects is to too literally interpret the medieval icon and in turn cut off from our understanding the study of the cultural significance of people who have affected our experience in iconographic ways. To say for instance that a poster of James Dean is an icon, that perhaps his role in *Rebel Without a Cause* could be, but that the living individual could not is to draw an all too literal line between life and death, person and object, thing and no thing, which circumscribes rather than enlarges our understanding. If we are to use the concept of icons to gain an understanding of the deep visions and values of our culture we must examine those individuals as well as those objects which we endow with our beliefs in their sacredness. As Fishwick put it, "what is central to the concept of icon is touching a center near man's essence."[2]

In contemporary America perhaps nothing touches the center of certain people as much as our popular music stars. American teenagers, especially girls, place on their walls pictures or posters of their favorite pop idols and surround them with other objects of devotions—concert tickets, record jackets, and perhaps, if they are lucky enough and impertinent enough, a lock of hair, a cufflink, a ripped piece of clothing. Like pieces of the True Cross or vials of the Holy Blood, these objects from the person of the pop star are deeply venerated. They may well be kept in specially designed reliquaries. Unlike their religious counterparts, though, these pop icons are only temporal. Their devotees grow up or find new objects of veneration. Even the most devoted admirer of Donny Osmond ultimately knows that some day the picture, tickets and other objects will end up in the trash can.

During most of the sixties there were probably no pop stars as high on the iconographic scale as the Beatles. Their devotees came from every class and age group. Many of them willingly had their hair clipped in imitation of their idols (whose haircuts resembled those worn by monks in many a Hollywood movie—perhaps that's why their imitators were called Monkees) or invested five to ten bucks in a similarly styled wig. Others bought collarless jackets and a type of leather boot which came to be called, appropriately enough, "Beatle boots." Original posters from their concerts sold in galleries for astronomical prices. Yellow submarines appeared on the sides of brick buildings. Thousands of children were named after them as were stores, free schools, amusement parks and a host of products. Above all, though, we bought their records—and in greater volume than we have ever bought records from a single group or individual. We made millionaires of four plain lads from Liverpool along with a multitude of managers, merchandisers and assorted hangers-on and rip-off artists. We made those records so popular that today they are still used to draw in customers when sold at a discount. Revivals on radio are so frequent one wonders whether they ever really "left" us.

Like true devotees we spent hours discussing and memorizing the verses of these recorded "texts." Decyphering them became a world-wide pastime. Even the photographs on the album covers were analyzed. When rumor spread that cypher experts had determined that certain messages spoke of Paul's death, even the real Paul had trouble denying it.

Then there were the rites at which the Beatles themselves presided: those live concerts where all one could hear were literally thousands of screaming, shrieking, hysterical people. Only at brief moments could you catch slices of the music, but since you had heard it before, your mind filled in the blank spots. What was important above all else at these rites was to show your devotion, to show how *they* moved you, how much you felt about *them*, what it did to you. Ushers spoke in awe of the wet seats left by teenage girls. As John Lennon tells it in *Lennon Remembers* many of these female devotees went a great deal further in satisfying their sexual stirrings. According to Lennon the Beatles on tour resembled something from Fellini's *Satyricon*: "We had four bedrooms separate from... tried to keep them out of our room. And Derek's and Neil's rooms were always full of fuck knows what."[3]

Iconic Modes: The Beatles 153

For all Lennon's efforts to set the record straight, though, most of the Beatles' fans preferred to keep their sexual stirrings in the realm of fantasy. This fantasizing about the private lives of pop icons, of course, has a long history. Its most prominent exponents have always been the gossip columnists and the Hollywood fanzines. For rock fans the biggest fanzine of all was and still is *Rolling Stone*, which comes in tabloid form like the *National Enquirer* and at its best is an articulate alternative to the regular press, while at its worst it is nothing but a gossip sheet and trend spotter.

It was in *Rolling Stone* that Lennon finally, as he put it in the language of these times, "let it all hang out." In his remarks about the Beatles one senses a strong self-destructive tendency—about which I'll say more later—which in its attempt at realism rings not unlike the criticisms of the Beatles that were issued throughout their reign as pop icons.

No icon is without its iconoclasts—you cannot have one without the other. They are the negative image of the icon and their attacks on the icon help to define it, many times help to fuel its power, and probably tell us as much about the icon as those who are its devotees. During the sixties these iconoclasts (who would, no doubt, become quite heated at being so labelled) were by and large represented by what was then known as the Establishment. These Establishment/iconoclasts decried the early Beatles in unison, viewing them as shallow popular artists bent on making money or as long-haired corrupters of youth. Then as the Beatles' music grew more complex, the Establishment splintered. Liberal intellectuals suddenly began embracing the Beatles, proclaiming their profundity in such journals as *The Partisan Review*. College campuses were full of professors lecturing about the musical and cultural significance of the latest Beatles album. Looking back on it one can see that this splintering of the Establishment presaged the deeper split which was to break out openly in 1968. Suddenly the Blue Meanies became real—Blue Meanies being the name given the Chicago cops by protestors at the Democratic Convention.

The Blue Meanies becoming real marked the beginning of the end for the Beatles. In the heated conflicts of the late sixties and early seventies their music became middle-of-the-road. The *White Album* is a good example of the Beatles' inability to cope with the new times. It never presents a consistent unified whole as *Pepper* did. Jann Wenner reviewing the album at the time prophetically remarked that the album seemed the work of four individuals rather than a group. So like the rest of us in those times, the Beatles fragmented.

Ironically it was the love of the intellectuals which helped to kill the Beatles. Even though they were embraced by only part of the Establishment, that embrace was a slow strangle-hold which eventually would kill them. Hearing their professors lecture about the Beatles, the students, who had been the largest group of devotees of the pop idols, began to wonder about the quartet. This is because there is perhaps no surer kiss of death in the pop music business than for a performer to be embraced by the Establishment—to be analyzed, lectured on and written about. I can remember my own sickness on seeing Poirier's article "Learning from the Beatles"—if the Beatles could be learned from like a book, if professors could write papers about them, then their music had no power.

In pop music above all, power, especially a power that had the magic of the Beatles, was not something that could or should be discussed logically. Like the devotees of medieval religious icons, devotees of contemporary pop icons relate to the power and the magic of their idols. The ultimate paradox of the pop idol is that in this business of packaging and selling music as if it were a car or deodorant, the pop idol must have that indefinable something that cannot be lectured about.

There must be what Erich Neumann in *Art and the Creative Unconscious* called a numinous quality in the pop icon. Neumann speaks of this quality throughout his book as being that transcendent, other-worldly element that all great art and artists possess.

> The need of his times works inside the artist without his wanting it, seeing it, or understanding its true significance. In this sense he is closer to the seer, the prophet, the mystic. And it is precisely when he does not represent the existing canon but transforms and overturns it that his function rises to the level of the sacral, for he then gives utterance to the authentic and direct revelation of the numinosum.[4]

Neumann borrowed the term numinous from the theologian Rudolf Otto who coined it to describe the essence of the religious experience. Otto's book, *The Idea of the Holy* is a lengthy attempt to outline the elements of the numinous experience, yet from the beginning he knew he was trying to articulate the inarticulatable. It was for him an attempt to describe a deep emotional and intellectual experience which went beyond our individual consciousnesses.[5]

This numinous quality which Neumann found in great art and Otto found in religion, Franz Neumann found in the charismatic leader.[6] The quality possessed by the pop icons is certainly quite similar to that possessed by charismatic religious and political—leaders figures as opposite and yet the same as Christ and Hitler—and by Erich Neumann's great artist figure of Leonardo Da Vinci.

That pop icons possess this numinous quality can be seen in looking at a figure like James Dean. As David Dalton describes Dean in his book *James Dean: The Mutant King*, Dean "like Gatsby...'sprang from his Platonic conception of himself' and in this form carried his incorruptible dream through the movies and into our lives.... What happened to Jimmy became a record of what was happening to America."[7] Dean was a mutant and "the mutant must arise to make transition from the old organism to the new,...Mutant derives its meaning from the same root as myth and James Dean became a myth through his mutations, a mystery we will never completely comprehend."[8]

It is interesting that Dean—a pop idol—should possess qualities that have been associated with charismatic leaders because Max Weber's original use of charisma—and Weber was the one who gave the term its contemporary context— was to describe leaders whose power went beyond bureaucratic structures in an irrational way. As Weber saw him, the charismatic leader was one who was opposed to the rational rules and normal routines of a bureaucratic society.

Iconic Modes: The Beatles 155

"In contrast to any kind of bureaucratic organization of offices the charismatic structure knows nothing of a form or of an ordered procedure of appointment or dismissal.... The charismatic leader gains and maintains authority solely by proving his strength in life."[9]

Like Weber's political charismatic leader who functions against and beyond bureaucratic society, so our popular icons function against and beyond popular norms. Like James Dean, the Beatles were as much a revolutionary force as any charismatic leader and their effect was a profound one which changed our cultural as well as our musical perceptions. Despite the efforts of people like Otto, Weber and the two Neumanns, we still only dimly understand the phenomenon of charismatic individuals like Dean and know even less about the numinous quality they possess. In the realm of popular culture it is this numinous quality which above all separates the great popular artist—the pop icon—from the run-of-the-mill. Elvis Presley had it. Bessie Smith had it. Certainly Louis Armstrong had it. The Beatles had it. While some people believe we can describe much of popular art as formula—taking the lead from John Cawelti's brilliant essays and his book *The Six-Gun Mystique*—it is the numinous quality in these popular artists which resists formulation and makes popular art so interesting. For Cawelti, "formula stories...are structures of narrative conventions which carry out a variety of cultural functions in a unified way. We can best define these formulas as principles for the selection of certain plots, characters, and settings which possess in addition to their basic narrative structure the dimensions of ritual, game, and dream that have been synthesized into the particular patterns of plot, character and setting which have become associated with the formula."[10] Understanding the formula will to some extent help us understand those who go beyond formula. The concept does not, however, help us understand the numinous quality of our pop idols. Formula tells us not what a popular artist's power is but what it is not. If all popular music, for instance, were mere formula then the record companies could predictably package one string of hits after another. They do this often enough that's for sure; but every once in awhile someone comes along who creates that special magic. Then we enter the realm of the numinous and they enter the Valhalla of pop iconography.

In that realm of the numinous, performer and audience do not need words to describe their mutual sharing of magic—as the behavior of the Beatles' concert goers shows so well. The attraction shared is not unlike that which one finds in charismatic leaders and their movements and mass rallies. The numinous performer and the charismatic leader have more in common than most of us care to admit. Yet if we could understand more of the nature of this quality in pop idols we might also come to a greater understanding of the power of a Hitler.

Looking back on the Beatles' reign as pop heroes, I believe that a great deal of their magic came from their talent as comedians. In fact they may well have been the greatest comedians since Chaplin. (In light of my previous comments about the numinous qualities of pop stars and charismatic leaders there is that curious relationship between Chaplin and Hitler—Hitler looked like Chaplin, Chaplin parodied Hitler in *The Great Dictator*.) Like Chaplin they were masters of timing and mimicry. There is even a parallel in their work—the early shorts, Chaplin's film *The Circus* and *Sgt. Pepper*, the *White Album* and *Modern Times*. (I have always thought of the *White Album* as a time capsule—a collection of observations about the world at that time.) Like Chaplin, the Beatles had a vision behind their work—an affirmation of the humanity of us all, a belief in freedom in its fullest sense and above all a spirit of fun. Like Chaplin's, the Beatles' vision sometimes slipped into sentimentality—in fact the same kind of winning sentimentality that Chaplin had. The audiences who left *Yellow Submarine* singing "All You Need Is Love" were not unlike the audiences who left *Modern Times* humming "Smile".

In the tradition of Chaplin and other truly great popular artists the Beatles were powerful because they were at once so different and yet so much like all of us. (Historians have speculated that this was also Hitler's great appeal.) Just as we all could see something of ourselves in Chaplin's little tramp, so the collective individuality of the Beatles fits those pop stereotypes that are deeply ingrained in all of us: Ringo, the folksy "good ole boy"; Paul, the teenage heart throb; John, the irreverent whippersnapper; George, the quiet intellectual who as some put it must be "deep". Each of them said things people wanted to say but couldn't. They put down all the pretensions of modern life. Chaplin's famous kick in the pants—the thing we all wanted to do to some pompous personage—was as much as the basis of the Beatles' humor as it was Chaplin's. When their own pretensions were getting a bit thick, the Beatles were not above poking fun at themselves just as Chaplin could do so well.

Coupled with their collective identities, the Beatles brought with them a great sense of timing. As with Chaplin the essence of their timing was the use of the unexpected. Certainly one of the most remarkable things about the Beatles' icon was how it varied.

The phrase that so many people uttered back then—"growing up with the Beatles"—was not an idle phrase, for perhaps unique among pop icons the Beatles ranged across all facets of twentieth-century music and created for us an amazing stew full of heady ingredients. They were constantly surprising us with their inventiveness. If Cawelti is right about the essence of popular art being convention and given in extreme cases the rote repeating of the same patterns, then the Beatles were superb—in the sense of being above—popular art, for they took the conventions, mixed them in that fabulous stew of theirs and produced works that turned the conventions back on themselves or went beyond them. Space, time, language, musical styles were mixed so freely they became irrelevant. Andre Bazin once said the essence of Chaplin's comedy lay in his irreverent use of objects—remember the immortal scene of Chaplin eating his shoe in *The Gold Rush*? So the essence of the Beatles' music was their irreverent use of the conventions of popular music. Chaplin eating his shoe left one laughing and crying at the same time, the same feeling one gets from songs like "Happiness is a Warm Gun" or "Maxwell's Silver Hammer." "Maxwell's Silver Hammer" is the food-feeding machine gone mad in *Modern*

Times or in the same film the Crazy Charlie tightening the buttons on a woman's dress with his wrenches.

As Chaplin helped us get through the twenties and thirties so the Beatles helped us get through the sixties. The sixties—two decades compressed into one—first the wild free times then the times of social upheaval. In the end both were superseded by evil not even their comedy could exorcise, (Spencer Bennett in an article "Christ, Icons and Mass Media" pointed to the Beatles' role of exorcism: "They have been molded as exorcisers of society by media just as Jesus was given stature by the Church as healer in iconographic form."[11]). Chaplin submerged by Hitler and the American McCarthyite fascists, the Beatles by Nixon, their song "Revolution" seeming a tame message after the deaths at Kent State. Black comedy became the style. Whimpy Mick Jagger singing "Street Fighting Man" seems a bit silly now but it was all the rage then as thousands of middle-class white college students who had never been closer to the streets or a fight than the nearest TV set donned fatigue jackets and Chairman Mao caps and exclusive dress chops sold cartridge belts to debutantes all bent on bringing about revolution. Such earnest figures, whether they be pseudo-revolutionaries, the ad men and lawyers who surrounded Nixon, or the stormtroopers and assorted deviants who surrounded Hitler are beyond comedy. (My father who escaped from Germany in the thirties said he thought *The Great Dictator* wasn't really that funny at the time, because Hitler couldn't be parodied.) You can laugh at cartoon Blue Meanies but the real ones are more deadly and not so humorous.

In considering the demise of the Beatles it is pertinent to remember that icons are above all objects. They can be plain and everyday or beautiful and unusual in their own right, but still they are only objects. These plain everyday objects do not become icons until we endow them with those other-worldly qualities that we ourselves find necessary to give them. The qualities, we choose and the reasons we choose them are as varied as all the vagaries of human nature.

So it was with four plain lads from Liverpool, each—as John Lennon put it—an individual in his rite. Collectively they became the Beatles and we made a cultural icon of them. For awhile they threatened to outshine even the most sacred of the old icons—remember when it was said the Beatles are bigger than Christ? The Beatles made the remark themselves at a press conference. To some it was blasphemous while to others it was a part of a press conference put-on, which stars like Dylan cultivated and whose precursors were the conferences given by idols like James Dean and Chaplin. The remark, though, was a bit more complex and profound than that. It illuminated the secular, popular nature of our society in a sudden dramatic way which hundreds of scholarly and not-so-scholarly articles could scarcely duplicate. In another way it alluded to the numinous quality the Beatles radiated; for they did seem to possess something given to them by contact with what Rudolf Otto called "mysterium tremendum." This relationship with the other worldly is something many would dismiss as sheer crap, but David Dalton was perhaps closer to the truth than he realized when he spoke of James Dean as a modern Osiris:

"It is through our eyes that we have taken Jimmy into ourselves, and he remains there magically present like Osiris, god of regeneration."[12]

Perhaps if we are to search for formula and conventions in figures like Dean and the Beatles we would do well to look at religious and charismatic archetypes. Dalton's brilliant insight could open the door to a whole area of cultural investigation which would serve to begin to illuminate the numinous side of our psyches: a revival of Otto's attempt on a secular level. As a beginning of such an attempt maybe we should differentiate between popular, political and religious charisma. It also might be more useful to refer to all these figures as charismatic icons to differentiate them from Fishwick's objective icons. Unlike those medieval icons which were paintings and objects, the Beatles were four living human beings. Ultimately they could not live as a collective idea and once again became mere mortals. Unlike Jimi Hendrix, Jim Morrison, Janis Joplin, and a host of burned out blues musicians, they at least were able to live with their humanity. That they are now less than perfect is not without its satisfaction.

In this light I wonder why so many of our charismatic icons die such untimely deaths. Even Hemingway—at once the strongest and the most vulnerable—succumbed. Those that do not die untimely deaths become sickening parodies of themselves like Elvis had become or like Mick Jagger is well on his way to becoming. The easy answer is that they could not live up to their own hype. No doubt there is a great deal of truth to that but it is still too simple. The fate of the human beings we choose to elevate to the status of charismatic icons reminds me more of the archetypal ritual Sir James Frazier described in his study *The Golden Bough*. In Frazier's story there was a ritual slaying of the old king by a newer and younger one. Reading Frazier's story one's mind conjures visions of two men in jaguar skins, bedecked with jewelry and gold fighting to the death under the ritual tree. Cultures like to create their charismatic icons, endow them with magic and mystery (perhaps send them on tour), and then find they must slay them because they're so heavy. The Beatles realized this as much as anyone when they wrote "Sexy Sadie" or "When I'm Sixty-Four"—and still they were caught in the trap. Luckily today's pop idols are not destroyed in ritual fights to the death, although the game and the results can be as deadly. All charismatic idols—like Frazier's old king—know their time is limited. The determination of that time is based on popular mood and on the appearance of a new challenger. When the inevitable happens their popular identity will be destroyed. If they become too wrapped up in that popular identity then death can become quite literal. So they burn the candle at both ends with sometimes fatal consequences. Jim Morrison's "Light My Fire" with that awful line "and our love becomes a funeral pyre" summarized the relationship between the pop star/icon and the audience.

Notes

[1] Marshall Fishwick and Ray Browne eds., *Icons of Popular Culture* (Bowling Green, Popular Press, 1970), p. 1.

[2] *Ibid.*, p. 4.

[3] Jann Wenner, *Lennon Remembers* (New York, 1971), p. 84.

[4] Erich Neumann, *Art and the Creative Unconscious* (New York, 1966), p. 97.

[5] Rudolf Otto, *The Idea of the Holy* (New York, 1958).

[6] Franz Neumann, *Behemoth: The Structure and Practice of National Socialism* (New York, 1966).

[7] David Dalton, *James Dean: The Mutant King* (New York, 1975), p. 375.

[8] *Ibid.*, pp. 377 & 379.

[9] Max Weber, *On Charisma and Institution Building*, (Chicago 1968), pp. 19-20, 22.

[10] John Cawelti, "The Concept of Formula in the Study of Popular Culture," *Journal of Popular Culture* III: 3 (Winter, 1969), p. 390.

[11] *Icons of Popular Culture*, p. 10.

[12] Dalton, p. 373. A lengthy comparison of Dean and Osiris appears on pp. 370-373. Dalton's book is full of intuitive insights of this sort and is highly recommended to anyone studying the power of popular charisma.

Me and the Devil Blues:
A Study of Robert Johnson and the Music of the Rolling Stones

John D. Wells

From one point of view it is not an exaggeration to say that the entire history of the Rolling Stones has been a debate with the ghost of Robert Johnson. The legendary Mississippi delta blues singer did not invent rock 'n' roll, but he was certainly among the first artists to develop the same standards of values and sources of commitment. Indeed, virtually every serious theme found in blues-based rock 'n' roll may be found in the music of Robert Johnson.[1] His songs involve elements of struggle and the search for meaning in an alien culture. This is not the safe, secure environment whereby protection may be obtained through ordinary channels of family, friends or religion. Johnson's songs reveal images of a world "as black as midnight," hellhounds on the trail, last fair deals going down, worried minds, love in vain, slaves chained and bound and chronic despair and damnation.

Very little is known about Robert Johnson except that he was a country blues guitarist who was murdered by a jealous husband in 1938. Paul Oliver reports in *The Story of the Blues* that Johnson spent his life traveling, gambling, playing and getting entangled with women. According to legend, Johnson was a mediocre guitar player who disappeared for a year. When he returned he was so proficient that his fellow blues singers claimed he had sold his soul to the devil in exchange for musical genius.[2]

There are several abiding thematic connections between Robert Johnson and the Rolling Stones. First of all, the Rolling Stones were obviously influenced by the blues tradition to the point of naming themselves after a Muddy Waters song and recording songs by such blues artists as Willie Dixon and Solomon Burke. However, the influence of Robert Johnson is particularly evident in terms of individual values and themes. Johnson's songs, like the Rolling Stones, are rooted in honesty and social realism which uncovers an often brutal account of the world through the expressive characteristics of the human voice. The human voice is extremely important in blues-based rock music because its value

Reprinted with permission from *Popular Music and Society*, Volume 9:3, 1983. pp. 17-24.

lies primarily in its emotional impact, not upon a linear development of theme or harmony found in composition music. The songs are improvised and spontaneously composed and voices are important for expressing emotions directly by moaning, grunting, screaming or howling and using full potential of the language. From their earliest records the Rolling Stones embellish Black expressiveness; Mick Jagger's vocals usually include an amount of distortion, groans, moans, howls and screams, often using phrasing that is barely intelligible. Again, emotional feeling is emphasized over and above articulation, and as in African music, the repetition of phrasing and rhythm often leads to a creation and resolution of tension, sometimes producing hypnotic trance-like states.[3]

Life Without Facade

The realism portrayed in Johnson's and the Rolling Stones' music deals with basic human problems and sometimes ecstasies. In *Blues Fell This Morning*, Paul Oliver reports that every conceivable aspect of Black life is exemplified in one blues or another—highways, lawyers, cities, rivers, beer, whiskey, voodoo, sex, gambling, boxing, hurricanes and floods.[4] Although one can perceive the blues as a reflection of sociological conditions and a commentary on the Black person's fate, the music itself is free from such protestations. Blues singers sing about individual problems; the loss of a woman, a job, being unable to pay the rent, or drifting without a home.

The portrayal of life without facade enables an audience to identify with the content and mood on a personal level even though the blues composition is usually an individual experience. Mick Jagger may have been speaking of his own problem when he sang, "I can't get no satisfaction," but many people felt he was speaking for their particular situation. In this sense many of the songs of Johnson and the Rolling Stones reflect a person that is out of tune with the universe without a great deal of faith. In "Stones in My Passway" Johnson sings:

> I got stones in my passway
> And my road seems dark as night
> I got stones in my passway
> And my road seems dark as night
> I got pains in my heart—
> They have taken my appetite.

In "The Last Time" the Rolling Stones proclaim:

> I'm sorry girl but I can't stay
> Feeling like I do today
> Staying here is too much sorrow
> Guess I'll feel the same tomorrow
> Well, this could be the last time
> Maybe the last time
> I don't know, oh no

These performers are not only alienated and out of touch with society at large but because of their emphasis upon basic human drives, they must in their own way deal with the contradictions and fears of our Puritan ancestry.

In *Mystery Train: Images of America and Rock 'n' Roll Music* Greil Marcus marks the distinction between music of the Church and the blues of Robert Johnson:

> Blues grew out of the need to live in the brutal world that stood ready in ambush the moment one walked out of the church. Unlike gospel, blues are not a music of transcendence; its equivalent to God's Grace was sex and love. Blues made the terrors of the world easier to endure, but the blues also made those terrors more real. For a man like Robert Johnson, the promises of the church faded; they could be remembered— as one sang church songs; perhaps even when one prayed, when one was too scared not to—but those promises could not be lived.[5]

William Faulkner once wrote, "You run without moving from a terror in which you cannot believe, toward a safety in which you have no faith."[6] This safety in which you have no faith is the Puritan ethic whereby salvation may be attained through good moral deeds, hard work, thrift, a denial of sensuality and a rigid code of ethics. Johnson and the Rolling Stones in not accepting the puritanical values were free to express and fulfill the body and the senses heretofore condemned by the Puritan Ethic. Accepting the Puritan Ethic is one way to deal with uncontrollable forces like temptation, sex and the devil; Johnson and the Rolling Stones had no such luxury. These performers may not have really believed in the devil, but they ran away.

Love in Vain

The blues idiom to a large extent does express the body and hence sexuality with a directly physical beat and intense emotional sound. Blues music and blues-based rock 'n' roll, according to Simon Frith, is an aesthetic of *public* sexuality as opposed to the development of private expressions of eroticism or literature and poetry—an aesthetic linked to puritanism itself.[7] This is one of the reasons why the Rolling Stones were considered the "bad boys" of rock music. Young persons were drawn to their public expressions of sex which was rebellion because these desires were supposed to be private sensations. In short, like Johnson, the Rolling Stones deal directly with the brutal, honest and yet ironic facts of sex and love.

Certainly, in the area of female relations Johnson and the Rolling Stones have similar attitudes. Women troubles abound in numerous songs. In "Kind Hearted Woman Blues" Johnson sings:

> I got a kind hearted woman, do most
>   anything in the world for me (repeat)
> But these evil hearted women, man
>   they will not let me be
> I love my baby, my baby don't love me (repeat)

But I really love that woman, can't
stand to leave her be.

In "No Expectations" Mick Jagger sings

...as I watched you leaving me
You packed my peace in mind
So take me to the airport
And put me on the plane
I've got no expectations
To pass through here again.

The two songs recorded by both Robert Johnson and the Rolling Stones are characteristic of their attitude toward women.[8] In "Love in Vain" the singer anguishes over the loss of his girlfriend:

When the train
Left the station
It had two lights on behind (repeat)
Well, the blue light was my blues
And the red light was on my mind
All my love's
In vain.

In "Stop Breaking Down," the singer is full of boastful pride, arrogance and self-confidence in his dealings with women:

Every time I'm walkin'
On down the street
Some pretty woman starts breakin'
Down on me,
Stop breakin' down (repeat)
Stuff I got will bust your brains
I'll make you lose your mind.

The Blues in general has often been accused of being sad music, and although there is usually a story to be told, blues songs rely heavily upon ironic twists of fate in male-female relations. Lines like "laughing just to keep from crying," "easy rider," "old time used to be," "I used to love her, but it's all over now" show up again and again in blues and rock 'n' roll.[9] In one song Robert Johnson confesses:

I'm going to stay around Jonesboro until
  my teeth is crowned with gold (repeat)
She's got a mortgage on my body, a lien on my soul.

On occasion both Johnson and the Rolling Stones fall hard for predatory "Honkey Tonk women" and as with all their subjects, when dealing with matters of sex and love, both artists are forthright and uncompromising. The fundamental Puritan streak in American life has persisted since Johnson's time and blues and rock 'n' roll are still in disfavor for flaunting matters that should be kept secret. Even today as sexual matters are more openly discussed, the tendency is toward more intellectual, self-conscious appraisal of sex drives and rarely do we openly celebrate our energies in such boastful fashion.

It has been contended that such forthright and uninhibited sexual language is a form of protest, and in the sense that they are meant to shock and assert the personality of the singer, there is some truth in this statement.[10] However, these artists include much of life that does not appear in a typical Tin Pan Alley song. They also sing about drugs, addiction, death, disease and alcoholism.

Sympathy for the Devil

Somehow the image of the devil is a striking yet logical connection between Robert Johnson and Mick Jagger of the Rolling Stones. The Puritan devil survives in the context of these performers and is played out in images of acts of violence, unsatisfied desires, boastful egos and struggles with women, sex, drugs, work and alcohol. Both performers side with the devil because they have no faith in puritanism, and besides it's more enjoyable anyway.

Again, Marcus writes:

> The Puritans came here with a utopian vision they could not maintain; their idea was to do God's work, and they knew that if they failed, it would mean that their work had been the Devil's. As they panicked at their failures, the devil was all they saw.
>
> ...The image of the devil was played out within the matrix of Johnson's struggle with women, and with himself. It was a drama of sex, shot through with acts of violence and tenderness; with desires that no one could satisfy; with crimes that could not be explained; with punishments that could not be escaped.[11]

In "Me and the Devil Blues" Johnson is very clear about his struggle with the devil and the acts of sex and violence.

> Early this morning when you knocked
>   upon my door (repeat)
> I said "hello satan, I believe it's time to go"
> Me and the devil was walking side by side (repeat)
> I'm going to beat my woman until I get satisfied.

If not the devil, then symbolic beasts torment and follow him everywhere:

> I got to keep moving, I got to keep moving
> Blues falling down like hail,
> Blues falling down like hail
> I can't keep no money,
> Hellhound on my trail
> Hellhound on my trail, hellhound on my trail.

As Max Weber recognized, the Puritan Ethic provided a sane, bearable solution to a problem which plagued religious cults throughout history, and that is, the control of all the evil forces, sorcerers, witches, devils and spirits at play in the universe. The Puritans, by repudiating magic and sorcery as a means to salvation, were able to deal psychologically with the demons and devils set loose in the world. As Weber noted:

...The reason for the entirely negative attitude of Puritanism to all sensuous and emotional elements in culture and in religion (is because) they are of no use toward salvation and promote sentimental illusions and idolatrous superstitions.[12]

The Puritans thus solved the problem of dealing with aggressive sexuality, the devil and symbolic evil forces by virtue of a strict asceticism to hard work and rugged individualism. Conversely, blues music, as Black music rooted in Africa and American slavery, did express belief in superstition and the supernatural. There was not a corresponding rationalization or asceticism to deny direct involvement and evocation of the gods. Robert Johnson, as a forerunner of not only the Rolling Stones but to the rock 'n' roll explosion, knew no such boundaries. To him, the devil and lust were as real as the Puritan work day. This particular attention to the devil as a symbol of cultural rebellion reached its apex in the 1960s when Mick Jagger himself was referred to as "the devil" and he even performed a song "Sympathy for the Devil."[13] This song could mean many things, but perhaps the Rolling Stones felt closer to the devil because of their obvious rejection of Puritanism, and of course the devil has been called the first rebel with a cause.

Although it has only been recently that the Rolling Stones have acknowledged even the fact that Robert Johnson exists, they have acknowledged their debt to rhythm and blues. Mick Jagger once said:

My father used to call it "jungle music" and I used to say, "Yeah. Good description." Every time I heard it I just wanted to hear more. It seemed like the most real thing I'd ever known.[14]

Certainly the themes and values portrayed in Johnson's and the Rolling Stones' music are real, if we mean by that the harsh realities of life set against a backdrop of a struggle between good and evil within the context of a person placed in a bewildered society.

Notes

[1]There is, of course, considerable discussion over the roots and influences of rock 'n' roll and nearly everyone has a different definition. Rock 'n' roll was really born a hybrid of country and western, gospel, Tin Pan Alley and blues music. I use the term "blues-based rock 'n' roll" to refer to rock music derived from early blues enthusiasts such as Muddy Waters, Arthur Crudup and Elmore James. This "type" of rock 'n'

roll is distinctly different from country-rock, new wave, gospel, folk-rock and doo-wop groups.

²Oliver reports that Johnson was twenty-four when he died, although other sources claim he was around twenty. For example, Sam Charters in his book *The Country Blues* states that Johnson was about thirty when he recorded. Don Law, who actually recorded Johnson, remembers him being around seventeen or eighteen at that time. See Paul Oliver, *The Story of the Blues* (Radnor, PA: Chitton Book Co., 1975). pp. 119-120.

³For an excellent musicological study of the relationship between techniques of pitch distortion and rhythmic repetitions on trance inducement see: Wilfred Mellers, "Pop Ritual and Commitment." There are also numerous studies done on the role of music in primitive societies. See Bruno Nettl, *Music in Primitive Cultures* (Cambridge: Harvard University Press, 1950); Sharon Schole and Sylvia White, *Music and Culture of Man* (New York: Rinehart and Winston, 1970).

⁴Paul Oliver, *Blues Fell This Morning* (New York: Cossell, 1960).

⁵Griel Marcus, *Mystery Train: Images of America in Rock 'n' Roll Music* (New York: E.P., Dutton, Inc., 1976). p. 33.

⁶Quoted in Marcus, *Ibid*.

⁷Frith also claims Western dance forms control body movements and sexuality with formal rhythms and "innocuous" times, whereas Black music expresses the body, and hence, sexuality. He also notes the censor's reaction to Elvis Presley's "form of sexual display" as one example of "public display." See: Simon Frith, *Sound Effects: Youth, Leisure and the Politics of Rock 'n' Roll* (New York: Pantheon Books, 1981), p. 19.

⁸The Rolling Stones recorded "Love in Vain" on albums *Let It Bleed* and *Get Your Yas-Yas Out*. "Stop Breakin' Down" was recorded on *Exile on Main Street*. In both cases, Johnson was not given credit. Either the author is listed as Payne or "traditional arrangement." In fact, the Rolling Stones have been very reluctant to give Johnson *any* credit. Only recently has Keith Richards applauded a screen play based on Johnson's life. See: Alan Greenberg, *Love In Vain: The Life and Legend of Robert Johnson* (Garden City, New York; Doubleday & Co., Inc., 1983).

⁹In addition to irony in sex and love relationships, the blues tradition is based upon a grimly ironic personification of the blues as when Johnson sings "Good morning blues, how do you do?" For an interesting view of the themes in blues music, see: *Feel Like Going Home: Portraits in Blues and Rock 'n' Roll* (New York: Random House, 1981), especially pp. 37-61.

¹⁰For an excellent analysis of sexual themes in blues lyrics see; Paul Oliver, *The Meaning of the Blues* (New York: Collier Books, 1960), pp. 131-153.

¹¹Marcus, p. cit., p. 34.

¹²Max Weber, *The Protestant Ethic and the Spirit of Capitalism*, trans. Talcott Parsons (New York: Charles Scribner's Sons, 1958), p. 105.

¹³In a recent book Robert Palmer addresses the "Stones as satan's messengers" themes. Palmer writes, "And since they'd been branded evil by the proper folk around them the blues people began to wonder: what *is* evil anyway? And if good means the hypocritical values of the proper folk, their tremulous faith and Protestant work ethic and all the rest of the bourgeois baggage handed down by the slave masters—if *that's* all good is, the blues people reasoned, then evil just might be worth investigating. Several decades later, the Rolling Stones would come to similar conclusions." See Robert Palmer, *The Rolling Stones* (Garden City, New York: Doubleday and Co., Inc., 1983), p. 6.

¹⁴Quoted in "Mick Jagger and the Future of Rock" *Newsweek* January 4, 1971.

References

Frith, Simon. *Sound Effects: Youth, Leisure and the Politics of Rock 'n' Roll*, New York: Pantheon Books, 1981.

Greenberg, Alan. *Love in Vain: The Life and Legend of Robert Johnson*. Garden City, New York: Doubleday & Co., Inc., 1983.

Guralnick, Peter. *Feel Like Going Home: Portraits in Blues and Rock 'n' Roll*. New York: Random House, 1981.

Jagger, Mick. Quote from "Mick Jagger and the Future of Rock." *Newsweek*, January 4, 1971.

Marcus, Griel. *Mystery Train: Images of America in Rock 'n' Roll Music*. New York: E.P. Dutton, Inc., 1976.

Mellers, Wilfred. "Pop Ritual and Commitment" *Journal of Royal Society of Arts* (January 1974) 80-89.

Nettl, Bruno. *Music in Primitive Cultures*. Cambridge: Harvard University Press, 1950.

Oliver, Paul. *Blues Fell This Morning*. New York: Cossell, 1960.

_____ *The Story of the Blues*. Radnor, Pennsylvania: Chitton Book Co., 1975.

_____ *The Meaning of the Blues*. New York: Collier Books, 1960.

Palmer, Robert. *The Rolling Stones*. Garden City, New York: Doubleday and Co., Inc., 1983.

Schole, Sharon and Sylvia White, *Music and Culture of Man*. New York: Rhinehart and Winston, 1970.

Weber, Max. *The Protestant Ethic and the Spirit of Capitalism*, trans. Talcott Parsons. New York: Charles Scribner's Sons, 1958.

Soul Music: Its Sociological and Political Significance in American Popular Culture

Portia K. Maultsby

One of the most innovative and generative forms of music that evolved from the 1960s Black Power Movement served to elevate the consciousness of an African heritage among black Americans. This music, coined "soul," established new trends and direction for the tradition of urban black popular music. Performers of soul music, in communicating the philosophy of the Black Power Movement, promoted the black pride or self-awareness concept. Their African-derived fashions and hair styles encouraged an identification with the mother country while their song lyrics advocated national black unity. Through their texts, soul singers not only discussed the depressing social and economic conditions of black communities but they also offered solutions for improvement and change. The overall awareness of an African heritage on the part of black performers influenced the conscious and unconscious revival and intensification of musical concepts that represented standards and aesthetics understood by the black community. The intense and emotional nature of songs performed by these musicians captured the new spirit, attitudes, values and convictions of blacks that later altered the social, political and economic structures of American society. Soul music, in the 1960s, served as a vehicle for self-awareness, protest and social change. In the 1970s, it provided musical resources for the evolution of new forms of American popular music. The sociological and political significance of soul music in American popular culture will be examined from three perspectives: 1) its use as an agent for advocating social and political change; 2) the path it paved for the acceptance of black music in an unadulterated form and 3) its impact on American popular culture. Since soul music is a by-product of the Black Power Movement, it will be discussed in this context.

Soul and the Black Power Movement

The foundation for the Black Power Movement was established by the Civil Rights Movement, which was an outgrowth of the Montgomery, Alabama, bus boycott of 1955-56. This boycott later proved to be the first of a series

Reprinted with permission from *Journal of Popular Culture*, Volume 17:2, Fall, 1983. pp. 51-60.

of organized efforts on the part of blacks to protest the "second-class" citizenship that defined their status. Discontented and frustrated with social, economic and political discrimination, black Americans began to organize non-violent courses of action to challenge these injustices. Leaders of the Civil Rights Movement adopted the "integration" philosophy—a philosophy they viewed to be the most effective strategy of achieving "first-class" citizenship. Integration was equated with emancipation and emancipation with full access to those rights and privileges granted to the larger society.[1]

Beginning in the 1960s, activities of the Civil Rights Movement drew national attention. Bombings, killings and the brutal treatment of blacks constituted the responses of white Americans. Such violent reactions coupled with poor enforcement of the Civil Rights Act of 1964 and the assassination of Malcolm X in 1965, provided the fuel for a major black revolution in America. Around 1965 blacks residing in large urban centers throughout the United States began to reject the non-violent approach of the Civil Rights Movement and retaliated to violent attacks by arming themselves and demanding immediate entry into society on their own terms. This change in philosophy and strategy gave way to the emergence of the Black Power Movement. Leaders of this movement encouraged the rejection of standards, values, beliefs and goals of the white society while they advocated the self-awareness or self-pride concept. The objective of the Black Power Movement as explained by Stokely Carmichael was to gain "full participation in the decision-making process affecting the lives of black people...."[2]

In view of this goal, black Americans sought to enter into the mainstream of American life as a unified group. Conditions for entry were to be guided by policies established and controlled by black people.[3] A philosophy inherent in the Black Power Movement promoted the concept of inclusion. In discussing this concept sociologist Talcott Parsons insists that "full inclusion and multiple role participation are compatible with the maintenance of distinctive ethnic and/or religious identity...."[4]

Although most blacks would agree with Parsons, white Americans generally, in theory and practice, are unwilling to act upon this interpretation of inclusion. The full implementation of the inclusion concept, however, can only occur when white Americans first recognize and accept cultural standards and values established and adhered to by blacks. Then black Americans must have the power to exercise control and to define their own needs, priorities, goals and courses of action. The concept of inclusion, therefore, necessitates social freedom and the re-distribution of economic and political power. The Black Power Movement was organized to promote these objectives.

The Concept of "Soul"

Urban black popular music traditionally has been subject to exclusion from the society at large. Representatives of record companies, the music industry and the mass media encouraged its exclusion by creating labels to identify black performers who *they* believed would appeal only to black communities. In addition, these representatives played a major role in selecting the listening audience and potential consumers of black music. *Billboard* magazine, for example, coined the phrase "Harlem Hit Parade" in the early 1940s to identify recordings made by blacks of urban black popular music. In the mid-1940s, this phrase was changed to "Race Records" then to "Rhythm & Blues" in 1949 and later to "Soul" in 1969.[5] Since the 1940s, music recorded by black artists, who modified their style to conform to musical standards and tastes of the larger society, has been classified as "pop." This music therefore was included in *Billboard*'s listing of songs that were recorded by white "pop" performers and distributed in white communities. It could be argued that these labels contributed to the identification of music style. But to the contrary, available evidence reveals that recordings made by white performers, when presented in a black or black-oriented style, became instant hits under the label of "pop." The Crew Cuts, Elvis Presley, Jerry Lee Lewis, Janis Joplin, Joe Cocker, the Bee Gees and Linda Ronstadt represent a few of many such artists.[6] Even when black artists modified their style to appeal to the white market, white performers, who recorded the music of blacks and in the same style, became benefactors of the "hit" in the "pop" market.[7]

Urban black popular music was first introduced to the larger society in the 1940s by white performers who presented "cover" versions of black hits. The performance style of these covers represented either diluted versions or poor imitations of the original song. When it appeared in the 1950s that black music played by black performers would gain acceptance in white markets, the term "Rock 'n' Roll" was coined by Alan Freed, a disc jockey from Cleveland, Ohio, to describe blues-derived black music with the black "beat." As explained by Gillett, when Freed first used the term,

> he was applying it to music that already existed under another name, "rhythm and blues." But the change in name induced a change in the music itself. "Rhythm and blues" had meant music by black people for black people. "Rock 'n' Roll" meant at first only that this music was being directed at white listeners, but then, as the people producing the music became conscious of their new audience, they changed the character of the music, so that "rock 'n' roll" came to describe—and be—something different from "rhythm and blues."[8]

After black performers provided the musical ingredients and style for the new treatment of "rhythm and blues," record companies began to contract white performers to record this music for white consumers who had discovered the "beat."[9]

Prior to the evolution of soul music, black performers of urban popular styles of black music had either been excluded from or assimilated into the American popular musical tradition. The music industry, mass media and the adult segment of white America refused to accept black music played by black musicians according to black definitions. Many adults regarded the commercial dissemination of black music to be "part of an NAACP plot to corrupt the nation's (and particularly Southern) youth."[10] The Citizen's Council of Greater New Orleans, Inc. distributed a circular that protested the air play of music recorded by blacks:

STOP
Help Save the Youth of America
DON'T BUY NEGRO RECORDS

(If you don't want to serve negroes in *your* place of business, then do not have negro records on your juke box or listen to negro records on the radio.)
The screaming, idiotic words, and savage music of these records are undermining the morals of our white youth *in America.*
Call the advertisers of the radio stations that play this type of music and complain to them!
Don't Let Your Children Buy, Or Listen To These Negro Records.[11]

In addition to this form of rejection, neither the mass media nor the music industry considered giving credit or sharing profits made from the creative efforts of black musicians.[12]

The rise of the Black Power Movement represented the first nationally unified group effort by blacks to directly counteract these and other forms of discrimination. "As black people became more immersed in social concerns and developed greater political activism, noticeable changes began to occur in their music." The music they created revealed "discernible impatience, courage and assurance."[13] Soul music emerged from this new spirit of social, political and economic liberation. Black performers of soul music were to serve as messengers who would communicate the philosophy of the Black Power Movement to the masses.

The term "soul" can best be defined as black nationalism. As a concept, it advocated the re-ordering of attitudes and values. As a symbol, it encouraged "the re-evaluation and re-definition of black identity, experience, behavior and culture" by blacks for blacks.[14] The term previously had been used in composition titles and group names not only to describe the "from the roots" character of songs but also to identify the source of inspiration and a black performance style of individual groups.[15] By the mid-1960s, soul nationally was regarded as a group attitude which mirrored the philosophy of the Black Power Movement.

The term "soul" was used consistently by black businessmen, who during the ghetto uprisings of 1964 (Harlem), 1965 (Watts) and 1967 (Detroit and Newark), identified their stores by displaying signs that read "soul brother." These signs served as a deterrent for potential looting and destruction of businesses owned by blacks. In July 1965, a black disc jockey from WOL in Washington, D.C. pioneered the national acceptance of the term "soul" when he identified his black-oriented station as "soul radio." The term was later used to describe various cultural trends, behavioral patterns and a particular style of verbal and non-verbal communication that evolved in black communities by and for black people. Although the term "soul" had become a household word in these communities by 1965, the mass media and music trade magazines did not give full recognition to its use until 1967, 1968 and 1969.[16]

The eventual acceptance of this term by the mass media, the music industry and the larger society signified an initial victory for the Black Power Movement. White Americans were to describe features distinctly unique to black culture by employing a term that had been *first* selected, sanctioned and used by black people. In the recording industry, the music that captured the essence of this victory was internationally known as "soul." The phrase "soul music", conceived by blacks, identified black vocalists and instrumentalists whose musical style corresponded to the "from-the-roots" concept. In returning to the roc s, they drew their musical ideas, vocal and instrumental styles from the gospel tradition. The emotional, intense, spontaneous and participatory nature of this tradition coupled with contemporary textual themes of black pride and protest provided the foundation for soul music.

Soul Music: A Force in Social Change

The period 1965-1969 witnessed the use of the phrase "soul music" as it was originally defined by blacks. When Sam Cooke recorded "A Change Is Gonna Come" in 1964 and the Impressions' "People Get Ready" in 1965, black artists were entering into the mainstream of the American society as politicians and spokesmen communicating the concept of "black pride." Prior to the era of "soul," black performers rarely addressed themselves to the social conditions and concerns of the black community. Performers of "rhythm and blues" sought to relate the realities of unfulfilled, broken and fantasized relationships, teenage romances, and good times in their texts.[17] Soul singers in establishing new roles for black performers discussed the reality of social and economic problems that plagues black communities. They called for community action and set examples for others to follow.

In addressing themselves to relationships, social problems, economic and political concerns, they gave advice and offered solutions for improvement and change. These performers preached the message that

> life is not to be accepted as it comes, hardship is not merely to be borne, but life is to be made worth living. Lessons are learned from unfortunate experiences which may either patch up existing failure, or give a better chance of success at a future date.[18]

This positive view of life reveals the fundamental relationship between gospel and soul music.

The two musical traditions served the same function, which is to console and comfort while providing direction and encouragement. Black performers of "soul," like black preachers, addressed themselves to the realities of the black community. Both related to their congregations and audiences in the same manner and their emotional approach to the delivery of their messages encouraged responses and activism. If for no other reason than its gospel roots, soul music penetrated through all social classes, religious denominations and age groups of the black community.[19]

Black performers and black preachers are in positions to serve as role models. They often coin phrases and influence the social behavior and life styles of the community. Given the acceptance and daily exposure of black performers in the community, they were able to communicate and elaborate upon the philosophy of the Black Power Movement.

James Brown was perhaps one of the greatest forces in advocating black pride, protest and social change. During his twenty-seven years as a successful performer, he never altered his unmistakenly black gospel-oriented style for acceptance in the white market. For this reason, he always had a solid black following and has earned the titles "Soul Brother No. 1" and "Godfather of Soul." His personal involvement with black communities extended from business investments, and financial donations to informal appearances.

Mr. Dynamite, as he was often called, re-invested a large portion of his earnings in the community. He gave large contributions to youth programs and charities and created jobs by establishing a variety of businesses. His interest in young blacks motivated him to make informal appearances in black communities where he discussed and emphasized the importance of education. The hardships Brown experienced resulting from the termination of his formal education after the sixth grade, coupled with his impressions from a 1966 tour through a ghetto area in San Francisco, motivated him to record his message. The recording "Don't Be A Drop-Out" sold over a million copies. His influence on the youth of America was recognized by the late Vice-President Humphrey, who invited Brown to lead a national anti-dropout campaign.[20]

Brown's first recordings that focused on the social problems of black communities encouraged blacks to be proud and to speak out against injustices. This message was expressed in his million-dollar seller "Say It Loud—I'm Black And I'm Proud" (1968) which was followed by "I Don't Want Nobody to Give Me Nothing" (1969). The call-response structure of the refrain section of "Say It Loud" encouraged blacks to participate by shouting "I'm Black And I'm Proud." After recording this song, Brown changed his hair style from a "process" to a "natural" and other blacks followed suit. Between 1969 and 1975 Brown continued to remind blacks of the reality of their condition and social status. Through his recordings during this period, he offered many suggestions as to how blacks could achieve social, political and economic independence. Brown's philosophy regarding community action is captured in his song titles: "Soul Pride" (1969), "Ain't It Funky Now" (1969), "It's A New Day" (1970), "Get Up, Get Into It, Get Involved" (1971), "Soul Power" (1971), "Talking Loud And Saying Nothing" (1972), "King Heroin" (1972), "Down And Out In New York City" (1973, "The Payback" (1974), "Funky President" (1974) and "Reality" (1975). The near and plus million sales of these recordings indicated that black America was listening.

Brown proved himself to be an elected spokesman for the black community when the mayors of Boston and Washington, D.C. called on him to help curtail rioting in these cities which followed the assassination of Martin Luther King, Jr. in 1968. His unusual ability to influence and control also was recognized by the late President Lyndon B. Johnson, who invited him to a White House dinner. On this occasion, a personally written and signed card, which read, "Thanks much for what you are doing for your country," was placed in front of him.[21] James Brown had the same kind of rapport with his audiences that black preachers have with their congregations. His experiences of poverty and hardship, of being black provided him with special insights into the problems and feelings of the black community. His songs were in the dialect and musical style that black people recognized and understood. They, consequently, responded to his messages, his music and to him as a successful black man with pride.

Other black performers[22] of soul music made significant contributions to the social awareness of the black community. In addition to employing themes of a social and political nature, they, as Brown did, spoke of unfulfilled relationships. In assuming the role of counselors, black performers provided a source of strength and encouragement through their words of wisdom and philosophical comments. Otis Redding and Aretha Franklin demanded "Respect" from their partners while Luther Ingram in "You Can Depend On Me," expressed his reliability and dependability. Other singers confessed their wrong doings but asked for forgiveness by declaring "I'm Gonna Do Better." Songs with these and related themes encouraged unity through expressions of "faith in love, hope for love, and the joy and happiness of love."[23]

The soul era was a productive period for black Americans. Group cohesion, political activism and community self-help programs were their responses to the messages of soul singers and leaders of the Black Power Movement. The music created by blacks and for blacks during this era communicated a general philosophy of refusal to accept the undesirable "and a determination to create a better future."[24] The Soul or Black Power Movement fostered black pride, black identity and black unity among black Americans. It also signaled to white America that blacks would now and in the future establish their own priorities and enter into the mainstream of the American society on their own terms.

Soul Music And American Popular Culture

In December, 1968,
...soul singer James Brown, 35, became the first black man in the 30 year history of *Cash Box* to be cited as the male vocalist on single pop records. For the uninitiated, "pop" means sales to the whole record-buying public, not simply in the predominantly Negro rhythm 'n' blues market....[25]

Brown's accomplishment established a precedent for other black performers. He was accepted on his own musical terms and did not alter his distinctive black style and dialect for inclusion and recognition in the popular music tradition. Although black music was subject to assimilation by white performers prior to the era of soul, the trend of the 1970s indicated that consumers of popular music were ready to listen to soul music played in its authentic form by black performers. Music critics credit the emergence of British musicians to be responsible for this change in attitude. Unlike earlier American white imitators and assimilators of black music, the Beatles and Rolling Stones[26] were the first to tell their audiences which Soul artists they were imitating—which led to the wider recognition of such greats as Chuck Berry, Muddy Waters, Little Richard, Don Covay, etc.[27]

With the advent of soul music, other British groups and individuals[28] attempted to acquire vocal and instrumental styles that characterized this music. In employing techniques associated with gospel singing, they incorporated the use of melismas and explored the potential of the entire voice. The blues and gospel traditions supplied them with a complimentary instrumental style. Soul music was the only available material that suited the vocal and instrumental techniques adopted by these British performers.[29]

The Vietnam protest of the 1960s also contributed to the change in musical taste of white Americans. In rejecting values and standards of the establishment, they increasingly turned to minority cultures for alternative lifestyles and values. This rebellion against establishment fostered the so-called "blues revival" which allowed many white Americans to hear blues and other contemporary forms of black music for the first time. Concerned promoters, local clubs and, later, universities engaged in a series of bookings of blues and soul performers. Artists such as Sam and Dave, the Staple Singers, Ike and Tina Turner, Aretha Franklin, Otis Redding, Sly and The Family Stone, Muddy Waters, Albert King, B.B. King, Jimmy Reed and many others appeared before predominantly white audiences at the Fillmores East and West, Central Park and large auditoriums and other parks throughout the country.[30] This trend even continues today under the bill of "Jazz Festivals" which are dominated by blues, soul and soul-based jazz artists.

This form of exposure to black artists, coupled with the popularity of British groups in America during the 1960s prompted American white groups to turn to soul and other forms of black music for their stylistic and musical resources. The Righteous Brothers, Boz Scaggs, the Rascals and Janis Joplin were among the many American whites to achieve fame from the use of black vocal and instrumental styles.[31] The imitation by white performers, and its international commercialization by record companies, gave soul music a new meaning by the 1970s. In the music industry, it was used to identify any performer—black or white—whose musical and performance style reflected influences of the blues or gospel idiom. The editors of *Billboard* magazine, in foreseeing that white Americans would eventually accept soul music in its authentic form and that larger numbers of white musicians would imitate its style, changed the magazine's chart heading from "rhythm & blues" to "soul." The editorial announcing this change reads:

> Beginning with this issue dated August 23, (1969), Billboard uses the designation "soul" in place of "rhythm and blues." The editorial department in making this change, is motivated by the fact that the term "soul" more properly embraces the broad range of song and instrumental material which derives from the musical genius of the black American.

> A valid music is dynamic. It changes and grows more complex with the years, even while it reflects root influences. Thus it is with soul music, a rich blend of Musical Americana incorporating in its ken many diverse influences from blues to gospel. The term, too, has relevance to a style of performances as well as to musical form.[31]

This change in chart titles called attention to a new style of black music that appealed to white musicians and, in general, members of American popular culture.

The impact soul music had on American popular culture was realized when disc jockeys of Top 40 stations began to program some of this music. They did so in an effort to retain that segment of their listening audience who began to tune in on soul stations. Between August 1968 and August 1969, "virtually every single making the top 20 on the R & B Chart was a 'Hot 100 Singles' Chart entry also, and a good many of these went to positions 50 or better."[33] By 1973, thirteen of the "Top 30 Artists" that were listed in *Billboard*'s Soul Charts were included in the "Top 30 Artists" category of "Top Pop Records." The influence of soul on the pop market was so great that major record companies who had never specialized in the "black sound" began to sign black artists to their roster. By 1979, Columbia records probably had retained the largest number of such performers. Warner Brothers, A & M, Epic, Mercury, Casablanca, ABC, Atlantic and Capitol also had many under contract.

The success of black artists in the white market provided the impetus for producers of record companies to contract and record white performers in a black style. Such practices have been the topic of heated debates among blacks because of economic and political implications. Recordings of these white performers received air play on both Soul and Top 40 radio stations. In addition, their recordings are promoted and sold in both communities. On the other hand, recordings of black performers receive air play on Top 40 stations only when program managers deem it absolutely necessary. Until recently, record outlets did not promote or sell recordings of black performers, whose style was distinctly black, in white communities. In view of these and other political trends, white performers reaped millions of dollars by imitating black artists and winning air play on Top 40 and black-oriented stations.[34] Chapple and Garofalo in their discussion on politics in the music industry attributed this practice to pervasive racism.[35]

In an effort for blacks to receive more recognition and financial rewards for their creative output, a non-profit Black Music Association (BMA) was formed in September, 1978, by black executives of the music industry. One of the organization's goals as expressed by its first vice-president, Jules Malamud,

> is to perpetuate and further black music on a national and international level, and...to work with schools and universities to bring blacks into music not only as performers, but also on the business end.[36]

In elaborating on these goals, co-founder and first President Kenny Gamble, chairman of Philadelphia International Records, stated:

In 1977, the music industry grossed more than $3.5 billion.... Approximately one-third of that gross volume was receipts on black music. If we want to reduce this issue purely to economics, the reality is that the industry has gotten fat off black music. It must not be exploited any longer. The world respects black music. It is time for the industry to respect black music.[37]

In view of the diverse forms of commercial music recorded by blacks and in a variety of black styles, BMA advocates replacing the term "soul" with the label "black music." Furthermore, the confusion regarding what styles and forms constitute soul music encouraged other blacks to endorse the proposed label substitution. The ambiguity surrounding the use of the term "soul music" resulted, in part, from the redefinition of the purpose, function and use of it. Its original message of self-awareness, protest and social change was transformed into quick dollars by the music industry. For white America, its beat, handclap, tambourine, language and musical style provided the ingredients for new forms of popular music. Black America's response to this exploitation of black music was the formation of the Black Music Association. The establishment of this association suggests that the philosophy promoted by leaders of the Black Power Movement continued to provide social, economic and political direction for black people throughout the 1970s.

Notes

[1] For a detailed account of philosophy, see Martin Luther King, *Why We Can't Wait* (New York: Signet Books, 1964).

[2] Stokely Carmichael and Charles V. Hamilton, *Black Power: The Politics of Liberation in America* (New York: Vintage Books, 1967), p. 47.

[3] For a detailed discussion about the philosophy of the Black Power Movement see Carmichael *Ibid.*, pp. 34-56.

[4] Talcott Parsons, "Full Citizenship For The Negro American? A Sociological Problem," *Daedalus: Journal of The American Academy of Arts and Sciences*, 94 (Fall 1965), p. 1016.

[5] Joel Whitburn, *Top Rhythm & Blues Records* 1949-1971 (Menomonee Falls, WI: Record Research, 1973), p. 5.

[6] For detailed information about this trend, see Steve Chapple and Reebee Garafalo, *Rock 'n' Roll Is Here To Pay* (Chicago: Nelson-Hall, 1977) and Lawrence Redd, *Rock Is Rhythm And Blues*, (Michigan State Univ. Press, 1974).

[7] Chapple, *Ibid.*, pp. 239-40.

[8] Charlie Gillett, *The Sound of The City* (New York: Outerbridge & Dienstfrey, 1970), p. 27.

[9] Gillett, *Ibid.*, pp. 15-20.

[10] Charles Gillett, "The Black Market Roots of Rock," in *The Sounds of Social Change*, eds., R. Serge Denisoff and Richard A. Peterson (Chicago: Rand McNally, 1972), p. 280.

[11] Lloyd Miller and James K. Skipper, Jr., "Sounds of Protest in Avant-Garde Jazz," in *Ibid.*, p. 28.

[12] Chapple, *Rock 'n' Roll Is Here To Pay*, pp. 231-267.

[13] William H. McClendon, "Black Music: Sound And Feeling For Black Liberation," *The Black Scholar*, 7 (Jan.-Feb. 1976), p. 23.

[14] Michael Haralambos, *Right On From Blues To Soul In Black America* (New York: Drake, 1975), p. 130.

[15] Ira Hoare, ed., *The Soul Book* (New York: Dell, 1976), p. 10.

[16] Arnold Shaw, *The World of Soul* (New York: Cowles Book Co., 1970), pp. 2-4.

[17] *Gillett*, The Sound of the City, pp. 24, 188.

[18] Haralambos, *Right On...*, p. 117.

[19] Haralambos, *Ibid.*, pp. 131-134; Phyl Garland, *The Sound of Soul* (Chicago: Henry Regnery, 1969), pp. 18-20.

[20] Thomas Barry, "The Importance of Being Mr. James Brown," *Look*, Feb. 18, 1969, pp. 56-62.

[21] Shaw, *The World of Soul*, p. 256.

[22] Such performers include: Impressions—"We're A Winner" (1968) and "This Is My Country" (1968); Marvin Gaye—"Inner City Blues" (1971); Staple Singers—"Respect Yourself" (1971) and "Be What You Are" (1973); Gladys Knight and The Pips—"Friendship Train" (1969); O'Jays— "Back Stabbers" (1972), and "Love Train" (1973), "Sly and the Family Stone," "Thank You For Talkin' To Me Africa" (1971), "Africa Talks To You" (1971) and "The Asphalt Jungle" (1971); Temptations—"Cloud Nine" (1968); Diana Ross and The Supremes—"Love Child" (1968).

[23] Haralambos, *Right On...*, p. 166.

[24] *Ibid.*, p. 117.

[25] Barry, "The Importance of Being Mr. James Brown," p. 56.

[26] The Animals, Fame and cream also attributed their early influences to black performers. David Bowie and Joe Cocker acknowledge black influences on their current style.

[27] Sue C. Clark, "Soul Sounds In The Mass Market Place," *Billboard*, (Sect. 2) "The World of Soul," August 16, 1968, p. S-6. The English groups were also the first to provide mass and consistent exposure to black artists by including them on their concert tours.

[28] These groups include performers John Lennon, Joe Cocker, Stevie Winwood, Mick Jagger, Roger Daltrey, Eric Burdon, Stevie Marriott, Rod Stewart, Tom Jones and Davie Bowie.

[29] Hoare, ed. *The Soul Book*, pp. 191-92.

[30] Clark, "Soul Sounds In The Mass Market Place," pp. S-6—S-8.

[31] Hoare, ed. *The Soul Book*, p. 194.

[32] *Billboard Magazine* (August 23, 1969), p. 3.

[33] Ira Trachter, "Soul Trends—The Widening Of Its Audience Into Pop," *Billboard* (Sect.2) "The World of Soul" Aug. 16, 1968, p. S-8.

[34] Ronald Kisner, "White Stars Cross Over And Get Rich On Black Music," *Jet*, April 13, 1978, p. 14.

[35] Chapple, *Rock 'n' Roll Is Here To Pay*.

[36] *Billboard Magazine*, May 27, 1978, p. 3.

[37] *Billboard Magazine*, Sept 23, 1978, p. 3.

"If Ya Wanna End War and Stuff, You Gotta Sing Loud"— A Survey of Vietnam-Related Protest Music

H. Ben Auslander

Rock music came of age in the sixties. Outgrowing its childhood of simple four chord progressions and inane lyrics, rock evolved into a complex art form that affected the lives of millions, simultaneously reflecting and shaping their political and social attitudes. Much has been written about the maturing of rock, but one area that has curiously been ignored is the study of protest music of the sixties, especially that directed against the war in Vietnam. A possible explanation of this neglect may lie in the difficulty of sorting Vietnamese-related material from general social protest music, the two genres being so inextricably intertwined. If one accepts as one's research criterion examining only those songs directly related to Vietnam, many important songs may be overlooked. On the other hand, to include all protest music of the period would be to obscure the significance of songs directly related to the war. A middle approach, then, one including material directly concerning the American involvement in Vietnam and also those songs depicting the side-effects of that involvement, would seem to be the best means of assessing the genre.

The roots of anti-Vietnam protest music can be traced back to those folksingers involved in the Civil Rights and nuclear disarmament movements of the late fifties and early sixties. Faced with the often violent reactions to civil rights demonstrations and the continual threat of thermonuclear annihilation by the Soviet Union, folk artists such as Bob Dylan, Joan Baez, Phil Ochs, Malvina Reynolds, Peter Yarrow, Paul Stokey and Mary Travers alike took firm stands for racial brotherhood and international peace. It was neither difficult nor unexpected, then, for such artists to shift the emphasis of their messages from "Stop oppressing our black brothers," to "Stop oppressing our yellow brothers," and from "Ban the bomb," to "Stop the war in which we'll probably use the bomb," as the American involvement in Southeast Asia intensified.

Reprinted with permission from *Journal of American Culture* Volume 4:2 (1981), pp. 108-13.

Phil Ochs' "Talkin' Vietnam Blues" has the distinction of being the first protest song to directly refer to Vietnam by name. The release date of that song is of particular note—April 1964, a full four months before the Gulf of Tonkin incident and the first major escalation of the American presence in Vietnam. Whether Ochs was mystically prescient or simply an excellent socio-political prognosticator is irrelevant; one should note, however, that rather than reflecting or attempting to direct public opinion, Ochs consistently seemed to second-guess it throughout his career.

Ochs' second album, released in February 1965, included two songs directed against the Selective Service that were both to become classics of the Draft Resistance movement: "The Draft Dodger Rag" and the album's title song, "I Ain't Marchin' Anymore." As draft quotas rose throughout the year, Ochs' outspoken anti-draft attitudes came to be shared by more and more potential draftees.

1965 was also the year of one of the decade's most controversial Top Forty hits, "Eve of Destruction." Released less than a month after the triumph of Gemini 4, the song included lyrics such as, "You may leave here for four days in space/But when you return it's the same old place." The singer-songwriter, Barry McGuire (another folksinger, formerly lead vocalist for the New Christie Minstrels), and his songs were immediately lambasted by the news media for expressing excessive pessimism, and the song was subsequently denied airplay on many radio stations. While attracting far less attention, "The War Drags on," by the English folksinger Donovan was also released during 1965, an event significant in that it marked the first time American listeners were exposed to criticism of the war from a non-American artist.

By 1966 America's involvement in Vietnam was no longer a peripheral issue for rock music's listeners. Rising troop commitments, rising casualty figures, and rising draft quotas all contributed to the growing anti-war sentiment of the young. The youthful "counterculture" became increasingly disaffected with and alienated from the "establishment" of American culture, and that schismatic tension was forcefully represented in several of the year's songs. Once again Phil Ochs expressed the feelings of many with his satiric songs "I'm Going to Say It Now" and "Love Me, I'm a Liberal," while the Fugs (charter members of rock and roll's lunatic fringe) pushed humor to the limit with their song "Kill for Peace." In sharp contrast to the Fugs' technique of aesthetic overkill, Simon and Garfunkel released two quiet anti-war songs, "Seven O'clock News/Silent Night" (juxtaposing the well-known Christmas carol with the narration of a topical and depressing news broadcast) and "Scarborough Fair/Canticle" (whose anti-war message was so subtlety presented that many never realized they were listening to a protest song). As troop commitments and troop ceiling figures increased, so did rock's attention to the war.

In terms of both the number of songs recorded and the artistic expressiveness of those songs, 1967 was decidedly the peak year for Vietnam-related protest music, and in the autumn of that year, public attention was concentrated on protest songs and singers like never before. The public's attention was first

A Survey of Vietnam-Related Protest Music 181

focused on the genre when CBS television executives banned folksinger Pete Seeger from performing his anti-war allegory, "Waist Deep in the Big Muddy," on a September *Smothers Brothers Comedy Hour* broadcast. The executives held to their position that the song's reference to the "big fool" (i.e. Lyndon Johnson) was disrespectful and should not be broadcast on a prime time show, then finally caved in under charges of censorship and allowed Seeger's performance.

During that same September Joan Baez's latest album, *Joan*, was receiving a good deal of attention, in part for the song "Saigon Bride." As if to counter charges that protest music was nothing more than noisy rock and roll, Baez co-wrote and recorded this gently poetic ballad about an American soldier bidding farewell to his Vietnamese wife as he leaves to fight in the jungles. Arlo Guthrie, son of the famous folksinger Woody Guthrie, also came into the public spotlight that month with the release of his first album, *Alice's Restaurant*, including the enormously popular monologue, "The Alice's Restaurant Massacree." Guthrie's humorous burlesque of the judicial system, the Selective Service, and the military establishment won him instant acceptance with the anti-war movement, but neither that movement nor the singer himself was spared a few stinging remarks (best expressed, perhaps, in a remark to his audience after an unsuccessful attempt at an audience sing-along—"If ya wanna end war and stuff, you gotta sing loud"). The month's activity was capped by the release of Peter, Paul and Mary's "The Great Mandala (The Wheel of Life)," a hagiographic account of a draft resister's life and death. Two months later, Country Joe and the Fish's song, "The I-Feel-Like-I'm-Fixin'-To-Die Rag," was released, providing the late sixties' anti-war demonstrators with an unofficial marching song.

Until 1968 the growth and popularity of protest music closely paralleled escalation of American involvement in Vietnam, then unexpectedly its intensity began to wane while the war's continued to increase. The number of anti-war songs recorded declined and those that were released lacked the immediacy and forcefulness of their predecessors. One explanation may be that performers and audiences alike were physically and spiritually exhausted by the war against the war and simply did not want to be reminded of the conflict any more than was necessary. Another possible reason may be that many shared the sense of manic resignation expressed by Phil Ochs in his last anti-Vietnam song, "The War is Over."

Whatever the cause, protest music declined as the sixties ended and the seventies began. Apart from Joni Mitchell's "The Fiddle and the Drum," 1969 was an aesthetically lean year for protest music. By the time of the Kent State University murders by National Guardsmen in May 1970, the anti-Vietnam song genre was effectively dead. The last Vietnam-related protest song, Neil Young's "Ohio" (recorded by Crosby, Stills, Nash, and Young and released as a single during the summer of 1970), commemorated the four murder victims and simultaneously provided an epitaph for the entire anti-Vietnam peace movement.

Disregarding chronology (see Appendix A) and looking at the body of Vietnam-related protest music as a whole, one can readily discern several major categories of songs. First are those songs that are general in their condemnation of war. This group includes such compositions as "Masters of War," "One More Parade," "Scarborough Fair/Canticle," "The Universal Soldier," "The Great Mandala (The Wheel of Life)," "The Unknown Soldier," "Minstrel" and "Rejoyce." Second are those which specifically refer to the war in Vietnam: "Talkin' Vietnam Blues," "Lyndon Johnson Told the Nation," "The War Drags On," "Waist Deep in the Big Muddy," "Saigon Bride," "The Alice's Restaurant Massacree," "The I-Feel-Like-I'm-Fixin'-To-Die Rag," "The War is Over," "White Boots Marchin' in a Yellow Land," "American Eagle Tragedy" and "Ohio" may all be included in this category. Third are those songs that are directed against the Selective Service, including "I Ain't Marchin' Anymore," "The Draft Dodger Rag," "The Alice's Restaurant Massacree," "The Great Mandala," and "To Susan on the West Coast Waiting."

Viewed from another perspective, the songs also reveal many of the attitudes and emotions felt by performers and audiences of the period. "What Have They Done to the Rain?" "Masters of War," "Eve of Destruction," "The War Drags on," "Requiem for the Masses," all express the same fear of sudden and unprovoked personal destruction by impersonal forces. Skepticism concerning "the American way" and calls for re-evaluation of the "American dream" underlie such songs as "I'm Going to Say it Now," "Love Me, I'm a Liberal," "The Universal Soldier," "For What It's Worth" (note: while not written about Vietnam protest, the intent of this song's description of the 1966 Sunset Strip riots is nearly identical to other Vietnam-related material), "The War is Over," "The Fiddle and the Drum," "Give Peace a Chance," "Chicago" and "Ohio." In response to the active militarism guiding U.S. foreign policy throughout the sixties, a domestic attitude of militant pacifism evolved in many of the young, an attitude expressed in songs like "I Ain't Marchin' Anymore" and many of the others discussed here. A few songs, most notably "We Can Be Together" and "Volunteers" even went so far as open calls to arms, urging the young to take to the streets and seize power before their elders destroyed the world.

Given the large body of Vietnam-related material, it is to be expected that a wide range of rhetorical devices were employed in the songs' lyrics to convey their anti-war messages, yet three (by virtue of their prevalence) are worthy of special mention. In those songs leveling political criticism against American involvement in Vietnam, satire and humor were frequently utilized, as in "Talkin' Vietnam Blues," "Lyndon Johnson Told the Nation," "Kill for Peace," "The Draft Dodger Rag," "Love Me, I'm a Liberal," "War Song," "The Alice's Restaurant Massacree," and "The I-Feel-Like-I'm-Fixin'-to-Die Rag." Such songs as "Seven O'Clock News/Silent Night," "Requiem for the Masses," "The Great Mandala," and "Sky Pilot" relied on religious allusions to focus attention on the moral issues involved in the war and the homefront effects of that conflict. Finally, the device of ironic juxtaposition was occasionally employed, setting harsh or cynical lyrics about the war against a beautiful melodic score, as in songs such as "Seven O'Clock News/Silent Night," "Scarborough Fair/Canticle," "Saigon Bride," "The Great Mandala" and "The Fiddle and the Drum."

Like the decade in which they were written and recorded, protest songs concerning the American involvement in Vietnam and the subsidiary effects of that involvement defy easy categorization. Many fall simultaneously into several classifications while others fit into none at all. Musically the songs ranged from beautifully melodic to jarringly dissonant, lyrically from idealistic to cynical. While their study is unlikely to provide the ultimate key to unraveling the enigma that was the sixties in America, the songs and their lyrics do chronicle many of the ideals and attitudes held by America's youth during the Vietnam war years, and as such should be included in popular culture studies of the decade.

APPENDIX B: A DISCOGRAPHY OF
VIETNAM-RELATED PROTEST SONGS

SONG TITLE	ARTIST	ALBUM	RELEASE DATE
"What Have They Done to the Rain?"	Malvina Reynolds	?	1963
"Masters of War"	Bob Dylan	the Free-wheelin' Bob Dylan	1963
"One More Parade"	Phil Ochs	All the News That's Fit To Sing	Apr. 1964
"Talkin' Vietnam Blues"	Phil Ochs	All the News That's Fit To Sing	Apr. 1964
"Lyndon Johnson Told the Nation"	Tom Paxton	?	1965
"I Ain't Marchin' Anymore"	Phil Ochs	I Ain't Marchin' Anymore	Feb. 1965
"The Draft Dodger Rag"	Phil Ochs	I Ain't Marchin' Anymore	Feb. 1965
"Eve of Destruction"	Barry McGuire	Eve of Destruction	July 1965
"The War Drags On"	Donovan	Catch the Wind	Dec. 1965
"Kill for Peace"	the Fugs	The Fugs	1966
"I'm Going to Say It Now"	Phil Ochs	In Concert	Feb. 1966
"Love Me, I'm a Liberal"	Phil Ochs	In Concert	Feb. 1966
"Seven O'clock News/ Silent Night"	Simon & Garfunkel	Parsley, Sage, Rosemary, & Thyme	Sept. 1966
"Scarborough Fair/Canticle"	Simon & Garfunkel	Parsley, Sage, Rosemary, & Thyme	Sept. 1966
"The Universal Soldier"	Donovan	Fairy Tale	Dec. 1966
"War Song"	the Fugs	Tenderness Junction	1967

Song	Artist	Album	Date
"For What It's Worth"	Buffalo Springfield	Buffalo Springfield	Feb. 1967
"Waist Deep in the Big Muddy"	Pete Seeger	Waist Deep in the Big Muddy	June 1967
"Requiem for the Masses"	the Association	Insight Out	Aug. 1967
"Saigon Bride"	Joan Baez	Joan	Aug. 1967
"The Alice's Restaurant Massacree"	Arlo Guthrie	Alice's Restaurant	Sept. 1967
"The Great Mandala (The Wheel of Life)"	Peter, Paul, & Mary	Album 1700	Sept. 1967
"The Dolphin"	Kenny Rankin	Mind Dusters	Nov. 1967
"The I-Feel-Like-I'm-Fixin'-To-Die Rag"	Country Joe and the Fish	I-Feel-Like-I'm-Fixin'-To-Die	Nov. 1967
"Rejoyce"	the Jefferson Airplane	After Bathing at Baxter's	Jan. 1968
"Sky Pilot"	the Animals	the Twain Shall Meet	May 1968
"The War is Over"	Phil Ochs	Tape from California	June 1968
"White Boots Marching in a Yellow Land"	Phil Ochs	Tape from California	June 1968
"The Unknown Soldier"	the Doors	Waiting for the Sun	July 1968
"The American Eagle Tragedy"	Earth Opera	The Great American Eagle Tragedy	Mar. 1969
"The Fiddle and the Drum"	Joni Mitchell	Clouds	Apr. 1969
"Give Peace a Chance"	the Plastic Ono Band	Live Peace in Toronto	June 1969
"To Susan on the West Coast Waiting"	Donovan	Barabajagal	July 1969
"We Can Be Together"	the Jefferson Airplane	Volunteers	Oct. 1969
"Volunteers"	the Jefferson Airplane	Volunteers	Oct. 1969
"Minstrel"	Richie Havens	Stonehenge	Mar. 1970
"Ball of Confusion"	the Temptations	(single)	June 1970
"Chicago"	Crosby, Stills, Nash, & Young	(single)	July 1970
"Ohio"	Crosby, Stills, Nash, & Young	(single)	July 1970

Sex Role Standards in Popular Music

Kathleen L. Endres

Recent research has focused on the sex-role standards portrayed in various elements of the mass media. Reacting to the American woman's movement criticism of traditional sex-role standards, researchers have scrutinized such elements of the mass media as television programming, films, comic books and fiction.[1]

Popular music seems to have escaped the systematic scrutiny of researchers. On the whole, discussions of the image of women in popular music have been impressionistic. In one such study, Marion Meade in "Does Rock Degrade Women?" concludes, "Rock music, in fact the entire rock 'culture,' is tremendously degrading to women."

The clearest indication of how rock music views womanhood is in its lyrics. Women certainly can't complain that the image presented there is one-dimensional. On the contrary, the putdowns are remarkably multifaceted, ranging from open contempt to sugar-coated condescension. Above all, however, women are always-available sexual objects whose chief function is to happily accommodate any man who comes along.[2]

This study sought to answer the question: What are the sex-role standards projected in the lyrics of popular music? Jerome Kagan, in "Acquisition and significance of Sex Typing and Sex Role Identity," determined a sex role standard as "...a learned association between selected attributes, behaviors and attributes, on the one hand, and the concepts of male and female, on the other."[3]

In order to gauge the sex-role standards portrayed in popular music, the author examined the attributes, behaviors and attitude of the males and females discussed in the lyrics of popular songs. In addition, the researcher examined the popular music in three different periods to discover if the attributes, behaviors and attitudes of the men and women figuring in the lyrics had been affected by the woman's movement and/or other factors in society.

The popular music of three time periods—1960, 1970 and 1980—was chosen for examination: 1960 because it preceded by three years the publication of Betty Friedan's *Feminine Mystique*, which has been credited by some historians as signalling the beginning of the current women's movement;[4] 1970 because

Reprinted with permission from *Journal of Popular Culture*, Volume 18:1 (Summer, 1984), pp. 9-18.

it followed Friedan's book and also because it allowed seven years to pass to give the woman's movement time to have had some effect on popular music; 1980 because, first, it was an election year and such "women's" issues as the Equal Rights Amendment and abortion figured prominently in the presidential campaign, and, second, because the year was the most current complete year for analysis.

A sample of 12 songs from each of the periods was taken from the record industry's trade publication, *Billboard* magazine. Each song was rated number one by the magazine in its "Hot 100s" during the first week of each month.[5]

In the 36 songs studied, the majority of the vocalists were men. In 1960 and 1970, 75 percent (nine) of the singers were either male singles or male groups.

Chart 1
Sex of Singers

	1960	1970	1980	Total
Male Single	7	3	3	13
Male group	2	6	4	12
Female single	3	1	3	7
Female group	0	0	0	0
Mixed male-female group	0	2	2	4

By 1980 that number had decreased to 58 percent (seven). In 1960 and 1980, three female vocalists (25 percent) recorded the number one songs studied. In 1970, however, only one female vocalist (Diana Ross) recorded the number one song examined.

These results should be considered in conjunction with another finding. Thirty-four of the 36 songs studied were written in the first person singular. In other words, men and women were singing about themselves and their relationships with members of the opposite sex. The male preponderance in popular songs, coupled with the fact that the majority of the songs were written in the first person singular, means that the presentation of both males and females is from a masculine perspective, a fact of key importance in understanding the sex-role standards presented in the popular music of each of the three periods.

In the majority of the songs studied, women seldom initiated the action. They were normally characterized as passive figures—important to the plot of the song but seldom active. Over the three periods studied, passive females outnumbered passive males four to one. In contrast, active males outnumbered active females by the same margin (see charts two and three).

Chart 2
Male Roles in Popular Music

Year	Passive		Active		Other		Total
	N	%	N	%	N	%	
1960	1	8	10	83	1	8	12
1970	2	17	5	42	5	42	12
1980	2	17	7	58	3	25	12

Chart 3
Female Roles in Popular Music

Year	Passive		Active		Other		Total
	N	%	N	%	N	%	
1960	10	91	1	9	0	0	11*
1970	5	45	1	9	5	45	11*
1980	5	42	3	25	4	3	12*

As chart three indicates, in 1960 only one female discussed in a song's lyrics was active and this particular song ("My Heart Has a Heart of Its Own") was recorded by a woman. In 1970 only one song had what the coders perceived as an active female figure. Again, this song ("Ain't No Mountain High Enough") was recorded by a woman. In 1980 three women were "active" figures and two of these songs were recorded by women. The other song with an active female was recorded by a mixed male-female group with a lead woman vocalist.

In contrast, songs recorded by males usually included women who were passive figures. In 1960, for example, the male singers invariably presented passive female major figures although two of the three songs recorded by women also presented passive female figures. In 1970, each of the songs presenting passive females was recorded by a male. In 1980 all but one of the songs portraying women as passive figures were recorded by men; the other recording artist was a woman.

As chart three indicates, fewer women in the 1980 songs were grouped in the passive category than in 1960. However, the passive female figure remains a major role assigned to women in popular lyrics. Certainly one explanation has to be the continuing domination of male recording artists.

In all three periods, the most popular subject discussed in the songs was emotion—or more specifically love. The majority of the men and women discussed were involved in some phase of a love relationship. And it is that which is the background for most of the attitudes, attributes and behavior of both men and women. Women's roles, however, have changed from 1960 to 1980. In 1960, women were most frequently portrayed as objects of unrequited love (4 or 33 percent). Women were unable to spurn their male admirers. As Bobby Rydell so aptly insisted in "Wild One":

> Oh, Wild One, I'm gonna tame you down.
> Oh, Wild One, I'll get you yet, you bet.

In another chorus, Rydell promises:

> Oh, Wild One, I'll clip your wings and things.[7]

---

*Two songs were not included because of lack of agreement on women's role among coders.

In the three 1960 songs in which women are part of the continuing love relationship, the male is clearly the dominant figure. Elvis Presley in "It's Now or Never" best exemplifies this theme:

> It's now or never.
> Come hold me tight.
> Kiss me, my darling.
> Be mine tonight.
> Tomorrow will be too late.
> It's now or never.
> My love won't wait.[8]

In the three 1960 songs, the love relationship had been ended by the man. Each of these songs was performed by female vocalists. In the two songs in which women ended the love relationship, females were presented in an insensitive, negative light. Again, Presley, this time in "Are You Lonesome Tonight?" shows this trend clearly by detailing the deception of the woman he loves:

> Honey, you lied when you said you loved me,
> And I had no cause to doubt you.
> But I'd rather go on hearing your lies than
>   to go on living without you.[9]

By 1980 women were taking a more active role in the love relationship. In 1960 and 1970 no woman sought a love relationship. By 1980, however, women in three songs openly solicited male companionship. The type of relationship varied from an evening's entertainment with a gigolo to a more lasting love. In "Call Me," Blondie sings the theme song from the movie *American Gigolo:*

> Cover me with kisses, baby,
> Cover me with love.
> Roll me in designer sheets,
> I'll never get enough.[10]

Another woman searching for a love relationship is Barbra Streisand in "Woman in Love," who will "do anything to get you into my world/And hold you within."[11]

Even as part of the continuing love relationship, women in certain 1980 songs assumed the dominant role. Olivia Newton-John in "Magic" is the bold, yet sensitive, leader in the relationship. As she calms her lover:

> Come to me, my pet, you should know me.
> I've always been in your mind.
> You know I will be kind, I'll be guidin' you.
> Believe your dream has to start now.
> There's no other road to take.

You won't make a mistake, I'll be guidin' you.[12]

The personality characteristics of the men and women in the lyrics did change over time. In 20 of the 30 songs examined, men and women displayed statistically significant differences in their personality characteristics in 1960 and 1970. By 1980, however, not one of the personality characteristics was significantly different between the sexes. Table 1 illustrates how males compared to females in 1960 on each of the 30 items. Table 2 shows the comparison in 1970 and Table 3 shows the findings for 1980. Table 4 details those 20 items where differences between the sexes were found to be statistically significant.

As can be seen in Table 1 men in 1960 were assigned action-related characteristics. Ambitious, competitive, adventurous and aggressive, these men possessed many of the traits commonly associated with the American frontier and its heritage of individualism and independence. On the other hand, women were assigned the passive, less daring roles. They were weak and dependent on their men. Women in the 1960 songs reacted to the actions of the men and seldom initiated any activity. Presley and Connie Francis, two of the most popular recording artists of the day, best illustrate these characteristics.

In "Stuck on You," Presley is the action figure, deciding that he wants the woman—whether she likes it or not. Presley is so confidant of his abilities to win his lady, he asserts:

> Hide in the kitchen, hide in the hall.
> Ain't gonna do you no good at all.
> 'Cause once I catch you and the kissin' starts,
> A team of horses couldn't tear us apart.[13]

In this song, the man scored high in ambition, competitiveness, decision-making, dominance and boldness. The woman, in contrast, was a weak, passive figure who was helpless to thwart the man's intentions.

Another weak, dependent woman was Connie Francis in "Everybody's Somebody's Fool." Despite the man's insensitivity, Francis cannot and will not forget him. No matter how many tears she cries, she "couldn't bring myself to say goodbye."[14]

The 1970 males, like their older brothers of 1960, possessed many action-packed characteristics but other attributes added new dimensions to their personalities. Like the 1960 males, the 1970 men were adventuresome, aggressive, dominant and self-confident. Not only were they knowledgeable but intelligent as well. The action characteristics, however, were softened by helpfulness, kindness, sensitivity and responsibility. These characteristics had also been present in the 1960 males but not strongly enough to make the differences in the scores between the sexes statistically significant. Part of the explanation for the emergence of these particular characteristics as significantly different from females in 1970 may be explained by the sex of the singers. Only one female vocalist recorded a song examined in 1970. In 1960, three females recorded songs analyzed. In each of these songs, women were as sensitive, kind and

American Popular Music

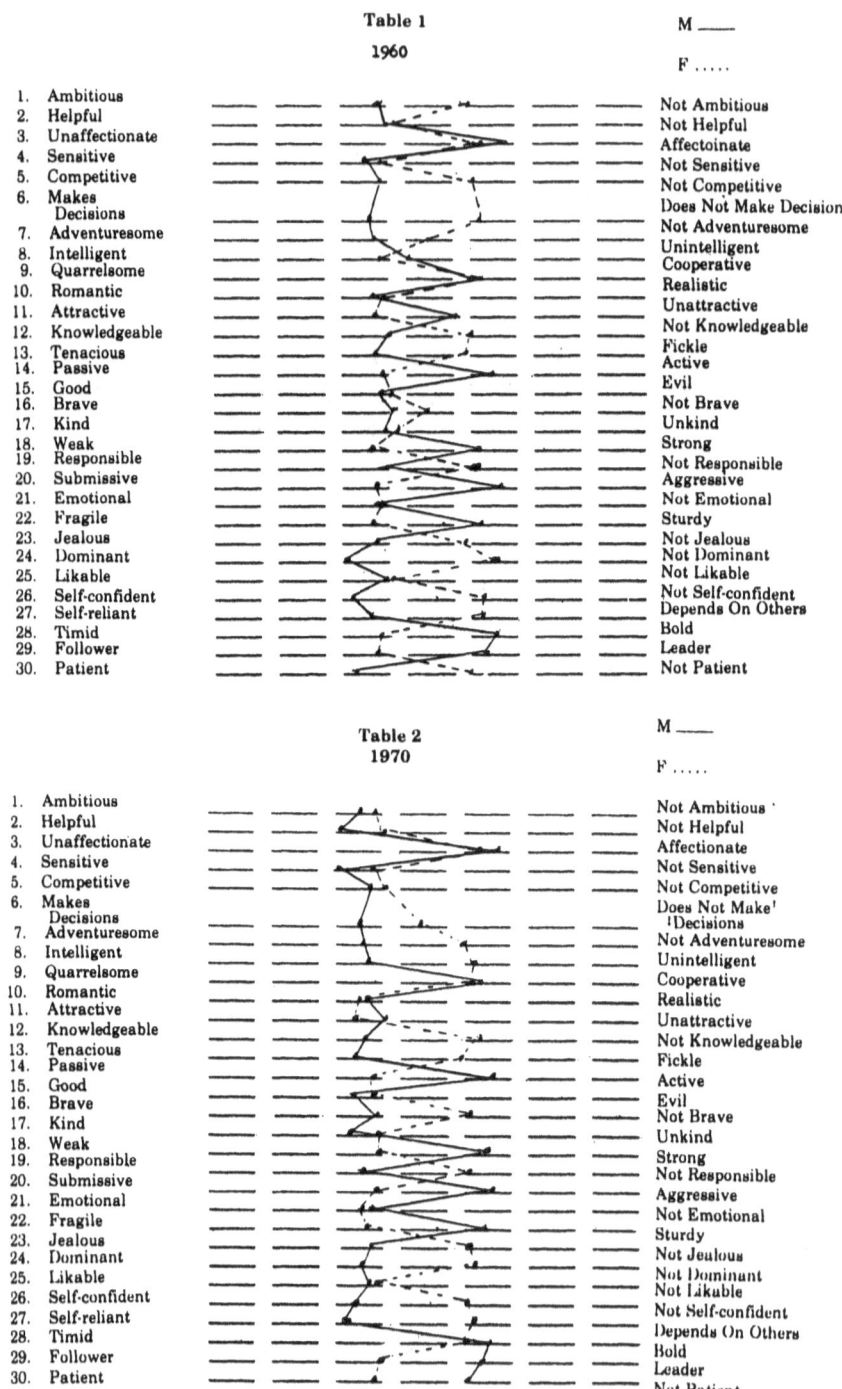

Sex Role Standards in Popular Music 191

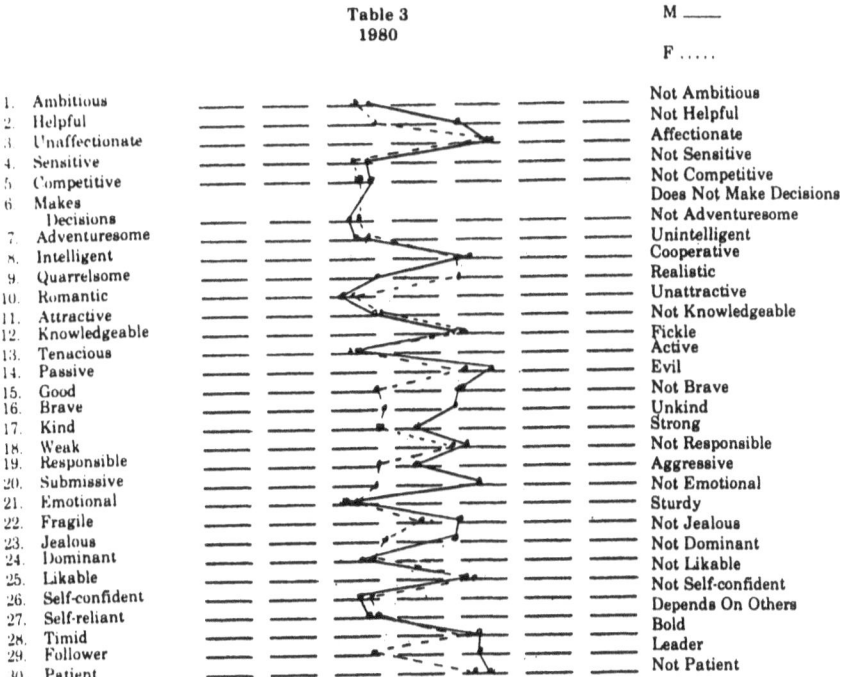

Table 3
1980

helpful as the men. The input of these women in the 1960 songs, again, did make a difference.

The hero—a male—in "Bridge Over Troubled Waters" is sensitive to the plight of his friend and represents a safe harbor from the troubles of the world. He will "take your part, when darkness comes,/And pain is all round."[15] Just as accommodating are the Jackson Five in "I'll Be There." The hero, again a man, offers protection and strength to the woman who, presumably, needs both:

> Whenever you need me, I'll be there, I'll be there.
> I'll be there to protect you, baby,
> With an unselfish love and respect you.[16]

It is in these kinds of songs that male singers ascribe to themselves—and their male characters—the sensitivity, kindness and helpfulness that become so strong in 1970. Women, according to this interpretation, somehow fumble along until sensitive—yet strong—men lead them in the right direction, a direction which is male-defined.

In contrast, the third song was recorded by a woman and presents a different picture of the woman. In "Ain't No Mountain High Enough," the woman is the helpful, sensitive, kind and responsible one. Diana Ross will risk any danger to get to her man who has left to seek his fortune:

Table 4
Significantly Different Characteristics

Male Characteristics	1960	1970	1980	Female Characteristics
1. Ambitious	p<.05	n.s.	n.s.	Not Ambitious
2. Helpful	n.s.	p<.01	n.s.	Not Helpful
4. Sensitive	n.s.	p<.02	n.s.	Not Sensitive
5. Competitive	p<.02	n.s.	n.s.	Not Competitive
6. Makes Decisions	p<.05	n.s.	n.s.	Does Not Make Decisions
7. Adventuresome	p<.05	p<.05	n.s.	Not Adventuresome
8. Intelligent	n.s.	p<.05	n.s.	Not Intelligent
12. Knowledgeable	p<.01	p<.01	n.s.	Not Knowledgeable
14. Active	n.s.	p<.05	n.s.	Passive
17. Kind	n.s.	p<.05	n.s.	Not Kind
19. Responsible	n.s.	p<.01	n.s.	Not Responsible
20. Aggressive	p<.01	p<.02	n.s.	Submissive
22. Sturdy	n.s.	p<.01	n.s.	Weak
24. Dominant	p<.01	p<.05	n.s.	Not Dominant
26. Self-confident	p<.01	p<.02	n.s.	Not Self-confident
27. Self-reliant	n.s.	p<.01	n.s.	Depends On Others
28. Bold	p<.02	n.s.	n.s.	Timid
29. Leader	p<.05	n.s.	n.s.	Follower
30. Not Patient	p<.05	n.s.	n.s.	Patient

> If you need me, call me.
> No matter where you are; no matter how far.
> Just call my name, I'll be there in a hurry.
> On that you can depend and never worry.

She concludes that no mountain is too high, no valley too low, no river too wide to keep her away.[17]

By 1980, however, things seem to be changing in the lyrics. None of the personality traits between the sexes is statistically significant. Beyond statistical significance, however, women seem to be asserting a more active personality. For the first time, women are more ambitious and competitive than men. Men continued to be stronger, more active and more dominant but women for the first time asserted characteristics of strength, activity and dominance. Men were more self-confident and self-reliant but women were gaining similar characteristics. Men, however, continued to be the aggressive leaders while women were coded as the submissive followers but the differences between the sexes were not large enough to be statistically significant. In a major shift from 1970, women were more sensitive and kinder than the men, although not enough to be statistically significant.

Three 1980 songs illustrate the diversity of approaches to women in the lyrics of popular music. The traditional sex-role standards may be seen in Michael Jackson's "Rock With You." Continuing the trends seen in 1960 and 1970, the male in this song scored high in the action-related characteristics of decision-making, strength, self confidence, self-reliance, leadership and boldness. In contrast, the woman is the passive follower, depending on others. Moreover the man is more sensitive, romantic and affectionate than his female companion. He tells her "Don't try to fight it." She should "Relax your mind. Lay back and groove with me."[18]

In sharp contrast is Olivia Newton-John in "Magic," who assumes the dominant role and says to the male, "Through every turn, I'll be near you/ Come anytime you call/And catch you when you fall./I'll be guidin' you."[19]

Between these two extremes is Kenny Rogers' "Lady." In this song, the man and woman share similar personality characteristics. Both make decisions; both are self-confident and self-reliant; both score the same in leadership; and both are affectionate and sensitive. Even though his "lady" has left him, Rogers pleads: "Lady, your love's the only one I need,/And beside me is where I want you to be."[20]

In these songs during these three decades, then, two elements appear to be the most important in determining the sex-role standard projection in popular music. First, male singers continue to predominate in the popular music industry. Second, songs are usually written in the first person singular. Male predominance in the industry coupled with the first person single approach to the music means that the sex-role standards are usually male defined.

This meant in 1960 that songs presented traditional sex-role standards. Males were active; females passive. Men were the leaders, were also sensitive, helpful and kind. By 1980 adolescents did not receive such a clear-cut message. There were not statistically significant differences in the personality characteristics between the sexes.

If these findings are indicative of trends developing in popular music, it would appear that in the future males and females will be portrayed in less traditional—and more diverse—roles than before. Certainly part of the explanation of this change has to stem from the sex of the recording artists studied in 1980. Only seven, or slightly more than half of the recording stars, were male.

Another part of the explanation may be audience preference. While other factors may also be important, it appears that changes in the portrayal of men and women in popular music in 1980 is also a product of buyer demand. As noted, the sample for this study was drawn from the best-selling records of that year. Thus, listeners, who were buying records for any number of reasons including the "beat," singer or peer pressure, were still hearing lyrics which offered a greater variety of roles for men and women. Such was not the pattern in 1960 and 1970. In those two years, record buyers turned to songs and singers that showed traditional sex roles. By 1980, such was not the case. Whether listeners purchased records for the lyrics alone or for any number of reasons, they still bought records which, perhaps, mirrored changes in American society. These changes may stem, at least in part, from women's great involvement in American economic, political and social life.

Notes

[1] See, for example, Mildred Downing, "Heroine of the Daytime Serial," *Journal of Communication*, 24 (1874), pp. 130-137; John F. Seegar, "Imagery of Women in Television Drama: 1974," *Journal of Broadcasting*, 19 (1975), pp. 273-281; Nancy Tedesco, "Patterns in Prime Time," *Journal of Communication*, 24 (1974), pp. 119-124; Joseph Turow, "Advising and Ordering: Daytime, Prime Time," *Journal of Communication*, 24 (1974), pp. 138-141; and Linda Busby, "Defining the Sex-Role Standard in Network Children's Programs," *Journalism Quarterly*, 51 (1974), pp. 690-694.

[2] New York *Times*, March 14, 1971.

[3] In *Review of Child Development Research*, edited by Martin L. Hoffman and Lois W. Hoffman (New York: Russell Sage Foundation, 1964), p. 138.

[4] According to William H. Chafe in *The American Woman: Her Changing Social, Economic and Political Roles*, 1920-1970 (New York: Oxford Univ. Press, 1972), p. 227, the *Feminine Mystique* sounded the ideological keynote of the feminist revival.

[5] Should the number one record be an instrumental or a repeat of the previous month, the number two song was included.

[6] Characteristics based, in part, on Busby's study, "Defining the Sex-Role Standard in Network Children's Programs," op. cit. In her study, she noted that these items "reveal general personality traits" or "are traits that researchers have found to be uniquely associated with males and females, respectively, in American society.

[7]"Wild One," as recorded by Bobby Rydell on the Cameo Label.
[8]"It's Now Or Never," as recorded by Elvis Presley on the Victor Label.
[9]"Are You Lonesome Tonight?" as recorded by Presley on the Victor Label.
[10]"Call Me," as recorded by Blondie on the Chrysalis Label.
[11]"Woman in Love," as recorded by Barbra Streisand on the Columbia Label.
[12]"Magic," as recorded by Olivia Newton-John on the MGM Label.
[13]"Stuck on You," as recorded by Presley on the Victor Label.
[14]"Everybody's Somebody's Fool," as recorded by Connie Francis on the MGM Label.
[15]"Bridge Over Troubled Waters," as recorded by Simon and Garfunkel on the Columbia Label.
[16]"I'll Be There," as recorded by the Jackson Five on the TK Label.
[17]"Ain't No Mountain High Enough," as recorded by Diana Ross on the Motown Label.
[18]"Rock With You," as recorded by Michael Jackson on the Epic Label.
[19]"Magic," as recorded by Newton-John on the MGM Label.
[20]"Lady," as recorded by Kenny Rogers on the Liberty Label.

Let It Be:
Rock In The '70s and '80s

Introduction

> The old music ain't got the same soul,
> Not like that old time rock 'n' roll.

That Bob Seger should sing these lines in 1978 is not surprising. The decade did not begin well: The Beatles had broken up, most of the "supergroups" (Blind Faith, Crosby Stills and Nash [and Young]) were set on the self-destruct course, students had been killed at Kent State and Jackson State during antiwar demonstrations, and rock luminaries Jimi Hendrix and Janis Joplin were dead of drug overdoses. The warm glow of Woodstock, of the final triumph of the new order where peace, love, and music would form the foundations for a new consciousness, was quickly replaced by an icy chill in the wake of the Rolling Stones' debacle at Altamont, where The Rolling Stones' "bodyguards," the Hell's Angels, presided over beatings and a fatal stabbing.

As the decade wore on things did not improve much. Oil embargoes reminded Americans how tenuous their hold on the world actually was. Nixon—never well loved—was forced from office 1974 following a third-rate burglary at the Watergate Hotel a couple of years previously. Finally, Americans and Vietnamese clambered aboard helicopters from the roofs of the American embassy and other locations in 1975 bringing to an end the most divisive war in modern times. Jimmy Carter took office during our Bicentennial and quickly found that an appreciation of the complexity of modern government and modern life did not make for an effective President; he "lost" the American embassy in Iran to the followers of a charismatic and fanatical religious leader. Earlier in his tenure in office he gave Americans the truth, that they were suffering a malaise, but he found out Americans didn't really want the truth but myths, and he was defeated in the 1980 election by Ronald Reagan, a man who articulated and seemed to really believe the myths.

So it is not surprising that Bob Seger should ask for some semblance of stability in a popular song in the late seventies. What is ironic is that he would hearken to that most revolutionary, that most destabilizing force—rock music—as a symbol of what was missing from contemporary life. As the culture seemed to be inexorably unravelling before our eyes, so did the music at times. There was, however, no real erosion of rock during the seventies. Record companies were indeed fully committed to rock now, and independent labels would quickly be gobbled up by the major companies. FM radio grew in power as well. Shedding itself of the Middle-of-the-Road image and format it perpetuated in the late sixties and early seventies, it became the format of choice for all types of rock music by the mid-70's.

Yes, all *types* of rock music. If there is a single major development that took place in the 1970's in popular music it is the fragmentation of rock music. The British invasion had provided the impetus with the Beatles introducing a sophisticated pop oriented style of rock, and the Rolling Stones, the Animals, the Yardbirds, and others providing the hard rhythm and blues based style. Groups working within these two large areas, and drawing variously on soul music or folk music, experimented more, and by the decade's end, one had their choice of acid rock, folk rock, country rock, art rock, to name just a few.

As groups broke up in the early seventies, the solo singer-songwriter appeared on the scene as the "next big thing." James Taylor got his picture on the cover of *Time*, and it seemed a new era was dawning. The singer-songwriter perfectly complemented the emergent "Me decade" as author Tom Wolfe described it. Folk based and confessional in manner, the singer songwriter laid bare his/her soul; it was like a musical rap session. It expanded the range of instruments in rock (Elton John and Carole King brought the piano back from the days of Little Richard and Jerry Lee Lewis); it expanded the musical vocabulary of popular music by introducing elements from rock, classical, and jazz (Joni Mitchell's *Hissing of Summer Lawns* owes as much to California jazz musicians as it does to her folk music roots). But it clearly was no longer rock music. It did, however, have the capacity to "crossover" on the charts and therein lay its power. It was able to reach large audiences because the music could be played on a variety of radio formats. Carole King's landmark album *Tapestry* (1971) could produce singles for the Hot-100 (i.e., top forty radio), cuts and/or sides for album oriented radio, and cuts for remaining middle-of-the-road formats, which would evolve gradually, as the baby boomers aged, into adult contemporary formats.

As the culture became more preoccupied with realizing one's individual potential and as students found that grubbing for grades to merely survive was the educational imperative rather than mobilizing and taking to the streets to force sweeping change in the system's infrastructure, so there seemed to be a music for everyone's taste, and it all was called rock. There was folk-rock, country rock (handled most smoothly by the likes of The Eagles and Linda Ronstadt), heavy metal, soul, funk, glitter rock, fusion jazz, art rock, disco, reggae, punk, new wave/new music. This was but a sampling of the types that emerged in the 1970's. In a couple of cases (disco and punk) mini-revolutions were spawned; they, interestingly enough, were contiguous explosions on the same axis, and were not able to generate the enthusiasm and following that rock 'n' roll and the Beatles had done previously. Each, however, did generate excitement and helped revitalize the form. But, as Bob Seger's song suggests, for many there was something missing.

That was the feeling that took us into the eighties, where we waited patiently for the next big thing. We spent the early part of the decade watching rock music on MTV and hoping that it might wreak some transformations in what seemed to be a staid industry. MTV, as Joan Lynch's essay here confirms, did indeed bring some new and interesting dimensions to rock music as well as bringing some new groups into prominence who might not have been heard otherwise. The eighties, in keeping with its waiting for the next big thing attitude, has also produced the rock superstar. Michael Jackson, Madonna, Prince, and Bruce Springsteen have all produced albums garnering phenomenal sales and have attracted media attention and hype and, in some cases, have set off mini-revolutions in style. Springsteen has been the most durable force and has probably done the most to keep the great traditions of rock alive in the eighties. His blend of basic rock 'n' roll, Phil Spectorish production, Dylanesque lyrics, and commitment to the concerns of the common man, have made him one of the most respected as well as most popular stars of the eighties. The simultaneous interest in 60's styled rock sounds (The Bangles, the db's, the Fleshtones) as well as an interest in the roots sounds (The BoDeans, The Long Ryders, The Stray Cats, and the music of John Cougar Mellencamp) are reminders that, like Seger, musicians and audiences need to find that music that's got the "soul" like old time rock 'n' roll.

The essays in this section attempt to deal with the fragmentation as well as the mini-revolutions that have affected rock music in the 70's and 80's. We begin with Hugh Mooney's very fine overview of the music of the 1970's, and then move on to William Kelly's perceptive look at how rock has attempted to redefine itself in this fragmented age through the medium of the motion picture. Julian Tanner's essay on punk discusses this dynamic music within the context of larger cultural issues and contexts. James Winders' essay on Reggae, similarly deals with the socio-political complexities of reggae music and what it means for its proponents and followers. Hugh Mooney's "Disco: A Style for the 1980's" deals with the cultural (and future musical) ramifications of this most incredibly popular and incredibly hated musical style. Joan Lynch's essay on MTV and music videos offers us both historical and cultural perspective on the art of the music video and what it means for the production of the music itself. Finally, Julie Lyons and George Lewis' essay on Bruce Springsteen shows us the interrelatedness of "The Boss's" music and his life, and how those personal experiences play a key role in his ability to communicate to his audience.

Looking ahead to the 1990's there are times when rock seems to be becoming the second fabulous invalid in American cultural life. There is a kind of torpor hanging over much radio programming and TV seems hopelessly ill equipped to deal with the music. Like Tin Pan Alley, the rock establishment has learned how to absorb and blend the many different voices creating the music into a palatable dish suitable for mass consumption. The tapestry of American popular music these days may strike some as owing more to black velvet art sold on roadsides than the bold, vigorous and thoroughly original strokes of the folk artist, but it, nonetheless, remains a vital force in the culture. It still animates our myths and rituals, and can inspire astounding collective outpourings of goodwill and concern (the music of U-2, Sting, and Bob Geldoff's efforts for the starving in Ethiopia). It, indeed, evokes the very myth of America as described by D.H. Lawrence: "She starts old, old, writhing in an old skin. And there is a gradual sloughing off of the old skin, towards a new youth. It is the myth of America." Thus, we are perpetually surprised and reinvigorated by the music: Paul Simon produces *Graceland*, Steve Winwood produces the best album of his career, and groups like the Talking Heads and R.E.M., moreover, are able to synthesize the best elements of classic rock with the adventurous spirit of the new wave and punk to create vital rock music, which, like Chuck Berry's, may still be able to deliver us from the days of old.

References

Coon, Caroline. *1988: The New Wave Punk Explosion*. New York: Hawthorn, 1978.
Cooper, B. Lee. "The Image of the Outsider in Contemporary Lyrics." *Journal of Popular Culture*, 12 (Summer 1978), 168-78.
Davis, Stephen. *Bob Marley*. New York: Doubleday, 1985.
Davis, Stephen and Peter Simon. *Reggae International*. New York: R & B, 1982.
Henry, Tricia. "Punk and the Avant Garde Art." *Journal of Popular Culture*, 17 (Spring 1984), 30-36.
Marsh, Dave. *Born to Run: The Bruce Springsteen Story*. New York: Dell, 1979.
The Rolling Stone Interviews: Talking with the Legends of Rock and Roll, 1967-1980. Intro. by Ben Fong-Torres. New York: St. Martin's Press, 1981.
Stevenson, Ray. *Sex Pistols File*. London: Omnibus, 1980.
Wolfe, Arnold. "Rock on Cable: On MTV: Music Television, the First video Music Channel." *Popular Music and Society*, 9 (1983), 41-50.

Twilight of the Age of Aquarius? Popular Music in the 1970s

Hugh Mooney

Before trying to summarize and assess the 1970s we should challenge rigid distinctions between this and past decades. The very fact it was so synthetic indicates continuities.

The so-called "mellow" 1970s saw hard rock continue, although dipping a bit into mid-decade and often diluted with other forms in the pronounced syncretism of the 1970s. Heavy rock is a much deeper part of our pop music tradition than an ephemeral tide of late 1960s radicalism. It is a form whose time had come by 1964 and which will be around forever. In distorting tones, improvising in (or rejecting) melodic line, pure tones, rhythm and tempo, it is a logical extension of jazz; a musical concept oncoming since at least 1900. Facilitated by electronics, it can slur sounds beyond the capacity of, but not the intent of, early acoustic jazz instrumentation. The Animals or Yardbirds' guitar runs over an R and B bass were derived from early jazz and are the basic source of a somewhat mellowed Boston or Fleetwood Mac in the 1970s. Electronic rock has merged into country, jazz-fusion, Disco, ballad.

The 1970s has been called "laid-back" in contrast to an iconoclastic, critical, rebellious 1960s. But from Paul Revere's "Indian Reservation" in 1970 to Johnny Paycheck's "Take Your Job and Shove It" in 1978/79 there has continued a strain of bitter—or warm—social concern. The 1970s have been called the "me" decade ("I Will Survive") against the communal-minded 1960s—an oversimplification which ignores not only the altruism of the 1970s but the egoism of the 1960s. From "T' Aint Me, Babe", to "My Life" is no great switch; nor for that matter is Billy Joel's "Honesty" in 1979 much different from Jeannie C. Riley's "Harper Valley PTA" in 1969. As there can be no one reading of either decade, so there can be few clear-cut distinctions between the 1960s and the 1970s. The Beatles' 1967 withdrawal unto the Maharishi anticipates the guru and "me" gambits of the 1970s. But in these same 1970s was the moral outrage of campus demonstrations against South African investments or nuclear power, of Randy Newman's 1972 slave-ship ballad "Sail Away". There were Stevie Wonder's "In The Ghetto" and "Red Man, Brown Man, Black Man";

Reprinted with permission from *Popular Music and Society* Volume 7:3 (1980), pp. 182-98.

Cher's "Red Man"; Queen's "White Man"; Dylan's "George Jackson" and "Hurricane"; Springsteen's "Born to Run". Nick Gilder's "Hot Child in the City", its theme child prostitution, seared the smug face of 1970s hedonist pop. Even Village People's "Macho Man" (1978) could be read as gay lib, or as an attack on male chauvinism, a new way of stating a feminist message explicit or implicit in the woman's ballads of 1970-1975. Just after Helen Reddy's platinum *I Am Woman* in 1971 came Carly Simon in "That's the Way I Always Heard it Ought to Be" torn between conventional marriage and her assertiveness.

> You'll cage me on your shelf
> I'll never learn to be just me, myself

After the fragile ballad became old hat, Chaka Khan (very third world) rendered the woman's vocal in the blues-with-beat "Woman in a Man's World" (1978). Of course lib worked two ways. Billy Joel's "My Life" raspberried "the American Way" of male domesticity. There was a certain decadence in the 1970s as in the 1960s. As a subversion of impersonal official optimism, it was in a sense a social as well as personal statement. Life was measured against Death-a theme recurring in Jackson Browne, in Kansas' "Dust in the Wind", in Raymond Moody, in avant-academia. All this wasn't exactly Moon-June-Spoon. Things were being said, or implied. "Killing Me Softly with His Song" was as poignant an evocation of urban loneliness as had been "Eleanor Rigby". Social comment wasn't gone.

So a view of the 1970s as casual, joy-of-sex, shake your booty and ring my bell is simplistic. On the one hand was a persistent 1970s idealism—or iconoclasm. On the other there was good old you needed me romance, from Fifth Dimension's soft soul "One Less Bell to Answer" (1970) through Jagger's "Angie" (1973), Humperdinck's "After the Lovin' " (1976), Carly Simon and James Taylor's "Devoted to You" (1978). Sentimentality may have slumped with the weakening of the ballad after mid-decade, but even Police in 1979 recorded "Can't Stand Losing You".

Although there is a contrast between (1) the rough, raunchy blues rock of indie labels and freeform broadcasting around 1966-1967 and (2) the commercialized Top 40 formulas and Disco packages of the 1970s, this contrast between decades is also overdrawn in several ways. First: The late 1960s helped popularize the blues which have been a real if watered-down element in Disco. Second: The Disco craze, beginning with Wild Cherry's "Play that Funky Music" in 1976, increasingly absorbed hard rock. Third: The electronic, overtaped, synthesized studio sounds created by 1969 for heavy rock recording were still used, albeit less aggressively, for much of the studio-produced music characteristic of the 1970s. Fourth, and most importantly: The Disco vogue was not unlike the heavy rock enthusiasm in one way. It was originally made at the popular level more than by the big media. Acid rock had been forced to the attention of big labels and radio by the grass roots audience enthusiasm at concerts or in parks. A decade later, youth and young adults in Disco clubs, although a changed audience to be sure, were also in effect telling the radio

Popular Music in the 1970s 203

what to play, the record companies what to record. Despite the heavier role of record companies in shaping product in the early 1970s, Disco by 1975 represented a consumer's movement more than a media conspiracy. In this sense, we can see that contrast between the "populist" 1960s and the "media controlled" 1970s must be limited. And, further to break distinctions between 1960s and 1970s, we recall that Disco music, like the clubs themselves, owed much to the tightly swinging bugaloo bands and the dancing clubs (less permissive to be sure) of the 1960s; and to the latin bands of the Perez Prado—Tito Puente 1950s.

Another cliche is that the 1970s were mundane in contrast to a metaphysical 1960s. But how does Neil Diamond's "Be", played against, say, the Stones' "Midnite Rambler" support the conclusion that the 1960s were spiritual, the 1970s sweaty? An early 1970s religiosity, sometimes touched with the hipness of the 1960s, come to mind: "I Don't Know How to Love Him", "(Mother Mary) Let it Be", "Take My Hand, Precious Lord", "Put Your Hand in the Hand of the Man Who Walked Upon the Waters", "Day by Day", "Amazing Grace".

Having questioned some rigid stereotypes about the 1970s we can begin to analyze it further. Rather than a refutation of the 1960s, it has been a period of breath-catching and consolidation, blending the streams of 1970s music: The horns of Santana, the ballads of Joni Mitchell, the rather simple sensual flow of the Beatles. Particularly in the shattered early 1970s, a nostalgia permeated the audience. The Beatles *Originals* album topped the charts in 1972-1973. This periodization—arbitrary, overlapping, incomplete—is a place to begin a summary of the 1970s:

1) Inconclusive, mushy years 1970-1973. Emphasis shifted from passive listening to active, physically responsive music (ragtime, Disco).
2) Mid-decade blendings of many forms—gentle commercial citybilly or countrypolitan, jazz-rock Fusion—typified in Brick's "Dazz" ("Disco! Jazz!" (1977).
3) Restless rumblings 1976-1978:
    a) punkish elements from the late 1960s surfaced with a harsh, strident updating of R and B;
    b) various avant-garde adventures marked a brief economic comeback
4) 1979? Once more as in the earlier 1970s, economic crunch and potential vinyl shortage seem to herald a conservative shift; fighting against the grain, however, of a renascent punkish toughness heard in Police's "Dead End Job".

Let's take up each of these periods in some detail:

1970-1973

These years were the harbinger for the entire decade with its ambivalences, its nostalgia, its blendings, its search for a dance beat. They introduced the fusions which lasted throughout the 1970s. But first a ballad revival topped with woman singers—Reddy, Simon, Melanie, Flack and Carole King, whose silken *Tapestry* (1971) was a commercial and artistic trendsetter for a time. The biggest selling album of these years, it wove softly introspective vocals

("Too Late Now") into the rich textures of a processed easy listening sound—vaguely latin lilt, grandiloquent keyboards, some guitar thumps and whines of a dentured rock. With Simon and Flack would come the strings.

Other slick-surfaced styles were emerging as the ballad, which had crowded rock aside, in turn palled. These included countryish, jazz Fusionist, soul and dance genres—the chief ingredients of the 1970s mix. Country was in there at the start: Night-club country (Glen Campbell); studio-rock-country (Waylon Jennings); country-rock mellowed from the 1960s (CSNY); philosophical hip-country (Kris Kristofferson). The 1970s were ready for it. The first new big male stars of the decade, James Taylor and John Denver, made it in 1970 with country-roadish titles. Why at this particular time? One of my students called it "ecologically oriented" for a Sun Day and Whole Earth generation. Its environmental connotations, so dear to the hearts of those youth still searching for causes; its simplicities for those who weren't; its nostalgic *Waltons-Roots* balm for the shocks of the 1970s; its increasing introspection in the "Feelings" decade, all enhanced countryish music.

And countryish blends throve perhaps because between the later 1960s and early 1970s attitudes toward white southern entertainers and eventually white southern folk as a whole had mellowed. Johnny Cash had worn the black for all oppressed people at Folsom Prison in 1968. Kristofferson, then Waylon Jennings and (by 1974) Willie Nelson's *Phases and Stages* won audiences still concerned for those "Born to Run" but now more willing, like liberals back in the Woody Guthrie 1930s, to include southern whites among them.[1]

Already in 1970, there was a strange empathy for the southerners' born-to-lose grit. Joan Baez, no less, did "The Night They Drove Old Dixie Down". By 1973 influential critics and college students no longer resisted country culture as "redneck". If many in the Birmingham Sunday—Barry Sadler—Lieutenant Calley eras had seen Georgians as crackers and praying hypocrites, such polarities eased with the winding down of the war and diminution of racial rhetoric—or maybe with the realization that southerners had no monopoly on racism. Country was permeating every form of pop music, proclaiming through Charley Pride its old affinity with blues and gospel. But the climax of it all was the thrust of southern white country rock bands between 1973 and 1975. Richard Betts' guitar for the Allman Brothers "Rambling Man" was literally instrumental in confirming and boosting the appeal of a country mix to heavy rockers. By mid-decade, as Americans sized up their new born-again candidate from Plains, there was a flood tide of southern groups: Charlie Daniels—who to be sure was anti-redneck in "Uneasy Rider" (1973)—Lynyrd Skynyrd, Marshal Tucker, ZZ Top. Later, between 1975 and 1977, America and The Eagles would win mellow rock fans for country: Dolly Parton, the ballad crowd. But by 1973 the die was long cast. County was In.

And country was nostalgic in the early 1970s, which loved to meander along the pathways of the past in every direction. The year 1972 carried over from the 1950s the romantic duet a la Eydie Gorme and Steve Lawrence, with a soul update in the Roberta Flack-Donny Hathaway "Where Is The Love?" (Duets were to peak in the late 1970s; among them the Streisand-Neil Diamond

"You Don't Bring Me Flowers Anymore" and the John Travolta-Olivia Newton-John "Summer Nights".) Nostalgic sounding things included John Denver's forthcoming "Annie's Song" (1974)—simple waltzes, if infrequent, were to be the top of later 1970s tops with Barry Manilow's "Weekend in New England" and Debbie Boone's "You Light Up My Life". Other vaguely reminiscent sounds of the early 1970s included ballads echoing Stephen Foster (Roberta Flack's "The First Time Ever I Saw Your Face"); lush pseudo-Beethoven sonatas ("Theme from *Love Story*"); Mozartian flutes (Ian Anderson's "Living in the Past"); 1920s concert pop (Moody Blues' "Nights in White Satin," a 1968 cut most popular in 1972). And there were echoes of the Mamas and the Papas' sweetly-chorded rock in the Carpenters. All had a good share of the market. They did not, however, clearly spell "trend".

Of the melange of styles in an aimless era, ragtime and more so revivals of 1930s to 1950s styles country and urban appear most important in the long run. In the Pointer Sisters', Bette Midler's and Manhattan Transfer's boggie and night club "vocadances" was a more sharply defined sound: Brisk but relaxed, breezy, fairly simple; with lyrics, if not always unsentimental, lighter than the metaphysics of the 1970s. Perhaps the most significant phase of the nostalgia craze was this focus on the 78 rpm or 45s formats of 1935-1964. It led into modern country, Disco, and Fusion.

So, like the other key forms of the 1970s, Disco style was also a growth from past roots. By 1974, its special time would come. People want to *move* again, not just listen or at best trance-dance at rock concerts, as the ragtime revival proved. It was heading for a big album in Marvin Hamlisch's piano soundtrack from *The Sting* (1974) on the very eve of the Disco rage. Ragtime's happy roll activated dancing as it had two decades before, under somewhat similar circumstances. Back in post-big band 1950 Teresa Brewer's "Music, Music, Music" and Kay Starr's "Piano Roll Rag," along with folksy country and western edged aside the pale ballads which had themselves edged aside overblown arty-progressive bands. Ragtime moved toward a simple, earthy dance rhythm.[2] But because, in 1953 and 1973, people wanted something more contemporary for dancing, they turned to boogie.

If ragtime was a transition from listening music to Disco, the times were ripe for such a progression. By 1971 whites more fully accepted music favored a few years before largely by blacks—dancing bugaloo. This funky but smart-and-sassy sound hadn't suited the general market of sombre 1967-1968, when many whites and some media people were in backlash[3] and more radical youth, revolting against social dancing, also eschewed twist and frug bugaloo. Most kids had preferred to take their rock from British sources, and more for listening than dancing. The two biggest blues rock singers, Joplin and Jagger, were white. Black artists were more absorbed in and with their own people.

But by 1971 the picture was changing in favor of black music. The Beatles, who could do everything for their broad audience, were gone, leaving it stranded. The "white" music which attempted to fill the vacuum, whether arty-progressive rock (Three Dog Night), heavy metal, or soft ballad, was not totally satisfying. There was a reaction toward simpler body music-ragtime, big band formats, gutty rock and roll (Oldies but Goodies, Sha-Na-Na); and for the now middle aged teenagers of 1955 an Elvis Presley revival. A spate of rock and roll oriented movies like *Let The Good Times Roll* and *American Grafitti* also reinforced an interest in rhythm and blues roots which reawakened in a mellower white audience an appreciation of joyous black dancing soul. Black artists and styles were rushing more heavily into the white market. Whites who bought Doobie Brothers' 1972 "Listen to the Music" enhanced the commercial potential of the black proto-Disco backups for B.B. King, the Jackson Five and Sly Stone's "Family Affair" (1972). So the ragtime revival, and more significantly bugaloo and rocking countryish blends, filled a physical need. The venture into vigorous, straightforward older forms by 1973 had also effected a big band revival (Maynard Ferguson) soon to influence Disco and Fusion. Ferguson, with some campus following, reopened interest in jazz by presenting it in its most easily comprehended big band setting. The crisp Spanish horns of Chicago and Santana also carried over from the late 1960s into a re-emerging salsa sound, not only enriching Disco but preparing the way for the Fusion which hit biggest after 1974 and will be dealt with later. It was nourished by the demand for a sharply defined sound, pleasant rather than polemical, favored alike among media and much of the public.

So music was heading into Disco, countryish and jazz-rock blends. All three "new" directions tended to be rhythmic, derivative, melded, deftly synthesized (in all meanings of the word), and tightly scored rather than wildly original. The media preconditions for such styles are well-researched.[4] The recession and vinyl crunch during 1971-1974 aggravated by the OPEC embargo and price hikes effected cutbacks in arty experimental albums in favor of finger-snapping one shot single cut material. The conversion of freeform radio to Top 40 also effected style, as did the demographic realities of the largely black and hispanic inner cores; and the growth of black radio for the burgeoning inner city minorities. (Martha and the Vandellas had once complained of acid rock "I Can't Dance to That Music".) Radio sponsors needed minorities' business, and black and hispanic taste (until 1976 at least) centered on danceable 45s rather than the more costly albums-oriented rock material. And (at that time more than whites) blacks and probably hispanics tended to buy records well into adulthood.[5] By 1972, not only blacks and hispanics but post-hip young suburban adults were getting into less millenarian or metaphysical, more mundane or physical music. White Top 40 radio took note and (although only later, by 1977 did it respond directly and specifically to the preferences of the all-important Disco club deejays and their patrons) was already shifting to smooth, uncomplicated, danceable sounds.

Black music was becoming less assertively pounding and driving, more melodic, less Nina-Simonish ethnic-stance. Marvin Gaye's "Let's Get It On!" (1973), for all its heavy soul, was a call not to black revolt but to a sensual liberation obsessing youth and young adults grown indifferent to high ideologies. Like him, Gladys Knight, Diana Ross, and Stevie Wonder moved toward a night club sound with sophisticated lyrics and orchestrations. Wonder, like the others a Motown product, more than did his share in reviving a dance music which not only moved soul inoffensively into major markets but appealed lyrically to the still socially aware.[6]

What about hard rock?

Many still-affluent students attended expensive rock concerts and bought albums by Grateful Dead, Steppenwolf, ELO, Led Zeppelin, Deep Purple. Chicago, Pink Floyd, Uriah Heep, Humble Pie, Yes, Ten Years After. Appealing to high school crowds were the unsubtle Grand Funk, Black Sabbath, and Raspberry. Very popular among older youth and typical of the every-whichways of early 1970s pop was Emerson, Lake, and Palmer, gorgeously Jekyll and Hyde, beauty and beast, sadist and symphonic. The deviate-culturists opted for Alice Cooper, whose sawing into a red paint-filled baby doll might be described in academese as a trendy rejection of family values! A more refined version of homoerotic anti-hero was David Bowie, tough but delicately painted like porcelain enamelled over heavy grit. With Blue Oyster cult ("I'm on the Lamb, But I Ain't No Sheep") and the New York Dolls also, punkishness was a rolling substream for those opting out of John Prine or Melanie. It had never been too far from the surface with the angry, sweaty, glittery grotesque of the Stones or even, more subtly, Dylan. Though extreme, Alice Cooper's 1970 "School's Out." ("I'm eighteen...got no ideals") illustrates that more popular heavy-metal bands had lost the minstrels-of-the-dawn aura of the acid days. It was this loss of rock's innocent social commitment which Don MacLean lamented in 1972's "American Pie"—"the day the music died". Rock now existed for sensory stimulation, not moral regeneration. It was less lyrical, much less preachy, in sync with the enhanced hedonism, or cynicism, which really was a bequest of the 1960s to the 1970s.[7]

There was plenty of hard rock around, much sound and fury. But even in the late 1960s it had to share the stage with Bacharach-Warwick and there was somewhat less rationale for it now. Many buyers were finding surcease from the 1960s in ballads with pianoforte effects persistent into mid-decade; or, tiring of these, in more danceable stuff. People wanted their "Bridge Over Troubled Waters"; then Tony Orlando and Dawn's upbeat "Knock Three Times" and—with its country-convict social consciousness more perky than preachy—"Tie a Yellow Ribbon"; the rinkey tink "Hey Babe, What Would You Do?" The down and up and down again economy of 1970-1974 was not an emboldening experience. Neither older rock groups, whose ranks suffered attrition, nor the relatively few successful newcomers like Supertramp who were replacing them, would risk really far out sounds. Heavy-decibel music was frequently as routinized and stagey as schlock. And there was much schlock. Even in a business always given to MOR, the uninspired drift of the earlier 1970s is notable. Economic and production problems crimped recording dates and personal appearances. Exposure was expensive; enterprisers hedged their bets. Recording experimental sounds, or any heavy sounds for that matter, involved a six-figure outlay slowly if at all recouped in album sales. Concert tours, with their electronic monsters, were also costly. Big sounds, overamplified and overtaped, derivative of the late 1960s, continued. There was still a demand for them and there were corporate technologists with a vested interest in them.

But with a public bathing in the balm of banalities, soft or loud, the electronic revolutions were being utilized less for the probings of a King Crimson than for such as John Denver and Tammy Wynette backups. The closest thing to a "new" trend—and this would last throughout the 1970s—was shorter, simpler (if more finely produced) numbers with greater sheen and sparkle than substance.

There were fewer concepts and more quick shots. Dance, ball, and get back to work was a strong recession mood. More and more post-Vietnam Americans wanted to forget polemics and politics, to play hard for a few hours and then get back to school or job. The three minute cut, like the old 78 rpm businessman's bounce of the 1920s, was a casual diversion not a way of life. It made new tracks with things like Abba's smooth "Dance (while the music still plays on)" (1974). And, speaking of the 1920s, booze returned: first, Boone's Apple Farm Wine, then lots of beer. Some say it encouraged music more "physical" than meandering acid rock. And the "in" drug, coke, was said to demand snappy, happy music. At any rate, with recession and vinyl shortage, this was a period of decline in indie records and in freeform broadcasting; of pulling-in-of-horns at Clive Davis' mammoth Columbia studios, of favoring the safest bet.[8]

Narrow, mundane, the state of the industry, attuned even more than usual to the tinkle of the cash box rather than the music of the spheres, matched the mood of a large public. Or did it determine that mood? Did the big media restrict taste, by elimination of potential product, more than they expressed it? Just how far did media concentration, the decline of freeform broadcasting, of indie labels, impel rather than merely reflect a trend away from experiment? A chicken and egg question? I asked an indies distributor of long experience how greatly the decline of indie labels effected musical conservatism. His answer was really, not too much.

"However," he continued—violating our strict chronology but to good purpose—

It's not axiomatic that indies make for experiment. They did in the 1950s and 1960s, sure, but remember the demographics. They were catering in the 1950s to age groups of 10-17 year old kids with cheap records. Then the 1960s revolts. Now my indies are into mellow. Peter Frampton, A and M; Barry Manilow, Arista. Big! They keep us going. We're mellow because that's where the demographics are. Indies are still down next to the biggies, Columbia. But that's not the reason for conservativism in music today. We're conservative too. Some guy, 25-40 years old, commuting to work, driving the car, all tensed up, house payments. Do you think he wants music screaming at him? Forget it! But he likes Disco, it's smooth-moving, relaxing, carries him along. I call it a mellow form, laid-back. Gutsy, yes, but not radical. You remember Glenn Miller.[9]

Thus in the mainstream of 1970-1974 and beyond, a factor much more relevant than the state of the indies was after all the mood of the market itself. A conservative pull was pronounced all through the decade, and certainly into the middle years.

But it was less reactionary, rigid conservatism than easy accommodation in music. Stevie Wonder moved into somewhat artier, "whiter" lyrics in *Innervisions*, Charley Pride into "redneck" country. Whites crossed into black boogie and bought Wonder's "Living for the City", with its picture of black migrants struggling for urban dignity. A more relaxed time, one of pause rather than push, the early 1970s prepared the way for the tranquil Earth, Wind and Fire or our next period—a group in no way to be harmed by a Nature-trendy name.

1974-1976

Music had now acquired a distinct coloration. Three leading forms had emerged: (1) Disco, (2) country, (3) jazz-rock Fusion. They often crossed and melded. All had intruded into the domain of heavy rock and were now challenging the somewhat wearisome ballad-for-listening which, to survive, was often moving to a soul beat: Barry White's "Just Not Enough" (summer, 1974), then Gloria Gaynor's "Never Can Say Goodbye" and (in 1975) Donna Summer's "Love to Love You Baby" were among the pace-setters.

Crossovers were strong. White country, salsa, synthesized rock, blues and boogie moved blandly into the pleasing commercial mix of Stevie Wonder's eclectic *Songs in the Key of Life*, which replaced *Tapestry* as the decade's biggest seller. (Its dancing "Sir Duke" then its lilting "Isn't She Lovely"—the least profound, the simplest cuts-were the hottest.) Although Wonder's Love Mentalism may have attracted the California and Cambridge crowd, we were now in the "Enjoy Yourself" and "Shake Your Booty" days of Chi-lites. Spinners, Funkadelics, Ohio Players. Contemporary rock groups like J. Geils ("Funky Judge") stressed a regular beat rather than the erratic, a rhythmic variations of a fading art rock Jethro Tull. People wanted to sing and dance rather than just passively to listen.

There was more consolidation than real new frontiering in such as Phoebe Snow's mix of jazz, Disco and country. Superstars tended mainstream: Captain and Tenille, blatantly (they were the Fords' choice for White House entertainment); Fleetwood Mac with more artistry. Earth, Wind and Fire, a black group increasingly committed to Disco, fused rock and country, as did America, Dolly Parton, Olivia Newton-John, Linda Ronstadt, Mac Davis, Maria Muldaur and the Eagles, whose "Lying Eyes" was a soft social commentary no more radical than the 1890's "Bird in a Gilded Cage ("Her Beauty was sold, for an Old Man's Gold"). By 1975 *Billboard* listed only three or four heavier bands on its Top 25 Artists of the Year. The Stones were slumping.[10] Hard rock had slipped somewhat, but not enough to deter ear-shattering cuts by Aerosmith ("Dream On"), Bad Company, or Bachman Turner Overdrive. New Riders and Grateful Dead had marked staying power.

But staying power in mid-1970s often involved retrenchment—with New Riders and the Dead, into softer, countryish sounds. Even such primitives as David Bowie, Alice Cooper, and Lou Reed, essentially cultist into mid-1970s, were not drastically innovative. An RCA contract tamed Bowie somewhat to give him "Fame". The company was doubtless ambivalent about its new artist in a market dominated by Neil Diamond. (With his symphonic score for *Jonathon Livingston Seagull*, Diamond was hailed by one of my students as a "genius" in the none too daring year 1975.)

The industry almost mandated routinized product. The electronics and multiple tape manipulations which had been used to produce novel effects during the late 1960s heavy rock years were now used by a vested bureaucracy and technocracy of producers and engineers to perpetuate a big, full, rich sound. Flawlessly banal, it would soon alienate some rock aficionados and performers. Slick studio people were in control in 1974. Billy Joel, then recording his first album, *Piano Man*, found the Columbia studios "a drag. Because the producer wanted technical perfection. I didn't know shit." This was not a time for artistic spontaneity. As 45s went stereo, as multiple tracks multiplied, engineers hovered evermore ruthlessly over performers for "sound".

A defensiveness compounded by economic squeeze swept an industry once more growing middleaged. "The day I have to market punk is the day I quit the business", a CBS promotions manager told me. But after all, as we have seen, the media interacted with a public eagerly seeking complacencies flawlessly reproduced. Even the Stones who, as this CBS informant told me, were "among the very few who could dictate to the studio producers" were not doing well in this market.[4] The center of mass taste ran to Disco-ballad with increasing touches of modest jazz, laid-back rock, citybilly. Top bands ran a narrow gamut from the mellifluous America to the ambivalent Fleetwood Mac whose real incursions into hard album rock were vitiated by some trite lyrics: "You Make Lovin Fun" (1977). The most novel breakthrough to larger sales in 1975— Fusion—was not all that new chronologically or musically.

Jazz-oriented rock had been around since 1968. Jazzman Miles Davis' absorption of electronic rock into *Bitches Brew* in 1970 had featured keyboard synthesizer Chick Corea whose *Return to Forever* (1975) went gold to really spark the trend. Two other "modern: jazzmen of the 1950s and early 1960s also were selling big Fusion albums—Herbie Hancock (*Headhunters*, 1973), and Ramsey Lewis, (*Sun Goddess*, 1974). In 1976 came Weather Report's big *Heavy Weather* and George Benson's platinum *Breezin*. "Fusion" was an appropriate word for these groups, which like John McLaughlin's adaptation of John Coltrane's 1963 *A Love Supreme* for Mahavishnu, blended the neglected advanced jazz of the 1960s with Afro-cuban, gospel, bossa nova, blues, swing, and the avante-garde "serious" music of Varese, Stockhausen, and Cage. Since the freely shifting rhythms and wavering tonalities of Coltrane; the free-floating melodies of Ornette Coleman; the sitar of Byrds and Beatles; and the fuzzed reverberations of acid guitar had similar effects, all these sounds were absorbed into 1970s Fusion—but smoothed and polished. Conventional chords and melodies in such mellifluous cuts as *Return to Forever's* "Celebration Suite or Benson's "This Masquerade" recalled the Beatles or even, with Deodato's symphonic flourishes, Paul Whiteman! "Pure" jazz has never made it on its own. Soft electronic blendings were good business.

As ballads continued to pall, Fusion won a deepening audience. It blended into *Songs in the Key of Life*, gaining terrific exposure.

Popular Music in the 1970s 211

Way out beyond fusion, revolutionary Ensemble's *Peoples' Republic* in 1976 probed new directions for an avant garde. Its Hindemith-like atonalism defied categorization in pop terms. But naturally the more moderate, listenable Fusion, just fresh enough to interest but not advanced enough to jolt or jar, held a much larger following. The appearance of Revolutionary on A and M was a straw in the wind, however, indicating some disaffection with standard studio sound.

1976-1978

Relative prosperity followed the 1973-1975 slump. The truism that the better the times, the more venturesome is capital and the more exploratory the market, seems to hold in this brief period.

There was a swelling of two counter-currents against mid-1970s mainstream: (1) back to various harder rock and driving R and B styles, and (2) on to more avant garde jazz orientations. We might call these disparate spinoffs from center the "scruffy" and the "cerebral" respectively—if we keep in mind these terms are more convenient than totally accurate.

The Stone's scruffy *Some Girls* illustrates the heavy surge of late 1970s. Newly-prominent if derivative heavy electronic rock groups were Boston. Foghat, Foreigner, Kiss, Styx, Queen, Heart. Recharging the voltage for a bored, restless youth in a more expansive economy, these groups were part of the AOR (album-oriented rock) renaissance as many radio stations shifted from tight Top 40. Single cuts on 45s often expanded to four or five minutes, allowing greater guitar and keyboards improvisation.

Beginning at its right wing with hard progressive bands like Foreigner carefully manipulating the dimensions of sound, heavy rock shaded raunchier into The Cars. At some fuzzy point beyond Cars, punk and new wave took over the leftward sweep of the spectrum toward the far out fringe of the Sex Pistols and the Ramones, anarchic, abrasive and to hell with technology and modulations. A sort of de-politicized spinoff of 1960s new-left, in British groups. Rotten and Vicious with the leering and sneering of the English music halls; in American, with the glitter of fag rock; either way, punk was the ultimate insult to MOR in life and music: To Rita Coolidge's coddled-egg soul; Chuck Mangione's salsa and Fusion gone spineless and slack with *Children of Sanchez*: George Benson's soft guitar and vocal ("This Masquerade") sellout of Jimi Hendrix. Its primal scream vituperated the more commercial, conservative product of Styx or of Boston, whose convoluted organ passages left the teenaged audience I witnessed in the fall of 1978 shrieking for more beat and bite. Punk supplied them. Punk had no baroque organ passages. It was content over style, feeling over form, a nosethumbing of art rock and commercialized Disco, sustained savagery. Trashy London and New York brat, lacerated, alienated, ("No Answer" yelled the Sex Pistols in "God Save the Queen") it came "in" 1977 just as Disco was starting to satiate the far out New York crowd. With Disco about to become the businessman's bounce in Topeka, punk was given the Big Apple hype in *Village Voice*, October 24, 1977. Androgynous leather punkers in chi chi Gotham apartments were a strange but not illogical lib replacement for the Panthers of several years before. The *Voice* shortly influenced some out of town college kids surfeited with the local record stores' Eagles, Carly Simon and James Taylor ("Liz and Dick" a student writer called them in December, 1977). "But alas," he continued, punk was "a trend which must be viewed from the outside."[14] Over a year later, the owner-manager and some of the staff of a large downtown Hartford record store agreed that punk was

not going out that far in the big market. The kids are screaming for more gut, yes. But how long does that last? The high school kids are low demographics now. They'll get older and come into the market that's buying big now, the 20s and 30s, even the 40s. The older market, they're oriented toward more mainstream—progressive, Disco maybe, jazz, big new classical sales here. Sophisticated forms are here to stay, more avant garde jazz albums. New wave (punk) may penetrate, but it won't dominate. Elvis Costello, yes, coming on; social criticism, ye-es; but not real raw punk; he's really something closer to progressive rock.[15]

Although I might place less distance between Costello and punk, there was a distinction to be made between conventional heavy rock and punk. New wave had strident vocals, emphasis on beat, on R and B or rock 'n' roll guitar licks. It was less electronic, more linear acoustical than progressive rock. Instruments might be amplified but the music often rejected synthesized sounds and chords. Punk rock thus recalled the original rock and roll rebellion from progressive jazz and mellow pop in the 1950s; but parallels are not cycles. Punk was bitter where its antecedents were merely exuberant, and it was more visually and lyrically outrageous (quite in keeping with the coterie cliche, "rage", which did denote a certain smoldering malaise of mavericks within a fairly satisfied majority culture). But while the old greaser rock had ridden demographic waves upward, punk now appeared to have demographics and, so far, majority attitudes against it. True, the Ramones had recently penetrated the lower ranks of the new sales-based *Rolling Stone* "100 Albums Chart" for late fall, 1978.[16] True, Kiss' absorption of gimmicky new wave and glitter theatrics had helped win it top billing among teenage boys in 1978. And true, there was something of punk new wave in Meat Loaf, and in The Cars' platinum album. But Cars melded it into an art-rock experimentalism. Disco absorbed some punk: I heard the heavy, rowdy, screechy hotrocks "Give It To Me" from Chee Chee Savalas and the Black and White Band's *Rock Solid* played for the live male dancers in a Time Square gay film house in March, 1979. But it was outbalanced even here, in this citadel of avant-rough, by dulcet keyboard-and-ballad hustles and bumps. Despite some gains for Patti Smith (her earliest breakthrough had been *Piss Factory* in 1974), punk appeared still not too far from what it had been ever since the early days of Velvet Underground, MC 5 and the New York Dolls in the late 1960s and early 1970s—a substream wave. Mainstream, rocker Rod Stewart's "Do Ya Think I'm Sexy?" smothered it in soft violins and Disco cliches. Said a college radio Program Director:

Punkish elements increased in 1978; but to hit most college listeners, even commercial power pop needs mellow mixed in. Your Queen and Heart can be heavy one cut, soft and pretty the next. You've got to be mellow, biggest new campus favorite is Anne Murray—nice sweet all-American girl image.

In a similar vein from the 22-year old college promotions man for A and M records:

The market's a bit restless but still pretty mellow. The Stranglers are something like punk with "Bring On The Nubiles", and you've got a comer with Police, *No Wave*, punkish with reggae. But you have to balance that with another big comer, Paul Winter.

Police did offer a scathing "Dead End Job"; but the Stranglers were closer to *Animal House* than to "God Save the Queen". And, as his example of the so-called "experimental" vogue on campus, *Winter Consort*, was less innovative than it was a beautifully textured reprise of chamber jazz. Its disciplined jazz samba arrangement illustrated the 1970s emphasis on techniques more than new statements. Collegians, if at all restless, were too used to flawless surfaces to be much more than ambivalent toward new wavepunk. "De-evolution", said a young man. "Rock's going Cro-Magnon."

If punk seemed in 1978 to be reaching a fairly low saturation point, there was good reason. The rather bland Americans didn't deeply share the earthy traditions of the British music halls; nor did our aspiring lower middle classes equate with cynical, class-bound British proles. And, for all the scruffy tastes of our male teenagers, demographics were moving us away from a wildly indisciplined cohort. (Only if an older group were to become embittered might we expect fireworks.)

Punk to be sure had some influence among the far-out as well as the juveniles. But this was diminished, as noted, by another, contrasting exoticism, jazz. And, because of its appeal among a larger, older cohort than punk's teenagers, jazz was gaining coast to coast,[8] perhaps more than punk.

The "cerebral" jazz revolt spun off mainstream mellow in the opposite direction from new wave scruff. It enlisted jazz buffs, new and old, frustrated by commercial Fusion and computerized electronics. The "new" jazz was more concerned with disciplined technique than was punk; however, both, often acoustical and performer-oriented, sought individualistic escapes from studio formats. If the Pistols pulsed stronger than more orthodox rock with the orgasmic Chuck Berry or limey punks, so on the other more cerebral side of the spectrum, did Revolutionary Ensemble go beyond sales-oriented Fusion. Closer to the mainstream, pianist Keith Jarrett was most widely known of the new jazz experimenters (or syncretists; he was as much melder and polisher as maverick). He appeared on network TV. His acoustical *Survivor's Suite* (1977) assimilated Coltrane and Coleman; fused near eastern, oriental, African, and latin modes with greater complexities than mainstream Fusion. He was not a big seller, but the popularity he did achieve, like that of his rebel counterpart on the scruffier side of the continuum, Elvis Costello, was because he excited people without pushing them all the way into *terra incognita*. And, with his subtle explorations of "third world" music, he accelerated for a small but growing audience elements of a cultural revolution continuing from the 1960s. Jarrett tapped the more sophisticated members of a very large cohort born between 1946 and 1960. Even Top 40 radio, realizing demographics, was filling slots with jazz. Jazz was fed by Fusion and Disco. Easing of relations with Cuba facilitated recording some strong Afro-Cuban jazz by Irakere (July, 1978), significantly on hyper-market research oriented Columbia. If punk attracted younger teens, attracted some 20s-30s, rock-influenced but moving beyond hackneyed pop. For these latter, Joni Mitchell's renditions of Charlie Mingus, in collaboration with Herbie Hancock and Wayne Shorter (Atlantic, winter, 1978-1979) might be it.s0[9] Attention to demographics, which had attracted the media to concept rock in 1968 and then to 45s, seemed to favor once again more esoteric concepts in 1978. The economy briefly appeared favorable to risk.

A few artists blended the cerebral and scruffy into something transcending the ordinary. Most favored of these was Elvis Costello, spearhead of an attack on mellow-artsy; a reaction back toward the rock and roll guitar of the 1950s and, at the same time, the intellectual social commentary of the 1960s. As a maverick guitarist and vocalist, Costello suggested his namesake. But again parallels are not cycles. Only so far was he an Elvis clone. Despite his leather jacket, Levis, boots (or red shoes), and greasey hair, the picture on his first album, *My Aim Is True* (1977) shows us a Woody Allen. The 1970s was not the macho 1950s: No gods or superheroes (at least among whites); lots of scared, bespectacled, rabbitty-faced little Philip Roth kids. Punk was of the ambivalent 1970s. The Ramone's stud gear foiled small, androgynous bodies. Costello didn't sweat and grunt, really; and he lacked the sentimental sexuality of the punk-with-heart-of-gold 1950s. He made cold statements like "Watching the Detectives", sneering at cow-eyed housewives planted in front of TV cop shows; delivered broadsides against the very mass culture which ostensibly he was reinvigorating. He assumed Presley's natural artless redneck tackiness; but self-consciously, artificially, artfully to manipulate acerbic moods more post-1960s than 1950s. "Detectives" was as elitist as the Beatles' 1967 "Fool on the Hill". Costello's concepts were as much for albums as quickie singles, or more so. He, too, was at once both scruffy and cerebral. (Successful artists, like politicians, intentionally or intuitively play both sides against the middle.)

With Elvis Costello on the one hand, and with Jarrett and Irakere on the other, we note some departures from the 1970-75 atmosphere. Earlier in the decade, we recall, hard rock had subsided somewhat in favor of the Top 40 ballad, nostalgia, urbanized country, soul, Fusion and finally, Disco. The record industry had reconcentrated, with much technical standardization of sound. Mood shifts, economic recession, a reciprocally conservative industry and public, the vinyl shortage of 1973-1976, had inhibited innovation and encouraged smooth blendings of extant products more than risky creativity.

But 1976-1978 was slightly less restrictive. As the economy eased, big labels diversified somewhat. Columbia was into jazz, as was Clive Davis' indie Arista. Recording contracts for new artists and some revival of AOR marked a rather

Popular Music in the 1970s 215

looser if still laid-back period. Hard rock rebounded in power pop (Chicago's *Hot Streets*) and in punk/new wave, its strong R and B penetrating some Disco. The straight ballad, waning since 1975, was at low ebb: A late 1978 Gallup Poll of teenagers found non-dance solo vocals swamped by heavy rock and Disco groups. (Girls favored Disco, but also liked the versatile Aerosmith and Fleetwood Mac.) Although the newer bands might be like Boston more mechanically programmed than truly experimental; like Foreigner, "powerful without passion...impersonally pounding every note to provoke a Pavlovian response",[20] they did cater to teenagers' rising threshold of sensation by hyping the sounds of the late 1960s and the funky 1950s. Sharper rebellions came from the punk rockers and the advanced eclectics.

But how far would these go?

End of the 1970s

"I couldn't sell Irakere" said my dealer, a jazz buff who admired its fresh re-exploration of just about all elements that have gone into serious pop: the latinate horn jazz of the late 1960s; the dance rhythms and shouts of Africa; the European symphonic treatment of jazz in spinoffs of the 1920s Roy Bargy "Rhapsody in Blue" piano concerts. All this is not really revolutionary; but, richly textured yet intricate and freaky, it pushed 1970s electicism beyond the mass market. Perhaps it had been released, at the turn of 1979, at the very wrong moment, in a spent economy.

Like much of the recent acoustic experiment, it was too extreme for most consumers. Virtually all my media sources saw in recondite jazz, not a major market trend in itself, but a stronger minority taste which might further meld into mainstream.[21] But how far left would mainstream be pushed in 1979-1980? Are we rapidly adventuring into newer forms?

Informed guesses say not too far. The majority of the biggest market, at present 22 to 35 or 38 and rising—the guys and gals with house payments—(or even the 30ish "swinging singles" so-called who are really past the fesity music stage) do not appear greatly to support the far out fringes. They may subsidize their kids' tastes now; but the teenager is a demographically endangered species. The enervation foreseen by Jon H. Rieger is apparent; due in no small part to the demographics and economics he analyzed.[22] Early 1979 developments in the record industry were not encouraging for groundbreakers. Among the newer successes, Dire Straits' "Sultans of Swing" was proficient, uninspiring country rock; Cheap Trick's just that—flashy "Hey! Wow" stuff for the kiddies young and old. Two older but now-cresting groups, Abba and ELO, personified a competent blandness. ELO's "Shine a Little Love" had that dilute Beach Boys-electronic-Disco-sound toward which the entire decade had moved.

At mid-1979, the short-lived business recovery of 1977-1978 is over. The record industry is reconcentrating, and there is little hope that in the recurring vinyl crunch, the biggies will be very exploratory. Heavy market research, activated by giant Columbia's monthly surveys, is more prevalent than in the 1960s. It eliminates much "intuitive", "artistic", "hit or miss" production in favor of crafty releases methodically tailored, even possibly computerized, to market specifications. As a matter of fact, majors—Warners and perhaps Columbia—are "cutting the fat" in anticipation of further business recession and probably of oil shortages. They are contemplating as much as twenty percent cutback on production; concentrating on easily promotable releases for surefire mass appeal,[23] (or to be more exact, for the affluent mainstream within the aging 22-to-38 hump of the demographic curve. Prices were raised at the turn of 1979 to $8.98 list per album). Students—once a huge, leisured, affluent cohort markedly solidified in opposition to the draft, are a smaller and blander factor in today's market. Blondie's mix of Disco in "Heart of Glass", Van Halen's in "Dance the Night Away" leads one to expect that easy-blend formulas derived from those promoted in the earlier recessions and vinly shortage will persist, as updated, into the 1980s.

This stringency will not rule out fresh talents who will polish the pioneering work of others. Rickie Lee Jones was summer, 1979's meteorite. A fascinatingly ambivalent singer-composer, her "novelty" is really a leap from the shoulders of giants. Her remote ancestry lies in the delicate-tough blues of the slick urban 1940s and 1950s; in Billy Holiday's facile bendings of phrase; and in Ella Fitzgerald's rhythmic variations revived in Natalie Cole. Hence, like Manhattan Disco in its own way, she evokes the night club ambience of the so-called "urban renaissance". With something of the tricky smooth album blues introduced by Stevie Wonder and Chaka Khan to a sophisticated black middle class, somehow very "Chic-Freak" but with more street talk, she might well strike a path into the 1980s. She owes much to Joni Mitchell's 1970 "Woodstock Generation" with its then not too popular sojourn into non-western musical ideas; and to the sultry sensitive, moody "rapping" of Tom Waits. Drawing from such talents old and newer she is arresting but not disruptive. We are catching up. She can please alike soul buffs, adolescent daydreamers, jazz cognescenti, younger adults past power pop, those who want a tender-toughness short of punk.

Barring cataclysmic upheaval, one thing will probably never change. At least it hasn't in the past century or two. As R. Serge Denisoff observed, successful music transcends—actually melds—genres; particularly so when market crises alarm the industry. In 1979-1980, as to some extent in 1929-1934 and 1947-1950, we may see radical change inhibited by older demographics among the consuming public; shaky economy; and, to a degree, media concentration.

These conclusions are hardly startling in view of the long range history of pop music from Stephen Foster through Paul Whiteman or Glenn Miller. Top pop must avoid going out on a limb. But I have also attempted to suggest some uniquely contemporary aspects of both shift and continuity in taste. Beyond a certain point one must be very tentative, however.[24] A fuller picture of the 1970s can only be revealed after the 1980s.

Notes

[1]R. Serge Denisoff, "Nashville Rebels" *Popular Music and Society,* 5 (1977), 79-

Popular Music in the 1970s   217

87; Charles Gritzner, "Country Music", *Journal of Popular Culture,* 9 (Spring, 1978), 860; Pete Axthelm, "Willie Nelson", *Newsweek,* August 14, 1978, 55, 57; Fred Davis, "Nostalgia, Identity", *Journal of Popular Culture,* 11 (Fall, 1977), 421.

[2]In July, 1973, I went to an outdoor "concert" by the old Preservation Hall Jazz Band. Almost 20,000 people, mainly 18-40, were packed into Stern Grove amphitheater in San Francisco, once home city of acid rock. As momentum built, a sudden, prolonged convulsion of dancing swept the audience—everything from jitterbugging or 1950s bopping to a bounced-up version of rock concert slither. Without having any new steps or new music, they were starved for vigorous dance. My observations were bolstered by Dick Springfield's presentation to my 1976 class. He was music p.d. for WPOP Hartford.

[3]Presentations to my classes by J.T. Lambert, deejay, WPOP Hartford, 1976-1977.

[4]Peter Hesbacher, Eric Simon, Bruce Anderson, and David Berger, "Substream Recording", *Popular Music and Society,* 6 (1978); 38; Richard Peterson and David Berger, "Cycles in Symbols Production", *American Sociological Review,* 40 (1975), 158-173; R. Serge Denisoff, "Evolution of Pop Music Broadcasting", *Popular Music and Society,* 2 (Spring, 1973) 222-223; 1975), pp. 63, 191; Peter Hesbacher, "Sound Exposure in Radio", *Popular Music and Society,* 3 (1974), 191-192, 195; Richard Peterson and Russell Davis, "The Contemporary American Radio Audience", *Popular Music and Society,* 4 (1974), 300; Erik Barnouw, *The Sponsors* (New York: Oxford University Press, 1978), p. 50 n.

[5]Steve Chapple and Reebee Garofalo, *History and Politics of the Music Industry* (Chicago: Nelson-Hall, 1977), chapter 7 analyzes buying habits of blacks. Also valuable for these considerations are R. Serge Denisoff, *Solid Gold: The Popular Record Industry* (New Brunswick, N.J.: Transaction Books, 1975), pp. 243, 248; John Landau. "Rock 1970" in Charles Nanry, ed., American Music; *From Storyville to Woodstock* (New Brunswick: Transaction, 1972), pp. 242-248.

[6]Clive Davis, p. 145; William Brasher, "The Black Middle Class: Making It", *New York Times Magazine,* December 3, 1978, 147-148.

[7]Denisoff, *Solid Gold,* p. 15; for insights into the sensationalism of the 1960s, see Dotson Rader, *Blood Dues* (New York: Knopf, 1973); Werner G. Albert, "Dimensionality of Perceived Violence in Rock Music", *Popular Music and Society,* 6 (1978), 27-38; and John Wells, "Bent Out of Shape...The Grotesque in the Songs of Bob Dylan", *loc. cit.,* 39-44. The late 1960s shift from moral sensitivity to mere sound is a theme of Jerome Rodnitzky, *Minstrels of the Dawn* (Chicago: Nelson Hall, 1977).

[8]Clive Davis, pp. 189-190, 206. Clive Davis' idea of catalogue was the snappy Lynn Anderson country cut "Rose Garden".

[9]The extended quote is from my interview with Tracy Garneau, Aquarius Distribution manager for indies throughout Connecticut, eastern upstate New York and western Massachusetts, January, 1979. Two indies who came up strongest—Casablanca and RSO at the turn of 1979 made it on Disco—hardly an esoteric experiment. Nor were these labels provincial in any sense. They were big city labels featuring urban professionals—not grassroots outlets for scruffy amateurs or havens for innovators like so many indies of the 1950s or 1960s. (See Andrew Kopind, "The Dialectics of Disco: Gay Music Goes Straight", *Village Voice,* February 12, 1979, 11.)

[10]Springfield interview confirmed my reading of the *Billboard* charts for 1975 (as presented in Daniel and Martin Miles, editors, *Chart Display of Popular Music,* vol. 2: Top 100, 1971-1975 (New York: Arno Press, 1977). The survey of the Top 25 artists listed War, Doobie Brothers, Sweet, Grand Funk). War however was strongly into jazz/soul; Doobie Brothers Disco-bound; Sweet something of a flash in the pan. See Ed Naha, compiler, *Lilian Roxon's Rock Encyclopedia* (Revised ed., New York: Grosset and Dunlap, 1978), 495, 526.

[11]Dave Marsh, "Billy Joel", *Rolling Stone,* December 14, 1978, 74.

[12]*Roxon's Encyclopedia* 426.

[13]Springfield: "In late 1978 radio stations are in flux. Some are going all Disco, some are getting more into AOR, some are mixing. But the mechanical Top 40 format is going out."

[14]Bill Burke, "Record Review: Punk Rock", *The Inferno* (Central Connecticut State College), December 1, 1977, 14. Youth still eagerly sought complacencies early in 1977. My own small class survey suggested a preference for harmony and melody (13) against beat (5) or heavy sounds (3)—which last, one student indicated, would be accepted "only if elegantly polished". Much of the mainstream rock honored the reservation.

[15]Interview with proprietor and staff, Al Franklin's Musical World, Hartford Civic Center Shopping Plaza, January 2, 1979.

[16]*Rolling Stone*, December 14, 1978, 101.

[17]Quotes: First, interview with David Hill, p.d., WFCS, Central Connecticut State College; second, interview with Jeff Haymes, A and M Records, Boston; third, conversation overheard. All February, 1979. Michael Bloom asserted that action for a rock group lay in a diplomatic balance between "studio chamber ensemble versus kick-ass rock and roll band" (I would add some jazz and Disco thrown in) for the widest possible market. *Rolling Stone*, December 28, 1979-January 11, 1979, 113-114.

[18]Information from retail clerk at Bananas, the Hillsdale Mall record store in a San Francisco suburb, January 16, 1979.

[19]Ben Sidren, "Charlie Mingus Finds a New Voice", *Rolling Stone*, December 28, 1978-January 11, 1979, 33-41; Robert Palmer, "Jazz, 1978: the Cubans are coming", *loc. cit.*, 48-55; Michael Segell, "Children of Bitches Brew", loc. cit., 43-47.

[20]In arriving at these conclusions, I've amalgamated and interpreted the following sources along with personal observation: A Gallup poll among teenagers reported in the New Britain (Connecticut) *Herald*, January 31, 1979, 8:1; article by New York rock critic Dave Marsh, San Mateo (California) *Times*, Weekend Section, 5 G, 1: 1,2, My observations of Boston are firsthand. On Foreigner, review of concert in New York *Times*, November 25, 1978, 15; 1-2. According to the Gallup poll, among the top fifteen choices for both boys and girls were Aerosmith, Fleetwood Mac, and Earth, Wind and Fire.

[21]*Billboard*, January 6, 1979 is indispensable for summary and projection. See Alan Penchancsky, "Classical Sales Moving Up". 8:3; Gerry Wood, "No Boundaries for Country Acts", 10:1; Jean Williams, "More Pop Exposure: Disco can Spur R and B Crossover"; 31:1 Elliot Tiegel, "Does It Sell? Criterion for Jazz Issues", 10:4.

[22]"The Coming Crisis in the Youth Market". Read at the Annual Meeting of the PCA, May, 1974. Published in *Popular Music and Society*, 6 (1978), 185-201.

[23]Going broke, ABC is being absorbed by MCA, and other indie capitulations are in the wind. See Marc Kirkeby, "The Changing Face of Record Distribution", New York *Times*, Section 3 (Business and Finance). February 18, 1979, 1: Robert Wallace, "Warner Bros. Cuts Back". *Rolling Stone*, March 8, 1979, 11. A and M is entering into a monster production—distribution conglomerate with RCA—on highly favorable terms for A and M, however; for RCA will distribute A and M products. I am indebted to observations on this by Russell Sanjek, Vice President for Public Relations of BMI, at the Joint PCA/ACA National Meeting, April 26, 1979. On market research in the late 1970s, Arnold S. Wolfe, "Rock Music and the Record Industry", paper delivered at the same meeting.

[24]For example, the impact of computerized music cannot yet be analyzed. The first all-digital popular album, Ry Cooder's *Bop Til You Drop* has just appeared in July, 1979.

The 1980s must also decide how valid is our prognosis for mild music. A mild forecast may hold for a mild recession, with relative social stability and a large enough pie to somehow go around. But a real depression, a shrinking pie—or a cold furnace or empty gas tank for frustrated Americans—could amplify the occasionally bitter snarls not only of minorities and radical intelligensia, but of middle Americans. There's already a harsh blue collar note in Johnny Paycheck's "Take Your Job and Shove It". Even if its specific message isn't too appropriate to a depression, the underlying spirit is anti-establishment. It's the pissed-offedness of small farmers' demonstrations, gas line violence, truckers' strikes, *China Syndrome*. "This is My Life"; a malaise crossing class lines. So far DEVO's art-punker antics ("Space Junk", "Corporate Anthem") can be dismissed as a youth minority also-ran subtrend. The 1980s may decide if it was instead a maverick stream from the 1960s flowing into a broader current of iconoclasm. An added note as of June, 1980: If in 1979 there were indications of nastiness, the question, "Was music at the end of the 1970s trending mild or heavy, bland or iconoclastic?" seems arbitrary and simplistic. Considering the demographics of the 1970s into 1980s— a larger adult population, a smaller but vociferously raunchy youth segment—the broadest sales appeal in an economic recession lies in catholic crossovers. Embracing adults and youth in one sweep, Queen's new mix of hard electronic rock, country, and richly chorded Beach Boyish vocals has paid off in a smash album literally playing the game of commercial mainstream pop. (As always, variations from the norm may depend on current events: Given resistance to the draft, and deepening budget squeezes, The Clash could be the keynote group of the 1980s to emerge from the late 1970s.)

Pop, Punk and Subcultural Solutions

Julian Tanner

In a decade devoid of major trends or shifts in pop-music styles, Punk Rock has emerged as the most significant social (if not musical) development to date; in the words of one recent reviewer, punk rock has provided the pop scene with a breath of bad air. What has made the Britain of the 1970's such a fertile breeding ground for the likes of Johnny Rotten and the Sex Pistols, the Clash and the Damned?

The purpose of this short paper is to try to answer these questions. The thrust of my argument is that punk rock is the outcome of two reactions. First of all—as most commentators have emphasized—it has been generated by the rapidly declining material position of working-class youth, particularly the unskilled and uncertificated school leaver. The working-class young represent the single most important component of British unemployment statistics, and it is from the ranks of the unemployed working-class young that the fans of punk rock are drawn—indeed, one commentator has characterized the punk phenomena as "Dole Queue Rock."

Nevertheless, although a deteriorating economic situation is an important pre-condition for its emergence, punk rock cannot be accounted for solely in terms of the retarded life chances of the working-class young. In order to provide a more comprehensive explanation for the rise of punk rock, the centrality of leisure to working-class adolescents' lives must be noted. More particularly, attention needs to be focused upon the nature of working-class adolescents' involvements in pop music.

Leisure and leisure styles, rather than delinquency, has been the central core of the adolescent subcultural solution[1] in Britain. From the Teddy Boys of the early 1950's onwards, deviant youth groups in Britain have fashioned oppositional styles on the basis of clothing and pop music. Hence the substance of the subcultural solution created by the Teds focused upon their distinctive adaption of the Edwardian suits and their undying commitment to the pioneers of American rock 'n' roll (Bill Haley, Elvis, Gene Vincent, etc.). Their mid-1960-s successors, the "Rockers," stylistically heavily influenced by the American "Biker" image (cf. Marlon Brando in "The Wild One"), have maintained this commitment. In a similar vein, the Mods style was created around Carnaby

Pop, Punk and Subcultural Solutions 221

Street fashions and rock groups such as The Who and The Small Faces. Leisure was particularly important to the Mods, as Gary Herman has noted in his book on The Who: "The Mod defined himself through his leisure activities, into which his work was an unpleasant, but necessary intrusion"[2]. The Skinheads—although less centrally involved with the more commercial aspects of "teenage culture"—forged their style around, on one hand, their conception of traditional proletarian manhood, and, on the other, West Indian reggae music.

Thus a cursory glance at the post-war urban landscape in Britain reveals that all the deviant youth groups have used the media culture surrounding pop music as a source of identity and style. In this regard there is a common theme which links the punk rockers with their predecessors. All the varieties of post-war working-class "youth cultures" have employed clothing and pop music to advance symbolic solutions to collectively experienced "problems" of, for example, failure in school and unsatisfactory jobs. Leisure-based subcultures thus operate as the "means of expressions through which groups in subordinate structural positions have attempted to negotiate or oppose the dominant meaning system."

They therefore provide a pool of available symbolic resources which particular individuals or groups can draw on in their attempt to make sense of their own specific situation and construct a viable identity"[3] Like their predecessors, British punk rockers have shaped a distinctive subcultural style around clothing and music. Moreover, the thematic line connecting the punks with their predecessors can be further illustrated by an examination of the content of the punk rock subculture.

For example, the Mods have provided punk rock with its most important inspirations. Much of the music is very reminiscent of British R 'n' B of the early 1960's, for example The Rolling Stones, The Yardbirds, and particularly, The Who. In fact, some early Who songs—for example, "The Kids Are Alright"—have been incorporated into the punk rock repertoire. Stylistically, one punk rock group, the Jam looks uncannily like the Who of 1965 on their album cover photograph.

More importantly, perhaps, punk rock groups deliver the same kind of social message that groups such as The Who used to make. The Mods emerged in mid-1960's Britain as an angry reaction to the much heralded classless, affluent society; a society which, nevertheless, was unable to provide the opportunities for upward mobility that it promised. Likewise, punk rock has emerged partly as a reaction to the possibilities of a lifetime spent in dead-end jobs or no jobs at all.

However, punk rock is not merely a product of economic conditions. It is also a response to changes within pop music. In this respect, punk rock shares a similar generating milieux to the Skinheads of nearly a decade ago.

Since its emergence in the mid-1950's British "teenage culture" has primarily been the preserve of working-class adolescents. Not only has pop music been at the heart of this culture, it has been organized and presented in a particular way. Thus in the years prior to 1967, British pop culture was characterized by the "45" rpm single and the Top 20. This pattern changed in 1967 with the rise of progressive rock. Organized around albums rather than singles, progressive rock emphasized experimentation and eclecticism in an attempt to break away from the formula pop of the Top 20. Whilst successfully attracting a more middle-class "intellectual" audience (ie. Grammar School sixth form), progressive rock also succeeded in alienating the working-class pop fan, whose conception of, and orientation to, pop music was very different.[4]

The relationship that working-class adolescents have with pop music is governed by patterns of leisure activity and value-systems rooted in the working-class community. Lockwood has described the tightly-knit patterns of work and leisure which characterize these communities. He notes that they emphasize "mutual aid in everyday life and the obligation to join in the gregarious patterns of leisure, which itself demands the expenditure of time, money and energy in a public and present-oriented conviviality and eschews individual striving 'to be different.' As a form of social life, this communal sociability has a ritualistic quality, creating a high moral density and reinforcing sentiments of belongingness to a work dominated collectivity."[5]

Post-war generations of working-class adolescents have responded to pop music on the basis of these traditional values and activities. Thus, pop music has been used to reflect and update typically working-class leisure activities and focal concerns: it provides the backclothe for drinking, meeting girls and dancing, for example. Conversely, working-class values and subcultural concerns provided the yardstick by which particular forms of pop music are to be rejected. Most importantly, involvement in pop music was not an intellectual activity—hence debates about the meaning of Dylan's lyrics were—and are—antithetical to working-class notions of pop. The Skinheads spearheaded the resistance to progressive rock. Their style and concerns were largely fueled by their reaction to the "bourgeoisification" of pop music. The industrial denims, work-boots, the close-cropped hair (which gave them their name) represent an extreme version of traditional working-class manhood; their endorsement of West Indian reggae reflected their conception of the nature of pop music: a symbolic context in which masculine solidarity could be expressed via drinking and dancing.

Thus the importance of pop music for working-class adolescents rests upon its ability to contribute to an overall and unifying style rooted in their conception of working-class masculinity. Paul Willis has made this point very well in his description of the relationship between pop music and other core concerns of a group of working-class motor-cycle boys:

Their attitude to music at the club matched their lifestyle. The quality the boys universally disliked in music was slowness and dreariness. The quality they prized was fastness and clarity of beat. They preferred singles to LP's: singles were more responsive to the listener. If you disliked a particular record, at least it only lasted for two and a half minutes, and to play an LP was also to be committed to someone else's ordering of the music. LP's are more popular with an audience prepared to sit and listen for a considerable period, and with extention of trust, so that unknown material can be appreciated and evaluated. Approximately since the Beatles' "Sergeant Pepper", Progressive groups particularly have tried to produce LP's imaginatively conceived as

Pop, Punk and Subcultural Solutions 223

units which are meant to be taken as a whole at one sitting. The Triple-X boys are not like this. They are usually moving about, engaged in other activities.[6]

This theme can also be illustrated by looking at the impact that a group like Slade had on its largely working-class audience. Their success was based on an ability to exploit the connection between pop music and other working-class adolescent leisure pursuits, particularly soccer. Slade's brand of "hard" pop shared with football an emphasis upon physical expression and a cheerful collective solidarity.

Nevertheless, the increasingly dominance of progressive rock, coupled with the discovery by the pop music industry of a sub-adolescent audience for bubble-gum pop (David Cassidy, The Osmonds, The Bay City Rollers) alienated the traditional working-class pop fan. Neither progressive rock nor "teeny-bop" pop were to prove, in the mid 1970's, very attractive to the generation of working-class adolescents passing through school without commitment and onto an increasingly depressed labour market. Accordingly, the scene was set for the development of a rock music form capable of resonating more closely with the feelings and experiences associated with the dole queue and the dead-end job. In this regard, punk rock has provided its participants with a set of shared meanings—a sense of community based upon an active, albeit symbolic resistance, to declining life-chances.

Punk represents a return to rock's original and distinctive quality as a symbol of "teenage rebellion". In this respect the punk rock bands are the heirs to the early American rock 'n' rollers (particularly Elvis Presley) and the more controversial of the British groups who followed the Beatles, notably The Who and The Rolling Stones. Moreover, in a similar vein to their predecessors, the style and content of the peer culture surrounding punk rock is illustrative of the core features of the delinquent subculture outlined by Albert Cohen. The Sex Pistol's hit single, "God Save the Queen", managed to offend precisely because it inverted deeply held values concerning the institution of Monarchy—particularly in Jubilee year. They hit, in other words, at the underbelly of the dominant normative order. Likewise, punk fashions—created by the calculated adaption of conventional clothing (suits are cut up and then held together by safety pins)—subvert more conventional notions of fashion.

The punk rock subculture, like the working-class youth cultures which proceeded it, strikes its blows by the imaginative use of leisure time. Formal ideological politics and statements about political alternatives—alternatives aimed at alleviating the structural roots of working-class impoverishment and subordination—are not the stuff of adolescent subcultural solutions. Similarly, its "reactive" origins ensures that is formal political content—when it does emerge—is couched in the negative; defined in terms of what it is against rather than what it's for. Punk rock, then, provides a limited and temporary "solution" to the ongoing problems of the working-class young. Focused upon the innovative use of leisure, it represents, in the words of Frank Parkin, a "symbolic acting out of discontent."[7]

Notes

[1] A.K. Cohen. *Delinquent Boys: The Culture of the Gang* (Chicago: Free Press, 1955).

[2] G. Herman. *The Who* (London: Studio Vista Limited, 1971) Page 21.

[3] G. Murdock. "Mass communication and the construction of meaning" in N. Armistead (ed.) *Reconstructing Social Psychology* (London: Penguin, 1974). Page 213.

[4] Pete Fowler has provided a good analysis of the consequences of the emergence in 1967 of the pop-rock divide in Britain in his "Skins Rule," to be found in G. Gillet (ed.) *Rock File I*, (London: Pictorial Publications, 1972).

[5] D. Lockwood. "Sources of variation in working-class images of society" in M. Bulmer (ed.) *Working-Class Images of Society* (London: Routledge and Kegan Paul). Pages 17-18.

[6] P. Willis. "The Triple X Boys." *New Society* 23 (54): 693-695. 1973.

[7] F. Parkin. *Class Inequality and Political Order* (London: Paladin), 70.

Reggae, Rastafarians and Revolution: Rock Music in the Third World

James A. Winders

They came to the main square, once an area of trees and asphalted walls, now full of parked motorcars and rough wooden booths. The reggae shrieked from a dozen amplifiers, now above the roar of motorcars and trucks, now below it. Diseased pariah dogs wandered about; some lay prostrate on the crowded pavements; and she studied one, dead-eyed, with a growth like raw flesh protruding out of its mangy yellow fur. The sea, when they came to it, gave no feeling of air and lightness: the fine red powder of bauxite, sheds of corroded corrugated iron, the reek of the burning rubbish dump, everywhere here—hillside, forest, sea, mangrove—turned to slum.[1]

V.S. Naipaul, *Guerrillas*, N.Y. Knopf, 1975.

The blood of the prophet/is on the shoulder of Babylon.

Max Romeo, "Blood of the Prophet,"
Open the Iron Gate. United Artists Records, 1978.

I heard the words of the Rasta Man say
Babylon you throne gone down, gone down

Babylon you throne gone down.
(Traditional) arranged by The Wailers,
"Rasta Man Chant," *Burnin'*. Island Records, 1973.

America gave birth to rock 'n' roll and, however revolutionary the rude sounds of early rock 'n' roll may have seemed to its first public, the actual flirtation of some forms of rock music with at least the appearance of revolution in the late 1960s was very brief. Today, as anesthetized Muzak versions of rock songs hover in office-building elevators, rock music seems about as revolutionary to us as Big Macs. Mick Jagger and Rod Stewart tumble out at us from newspaper gossip columns along with Truman Capote, Andy Warhol, Lee Radziwill and other objects of our jaded curiosity. Rock music—shocking? Compared to what?

But that's not the whole story. What might hold true for American popular culture cannot always be applied to other settings. For example, in England, through such activities as the participation of a number of punk or new wave groups in the "Rock Against Racism" movement, the music maintains a strong

Reprinted with permission from *Journal of Popular Culture* Volume 17:1 (Summer, 1983), pp. 61-73.

identity with the forces of social and political change. But let us turn to a more unfamiliar milieu, which we will categorize as "Third World." Here I am thinking of the specific use of the term—*tiers monde*—by the Algerian revolutionary theorist Frantz Fanon; referring to those areas of the world in which the native populations of newly-emerging nations are struggling with the legacy of a dying colonialism.[2] In such a setting, the potentially revolutionary appeal of rock music is thrown more sharply into focus.

Such a case is provided by the tiny Caribbean island country of Jamaica, and Jamaican rock music is called Reggae. Formerly a British colony, Jamaica attained independence in 1962,[3] and has had to struggle toward a separate identity over many obstacles. It is a country full of contradictions and ironies, many of them to be found in the capital city of Kingston, where the stately homes of the white colonizers sit on hills that overlook Trenchtown—one of the worst slums of the Western hemisphere. Reggae is the music of Trenchtown, chiefly the music of displaced rural Jamaicans who have streamed into the slums of Kingston over the years to escape an even more frightful rural poverty. Reggae is thoroughly Jamaican, despite its obvious debt to black American rock forms. Reggae records are produced in independent Jamaican studios by Jamaican producers and engineers, with skilled, seasoned native studio musicians. It is a *recorded* music—only very recently have Reggae groups begun touring, and for concert tours they must go outside Jamaica. These studios release some thirty singles a week, and most of the copies are sold in Trenchtown.[4]

But in recent years, Reggae has become Jamaica's major new export—rivalling bauxite. As a result of this exposure of the rest of the world to Jamaica through this recorded music with growing participation of British and American record companies, people outside Jamaica have learned something of the explosive nature of Jamaican society. In particular, it is through the music that we have become more acquainted with the beliefs and customs of one of the world's most unusual subcultures: the Rastafarians (Brotherhood of Rastafari). The Rastafarians, concentrated in Jamaica but with many followers among large Jamaican immigrant population centers such as London and New York, are variously described as a religious cult, as a political movement within Jamaica, as a criminal element associated with drug dealing and violence, or as irresponsible dropouts. They are objects of considerable scorn among many segments of Jamaican society—black and white alike—and their extensive cultivation and use of ganja/marijuana brings them frequent clashes with the police.[5] Rastafarians are characterized by the police as violent and a threat to Jamaican society, yet many of the nation's leading artists, craftspeople, athletes and especially musicians are Rastas ("Rasta" or "Rastaman"; terms used more frequently than "Rastafarian").[6] They are the leading critics of Jamaica's government—the forces of Babylon to them—and their ideas dominate the lyrics of reggae songs to such an extent that recent albums by groups like Bob Marley and the Wailers and Burning Spear and artists like Peter Tosh and Max Romeo appear to have been intended more as Rastafarian sermons than as popular record albums.

There is no "official" Rastafarian theology; no canon; no church structure. Rastas agree on two principles of faith only (with wide differences on everything from personal appearance to whether or not Haile Selassie was the incarnate Christ or a god in his own right): 1) that Haile Selassie I—the king of kings, the lord of lords, Conquering Lion of the Tribe of Judah,—is the living God, and 2) that Africa is the real home of the Black Man; his paradise.[7] They see themselves as the lost children of Israel captive in Babylon, awaiting deliverance and repatriation: when "Jah" (Rastafari: Haile Selassie) leads them back to "Zion" (Ethiopia).

The story of the Rastafarians begins with the career of a self-styled black prophet from Jamaica who gained great prominence in Harlem in the 1920s: Marcus Mosiah Garvey—a man much maligned and misunderstood in this country, but much beloved and esteemed as a prophet by his fellow black Jamaicans.[8] Born in Jamaica in 1887, Garvey emigrated to the United States in 1916, and, the following year, founded the Universal Negro Improvement Association. Under Garvey's leadership, this organization became the leading exponent (to the horror of many middle-class blacks and liberal whites and to the delight of the Ku Klux Klan) of "redemption through repatriation" for blacks: Garvey taught that the Negro would always suffer as long as he was divorced from his true homeland—Africa.

Garvey wasted little time in taking steps to put his beliefs into practice. He founded his own newspaper, *The Negro World*, in New York soon after founding the U.N.I.A. Garvey's black nationalist slogan, "One Aim, One God, One Destiny," became the official motto of the newspaper. But the venture that proved his undoing was the establishment in 1919 of the Black Star Line to "link the colored peoples of the world in commercial and industrial discourse." Garvey sold shares in this company, which he promoted to potential backers as the means for returning New World Blacks to Africa. He even held meetings with the Klan to secure their investment in repatriation. Garvey traveled widely throughout the United States speaking in support of his schemes, even appearing in Harlem and elsewhere in what could only be called Napoleon regalia. Garvey was a short, powerfully-built man of regal bearing. His critics of course called him ostentatious. A proud man, he preached black pride and black consciousness in a Jim Crow era. As a result, the federal authorities were gunning for him. In 1922, after the Black Star Line went bankrupt, Garvey and three associates were indicted on several counts of mail fraud stemming from the sales campaign for the company's shares. Garvey was indicted of mail fraud in 1923, but was free on bond until 1925, when the conviction was upheld and he began serving a sentence in the federal penitentiary in Atlanta. President Coolidge commuted his sentence in 1927 and Garvey was deported to Jamaica.

Garvey was nevertheless a prophet with honor in his own country; indeed he had become something of an international celebrity. For example, in Kenya no less a personality than the young Jomo Kenyatta listened with great interest to Garvey's message of black strength and solidarity. Jamaicans listened enthusiastically to Garvey's talks in the months after his return, and he made something of a splash in Jamaican politics. He eventually grew impatient with his native country and moved to England in 1935, where he oversaw his dwindling international movement. He died there in 1940.[8]

But before Marcus left Jamaica behind he made a speech in Kingston that became the launching pad for Rastafarianism. In a Kingston church on a Sunday, in 1927 Garvey proclaimed (prophesied), "Look to Africa, where a black king shall be crowned." Garvey's followers were thus extremely interested in November of 1930 when the Kingston *Daily Gleaner* ran on its front page the story that a relatively unknown tribal chieftain named Ras Tafari Mekonnen had been crowned Haile Selassie I (The name means "Power of the Holy Trinity"). Was this the black king Marcus had prophesied, the Garveyites wondered?[10] The faithful, like all Jamaicans steeped in a tradition of Bible-thumping revivalism, pored over the scriptures to find some clue about this Haile Selassie. And in Revelation 5:5 they found this:

Then one of the elders said to me, "Weep not; lo, the lion of the tribe of Judah, the Root of David, has conquered, so that he can open the scroll and its seven seals."[11] (R.S.V.)

When Ethiopia won the world's admiration for its heroic resistance to Mussolini in 1935, the excitement in Jamaica over Haile Selassie increased. Some began to call him "Jah," a word whose origins are obscure. It may, however, be related to a word used in certain Masonic rituals. The Masons, in fact, had been active in Jamaica. His followers regarded him as the Living God, and Marcus Garvey was elevated to a kind of John the Baptist status. Thus was born the brotherhood of Rastafari.

Only gradually did other Jamaicans learn of the existence within their country of a growing body of people who rejected Jamaican society and longed to be transported to Africa. Through periodic confrontations with the law the Rastas began to intrude more and more into the Jamaican consciousness. In 1933 a Rastafarian named L.P. Howell was imprisoned as a result of his attempt to sell 5000 pictures of Haile Selassie purporting to be exclusive passports to Ethiopia. When Howell got out of prison in 1940, he moved with his followers into the remote hills of Jamaica; the historic place of refuge for the runaway slaves who came to be called "maroons," and founded a settlement called Pinnacle. The police raided this settlement in 1941 and arrested 70 people on charges of growing ganja and violence.[13]

From this point on the Rastas began to be associated in the popular mind with violence and crime.[14] In the 1950s Rastas were often arrested, and sometimes flogged and forcibly shaved. Rastas even charged that in Trenchtown the police deliberately burned many children to death.[15] 1955 in particular was a violent year of demonstrations over the subject of repatriation.[16] In 1960, several Rastas, anxious to alter the violent prejudices most Jamaicans had against them, asked some scholars at the University of the West Indies in Kingston to prepare a report on the Rastafarian movement. The results of the report, which concluded that most Rastafarians were non-violent, that they were an important part of the cultural life of Jamaica, and that their cannabis cultivation and use posed no great threat to society, and that they really were sincere about repatriation and ought to be supported by the government in moving to Africa, did not please the government, either in Kingston or London, and the report was largely ignored.[17]

On April 21, 1966 one of the most extraordinary spectacles in post-colonial Jamaican history unfolded at Palisadoes Airport where thousands of Rasta were on hand to greet the arrival of Emperor Haile Selassie I, who was on a state visit. When pandemonium erupted upon his landing, Selassie at first refused to leave his plane. He expressed dismay over the hysterical crowd who were worshipping his divinity (he later emphatically denied his own divinity, but the Rastas were not swayed by this; even Jah, they said, could not gain say the prophecy), but he finally relented and basked in the outpouring of affection from this and other gatherings in Jamaica. He appeared to enjoy himself immensely during his stay, and while some Jamaicans expressed surprise that "Jah" was a mere 5 feet 4 inches..., most were pleased with his kingly demeanor.[18]

Ethiopians occasionally expressed some interest in the desires of the Jamaican brethren to settle in Ethiopia. In 1955 the Ethiopian government had set aside some 500 acres of land for "the black peoples of the West," but only a few ever came. This was at the same time that large numbers of Jamaicans began to emigrate to London.[19] While Haile Selassie was willing to accept a few settlers from Jamaica, the thought of thousands of ganja-smoking unemployed aliens living in his country made him reluctant to make overtures to the eager Rastafarians. The Jamaican government of Prime Minister Michael Manley, while—like its predecessors—opposed to the idea of wholesale repatriation of large numbers, was willing to play up the "Ethiopian connection" to win the support of the Rastas. When Manley visited Ethiopia before Haile Selassie was overthrown in the coup of 1973, Selassie gave him a handsome walking stick that Manley, with his flair for adopting the Biblical style of the Rastas, called "the rod of correction."[20] But, despite signs from Manley that he, like the present more moderate government of Edward Seaga, was interested in maintaining good relations with the brotherhood of Rastafari (though not willing as yet to legalize marijuana, one of their chief demands), most Rastas still say they await the "return to Zion."[21]

If I dream, mon, every Rastamon's dream, to fly home to Ethiopia and leave a-Babylon, where de politicians doan let I an' I brethren be free an live we own righteous way.[22]

Although there is not universal agreement among Rastas concerning specific religious practices, the movement as a whole is known in Jamaica and abroad for two things in particular: the extensive use of and devotion to ganja as a way of life, and the practice among male members of wearing the hair, which they refuse to cut, in "locks" or "dreadlocks." Not all Rastas adopt this style, while many "false Rastas" do, and differences can be found among Rastafarians on matters of diet, sex, children and work. Use of ganja, however, is universal—true of many non-Rasta Jamaicans as well.[23]

Ganja has long been a part of Jamaican folk culture, though a likely explanation is that immigrants from India introduced cannabis to Jamaica in the mid-19th century. "Ganja" is the Hindu word for marijuana, and "Kali," the name for an Indian black goddess, is also the name of a particularly potent grade of dark-colored ganja. For generations in Jamaica ganja has been not only smoked, but brewed as tea and eaten as seasoning in soups and stews. Most of its uses have been medicinal (note recent discussions of marijuana and glaucoma), including use of ganja tea to calm upset stomach in children. Ganja is cultivated on a grand scale in Jamaica and, despite the activities of Jamaican and American authorities, ganja is the island's true cash crop.[24]

For Rastas, ganja—"herb"—has sacramental importance. The marijuana high is valued as something more than pleasurable; it is cherished as a "righteous" state; prayerful and contemplative. Much of Rasta theology is composed of specific and curious verses of scripture, and interpretations thereof, from the Old and New Testaments. Nowhere is this more obvious than on the subject of "herb." The specific verses used to support the copious sacramental use of marijuana are Psalm 18:8 and Revelation 22:2.[25] The 18th Psalm finds David giving thanks for a victory in battle, and then the Lord appears to David in anger. In verse 8 we are told that "Smoke went up from his nostrils, and devouring fire from his mouth," and this is taken by Rastafarians as evidence that God himself smokes the herb and urges his children to do so. The passage in Revelation is the "river and the tree of life" passage where "The leaves of the tree were for the healing of the nation." Ganja again?

Numbers 6:5 is another source from which the Rastas extract the scriptural authority for one of their most curious practices. This verse begins, "All the days of his separation no razor shall come upon his head."[26] Since Rastafarians take themselves to be "Israelites" separated from "Zion," this has been used as the scriptural basis of the refusal of many male Rastas to cut their hair. Many are "locksmen"; wearing their hair in plaits, which they themselves smear with lard, called "dreadlocks," often for convenience stuffing the mass of hair into large woolen caps, frequently in the red-green-and-gold of Ethiopia.[27] Other Rastas are "beardsmen," keeping the hair short above but allowing "no razor upon the beard." Some Rastas have both locks and beards, and some are "baldheads."[28] But tonsorial considerations should not be allowed to override concern with what lies within, as the Rasta saying about "false Rastas" who adopt the style without the real commitment reflects: "Him have locks on head but not in heart."[29]

Native Jamaicans speak a thick *patois* that reveals certain African survivals in their dialect, and Rastas have a dialect all their own. These Rasta linguistic inventions frequently find their way into reggae songs, where they provide the uninitiated with no end of confusion. Words like "Jah" we have mentioned, but then there is the mystifying tendency of Rastas to use the nominative case exclusively: "I," "I and I," "I and I brethren."[30] This extends to the substitution of an "I"-prefix for the first syllable of a word, e.g.: "I-dren" (children) or

Rock Music in the Third World 231

"I'tal" (natural).[31] Reggae songs are literally peppered with Rasta slogans such as "I-Ree-Ites" ("Higher Heights" or perhaps "Israelites").[32]

Many Rastafarians are vegetarians, and insist on "I-tal" food, emphasizing vegetables, fruits and grains. Some refuse to drink alcohol, while many enjoy Jamaica's Red Stripe Beer or Dragon Stout. Some, like Orthodox Jews and Muslims, will eat no pork, often preferring goat as their choice of meat. Such prohibitions are of course biblical, and many Rastas go beyond the dietary laws to enforce certain taboos such as the Old Testament admonition against sleeping with a woman who is menstruating. This stricture carries over into Jamaican popular culture generally, for the most violent curses and epithets are menstrual (Blood clot! Ras clot! Bumba clot!—all eligible for use as either nouns or adjectives). Some Rastafarians are polygamists, and there is generally no marriage ceremony.[33] Rastas are very much opposed to birth control, which they suspect is part of a white program to limit the size of the black race.[34] In V.S. Naipaul's novel *Guerrillas*, set in Jamaica, this item is noted among the graffiti along a busy Kingston thoroughfare: "Birth Control is a Plot Against the Negro Race."[35]

Of crucial importance to Jamaica is the debate within the Rastafarian movement over whether to cooperate at all with "Babylon" and, if so, to what extent. Most Rastas are unemployed, chronic unemployment being a basic feature of Jamaican life, but many reject the idea of working "for Babylon" anyway. "Don't vote" is another familiar slogan found in places like Trenchtown, and yet reggae songs have been used by both major political parties in recent elections,[36] an acknowledgement that reggae music, Rastafarian influences and all, has become a major cultural force in Jamaican life. For example, Prime Minister Michael Manley's campaign song in the 1972 election was a reggae hit called "Better Must Come."[37] Most recent reggae songs trumpet the certain downfall of Babylon, the Armageddon that will surely come, in much the same way that punk rock groups in Britain gloat over the diminishing power of the U.K.

Reggae is the music, part journalism, part prophecy, that captures the cultural contradictions of the new Jamaica, pounding them into the consciousness with a hypnotic beat.

Reggae

"Reggae" is the latest form of Jamaican rock 'n' roll, evolving over a period of 15 years or so and including African, native Jamaican and American influences, not necessarily in that order. Traditional Jamaican music called Mento, uses African drumming techniques and is somewhat akin to calypso, until now the best-known Caribbean music. The Rastas scornfully regard calypso as the music of the "rum culture"; of the tourists who never see places like Trenchtown. If you go to hear live music in Jamaica, you will hear calypso, not reggae, for live reggae is banned in Jamaica. Calypso is considered "safe," reggae subversive. Because of the concert ban, in effect because of the violence associated with some concerts and dances, and the policy of the J.B.C. of restricting the playing of reggae records to certain times (recently, after midnight) virtually the only way to hear reggae is to buy the records. Thus, the history of reggae is the history, primarily, of a recorded music.[38]

In the 1972 Perry Henzell film *The Harder They Come*, whose soundtrack provides a wonderful sampling of reggae music (for that time), offers a look at several aspects of the Jamaican recording industry. Jimmy Cliff, the reggae singer who plays the lead character in the film, Ivan Martin, arrives in Kingston a naive "country boy" eager to interest a record producer in his singing-songwriting talents.

When he submits songs, after a humiliating period of waiting, he is rebuffed only to discover later that one of his compositions has become a hit. He will receive no royalties; the song was simply stolen. This portrait of a recording industry in which copyrights did not exist, songs were sold by their composers for a few dollars, and musicians were victimized by hidden clauses in contracts they had been forced to sign but had not understood is apparently no exaggeration of the situation in Kingston at that time. Conditions have improved somewhat since reggae has entered its "international phase."

Most of these independent recording studios also own record shops in Kingston, and a single record can be made, mastered, printed and delivered to the shop in a matter of hours. Many of the producers themselves began as sound-systems men. These flourished in the early 60s when whatever rock music was to be had was coming from the United States. Jamaicans could not hear rock 'n' roll on the radio in Jamaica, but, at certain times, broadcasts from Louisiana or Florida strayed over the airwaves, and, in this way, Jamaica was exposed to the American popular forms. Jamaicans were interested in black American music and in rock 'n' roll. This began as "rhythm 'n' blues" and later came to be called "soul music." New Orleans was of special importance. Black people in New Orleans, more so than in other American cities, had maintained many African qualities in their music. Thus, radio broadcasts from New Orleans, which could frequently be picked up in Jamaica, featured a kind of "New Orleans version" of "R & B," rhythmically more complex than other American forms and related to mento and other Jamaican folk forms.

These influences created the development of a succession of musical styles in Jamaica throughout the 1960s. The earliest form of Jamaican-flavored rock 'n' roll was called "ska." The beat was much faster than reggae; in fact much of "ska" seemed similar to calypso. In the mid-to-late 60's the beat slowed down to a much more strident pace, and the label "rocksteady" was applied. This was the music associated by Jamaicans with the "rudeboys": gangs of Kingston youths who clashed with the police on several occasions (Bob Marley and the Wailers were once called "The Wailing Rudeboys"). Very few people outside Jamaica paid any attention to "ska" or "rocksteady." There was, however, one ska hit and one rocksteady hit internationally. A singer called Little Millie Small recorded "My Boy Lollipop" and this enormously popular record was just about the only sound the world heard from Ska. Then in 1968 it was Rocksteady's turn when Desmond Dekker and the Aces scored a triumph with "The Israelite," a song of intricate rhythms whose references to Rasta theology were lost on most non-Jamaicans.

Rock Music in the Third World 233

In Jamaica in these years the records were being played by a few disc jockeys and by the "sound systems men." These men, many of them to become record producers later, outfitted vans and trucks with stereo systems, and, having obtained copies—sometimes illegally—of the latest American and Jamaican records, drove their vehicles, equipped with the latest in sounds to provide the music at neighborhood dances in Kingston. The Reggae sound was, in a way, born at such dances. The sound systems men began to notice that people most enjoyed dancing to records when they exaggerated the bass level of the "system." Because of this preference, when these men became record producers themselves, they mixed the sound on each record to accentuate the bass and rhythm tracks. Eventually, the beat slowed some more, and, in 1968, singer Toots Hibbert, leader of the reggae vocal trio Toots and the Maytals, recorded a single called "Do the Reggay" (he says he was thinking of "regular"; to celebrate everyday people), and the present label for Jamaican rock came into being.[39]

This preference for the bass and rhythm tracks of a reggae song led to one of the most unusual genres within reggae. This music is called "dub," and it was developed by the sound systems men to satisfy the demand for dance music. It became customary for single records to be released with a "dub" side. The "A" side contained the "hit," and the "B" side was the dub version: lead vocal tracks were removed, and the sound was remixed to provide special emphasis on the bass and rhythm tracks. A good dub record gives the impression that it is on the verge of blowing out the bass channel of a stereo speaker, and the best dub records feature layer upon layer of rhythmic jamming: the overall effect giving the impression of flavorings of sound bubbling up out of some mysterious cauldron. Dub records also gave rise to a special kind of reggae star: the disc jockey. At dances or on radio programs the person playing the record would improvise a kind of talk-song over the rhythm tracks, and in some cases became a celebrity in his own right, overshadowing the musicians on the record itself. Some of these dub stars include Prince Jazzbo, Dillinger, Scotty, U-Roy and Big Youth.[40]

Hypnotic rhythm is Reggae's trademark. Reggae is slower than rocksteady,[41] and the bass guitar and drums are the true lead instruments. Guitars and keyboards are usually limited to rhythm and, together with the occasional use of horns, are used to flavor the basic rhythmic structure. Drumming is one of the most unusual features of reggae, and bears some relationship to the African-style native drumming of Jamaica: the sounds associated with the Niyabingi—or "Niya men." Ras Michael and the Sons of Negus are the most popular group in this tradition.[42] One reason that reggae takes some getting used to is that the accents fall on the first and third beats, unlike the accented second and fourth beats in standard rock drumming. The reggae beat is closer to an African syncopated style, and demands a level of musicianship that only the most skilled rock drummer could approach. This attention to rhythm and percussion is a constant reminder of African roots, and, in Jamaica, music that adheres closely to this tradition is accorded the affectionate label of "roots" music. The Reggae groups that play true roots music are valued highly, while groups that venture closer to mainstream rock are sometimes criticized for abandoning "roots." Criticism of some of the music of the leading reggae band, Bob Marley and the Wailers, especially since they began to attract a following in the United States, runs along these lines. Reggae has also shown a tendency over the years to reflect increasingly the emphasis of the Rastas, and to offer many criticisms of Jamaican society from the point of view of the Rastafarian sub-culture. As the popularity of reggae has grown, so has awareness of the Rastas' discontent and of the divisions within Jamaican society.

Not all reggae stars are Rastas, but most are sympathetic to them, and the musicians certainly share the Rastas' enthusiasm for ganja. One of the most popular reggae artists internationally is Jimmy Cliff, although he is *persona non grata* among many Rastas for his espousal of the Black Muslim faith. He also lives in England, while every other reggae celebrity lives in Jamaica. But the film *The Harder They Come*, in which Cliff starred, offered a very sympathetic look at the Rastafarians, and in his songs, such as the hits "You Can Get It If You Really Want," "The Harder They come," "Sitting in Limbo" and "Many Rivers to Cross," he certainly seems to share the Rastafarian emphasis on black liberation and opposition to the powers of Babylon. One of the most popular Jamaican groups is Toots and the Maytals, featured in *The Harder They Come*. Their music, in such classics as "Pressure Drop" and "Reggae Got Soul," is recognizably close to American "soul" music, and lead singer "Toots" Hibbert acknowledges his debt to such singers as Otis Redding. Toots is a recent convert to Rasta, though he doesn't wear locks.[43] Toots, as noted above, is given credit for coining the word "reggae."

Certainly the best-known group is Bob Marley and the Wailers, and the face of Bob Marley, locks flashing, on the cover of magazines and record albums is the only look most people have had of a Rastaman. In some circles in Jamaica, Marley has acquired a near-prophet status. The peak of this adulation of Marley as an exemplary Rasta man was reached in 1975, when Bob Marley released a single immediately after the death of Haile Selassie called "Jah Live."[44] Of late he has slipped in the estimation of some brethren, because of his commercial success with the Wailers. The spectacle of a wealthy Rastafarian is rather paradoxical.

Marley was not always in the center of the spotlight. Originally, his group was called The Wailing Rudeboys, then The Wailers, and Marley was but one of a superb vocal trio that included Peter (MacKin) Tosh and Neville "Bunny" Livingstone. The Wailers were groomed for stardom by Coxone Dodd, a legendary Kingston producer. In the mid-sixties they were wearing matching suits and ties and singing versions of American pop songs like "Ten Commandments of Love." Late in the Sixties they became Rastas and expanded from a trio with pickup backing musicians. Most notably they added the Barrett Brothers—Ashton "Family Man" Barrett and Carlton Barrett—one of the greatest Jamaican rhythm sections. The Wailers thus had a hand in forging the basic reggae sound, and their recorded work, like that of other reggae groups, moved more and more in the direction of "Natty Dread"; defying Babylon. The last two albums by the original group, *Catch a Fire* and *Burnin'*, are filled with images of "Burnin' and-a-lootin' " and suggest that Babylon will pay for its sins with violent revolution.

In 1974 Bunny Livingstone and Peter Tosh left the group, and Marley, now pushed to the forefront, altered the group's (now Bob Marley and the Wailers) sound by adding a back-up trio of the best women reggae singers in Jamaica: The I-Threes (Rita Marley—his wife—Judy Mowatt and Marcia Griffiths). It is this new group that has gained international fame and success. The greatest reason for this success is Marley himself. Through the lyrics of his songs he has become a major spokesman for his fellow "Israelites," and his personal magnetism helps to make Wailers' concerts sensational. At times, on a stage that features Ethiopian flags and blow-up photos of Haile Selassie, Marley stands riveted to one spot, holding tightly to his Gibson Les Paul and testifying for Jah. Then he is off in a frenzy of motion, dreadlocks flying, looking like some Rasta Dionysus dancing the dance of doom for Babylon. The irony of making his fortune in the wider Babylon (America, Europe, etc.) is not lost on Marley, however, and the title of the last live concert album of Bob Marley & the Wailers is *Babylon By Bus*.[45]

But Marley cannot escape the ironies of success within the wider rock audience. Some Jamaicans feel he has moved too far from roots music, and have shifted their enthusiasm to groups like Burning Spear and the reggae singer Peter Tosh, Wailer-alumnus. Burning Spear are from the Jamaican hill country, and their songs evoke a different milieu than Trenchtown slums'. They make use of African rhythms, and are hailed as true "roots" artists. Their name is from Jomo Kenyatta, the Burning Spear of Kenya, and they refer constantly to Marcus Garvey.[46] In 1975 they released the album *Marcus Garvey*, and later a dub version called *Garvey's Ghost*. Peter Tosh is valued by those who want to insure that reggae will continue to be the music of protest, and his "Get Up, Stand Up" ("Stand up for your rights/Get up, stand up/Don't Give up the fight"), is one of the most strident Rasta anthems. Additional themes and genres will likely emerge as long as Jamaica's troubles persist.

Today reggae is in conflict with itself. It is bringing lots of attention and some money to Jamaica. Michael Manley's government wants to count on the reggae celebrities for support and contributions. But reggae is still in many respects outlaw music, which some feel is rock's rightful stance. This was made clear in 1976 when Peter Tosh's single "Legalize It" was banned in Jamaica.[47] Among other reasons given for legalization, Tosh suggested that the sale of marijuana could revive the island's failing economy.[48] Reggae songs call attention to certain features of Jamaican life that the government, anxious to attract tourist dollars, would like to hide. By reminding its audience of the conflicts within society, reggae plays a Voltairean role: mocking the government for its short-sightedness and its stubborn clinging to colonial traditions.

Reggae songs are bits of journalistic commentary, heeded at times more closely than the Jamaican press, as Prime Minister Manley has acknowledged. And, as reggae star Max Romeo says, "People will pay a dollar for my message and reject the politician they can hear free of charge."[49] As Jamaica walks a "thin wire"[50] between its colonial heritage and what lies ahead, reggae should provide a critical look, if not a revolutionary impetus for change.

We may draw some lessons from this for the Third World generally. Could some native adaptation of rock music flourish in some other potentially revolutionary neo-colonial setting? The fact that rock is on America's main street now is no guarantee that it will follow that model in all other countries. Rock 'n' roll began with a strong revolutionary potential. The New Wave rockers in England are now trying to reclaim that legacy. But perhaps the future of rock lies not in the West but in the changing Third World, where the music, fusing a strident beat with native rhythms, can become the voice of previously voiceless peoples.

Epilogue

Since I presented an earlier version of this paper, at the October, 1979 meeting of the Midwest Popular Culture Association, two key changes have occurred in Jamaica. In the 1980 elections Prime Minister Michael Manley's part was defeated, and the more conservative Jamaican Labor Party, under Edward Seaga, came to power. Many have interpreted this as a repudiation of the policies of Seaga's predecessor. Nothing in Seaga's remarks or political style, however, indicates any change in policy for reggae or the Rastafarians.

More recently, death has claimed reggae's greatest star, Bob Marley, who died May 11, 1981 of brain cancer. More than 30,000 Jamaicans viewed his body as it lay in state, including both Michael Manley and the new Prime Minister. This underscores the importance of reggae in Jamaican culture. An equivalent gesture would have been the attendance of both President Carter and President-elect Reagan at the memorial service for John Lennon. Yet the removal of Marley from the scene need pose no greater threat to the survival of reggae than the deaths of Lennon and Elvis Presley did for rock and roll. It may be that Toots Hibbert or Peter Tosh will now receive greater recognition, or that some new star will emerge.

Earlier I suggested that we might look to the Third World for the revolutionary spirit many feel is the essence of rock 'n' roll. Recent trends demonstrate that perhaps a fusion of Third World styles and British or American rock 'n' roll is developing rather than the widespread appearance of isolated styles. "Ska" has enjoyed a revival in England, where bands such as Madness, The Specials, The English Beat and The Selector play a frenzied, ska-flavored variety of rock 'n' roll dance music. Many of these groups consist of both Britons and Jamaicans.

Other New Wave bands, notably The Clash and Public Image, Ltd., employ "dub" effects or offer cover versions of reggae standards, as in The Clash's recording of Toots Hibbert's "Pressure Drop."[51] Stateside, the recent work of Talking Heads and the collaboration of David Byrne of that band and Brian Eno on *My Life in the Bush of Ghosts* (Sire Records, 1981) offer the best examples of rock 'n' roll that directly appropriates African and Caribbean influence.

Reggae may never receive the level of commercial success outside Jamaica that it merits. However, its survival seems assured there. Perhaps this fusion of Anglo-American and Third-World styles, which is what Brian Eno may be thinking of when he refers to "Fourth World,"[52] will produce the most artistically significant, if not the most popular, rock 'n' roll in the years to come.

Notes

[1]Naipaul's novel, set in Jamaica (though the location is not named) highlights the bleak social landscape.

[2]See Frantz Fanon, *The Wretched of the Earth* (New York: Grove, 1968), also G. Llewellyn Watson, "Social Structure and Social Movements: The Black Muslims in the U.S.A. and the Ras-Tafarians in Jamaica," *The British Journal of Sociology*, XXIV: 2 (June 1973), p. 190.

[3]Rex M. Nettleford, *Identity, Race and Protest in Jamaica* (New York: Morrow, 1972), p. 157.

[4]Stephen Davis and Peter Simon, *Reggae Bloodliness: In Search of the Music and Culture of Jamaica* (Garden City, N.Y.: Anchor, 1977), p. 111. This is the most useful book on reggae.

[5]Sheila Kitzinger, "Rastafarian Brethren of Jamaica," *Comparative Studies in Society and History*, IX: 1 (Oct. 1966), 33-39. See also Nettleford and Watson.

[6]Davis, p. 72.

[7]Ibid., p. 72.

[8]Literature on Garvey is fascinating and extensive; see especially Edmund David Cronon, *Black Moses: The Story of Marcus Garvey and the Universal Negro Improvement Association* (Madison: Univ. of Wisconsin Press, 1955); *Marcus Garvey*, ed. E.D. Cronon (Englewood Cliffs, N.J.: Prentice-Hall, Inc., 1973), in Prentice-Hall's "Great Lives Observed" series; Amy Jacques Garvey, *Garvey and Garveyism* (New York: Collier, 1970); Tony Martin, *Race First: The Ideological and Organizational Struggles of Marcus Garvey and the Universal Negro Improvement Association* (Westport, CT: Greenwood, 1976); and Elton C. Fox, *Garvey: The Story of a Pioneer Black Nationalist* (New York: Dodd, Mead, 1972). For speeches of Garvey and his followers see: *Philosophy and Opinions of Marcus Garvey*, ed. Amy Jacques Garvey (New York: Atheneum, 1970); *More Philosophy and Opinions of Marcus Garvey*, ed. E.U. Essien-Udom and Amy Jacques Garvey (London: Frank Cass, 1977); and *Black Redemption: Churchmen Speak for the Garvey Movement*, ed. Randall K. Burkett (Philadelphia: Temple Univ. Press, 1978). Reggae recordings are peppered with references to Garvey, especially the recordings of the Burning Spear, including their albums *Marcus Garvey* (Island Records, 1975) and *Garvey's Ghost* (Mango Records, 1975). Additional references may be heard in Peter Tosh's recording of "The Prophets," *Bush Doctor* (Rolling Stones Records, 1978) and in Bob Marley and the Wailers' "Kinky Reggae," *Catch A Fire* (Island Records, 1973).

[9]This summary is based chiefly on E. David Cronon, "Introduction" and "Chronology of the Life of Marcus Garvey," *Marcus Garvey*, ed. Cronon, pp. 1-16, 17-18; Davis, pp. 66-68; and "Would You Believe Rasta Theology?" *High Times* (Sept. 1976), pp. 58-59.

[10]Davis, p. 69.

[11]"Would You Believe Rasta Theology?" p. 59. See also Leonard Barrett, *The Rastafarians: Sounds of Cultural Dissonance* (Boston: Beacon, 1977), p. 83. Although this book has its flaws, the author demonstrates the ways in which Rastafarianism is rooted in various Jamaican revivalist traditions.

[12]"Would You Believe...?" p. 59.

[13]Kitzinger, p. 33.

[14]The growing tension between the Rastafarians and the Jamaican authorities is treated in Nettleford, pp. 39-111.

[15]Kitzinger, p. 33.

[16]Ibid., p. 34.

[17]Ibid., p. 36.

[18]Davis, pp. 76-77.

[19]Kitzinger, p. 34.

[20]Michael Thomas, "The Rastas Are Coming! The Rastas Are Coming!" *Rolling Stone* (Aug. 12, 1976), p. 34.

[21]Ibid., p. 37.

[22]Bob Marley, quoted in Ed McCormack, "Bob Marley With a Bullet," *Rolling Stone* (Aug. 12, 1976), p. 34.

[23]Davis, pp. 70-75. See also Kitzinger, pp. 37-38.

[24]Ibid., pp. 179-81.

[25]Ibid., p. 75.

[26]"The *High Times* Guide to Jamaica" *High Times* (Sept. 1976), p. 51.

[27]Kitzinger, p. 35.

[28]This terms is also used to express disdain for non-Rastas, as in Marley's song "Crazy Baldhead," *Rastaman Vibration* (Island Records, 1976).

[29]Davis, p. 75.

[30]Kitzinger, p. 35.

[31]"*High Times* Guide to Jamaica," p. 51.

[32]This last phrase is sung, e.g. by the "I-Threes"; the three female singers in Bob Marley and the Wailers, as a refrain in the song "Positive Vibration," *Rastaman Vibration* (Island, 1976). One of the most popular songs of the Jamaican band "Third World" is called "Irie Ites," and can be heard on the 1979 Island Records release *The Story's Been Told*.

[33]Davis, p. 75.

[34]Kitzinger, p. 37.

[35]V.S. Naipaul, *Guerrillas* (New York: Knopf, 1975), p.3.

[36]"Singing Them A Message," *Time* (March 22, 1976), p. 84.

[37]Davis, pp. 172-73.

[38]Ibid., pp. 12, 99.

[39]Ibid., pp. 13-17.

[40]Ibid., pp. 103-106.

[41]Ibid., p. 17.

[42]Kitzinger, p. 35.

[43]Davis, pp. 85-93.

[44]Ibid., p. 79.

[45]Ibid., pp. 31-37.

[46]Ibid., p. 54.

[47]Ibid., p. 126.

[48]Peter Tosh, "Legalize It," *Legalize It* (Columbia Records, 1976).

[49]"Singing Them a Message," p. 83.

[50] Thomas, p. 35.
[51] The Clash, *Black Market Clash* (Epic Records, 1980).
[52] John Hassell and Brian Eno, *Fourth World, Volume I: Possible Musics* (E.G. Records, 1980).

Disco: A Music for the 1980s?

Hugh Mooney

There's no doubt that Disco has been a style for the 1970s. This paper attempts primarily to suggest why. Then, warily—any self-appointed seer in the music game is in the risky position of plotting a path on quicksand—it will venture a note on Disco's chance of survival in some form into the 1980s.

First, in analyzing the major question of Disco's popularity in the 1970s, we'll have to observe 1968 to 1974's shifting, amorphous musical scene: some of the current events; changes in popular moods and in media responses to them; the increasing impact of minority tastes and womens' lifestyles; changes in entertainment patterns—all of which combined to produce the Disco vogue by 1975. We'll then touch on the extent to which Disco repudiated the 1960s; seek reasons for Disco's ever-increasing success throughout the last half of the 1970s; and finally, prognosticate on its near future.

Of course the term "disco" (usually in the full form "disco-theque") had been used in the earlier 1960s to denote nightspots where a jukebox or small combo played for the Twist dancing. True, neither the dances nor the social setting—usually, in the "better" spots, for date-dancing—were the milieu of modern Disco. But a Motown and Memphis bugaloo was coming on. So why, then, was Disco as we know it today—I use the term to refer to the music but it is part of an entire ambience—why was Disco to await the 1970s? The answer involves social and racial issues. For all the popularity in the 1960s of an increasingly latinate black dancing soul band style, the very fact that the two biggest heavy blues or soul singers—Joplin and Jagger-were white rockers indicates something. The mid to late 1960s were a time of racial unrest when the whims of consciously or unconsciously racist (or timid) white program directors and disk jockies with demographic heads in the sand might still somewhat resist trends. But this is a bit unfair to the deejays. Much black music was dance music, earthy perhaps but heavily "produced" in a rather routinized formulas unsuited to, demeaned by, freaked-out white middle class youth. Many carelessly affluent (or militantly seedy) college kids felt they had risen beyond the satiny bourgeois trappings so glamorous to the Supremes and other black boogie groups. And formal dancing, as distinct from the

Disco: A Music for the 1980s? 241

impromptu "when you feel like it" of rock concerts, just wasn't popular among the "in" young. They regarded it as inane or "obscene". Demonstrations supplanted proms or bar and hotel hopping. The nightclub scene became a middle-aged diversion. So many black artists, heavily devoted to slick vocal and dance groups, suffered neglect from "radical rock" whites.[1] without compensatory gains among "backlash" whites. For a time, it looked as though white and black tastes were travelling far apart. In 1968 Martha and the Vandellas castigated acid rock: "I Can't Dance to that Music." But by 1969 (after the smash success of Otis Redding's heavy brass-and-boogie soul "Respect") the Temptations' protest song, "Cloud Nine" and James Brown's "Say it Loud (I'm Black and Proud)" had crossed over from black into liberal white markets. With their soul band settings, they helped deepen liberal white demand for "bugaloo." This was now also more readily and frequently heard because black soul stations emphasizing the Motown sound had proliferated in the later 1960s[2]. By 1971 proto-Disco numbers like Sly Stone's "Family Affair" were on the charts more regularly. Soul boogie was favored by trendsetting gays in their dancing bars, which after the Gay Liberation street rebellion in New York City in 1969 were tolerated by the authorities in Manhattan and soon in San Francisco. Of this, more later.

Such *ur*-Disco, often spiced by latin *salsa*, was in the very early 1970s a comer not yet considered as the national trend by my students or by the industry either. Clive Davis, pop production chief at Columbia, in his 1974 autobiography gives it no special mention although he did stress the need for snappy, viscereal singles. Back in 1972-1973 when a retailer told me, "Trend? There is none," the Motown revival might well appear a victory by default, merely the most recent of many older forms (country, ballad, ragtime, mild jazz and swing band formats) which rushed in to fill the vacuum left in the wake of the catholic Beatles and the crested heavy rock wave. The "new" dance music had no name. It was sometimes called "party music." This term distinguished it from the pontifical, abstruse, prolix, tortuously philosophical rock once favored so heavily among the upper middle class youth of the later 1960s.

The rise of Disco paralleled the growing disfavor with stoned rock in the market place (and then with the languid ballads which succeeded such rock). Concept rock—acid, folk, progressive, art, heavy metal, whatever—had flourished in a prosperity which nourished diversity and innovation in product; in a temporarily radical anti-war market which may well have been magnified by those who catered to and sought to profit from it. Promoted first by indie labels and then, more warily, by big labels who kept a sharp eye on its sales, folk rock and heavy progressive could not remain unchallenged. In the early 1970s they were diminished by more conservative attitudes, and by the decline of the indie labels during two early 1970s recessions (that of 1973 compounded by a vinyl shortage).[3] The offensive during 1970-1976 passed from the (often provincial) independents of the 1960s to the labels who could afford the production expenses—and even then, took only very calculated risks. The industry was under a double handicap now. It faced a market diminished by inflation and it faced a rise in production and marketing expenses. Certainly more than in the mid-1960s cost accountants influenced the business—indeed, all but ran it.[4] These are not advocates of risk-taking for the joy of it. They have to convince bankers of their company's soundness.

It may seem puzzling that the black and hispanic music vital to Disco was to gain in so conservative a business climate. One doesn't easily connect boogie and banker. But, the validity of stereotypes aside, this was business, not esthetics. The recessions of 1970-1974 sharpened the industry's attention to demographics. Business people inside and outside music became more aware of the minority market concentrated in the inner cities. Blacks bought records later into adulthood than whites, as probably did adult hispanics. Less inhibited by Calvinist ideas of disciplined maturity, they carried transistor radios and sang on the streets. The media couldn't ignore them in favor of middle class whites who in the urban cores were no longer major consumers.[5] Once considering it "uneconomic" to advertise to poor blacks by using music offensive to the more "important" white market, white radio was discovering the necessity of beaming to "minorities" who were often in fact urban majorities![6]

So, preconditional for Disco were more black and hispanic (as well as feminine and gay) influences on and in the music media. What came to be called Disco emerged as media responded to an increased early 1970s demand for quick-shot, physical music. During the recessions and oil crunch, output and promotion must be centered on relatively few singles, or albums containing obvious potential Top 40 radio cuts; not on "uncommerical" concepts for freeform radio. How economic and media changes interacted with social and psychological shifts to affect musical trends has been well researched and analyzed elsewhere.[7] Suffice to note here that record production and consumption was already favoring short, tight 45s type music again, as in 1960, when dancing Disco hit full force in 1974/1975. Disco was to both gain from and contribute further to this tightening tendency. It was of course a tendency stimulated through black radio for one thing. But black radio also beamed into suburbia.

By 1971-1972, program directors might perceive that white suburbanites too were ripe for change.[8] "Respectable" women were taking Belly Dancing for night school credits and going into touch and feel encounter therapy. So much for Calvinism in suburbia. These new homemakers, the youth of the 1960s, were now more receptive to the pure joy of an afro-latin dancing beat. The 1960s neo-puritans and the hip millenium were gone. The world continued, neither regenerated nor blown up either. It was time for the Restoration, time to "Enjoy Yourself", to "Listen to the Music" (of the 1972 Doobie Brothers' almost-Disco hit); to take up where the gawkier gyrations of the Twist or Frug had left off. "Shake Your Booty". It was time to recall and revive Gladys Knight and the Pips, Marvin "Let's Get it On" Gaye, the Jacksons, and above all, Stevie Wonder, and mix with a touch of the old samba or conga. Sparked by inner core taste, geared to 45s rather than freeform albums, dancing soul was to be a winner, catapulting Wonder's "Boogie On, Reggae Woman" in late 1974. Already that summer had come Barry White's "Can't Get Enough"; soul to a samba beat with electric guitar thump, softly synthesized brass and strings playing more than a background to the vocal.

Disco: A Music for the 1980s? 243

The sound was arriving, as yet without a name. It should be reemphasized that the update bugaloo-with-latin, like the ballad and country upsurge, were indicating a reaction among many buyers away from heavy power back to a more acoustical sound. And yet, in order to cross over into the electronic sounds still in favor among many buyers and (naturally) studio engineers, the "new" products had their own synthesized and amplified sounds (smoothed).

With some easing of racial tension; with public overexposure to and boredom with a white music either too lack-lustre or too far-out; with subtle changes in black product; and finally, with the renewed urge to dance, Motown and Memphis sounds heightened between 1969 and 1974. Their stars, listened to and bought outside the ghetto, would become the driving force of Discomania.

Faintly anticipated in the "society" rumba craze of the 1930s, the way for Disco had been prepared in the 1950s, first by the Perez Prado mambo band and later by Mongosantamaria, favorites among New York's growing Puerto Rican community. With blazing horns, intricate but withal slick and easy to follow polyrhythms these were more appreciated by blacks than the convolutions of their own Jimi Hendrix. By 1969 Santana had brought something of this sound to white middle class youth.

But by 1974, these youth, tired of the concert approach of the more grandiose jazz-rock groups, wanted something to *move* to—one reason for the ragtime revival that year—a simple, physical music. But, nostalgia craze or no, ragtime was too old-timey. Many kids felt stranded and neglected by what was to them dull or incomprehensible music scene: arty ballads, arty rock, good at best for listening; dense post-Beatles avant garde, superfluous hold-overs from the outmoded acid rock be-ins.[10] Then came the fuse lit by "Boogie On", by Tower of Power, and Average White Band the winter of 1974-1975; and the "Disco" explosion. In analyzing the force of this explosion, we should consider that, due to Top 40 policy, lack of exposure to good album rock concepts might have compounded indifference to progressive rock and programmed the ears to a more rapid-impact music. Whatever the reasons, however, there was a place for Disco.

Was Disco, then, a repudiation of the 1960s and its social rock? Yes and no. For the socially aware 1960s radical, Disco might empathize with the two minorities who earliest embraced it—the Puerto Ricans and gays concentrated in the media center of the nation. Gays had danced to the vibrant *salsa* of a people who (in the contemptuous eyes of straight, square Americans) flaunted an "offensive" physical freedom. Legitimatized and wide open after the Greenwich Village gay riots in 1969, gay dancing bars soon attracted a straight "in" crowd. Their no date pattern, ideal for men coming out of the closet, was also a boon to "liberated" urban women. Although the music was tightly structured, the dancing, while graceful, was not; and the light shows suggested the 1960s.

Disco is a commentary on the ambivalent cross-currents of the 1970s, a decade desiring pleasure but largely past the banalities of the 1950s. The sensualism of the 1970s was tougher and, with the disintegration of 1960s idealism, more skeptical. For the socially-concerned holdovers of the 1960s,

Disco may have suggested gay rights, women's liberation, and latino pride. But for many other youth it expressed, if not total disillusion with the utopian-rural-commune syndrome, an urbane, realistic, even cynical acceptance of life as it is rather than as it should be: Between Disco and the renascent Night Club was a symbiosis of the 1970s.

It was almost a replay of the brisk apartment living, the brash music of the 1920s. For a revived interest in Big City games was impelling some suburbanites back into town for the pulse of Hot Streets, the chance of pursuing and living close to an urban career, the glamor, the clubs. That's what Disco was about—New York above all. The early 1970s had seen reconcentration in the record industry; and while Los Angeles and Nashville shared in the scene, the Big Apple was the focal point for business, for talent, for the ambience of the new Disco. It wasn't the hicks and sticks Sun Records days anymore, it was satiny, slithering 1933, except Billy Joel moved the old "42nd Street" up ten blocks. Disco was the hard, exuberant but dressy city of Odyssey's "Native New Yorker" reasserting itself against the cowpastures of an all but forgotten Woodstock. Perhaps this is poorly put: New York didn't oppose the boondocks, it co-opted them. Alan O'Day's "Undercover Angel" (1977). Slickly packaged big-city sex, country lovin', latin, soul, and electronic rock, with a touch of Brick's "Dazz" (Disco, Jazz). But the major thrust of the new dance music was urban black, with assists from other "minorities"—women, gays, and especially "hispanics" (afro-latin, Indian). From media strongholds in New York City and Los Angeles, they assaulted the "white middle class hinterlands" (to use a cliche inapplicable to Chicago, Detroit, Cleveland, Kansas City!) New York meant two different kinds of slickness: not only ASCAP-Broadway's finely-crafted little tunes; but also the hard, staccato, non-philosophical yet city-wise vernacular of neighborhood streets and Saturday night blasts. This street-smartness put down hick amateurs—with reservations, since urban rock and soul do have gutty country roots.

Ambivalent in many ways, Disco recalled the 52nd Street *boite* styles of the 1920s and 1930s which, smoothly processing raw materials of ghetto life uptown, blended upper middle class and outcast folkways. The night club renaissance in New York was underway by 1975. Preconditional to the music heard there was as we have seen the Top 40 radio format and its exposure of Afro-latin dance music. But beyond this, radio was to do little until 1977-1978 and the smash success of *Saturday Night Fever* specifically to exploit Disco. (After 1977 radio's large Disco time slots and even all-Disco stations would help the vogue to peak). Much more potent in the early days of the craze were records; or, more basically, the demands of the newly-powerful deejays in the Disco clubs who at last gave the music a name.

How did these deejays—some of them products of the gay bars attuned to dancing soul and Spanish Harlem sounds—become so powerful? Because they had practically grown up psyching the tricky currents of a shifting social life where ambivalences titillated; where 1960s emulation of outcast somehow was somehow mixed in with a newly-conspicuous consumption; where in-crowd snobs-in-reverse absorbed a smattering of ghetto culture and flaunted

Disco: A Music for the 1980s? 245

it in the face of middle-Americans who then simply had to join the parade—an old story. The new discos, like the old Peppermint Lounge where Jackie and her beautiful people loved to be photographed doing the Twist, became the haunts of the incrowd by 1975. The Disco deejays became ever more important of Harlem, smoothed for the smart set, began to penetrate middleamerica. The deejays practically told the record companies what to produce for this growing market. Their rejection could be the kiss of death, their approval the beginning of a million dollar sales spiral.[11]

Disco has been more than a flash in the pan since 1975 because in so many ways it's moved to the contemporary pulse. Disco lured—among others—working class youth desiring status—even "law and order"—unlike 1960s acid rocker coupon clippers rejecting it. Recession can take the glamor from poverty clothes. Disco "dressed up", sartorially and musically. It well suited those with only so much time and money to spare, wanting instant action; rather than endlessly stoned youth passively receiving attenuated, time-obliterating rock. It was scored precisely arranged; the very antithesis of improvised, literally disorderly 1967 rock. But while Disco may have contrasted to the 1960s in many ways, it still might express many white upper middle class youths; empathy with minorities. "Disco's a perfect medium for street kids and at the same time for West Hartford kids who want to be like them."[12] (The middle, as usual, followed along). And the high high-impact, continuous flow music of the salad days of Jagger and the New York Dolls continued with Rod Stewart and Village People. The dancing, more graceful and ritualized than in the 1960s, and with somewhat more physical contact, nevertheless drew some inspiration from the non-coupled, spontaneous movements of a decade ago. Saturday night fever could be fun and pure escape; jiggle on the dance floor like jiggle on the tube. But Disco might liberate girls; or glamorize the status race of a humdrum outside work world in a dazzling competition under magical spotlights where triumphs were more rapidly attainable than Out There.

Disco was a music made for the 1970s. Behind this apparently simple statement were two agents: the public itself with its sensual mood, and the "makers" who exploited and intensified that mood. The makers—New York entertainment executives and gays (sometimes one and the same)—were the avant garde of the in-the-know, sexually "open" nightlife cosmopolities who somehow were able to sense, anticipate, and influence tastes. Americans were ready for mellow night club dancing; weary of 1960s preachments, polarizations, and poverty garb; ready to be gay in the old, perhaps the new, sense. And, since for one thing the Big Apple rather than the cowpastures was once more the cynosure of their eyes, the cultural leadership of New York City was more secure than a decade earlier, when more trends had been made in the provinces. New York's *Billboard* was first among the media publications to grasp the significance of the trend. In emphasizing the rising profits of the Disco-night club industry, *Billboard's* reporting actually pushed the commercial expectations even higher: by 1977 Disco clubs opened throughout the country in anticipation of ever higher profits, and small bar jukebox jobbers were busy supplying product. Though I can at present find no explicit documentary evidence, at least one knowledgeable student of pop music has indicated that future scholarship would do well to investigate the obvious support given to Disco promotion by electronic equipment manufacturers, lighting systems people, and others profiting from reestablishing night club enterprise.

City-smart Disco would continue to draw support from the strong gay communities in Los Angeles and Hollywood as well as San Francisco yet such things as Village People's "YMCA" were eventually to Bronx-cheer for a much larger market the overbred music of what one Disco enthusiast termed the "wailing art-rockers" so typical of introspective Californians, of breakroots kids without neighborhood ties seeking "identity" on indie labels on the coast in the late 1960s. This youth's tendermindedness was sabotaged in Disco. While some California pensiveness and lyricism lingered, most mainstream Disco derived more strongly from the neighborhood street-savvy traditions of tougher, more self-assured, extroverted and close-knit east coast youth. Ready to face life with fewer questions or disquisitions and more "shove it", Disco's arrogant grace shafted not only the slow-witted bucolic but the angelic Wordsworthian man-made and woman-child of Big Sur. The New York stance meant more of Rocky and the Fonz, of Billy Joels from working-class Levittown, Long Island; less of the fragile poetry still heard in California Jackson Browne, less groping for Ultimate Wisdom. It meant less of Neil Young's "See the Sky"; more wised-up techniques for "Stayin Alive". For all his social protest, Bruce Springsteen's philosophy was, "You gotta be tough or you get trashed, ya know."[13] Billy Joel, ambivalent in his love for 52nd Street, might lament its loneliness and cynicism in "Honesty"; but he enjoined his audiences, "Don't take any shit from anyone".[14] The 1970s trended worldly.

Disco was worldly. It was out of New York and Oakland—not the California of suburbanites but West Oakland with its large black and Chicano communities, served by well established urban core indie radio and records. Tower of Power, whose "Only So Much Oil" in 1974 referred to the crisis which would in effect facilitate its classy style, was a mixed black-white Oakland group in the 1960s chicano-blues band tradition of Nat Hendrix, who had recorded locally to back up Sugar Pie Desanto.[15] Linking coast ghetto and Gotham splash, Tower had heralded a glossily recorded music for no date dancing in bars which, despite an image of high fashion, were cheap in a recession. In Disco, polemics were out, sound was in. There was less need for the "I Am Woman" thing. Women celebrated new freedoms by dancing where unescorted girls were no longer barred outright or branded as prostitutes and open game. For autonomous girls Disco replaced the stoned vagaries of the rock concert. Special Disco albums of short cuts replaced protracted concepts. Music was compressed into finely honed little gems reminiscent of the swing era: Tuxedo Junction's version of Glen Miller's "Chattanooga ChooChoo" and Duke Ellington's "I Don't Know About You" hit the jukeboxes in 1978. (If in the bigger Disco clubs, deejays in engineering control booths selected a constant flow of specially amplified records, in small bars the juke box was stronger than ever. Either way, the emphasis was on short-play 45s or album cuts.)

Disco: A Music for the 1980s? 247

So, sometimes with an assist from the brass of the old big bands, Disco was an often latinate updating of R and B; largely a descendent of soul bands. As in K.C. and the Sunshine Band's "That's the Way I Like It", vocalists were merely part of the rhythmic sound. For *The Sensuous Woman*, the Disco years, despite the "Misty Blue" moods, would be at least more buoyant than the lugubrious Grace Slick and Janis Joplin "Women is Losers" 1960s. Like the lives more "successful" women were approaching in the 1970s, like their couture, Disco music and dance had a formal gloss. Like the smooth-tough "Savoir-faire" of the new fashion models, "lib" without doleful diatribes. "I Will Survive" said it all.

Disco accompanied a drug shift. More alcohol (often beer) was consumed than acid. Disco eliminated the prolix lyrics and dense psychedelic sounds of the old open air acid concerts or the protracted acid-and-stereo zonkouts. Coke was the new "in" thing and, unlike acid, it was stimulating, making you dance faster and faster to a breezy, happy aphrodisiac music.[16]

The musical texture was satiny. Flowing over an often (deceptively) simple beat, it recalled svelte-but-swingy Astaire-Rogers. The dance, the music, the dress was sensuous, slinky, stylized, status-aspiring; but with a dash of the funky-butt so natural in the streets and so glamorous in the salon. Its "Chic-freak" ambivalence was for everyone.

Its rehearsed precision, so unlike unscored acid freeform, demanded conformity. Its heavy chording was a prime example of the arranged sounds favored by the big recording studios in New York, Hollywood, and Nashville. For all its snap, spring, and sparkle it was, at least during its first years in the mass market (1975-1977), a rather innocuous mainstream music. As prosperity revived somewhat, MOR was in 1977/1978 agitated by a tougher new wave of heavy "power pop" whose left fringe, punk, was growing stronger in the currents of 15 to 24 year old male taste. Without losing its identity, without sacrificing its sleek, bourgeois, pan-sexual appeal, Disco reached for a larger market. In a late 1978 New York concert by Blondie and guitarist Robert Fripp, it was fused with punk.[17] Less extreme, Mr. MOR, Billy Joel brought to Disco a scruffier street life realism. The end of 1978 belonged to his smart-assed salsa. "My Life". It was eclectic—Disco, country, somewhat punk; and it could attract the same blue collar audience as did "Take That Job and Shove It". It could also attract the post-hip individualists who read Wayne Dyer or Robert Ringer; and in a way any streetcorner kid could understand it said much the same thing as John Updike's precious novels about Connecticut or Marin Country couples. Joel's tribute to Disco was tribute to the self-centered, life-as-smorgasborg, single-blessedness aspects of the 1970s; it was a raunchy spin-off of the Declaration of Independence, the Pursuit of Happiness, the "new life-style" which had seeped down from the rarified Village People of 1915 to the "Do your own thing" of middle class 1960s universities, and now to more of the working class: Go ahead with your own life, leave me alone.

So Disco was not static. John Rockwell felt MOR was moving left in 1978 with Disco shifting from the more mellow mainstream of Van McCoy's tepid 1975 "Hustle" into a world closer to Chicago's new power pop *Hot Streets*, the Stones' *Some Girls*; to Elvis Costello or even the Sex Pistols; to the harse imperatives of "Stayin Alive" on 52 Street. The abrasive vitality of the sneering street punk stirring restlessly in 1978, surged into Joel's "My Life", the tough, sharp Disco a perfect medium for Joel's caustic rejection of American Domesticity. Of course, as a record distributor warned me, "Don't go overboard on Rockwell's idea. Disco is far from punk. Joel and Disco are fundamentally mainstream. Punk isn't going very far."[18] Disco was absorbing some ripples, but in its bid for the mainstream, appeared not about to be swept away by a chancy New Wave.

A good point going for Disco was its ability to transcend, actually to combine, specialized markets. It was not only a great dancing music but, with Donna Summer, it could move into the concert arena with a wide 17 to 35ish audience. Summer tantalized it, exploiting Disco's mix of soul ballad, electronic sound, gut rhythms, high styled classical chords, street-sophistication, insouciance and toughness. You saw a far more catholic audience for her than for Boston late in 1978: black and white, high school and college, gays and straights, urban swingers and married suburbanites nearing middle age. Power pop on the other hand had mainly white males 15 to at the very most 24. Or did it "have" them? Many of the young audience were physically, audibly restless during Boston's prolonged, arhythmic organ passages.[19] So Hall and Oates saw fit to hop on the Disco bandwagon in their misleadingly titled "Serious Music". Disco, like its nearest rival (or close comrade) in the mass market—the synthetic country of Waylon Jennings—stayed toward the middle of developments; lightly toying with them all, but pulling back from ultimate commitment to extremes. The cent is where the big action is, over the long run; and particularly so after the traumatic accelerations of the 1960s. The 1970s left radicals depleted, conservatives scared, and most people, your "average", hardened, sensual-minded people going about their business. But, more hedonistic, more iconoclastic, they were ready to take their pleasures. Disco suited them fine.[20]

Drawing vibrancy from its immersion in R and B, Disco has been the biggest breakthrough for this genuinely black music. But R and B in Disco, while bringing a "tougher" sound to white music—by 1978 it was more and more a driving force for ballads—has continued to mellow and to blend with much white—and black—middle class taste. And as a result it seemed to be facing its biggest market; more radio, TV and Broadway exposure in 1979.[21]

So how about Disco in the 1980s? As an established form with a good beat, capable of further mild fusions with other accepted forms—jazz, country, soul, ballad—I'd say it stands a reasonable chance of survival into a new decade which probably will not be looking for boat rockers. Early 1979 developments have appeared to indicate the media won't be seeking wild men. The short-lived business recovery of 1977-1978 may be over. There is little hope that in the oil/vinyl crunch to come the biggies will be very exploratory; a good chance that mild Disco, mild Jazz-Rock Fusion, citybilly, and fusions among them all-indeed, the very safe formulas promoted in the earlier recessions and vinyl crunch of 1971-1974—will be around for some time. (What may happen in a real depression is beyond conjecture). As a matter of fact, in a once more slipping economy threatened with oil price rise as in 1973-1974, major labels—now Warners and probably Columbia—are contemplating as much as twenty percent cutback on production and concentration on relatively few, easily promotable releases for use—fire mass appeal. And the younger, raunchier buyers are declining demographically; a dwindling portion of the consuming work force and a diminishing student population. This means the mass market is being skewed toward a 22-39 cohort, hedonistic but rather past the age of seething experiment.[22] One may foresee pleasant, danceable, familiar music in the 1980s; with good audio-visual appeal for stay-at-home TVers, also. If so, Disco or an updated synthesis of it with other forms-may be right there.[23]

Notes

[1]Clive Davis, *Inside the Record Business* (New York: Morrow, 1975), p. 171. In a presentation to my class in 1976-1977, WPOP Hartford program director Dick Springfield said that before 1970 white p. d.'s and deejays, less subject to Top 40 mandates, had felt freer to indulge (perhaps unconscious) racism. "If many of us had a choice between a white and a black record, we automatically reach for the white." This reinforces Steve Chapple and Reebee Garofalo's discussion of racism in *History and Politics of the Music Industry* (Chicago: Nelson-Hall, 1977), chapter 7, although it doesn't clearly support their allegations of continued suppression. They state (p. 264) that radio racism continued (although on AM rather than FM) to minimize the popularity of black records after 1972. If so, the example they have given (WRKO Boston) seems atypical: Boston during the busing crises of 1974-1975 was probably more virulently and openly racist than any other large city with South Boston and Dorchester/Roxbury pitted against each other.

[2]Henry McNulty, "Beatles and Dylan Made the Music", Hartford *Courant*, December 20, 1969, 20: 1-8 is based on interviews with a radio p. d. and record retailer, to which I've added information from the p. d. of black soul station WKND Hartford-Springfield, James Jack.

[3]Clive Davis, pp. 140-144. I draw on insights from Dick Springfield and his deejay from WPOP, J.T. Lambert in presentations to my class. The stereotype of a widespread, deeply lasting revolutionary impact of folk rock has been shaken in surveys by Denisoff, Robinson, Hirsch and Levine. See R. Serge Denisoff, *Solid Gold: The Popular Record Industry* (New Brunswick, N.J.: Transaction, 1975), pp. 243, 248, 424, 471. Also on the media as economics and demographics, Denisoff, "Evolution of Pop Music Broadcastion", *Popular Music and Society*, 2 (Spring, 1973), 222-223; Jon Landau, "Rock, 1970", in Charles Nanry, ed., *American Music: From Storyville to Woodstock* (New Brunswick: Tranaction, 1972), pp. 242, 243; Richard Peterson and David Berger, "Cycles in Symbol Production", *American Sociological Review*, 40 (1975), 158-173.

[4]Insights on media preconditions for Disco are dependent upon the early 1970s researches of Denisoff in *Solid Gold*, particularly chapters three through five; Clive Davis; Peter Hesbacher, Robert Rosenow, Bruce Anderson, David Berger, "Radio Programming", *Popular Music and Society*, 6 (1978), 138.

[5]Clive Davis, p. 145; Landau, *loc. cit.*, p. 260.

[6]Denisoff, *Solid Gold*, p. 233; Peter Hesbacher, "Sound Exposure in Radio," *Popular Music and Society*, 3 (1974), 191-192, 195; Rechard Peterson and Russell Davis. "The Contemporary American Radio Audience", *Popular Music and Society*, 4 (1974), 300.

Erik Barnouw, *The Sponsors* (New York: Oxford University Press, 1978), p. 50 n., discusses the demographic reassessments of the media. He minimizes idealistic liberal zeitgeist: "Behind these shifts was one unchanginging element: the assumption that merchandising factors must determine policy." On advertisers' pressures see also Hesbacher, Rosenow, et. al., *loc. cit.*

[7]See Clive Davis, pp. 189-191, 206; and adjacent footnotes here for citations from the literature on the significance of media policies.

[8]Dick Springfield told my class in 1976, "1972 was the real breakthrough for black soul records."

[9]"Monga Santa Maria Afro-Cubans" were recording in late 1950s New York on the obscure indie Tico label which termed itself "King of the Cha Cha Mambo." The material was purely ethnic (Album TR-LP 1037).

[10]In July, 1973 I went to an outdoor "concert" by the old Preservation Hall Jazz Band. Almost 20,000 people, mainly 18-40, were packed into Stern Grove amphitheater in San Francisco, once home city of acid rock. As momentum built, a sudden, prolonged convulsion of dancing swept the audience—everything from jitterbugging or 1950s bopping to a bounced-up version of rock concert slither. Without having any new steps or new music, they were starved for vigorous dance. My observations were bolstered by Dick Springfield's presentation to my 1976 class. On 1970s nostalgia, Fred Davis, "Nostalgia, Identity," *Journal of Popular Culture*, 11 (Fall, 1977), 421.

[11]Andrew Kopkind, "Disco Dialectic: Gay Music Goes Straight," *Village Voice*, February 12, 1979, 12; Martin Weinberg and Colin Williams, *Male Homosexuals* (New York: Oxford University Press, 1974), pp. 40-43. The "snob value" of disco as a what used to be called jet set image is perhaps reflected in and enhanced by the large imports of French and German Disco—also an old story as new as the latest Public TV fixation on Culture across the Atlantic. The Eurodisco sound is High Fashion.

[12]My interview with Dick Springfield, WPOP, December, 1978.

[13]Dave Marsh, "Pat Sounds...How the Middle class won the battle but lost the war", Boston *Phoenix*, Music section, 6 ff; Jack McDonough, Review Essay of Jackson Browne, *Popular Music and Society*, 4 (1975), 242-250. Bruce Springsteen interview CBS-TV November 21, 1978.

[14]Stephen Holden, "Records: Billy Joel Bites the Apple", *Rolling Stone*, December 14, 1978, 83; Dave Marsh, "Billy Joel", *loc. cit.*, 79.

[15]1963 Hendrix-Desanto recording in Oakland: Gedinson GD 100XX, "A Little Touch of Soul".

[16]Springfield interview; Hartford *Courant*, December 10, 1978.

[17]John Rockwell, "Pop Music", New York *Times*, December 31, 1978, Section D (Arts), 10:4.

[18]Tracy Garneau, Aquarius distributors manager for Connecticut-Albany New York and western Massachusetts area: "Punk doesn't and won't have the demographics to make real big waves." (Interview January 3, 1979.) An R and B infusion is however more and more noticeable in Disco (see next f. n.)

[19]Springfield interview. My own observation of Boston's Garden concert audience, November 6, 1978. On audience for Donna Summer concert held the same night in Boston, see James Isaacs, "A Cinderella for the '70s", Boston *Phoenix*, November 7, 1978, section 3, 8: 2. *Billboard*, January 6, 1979 was full of indications of Disco's power. Doug Hall, "Airways Jumping with Disco Beat" 6: 3, refers to all-Disco stations; Jean Williams, "Disco can Spur R and B Exposure", 31:1.

[20]Evidence that Disco was entering the more progressive market in 1978 (at which time blacks were producing and buying more albums and not just 45s) was FM radio's going into fuller, album-oriented Disco cuts as part of the new (or revived) tendency toward AOR/ William Brashler, "The Black Middle Class: Making It", *New York Times*

Disco: A Music for the 1980s?   251

Magazine, December 3, 1978, 147-148; Laurene LaPorte, "Disco Fever", *TV Week* (Hartford *Courant*), December 31, 1979, 36: 1.

[21] Williams, *loc. cit.*; Radcliffe Joe, "Broadway Shows, DJ Producers, Pool Collaboration Seen in 1979", *Billboard*, January 6, 1979, 18:2î. An interesting sidelight on the Disco movies and projected stage show(s) is that, as Tracy Garneau told me, "the record industry now controls and capitalizes films rather than vice versa as in the past" Garneau (Aquarius indies distributor) interview, Jan. 3, 1979. Extend this control to Broadway musicals: Spring/Event Records is producing *Gotta Go Disco* for early 1979, and will shortly release an exploitation album for the 1.8 million dollar stage show.

[22] Marc Kirkeby, "The Changing Face of Record Distribution", New York *Times*, Section 3 (Business and Finance), February 18, 1979, 1.; Robert Wallace, "Warner Bros. Cuts Back". *Rolling Stone*, March 8, 1979, 11.

[23] Since most of this prognosis was written in early 1979, some qualifications are in order. The idea that Disco may survive in "an updated synthesis with other forms" is timely. "Pure" (if one can so call it) Disco is now past its peak. There's been an upsurge of new wave—although little more surprising than The Knack—among my college students. Disco has aroused resentments among 18 to 34 year old males according to Dave Marsh because it is too specifically gay, black, and latin; and radio has found it centered in an audience older, younger, more female, or less affluent than broadcasters feel desirable for sponsor appeal now. (Dave Marsh, "The Flip Side of '79", *Rolling Stone*, December 27, 1979—January 10, 1980, 27ff.) But, on the other hand, heavy rockers have absorbed a Disco beat. I checked with a young retailer and performer, Bob Bucheri, on record sales. "The typical Disco formula's saturated the market", he said in March, 1980, "but the beat goes on forever in mainstream, even new wave. It was in Rod Stewart's "Do Ya Think I'm Sexy", Kiss' *Dynasty* for the kids, now it's the new Angel's "20th Century Foxes" (Casablanca), new wave and Disco beat. And of course soul is always part of it, Whispers, you have a Disco roots beat and sound there". Also in March, 1980, Phil Balsam, New England promotions, CBS records, Hartford: "As a total musical style, Disco's down; as a radio thing, down, way down. But as a club music, dance music, a beat, it's going to be around. Radio is getting into big band styles—*and that's a spinoff of something in Disco—hard, sharp,. tight, with those soul band horns*".

Music Videos:
From Performance to Dada—Surrealism

Joan D. Lynch

The music video is still in its early childhood, born out of necessity in 1980 when the record business slumped for the second year in a row and the lessening appeal of radio was blamed.[1] Its ancestors are music, particularly rock movies both main-stream and avant-garde, television, radio and commercials. In many ways music videos most resemble commercials. They are short, usually three to four minutes, aim to engage the viewer in a direct, immediate experience and their major "raison d'etre" is to sell. Their product is the music, more particularly the record of the music. Since the birth of music videos, the record industry has climbed out of the doldrums and is thriving once again.[2]

The record companies, instead of being grateful to the child prodigies they spawned, are beginning to see them as the albatross in their budgets. The cost of making them has climbed to an average of $40-$50,000.[3] What was once a day's shoot can now extend to three weeks with pre-production time.[4] The record companies' solution to the budget explosion is to propose that television stations pay for the videos as they would any other programming, and alternately to begin brain-storming marketing strategies to sell the videos themselves.[5] Thus far, only Michael Jackson's "Thriller" and a concert video by Fleetwood Mac have sold any appreciable number in the videocassette format.[6]

The economic struggle will continue to be waged as it is in any other industry, but other problems are also cropping up. Directors for whom making a music video was once just another commercial gig are beginning to think of themselves as artists and they sometimes find themselves in conflict with the performers whom they serve. Directorial concept is pitted against the musician's wish to keep the band and the instruments central.[7] The history of music video is becoming a microcosm of that of the movie industry; star and director battle for control. The musician, whose song may sell records regardless of the quality of the video, has, of course, the upper hand.

Reprinted with permission from *Journal of Popular Culture* Volume 18:1, (Summer, 1984). pp. 53-57.

This conflict points to the central issue in the development of the video as an art form. The video itself, unless the record companies come up with marketing strategies, has no intrinsic commercial value. When one hears of the top twenty music videos, that figure is the result of the audience survey polls taken by stations such as MTV or of record sales, not music video sales. A really amateurish video may stay on the top twenty for weeks; yet an extraordinarily stylish video may never make the list at all. There may not even be any relationship between the way the record sounds and the style of the video. "Eyes Without a Face," by Billy Idol, is a very pleasant ballad when heard on the radio. In the video one is treated to Billy's curled lip, leather and chain costuming and the imagery of Heavy Metal-fire, entrapment and sado-masochism.

There are literally thousands of music videos. Some are worthy of being hailed as examples of a new art form; others deserve being reviled as trash both in form and content. Making generalizations about them is like trying to draw the average American face. Nevertheless, certain common features, formally and thematically, do emerge.

To date, three basic structures can be identified. The most common one by far, with multiple variations, is centered on the performance itself. There are also narrative videos and videos that are strongly influenced by experimental film.

The cinematic processes are heavily used to create visual interest in the performance video. There are dissolves, lap-dissolves, split screens, masked screens, superimpositions, extreme angle shots, backlighting, intercutting, rapid cutting and so on. The repertory of cinematic tricks may be exhausted in the effort to hold the audience's visual attention. There are also other ways to keep the performance intact while giving the audience something to watch. The performance may be done in a setting appropriate to the lyrics. "Almost Over You" is set in the singer's apartment; her lover's face appears in every reflective surface. Unusual settings may be utilized, such as rows of lit candles or a constructivist set that resembles a huge pile of junk.

The performers may work with extras to whom they can relate. Grace Slick's "All the Machines" is set in a primitive environment surrounded by machines. Extras run the machines or become machines themselves. The theme is nature versus technology, a not uncommon one in videos. A much simpler video is The Romantics' "Talking in Your Sleep." The performers move through rows of girls in night clothes; the climax comes with the appearance of a Marilyn Monroe look-alike.

The performance may be intercut with visuals relating to the lyrics or with images that bear little relationship but are there for humor or shock value. Van Halen's "Panama," is an example of the latter. The dominant images are of travelling but occasionally an outrageous one appears, such as a man peaking through a woman's leg in a toilet. Def Leppard's "Bringin' on the Heartbreak" is set in an industrial area dominated by huge oil drums. The pain of heartbreak is concretized for the audience in the image of the lead singer tied Christ-like to the mast of a boat ferried by two medieval-looking masked men.

Dance is a strong element in most videos, and at times the entire performance is choreographed. "The Warrior" by Scandal resembles a modern dance piece far more than a rock concert.

The line between performance and narrative videos becomes thin when the performers tell the story or appear in the setting where the narrative takes place. The group Night Ranger narrates an episode in the life of "Sister Christian," a straight convent girl who longs for the world of cars and boys and succeeds ultimately in breaking away. Liberation from the shackles of a constraining environment is a recurrent theme in videos. The musicians of ZZ Top not only tell the story of the girl they call Legs, they act as the catalysts or fairy godfathers who spring her Cinderella-like from a repressive and even cruel environment, metamorphose her from a plain Jane to a slick chick and give her a pumpkin-coach in the form of a little red sports car to go off with her Prince Charming.

This notion of the performer as a magician or Christ-like power figure is pervasive in the genre. In "Magic" by the Cars, people of all nations reach out to touch Rick Ocasek, who proves his worthiness of this adoration by walking on water. Deniece Williams in "Let's Hear It for the Boy," has the power to turn dunces into slickly outfitted dancers and wimps into athletes, a combination of the performer as power figure motif and the transformation or Cinderella motif. Michael Jackson seems clearly to be a Christ figure in "Beat It." Warring gangs prepare for action, climaxing in a fight in a warehouse. Michael, with a single touch, separates the fighting leaders who join him in a dance as do their followers.

Pure narrative videos are mini-movies with the performers playing the heroes or heroines. In "Love Is a Battlefield," Pat Benatar rejects her working class parents to work as a prostitute. She becomes the leader of a rebellion against the pimp and returns home saddened but wiser. Cyndi Lauper is also the child of working class parents in "Time after Time," as she was in "Girls Just Wanna Have Fun." Her transformation is from plain Jane to Punker. Even her boyfriend finds her partially shaved head and dyed hair hard to accept, so she ends up going off alone presumably to seek others of her kind.

In the hundreds of videos I have watched, the parents were portrayed as lower middle class. The icons of motherhood are an apron and a broom. Fathers typically sit around in undershirts and swill beer. Marriage and a family are traps which the wary and the hip avoid. One exception to this is Tracy Ullman's "They Don't Know." Tracy, the performer, tells the story dressed in a succession of chic outfits. She also plays the heroine who falls in love, marries and ends up like the rest of the lower class parents, pushing the baby in a supermarket dressed in the obligatory shapeless dress and apron with stringy hair and bedroom slippers.

When the upper classes appear in a video they are figures of fun to be mocked and their rituals are set up to be disrupted. In the anarchic "Round and Round," by Ratt, Milton Berle plays both an aristocratic paterfamilias and a well-corseted, snooty dowager. Chaos occurs during a dinner party when the butler serves live rats in a serving dish; the lead Ratt at this point crashes through the ceiling onto the table. Exchanging his tux for a Ratt's costume, the butler joins the band.

Work in videos is something to be avoided, even the glamorous work of the pop star himself. In "Love Somebody," Rick Springfield is engaged in the arduous task of watching his own concert on a studio monitor to which he lip synchs. His eye catches a poster of a tropical island and he imagines himself there with a beautiful girl. The remainder of the video intercuts between studio, concert stage and island until the end when an explosion occurs in the editing room. Rick leaves, grinning happily, film strung around his neck, presumably glad to be freed from the onerous task of editing his own footage.

The most interesting music videos are those influenced by experimental film. Descendants of "Entr'acte," An "Andalusian Dog" and "Ballet Mecanique," they borrow the techniques of Dada, Surrealism and abstract film. Those that opt for pure abstraction are less compelling than the abstract video that builds a pattern that may be discerned in repeated viewings. In "Miss Me Blind" by Culture Club, oriental images dominate. The images, which are very harmonious at the opening, change to violent ones centering on the possibility of one character blinding the other physically. Various blinds (window shades) are pulled up and down. The word "blind" flashes on and off the screen. Intercut with these images are masks, strips of film and oriental letters. The piece ends with Boy George donning a white oriental mask. In the next frame, the mask is empty save for a fake blue eye which drips tears.

Many surrealistic music videos are more confusing than amusing. The best exploit spatial and temporal disjunction to create meaning. In "Harden My Heart" by Quarterflash the lyrics concern a girl's need to leave her lover psychically as well as physically. A narrow corridor symbolizes her confinement and restriction; the desert represents freedom and a third space set in a future time, a garage with the band on motorcycles, will become her means of escape. There is rapid cutting in the piece from one space and time to the other until the final frame when we see that the narrow corridor is in the desert. The heroine walks out the door to freedom and climbs aboard a motorcycle. A bulldozer then collapses the building and a flame thrower burns it.

Freudian imagery, the hallmark of Surrealism, is not found very often in the music video. Sexual symbolism was necessary in an age of censorship; the erotic was suggested in an oblique, indirect way. Today, if there is any one element that characterizes music videos, it is their blatant sexuality, though some censorship still exists. Kevin McVaney, programming director for MTV, claims that his primary concern in choosing the videos that will play is quality of the music; his next greatest concern is compliance with community moral standards.[8] One wonders exactly how explicit material needs to be before it is banned, since some videos such as "Gloria," by The Doors, leave little to the imagination. "Gloria" is the story of a groupie who gets very close to her idol.

A striking exception to the general rule that little Freudian sex symbolism is used in music videos today may be found in "When Doves Cry," by Prince and the Revolution. The ending of the piece finds Prince and the band dressed in very stylish costumes in what appears to be a concert setting. Very quickly the screen splits and images merge to create highly suggestive sexual symbols. The image of Prince himself splits and then merges to create a phallus. As a woman plays a guitar, there is a cut to a close-up of that musical instrument which then splits creating the female sex symbol.

By far the most effective of the music videos is a piece that is pure Dada, "You Might Think," by The Cars; to give tribute to public taste, it was also number one on the MTV audience survey poll for many weeks. "You Might Think" resembles a painting by Magritte. The colors used are bright pastels. Change of scale, scale dissociation and displacement are the techniques used to create Dadaist surprise and humor. Voyeurism pervades the piece. The lead singer spies on his beloved through her window in which he appears gargantuan and through a periscope in her bathtub. He becomes the lipstick in her tube, then, as a fly, lands on her nose. He perches with her on the sink, and when they fall in, a canoe appears and they row off. Like King Kong, he snatches her from her bed and clinging to a nearby building holds her Fay Wray-like in his hand. He displaces others in her affection, turning into a screen character in a movie she is watching and knocking her current boyfriend out of a photograph, to replace him. The band backs him up. They serenade her while in her medicine chest and from her soap bar. It comes as no surprise that The Car's next video to be released will be directed by Andy Warhol.

Music videos are the strongest and the weakest of pop art. Many are crude, vulgar, offensive or just plain boring. Some few are three minute masterpieces. In the summer of 1984, the Whitney Museum in New York ran a video art retrospective that showed the full capacities of video as an artistic medium. It is my hope that some archivist is collecting the most artistic of the music videos and that they, too, will someday be shown in a museum setting.

Many predict that credits will soon appear at the end of a video. When the choreographer, art director, scene designer and director are named, the videos will drop their disposable status as commercials and move toward being potentially recognized and collected as art. This would also open the door to videos being anthologized, labelled and sold as representatives of the work of a particular artist other than the performer.

Notes

[1] Jay Cocks, "Sing a Song of Seeing: Rock Videos are Firing up a Revolution," *Time*, 122 (Dec. 26, 1983), p. 54.
[2] Ibid., p. 56.
[3] "Music Video Director's Symposium," *Variety*, March 14, 1984, p. 88.
[4] Ibid., p. 70.
[5] "Beautiful Model Meets Sumo Wrestler," *Forbes*, Sept. 12, 1983, p. 38.

[6]"Music Videos: Growth of a New Art Form," *Rolling Stone*, Sept. 15, 1983, p. 90.

[7]*Variety*, p. 70.

[8]Symposium on Music Videos held at the Young Filmmakers by the New York Film Council, New York City, New York, June 21, 1984.

The Price You Pay:
The Life and Lyrics of Bruce Springsteen

Julie Lyons
George H. Lewis

In the world of rock and roll, and in a larger sense popular culture itself, Bruce Springsteen is sometimes viewed as a messiah. With a little knowledge of Springsteen's artistry and the downward course rock has recently taken in this country, it is easy to see why this is so. Springsteen is genuine. He is living proof that rock music can give someone who previously had none the will to survive and be successful. And, in a day when rock is gradually being watered down to almost unrecognizable, commercial forms, it is a welcomed treat to hear music being played from the heart, for Springsteen has lived his music, and more importantly lives for his music.

Though this reflects my own, personal attitude toward Springsteen as an artist, this attitude is prevalent enough to make him significant to the study of popular culture. In my essay, I will illustrate this significance by examining Springsteen's early musical influences, possible explanations of his popular culture impact, and the major themes and content of his three most popular albums, *Born to Run*, *Darkness on the Edge of Town* and *The River*.

The Early Years

Bruce Springsteen has been quoted as saying: "Rock and roll has been everything to me. The first day I can remember looking in a mirror and being able to stand what I was seeing was the day I had a guitar in my hand."[1]

That day came in 1963, when Bruce was thirteen. The son of working-class parents, he was born in Freehold, New Jersey, 20 miles inland from the city he has since made famous, Asbury Park. Freehold, which has been described as "sliding downhill for years,"[2] is typical of the small towns Springsteen often writes about in his songs.

Springsteen's father, who worked at various jobs such as factory worker, prison guard and bus driver, also heavily influenced his music, as Bruce inherited his obsession for driving. "My father was a driver," Bruce has said. "He liked to get in the car and just drive. He got everybody else in the car too, and

Reprinted with permission from *Popular Music and Society* Volume 9:1, (1983). pp. 13-24.

made us drive. He made us all drive."[3] His music clearly reflects this in its extensive car and highway imagery.

As a child, Springsteen attended parochial schools where, headstrong and idealistic, he wasn't well accepted. "I lived half of my first thirteen years in a trance," he has said. "People thought I was weird because I always went around with this look on my face. I was thinking of things, but I was always on the outside looking in."[4]

Bruce's home life wasn't great either. His father was often out of work, causing financial problems and leaving him home to argue with his headstrong son. And cultural escape, as in many working-class households, was practically nonexistent. Springsteen himself admits, "I wasn't brought up in a house where there was a lot of reading and stuff. I was brought up on TV."[5]

It's no wonder that Bruce turned to rock and roll as a release from all these problems. And the fact that he was influenced by the originals in this musical form has to be significant.

His first exposure to rock was Elvis Presley's appearance on the Ed Sullivan Show. "Man, when I was nine, I couldn't imagine anyone not wanting to be Elvis Presley," Springsteen remembers.[6] Later, after purchasing his first guitar from a pawnshop for $18,[7] Springsteen picked up musical knowledge from the radio. Artists such as Elvis, Chuck Berry, the Beatles, the Rolling Stones, the Animals, Manfred Mann, the Byrds and the Who were all his favorites, as well as Phil Spector, Roy Orbison, Sam Cooke, Eddie Floyd and others.

Absorbing all the music he heard, Springsteen had developed enough talent to join a local Freehold band, the Castiles, at the age of 15; with the Castiles, Bruce wrote his first songs, learned licks, and developed the beginnings of his musical style. Though the group had a fairly strong local following, the Castiles broke up and went their separate ways after graduation from high school.

For Bruce, this meant New York, where he worked in a series of bands until he returned to New Jersey, this time Asbury Park. Here his musical style developed even further as he came in contact with many musicians attracted to the city's clubs and nightspots. It was during this period Springsteen met many of the E Street Band members, his back-up band, who, for the most part, are also Jersey locals. Forming a group called Steel Mill, the band was fairly successful, but eventually folded in 1971. After attempting to form another band, Springsteen then went solo for a while. It was during this "solo flight" that Springsteen was "discovered," signing a contract with CBS in June, 1972.

I will not go into the details of Springsteen's discovery and early recording experiences as it is not entirely pertinent to this popular culture analysis of his music. It needs to be mentioned, however, that Bruce's two early albums, though meticulously done in typical Springsteen manner, were not to his liking. Springsteen felt deprived of his musical freedom in making these albums, *Greetings From Asbury Park* and *The Wild, The Innocent* and *The E Street Shuffle*. His manager-producer Mike Appel, and CBS tried to promote Springsteen as a folksy singer-songwriter, the "New Dylan," in accordance with the major record company's traditional avoidance of rock. As a result, these records did not sell well, causing CBS to loose faith in its "New Dylan." Springsteen's amazing performance ability, however, and some words of praise from rock critic and writer Jon Landau helped in establishing a growing Springsteen audience.

After seeing Springsteen live, Landau wrote, "I saw rock and roll's future and its name is Bruce Springsteen."[7] These words renewed Springsteen's faith in himself as well as launching an extensive promotion by CBS. Springsteen somewhat resented the resulting promotion, as it capitalized on "a very personal thing," but appreciated Landau's enthusiasm. "It came at a time when a lot of people—including the record company—were wondering whether I really had it. It gave me a lot of hope. Landau's quote helped me reaffirm a belief in myself."[8] It was also the beginning of a strong friendship and professional relationship with Landau, who later became Springsteen's producer.

With this growing reputation as a great performer, his alliance with the respected *Rolling Stone* writer Jon Landau, and the extensive CBS promotional campaign, the road was paved in 1975 for Springsteen's next album, *Born To Run*, to really catch on commercially. As a result, Springsteen found his niche in the rock industry and, in doing so, made the cover of both *Time* and *Newsweek*, quite a feat for a rock newcomer.

Springsteen's Impact on Popular Culture

It was April 1974 when Jon Landau discovered Springsteen. Considering Springsteen's current popularity, I have to believe the future to which Landau was referring has arrived. The rock audience has come to appreciate Springsteen's authenticity, pertinent yet poetic lyrics, and plain, gut-level emotion. Beyond this, those who have seen Springsteen in one of his famous, four hour high-energy concerts as in the recent "The River" tour, have to be converted, no matter how skeptical they may have been originally.

A product of popular culture itself, Springsteen is proving to be highly significant to the popular culture audiences of today, as well as purifying and rejuvenating one of the most original forms of popular culture, rock and roll.

In analyzing Springsteen's impact on popular culture, I have isolated several unique aspects of the man as artist and performer which may explain his present popularity.

The first aspect deals with Springsteen's "assimilation" of early rock styles and other forms of popular culture to form his present musical style. "It's all just assimilation. I've been playing for eleven years and you just assimilate all these things," Bruce said in 1974. "It goes through something in you and it comes out with something of what you've been watching,"[9] Through this assimilation, Springsteen has breathed life into an endangered species—not endangered because of lack of audience desire, but because of the commercial corruption in rock music today.

According to Dave Marsh, author of *Born To Run: The Bruce Springsteen Story*, in the late 60s and early 70s "mainstream rock went into decline. As the Beatles became baroque and the West Coast bands seemed unable to come up with anything visceral, only a few standard-bearers of the old sound remained:

Even the Rolling Stones fiddled with sitars, while the Who toyed with rock opera."[10]

With his early rock influences and working-class upbringing ("Levis make more sense for people who ride in cars than flowing robes do"),[11] Springsteen returned rock and roll to its original state. The following passage from the 1975 article from *Time* magazine summarizes the situation:

> Springsteen represents a regeneration, a renewal of rock. He has gone back to the sources, rediscovered the wild excitement that rock had lost over the past few years....Springsteen has taken rock forward by taking it back, keeping it young. He uses and embellishes the myths of the '50s pop culture: his songs are populated by bad-ass loners, wiped-out heroes, bikers, hot-rodders, women of soulful mystery.[12]

Springsteen represents rock in its pure and original form, popular for the same reasons rock and roll caught on in the first place: as a release, an escape, hopeful means if not an end to triumph.

Springsteen's impact on popular culture can also be attributed to the influence of his working-class background on his music, as a significant portion of society can relate to the messages and imagery it contains. Even taken out of a working-class context, the themes of his music also have great appeal, as many songs speak of struggles and aspirations that people in all classes experience. Springsteen's messages, however, are particularly pertinent to Middle America's young adults. His highway images and struggles to break away are very real to this group, and his words of triumph can't help but instill hope for their own success in breaking loose. They know what working nine to five is like, and they can feel as headstrong as Springsteen did about growing up and out of their environment. At a 1975 concert, a 23-year-old telephone dispatcher from the Bronx had this to say about Springsteen: "He's able to say what we can't about growing up. He's talking about hanging around in front of cars in front of the Exxon sign. He's talking about getting your hands on your very first convertible. He's telling us it's our last chance to pull something off, and he's doing if for us." His friend added, "The peace and love movement is gone. We have to make a shot now or settle into the masses."[13]

Other evidence of Springsteen's cultural significance is the fact that his attitude toward money disproves the mass culture critique. According to Herbert J. Gans, author of *Popular and High Culture*, mass or popular culture is often criticized as being "mass produced by entrepreneurs solely for the gratification of the paying audience."[14] Gans disagrees with this critique, however. "Popular culture creators want to express their personal values and tastes in much the same way as the high culture creators, who want to be free from control by the audience and media executives."[15]

Springsteen's concern for perfection and excellence in his music rather than the profit he could derive from it certainly supports Gans' argument against the critique. Springsteen never pursued a rock career for the money involved; he signed his first long-term management contract on the hood of a car in a dark parking lot. Later this contract would lead to court action between Springsteen and his first manager-producer, Mike Appel. Though Springsteen was being taken advantage of financially, it was his musical freedom about which he was primarily concerned.

This is characteristic of Bruce's overall philosophy: musical perfection first, money far behind, never really a concern for other than reasons of survival. For Springsteen, carrying out this philosophy means playing in small clubs though he could sell ten times as many seats, and working painstakingly long months, even years, to achieve perfection on his albums. Once he even refused to show up for a concert Appel had booked in a 10,000-seat auditorium, and although his albums are too few and far between for most of his fans, they're always worth the wait. Famous talent scout John Hammond, who signed Springsteen with Columbia, has commented on the matter: "In all my years in the business, he is the only person I've met who cares absolutely nothing about the money."[16]

In terms of audience appeal, Springsteen's non-monetary tendencies magnify his popularity. His dedication to his music in itself is admirable and the attraction of a major performer playing small halls in order to achieve the best sound quality and contact with the audience is undeniable. Springsteen, who has been viewed as "the last of rock's great innocents,"[17] appears to be an artist concerned only with pursuing his music to enrich the lives of his listeners, which, in turn, enriches his own life.

Not only is Springsteen living proof of the error of the mass culture critique, he is also living proof that one can rise above the limits and constraints of working-class life, in his case, through his music. This, I personally believe, is Springsteen's greatest appeal. When he sings, as he does in "Badlands," about not giving a damn for played out scenes and in between, but just wanting control, wanting the heart and the soul, you know he really means it.

The audience recognizes this in Springsteen, whose music is a release from their lives, as well as symbolizing the hope of overcoming. After all, this is what rock did for Springsteen: "Rock and roll came to my house where there seemed to be no way out. It just seemed like a dead-end street, nothing I liked to do, nothing I wanted to do, except roll over and go to sleep or something. And it came into my house—snuck in, ya know, and opened up a whole world of possibilities."[18]

Nowhere is this more apparent than seeing Bruce in concert, where he puts everything he has into every second of music he plays. Of his concerts, Springsteen says: "This music is forever for me. It's the stage thing, that rush moment that you live for. It never lasts, but that's what you live for."[19] And anyone who has seen Springsteen in concert knows this to be true.

More than merely a symbol, though, Springsteen allows the audience to also triumph through his music, if only temporarily. About this temporary triumph, Springsteen says, "It's great because all the people in their gray little houses come down to the show and it's wild for a few hours. Then you go back to your room and you see that gray skyline and you feel you whipped it, just for a night. For a little while you feel like you won something."[20] This is true for the audience, as well.

To me, Springsteen's impact on popular culture can best be summarized in the following words: "It ain't no sin to be glad you're alive."[21] When you hear him sing these words, you can't help but feel this gladness and share his exhilaration, no matter how bleak your existence may have been looking.

Content Analysis:
Born to Run, Darkness on the Edge of Town and The River

Table One depicts my content analysis of these three albums. For each album, I identify what seem to be the major themes running through the songs. I have identified these themes as eight in number, and they include: 1) breaking loose; 2) hope of overcoming; 3) the bottom line; 4) the working life; 5) family ties; 6) road machines; 7) we can do it together; 8) mysterious women. Songs that typify the theme are identified, and the emphasis in each specific album on each theme is indicated. Finally, I note what I consider to be a significant progression of themes through the three albums. The following section explains in more detail these themes, how they are interrelated in the albums and shifts and changes in theme that seem evident in Bruce's career.

Born To Run
Springsteen's third album, *Born To Run*, was a tremendous commercial success, establishing his artistic capabilities and receiving extensive press attention. A favorite of the critics, Springsteen's praises were sung loudly, including cover stories in both *Time* and *Newsweek*. The praise was well earned, however, as Springsteen had labored on the album for almost two years. With Jon Landau's added help, *Born To Run*, finally released in October 1974, was an "instant classic."

Springsteen himself describes the difference between this album and his earlier works in the following way: "My early albums were about being some place and what it was like there, *Born To Run* is about nowhere at all,"[22] But, as author Dave Marsh points out, "Nowhere is not Anywhere," implying that "nowhere" is certainly an American image. "*Born To Run* is as locked into an America of screen doors, fast cars, and casual violence as the Beatles" 'Penny Lane' is locked into the English everyday."[23]

The Album is composed of eight songs all adding up to one big story, following a guy and his girl through one long, brutal day in middle America. The opening song, "Thunder Road," a morning song, is full of hope and possibilities, if Mary will only accompany the guy on his ride down the highway, leaving the town full of losers behind. He's pulling out to win. This song also mentions an early tune of Roy Orbison's, a reflection of Springsteen's original influences.

The other songs on the first side continue through the afternoon: "Tenth Avenue Freezeout" suggests glaring noonday sunshine, "Night" the longing for evening that early afternoon brings, and "Backstreets" has the heat of late afternoon.

264 American Popular Music

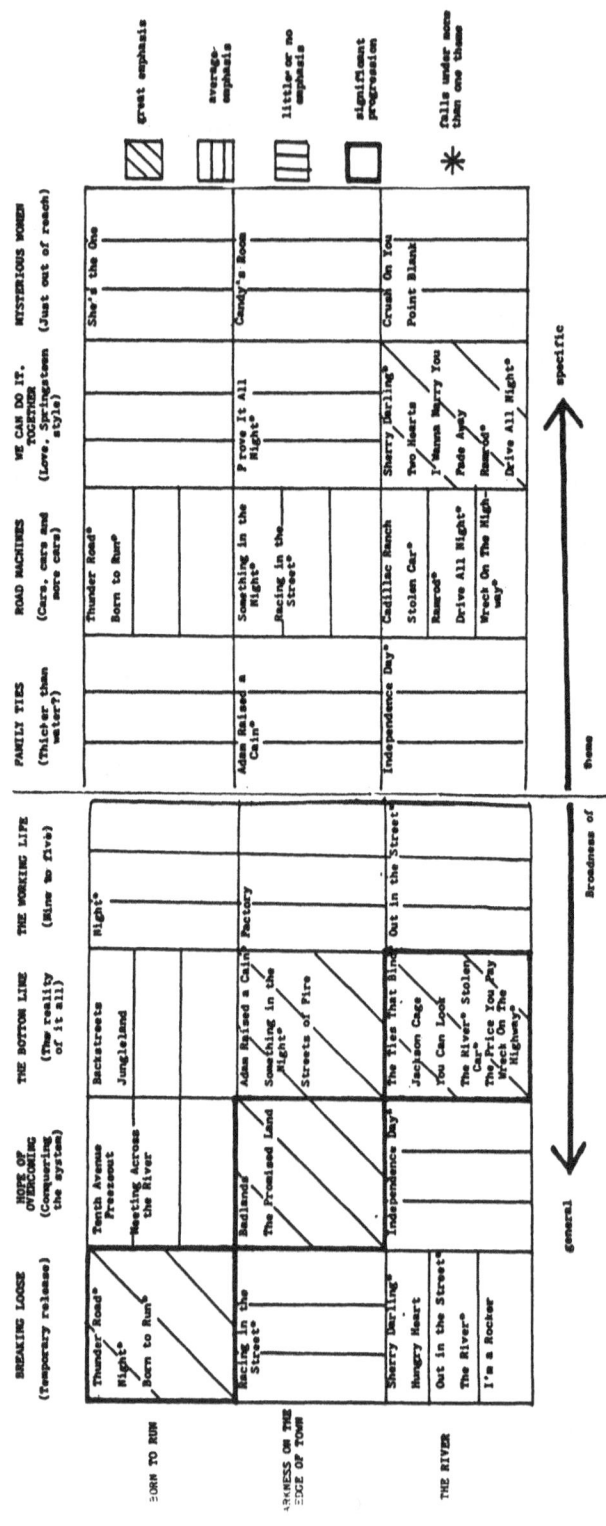

The album's second half, beginning with the classic "Born to Run," takes up the story at dusk and deals with escaping from "nowhere." Springsteen likens the town to a death trap, a suicide trip that "rips the bones from your back." He knows that, with such towns, you've got to get out while you're young. Dave Marsh's description of the song seems very appropriate: "It is a message of hope, but also a message of doom,"[24] especially with night closing in with the rest of the album's second half.

"She's The One" and "Meeting Across The River" provide a lead into the album's finale at dawn the next morning. The finale, "Jungleland," deals with the wounding of "Magic Rat" for an unstated crime, leaving him lying in the street, but with a hope for survival. The symbolism here seems to be as he wails the final passage of the song, that life may drag you down but you must survive to fight back.

Darkness on the Edge of Town

Springsteen does fight back with his fourth album, *Darkness on the Edge of Town*. It's interesting to point out here what happened between the making of these two albums, as Springsteen was fighting for his musical freedom as well.

A conflict between Springsteen and his manager-producer, Mike Appel, developed toward the end of 1975, dealing with the disadvantageous contract Springsteen had signed earlier. Springsteen was receiving a totally disproportionate share of his record royalties, 10 cents per album compared to Appel's company's 40 cents. The fact that Appel was both Springsteen's manager and producer was also a conflict of interests. What really upset Springsteen, though, was that Appel's company, Laurel Canyon, controlled the rights to his music. As Marsh states, "Bruce was willing to forgive whatever financial wrong-doing might have been done him, but the moment he realized that he did not own his own songs, he realized that he was fighting for his creative life."[25]

During these contract litigations, which lasted for over two years, Springsteen was prevented from recording with Landau and had to support himself with live performances. In the end, the final settlement granted concessions to both sides—Appel received money and retained profit shares for the first three albums, while Springsteen gained control of his music, both publishing and production. Free to work with Landau, the pair entered the recording studio on June 1, 1977, five days after the settlement was made.

There is a tie between the legal battle and the album which followed it, *Darkness on the Edge of Town*. Both deal with the struggle for control, for the predominant message behind *Darkness* is resisting submission and not allowing one's life to be controlled by others. Springsteen explains this in the following manner: "They throw dirt on you all your life, and some people get buried so deep in the dirt that they'll never get out. The album's about people who will never admit that they're buried that deep."[26]

The songs on this album are very powerful with an overall, relentless, pounding sound. This is true of the album's entire first side, except for the final song, "Racing In The Streets." This song sums up the necessary release that prevents one from giving in and being "broken," as it contrasts those who give up life and die, "little piece by little piece" to those who come home after a soulless day's work, wash up and go racing in the streets.

The second side begins with the hope of breaking free to "The Promised Land," then reminds us of the daily grind we must submit to in "The Factory." "Streets of Fire" represents the agony of the impending struggle, with "Prove It All Night" returning hope. At the end of the album, however, a man stands alone at the bottom of a hill in the title track, "Darkness On The Edge of Town." Surrounded by ruin, he looks to the top of the hill to see beyond the devastation wanting things that he can only find in the darkness on the edge of town.

The song ends with a wordless moan, symbolizing the effort of the struggle. The question to ask is how does the struggle end in success?

The River

Springsteen's fifth and most recent album, *The River*, seems to answer this question almost by avoiding it. The first double album, many songs are lighter than in the past and view the situation in a humorous way. The very existence of this lightness as well as some of the themes of the more serious songs lend a tone of acceptance to this album. Perhaps this is where success lies, in having the strength and insight to be happy and enjoy yourself under any circumstances.

There are also several recurring themes from previous albums. "Jackson Cage," for instance, deals with suppression, but establishes hope in the final lines in which Springsteen shows someone, locked in Jackson Cage, waiting to see the sun, never knowing if the day will come becoming "the hand that turns the Key." "Independence Day," written much earlier but never recorded, is about growing up and away from the life your father had. "Out In The Street" deals with the familiar release night time brings from the working grind, and sides three and four are rampant with car imagery: "Cadillac Ranch," "Stolen Car," "Ramrod," "Drive All Night," and "Wreck On the Highway."

The album contains quite a few songs about love and binding, never really a predominant theme before. Perhaps this is another way to overcome, by sharing your life with an understanding heart. Also, the idea of acceptance lies behind several songs, including the title song, "The River," in which he sings of memories that haunt him like a curse and that send him down to the river, even though he knows it is dry.

Perhaps the final song once again, as in the previous two albums summarizes the major theme of the album, as seen in the last lines of "Wreck On The Highway," a radically changed version of the classic Roy Acuff tale in which Springsteen, after seeing the wreck and driving home, sits in the darkness and watches his love as she sleeps, then climbs in bed to hold her tight, thinking all the time about that wreck on the lonely highway.

The themes of these albums, though very much generalized in this analysis, are evidence of Springsteen's pop culture significance. Absent are the drugs and frivolity associated so often with recent rock music, being replaced by more dynamic, life or death issues. This is Springsteen's great appeal, and the key to his cultural impact. As devoted fan Dave Marsh writes: "Rock saved my life. It also broke my heart. So then the advent of Bruce Springsteen, who made rock and roll a matter of life and death again, seemed nothing short of a miracle to me.... There can never be another quite like him."[27]

Notes

[1] Dave Marsh, *Born to Run*, p. 16.
[2] *Ibid.*, p. 12.
[3] *Ibid.*
[4] *Ibid.*
[5] *Ibid.*, p. 14.
[6] *Ibid.*, p. 16.
[7] *Ibid.*, p. 89.
[8] *Ibid.*, p. 91.
[9] *Ibid.*, p. 16.
[10] *Ibid.*, p. 22.
[11] *Ibid.*
[12] "The Backstreet Phantom of Rock," *Time Magazine*, (Oct. 27, 1975), p. 51.
[13] "Making of a Rock Star," *Newsweek*, (Oct. 27, 1975), p. 63.
[14] Herbert J. Gans, *Popular Culture and High Culture*, p. 19.
[15] *Ibid.*, p. 23.
[16] *Time*, op. cit., p. 58.
[17] Marsh, *op. cit.*, p. 6.
[18] *Ibid.*, p. 62.
[19] *Time* op. cit., p. 51.
[20] Bruce Pollock, "Poet of the Mean Street," *Family Weekly* (April 4, 1981), p. 7.
[21] Bruce Springsteen, *Darkness On The Edge Of Town*, "Badlands".
[22] Marsh *op. cit.*, p. 109.
[23] *Ibid.*
[24] *Ibid.*, p. 112.
[25] *Ibid.*, p. 137.
[26] *Ibid.*, p. 155.
[27] *Ibid.*, p. 6.

Bibliography

Anonymous, "The Backstreet Phantom of Rock." *Time Magazine*, October 27, 1975.
Anonymous, "Making of a Rock Star." *Newsweek*, October 27, 1975.
Gans, Herber J. *Popular Culture and High Culture*. New York: Basic Books, Inc., 1974.
Marsh, Dave. *Born To Run: The Bruce Springsteen Story*. Garden City, NY: Doubleday, 1979.
Pollock, Bruce. "Poet of the Mean Street." *Family Weekly*, April 4, 1981.

www.ingramcontent.com/pod-product-compliance
Lightning Source LLC
Chambersburg PA
CBHW031600170426
43196CB00031B/243